Praise for *Market-Driven Health Care*

"Herzlinger debunks the myth that free market health care hurts consumers. No pointy-headed academic, she uses real world examples to show how market mechanisms and consumer preferences drive behaviors to improve efficiency, cost, and outcomes. Herzlinger is our "no ax to grind" master chronicler of the fast moving, fast changing business of health care."

> —Jeff Schwartz, Managing Director, New Health Ventures
> Blue Cross and Blue Shield of Massachusetts

"Fresh prescriptions based on market-tested principles. Regina Herzlinger offers innovative approaches, such as "focused factories", that have been successful in the true marketplace, where people vote with their pocketbooks."

> —William A. Schreyer, Chairman Emeritus,
> Merrill Lynch & Co., Inc.

"Professor Herzlinger has an unparalleled insight into the workings of the American health care industry. This highly readable book will contribute greatly to the dialogue about its future."

> —Robert P. Luciano, Chairman of the Board,
> Schering-Plough Corporation

"Regina Herzlinger fearlessly analyzes what is wrong in health care. She mercilessly exposes greed, lack of compassion, and resistance to change. She argues that the free market system will finally correct our system if it is consumer controlled. I hope she prevails."

> —William J. Kolff, MD., Ph.D., Distinguished Professor
> of Medicine and Surgery, The University of Utah,
> Inventor of the kidney dialysis machine

"Indispensable to anyone trying to figure out the future of health care."

> —Carol Raphael, CEO, Visiting Nurse Service of New York

Market-Driven
Health Care

Market-Driven
Health Care

WHO WINS, WHO LOSES IN THE
TRANSFORMATION OF AMERICA'S
LARGEST SERVICE INDUSTRY

Regina E. Herzlinger

ADDISON-WESLEY PUBLISHING COMPANY, INC.

Reading, Massachusetts   Menlo Park, California   New York
Don Mills, Ontario   Harlow, England   Amsterdam   Bonn
Sydney   Singapore   Tokyo   Madrid   San Juan
Paris   Seoul   Milan   Mexico City   Taipei

Many of the designations used by manufacturers and sellers to distinguish their products are claimed as trademarks. Where those designations appear in this book and Addison-Wesley was aware of a trademark claim, the designations have been printed in initial capital letters.

Library of Congress Cataloging-in-Publication Data

Herzlinger, Regina E.
    Market-driven health care : who wins, who loses in the transformation of America's largest service industry / Regina Herzlinger.
       p.   cm.
    Includes index.
    ISBN 0-201-48994-5
    1. Medical care—United States—Cost control. 2. Patient satisfaction—United States. 3. Health services accessibility—United States. 4. Medical economics—United States. 5. Medical care—United States. I. Title.
RA410.53.H485   1997
362.1'0973—DC20   96-30199
                                                      CIP

Jacket design by Suzanne Heiser
Text design by Karen Savary
Set in 11-point Minion by Pagesetters, Inc., Brattleboro, VT

7 8 9 10 11 12-MA-0100999897
Seventh printing, November 1997

Addison-Wesley books are available at special discounts for bulk purchases by corporations, institutions, and other organizations. For more information, please contact the Corporate, Government, and Special Sales Department, Addison-Wesley Publishing Company, Reading, MA 01867, 1-800-238-9682.

CONTENTS

Why *Market-Driven Health Care*? If this is the market that brought us managed health care, with its focus on the bottom line, do we want it driving life and death decisions?

I have chosen this title to explain how the market—not managed care, but a true market, the great organic confluence of consumers and providers that characterizes virtually every other sector of our economy—will provide the solution to the deep problems that plague the American health care system. Just as the market revived our flagging manufacturing sector, once given up for dead, and created our world-class service and high-technology firms, the market and only the market can provide the health care that the American people want at a price they are willing to pay.

American consumers have steadily rated hospitals, doctors, and insurance as the lowest values for the money among the many goods and services they commonly purchase. They bemoan the system's inconvenience, which robs them of their good health and limited free time, almost as much as they bemoan its inefficiency. And while they have rejected government attempts to help the 40 million or so Americans who lack any health insurance, many Americans, including those who are insured, still cannot afford all the health care they need. The abundant information that is available for other sectors—data about prices, cost, quality, availability—is stunningly absent in health care too. The system's expenses recently broke a record trillion dollars. Yet the cost of a single episode of care remains unknown. Oh sure, you can find the cost of an aspirin, but what is the full cost of caring for a cancer patient? An AIDS victim? A premature baby? The quality of that care? Its convenience? Its effectiveness? *Nada*. Even prices are generally quoted only on an *à la carte* basis, not for the full episode of care.

Yet, paradoxically, Americans admire other aspects of our health care system. They greatly respect medical research and the drugs and devices it creates; they are very satisfied that they can receive the high technology health care services they need, more so than the citizens of many other countries; and they think highly of health care providers, such as doctors and pharmacists.

This book is for people who care about the American health care system—the providers, users, and payers who would like to reconcile these paradoxical characteristics. It tells the story of the activist consumers, entrepreneurial managers, and innovative technologies that are altering the system, and it maps out the new market-driven health care system that these forces are creating.

This book is intended to hasten the departure of the contradictions in the American health care system: to keep what is so good about it and to purge what is so bad.

I first noticed the contradictions in the American health care system twenty-five years ago, while I was doing my doctoral thesis at a neighborhood health center in a working-class town located across a river from a great metropolis. The center was founded by a renowned teaching hospital located in the city to provide routine health care services to the people of the town.

There I saw scarcity amid plenty: Although the town was just across the river from the city, the distance between the health care systems of the two was as vast as the Grand Canyon. While the city was loaded to excess with hospitals, doctors, and the very latest high-technology medical care, the town's residents had so few sources of regular health care that they would visit the hospital's emergency room just to see a doctor for a cold. The health status of the town's working-class community was shockingly low: Many adults had no teeth, or not enough of them, and alcoholism was rampant.

I saw insensitivity in the midst of compassion too. The center's talented practitioners were clearly committed to serving the community. After all, they had given up big-bucks careers in idyllic suburbs in favor of modest, salaried staff positions in the working-class town. And yet, like other health care users, the center's customers were sometimes kept waiting for hours. Lost X-rays and unrecorded appointments were all too frequent. No wonder patients are called patients.

Although the center integrated its services relatively well, some of its frail patients with chronic diseases were themselves forced to integrate the many different medical services that could help them. Other medical institutions too were untouched by the systems perspective that had begun to revolutionize business education and practice. Rarely could their patients find an already-existing organized system of care. Why did they call this a system? I wondered.

Although the center was clearly focused on providing health care, its proud parent, the great hospital across the river, didn't quite get it. Community work is expensive because it brings in no revenues, that hospital thought. Then as now, our health care system pays primarily for therapy, not for prevention. For example, to reduce the town's high rate of alcoholism, the center's mental health workers spent considerable time familiarizing the reluctant community with their services. But, after one hospital administrator reviewed the high costs of the center's community mental health work, he snapped, "What the hell do those shrinks think they're doing?" To him, real doctors don't provide preventive health care; they provide medical care—they cut people open, give them shots and drugs, sew them up, and send them back to the street. Real doctors practice in hospitals and offices—they don't wander the streets of the community, for heaven's sake. Patients should come to them, not the other way around.

The final contradiction I saw was that between dogma and art. Although medicine has been practiced for centuries, it is still a young science. It has gained real therapeutic powers only relatively recently, with the development of antibiotics after World War II. Even the anesthetics and antiseptics that enable modern surgery are only a little over a century old. Despite the hundreds of billions of dollars spent on medical research and the brilliance of our scientists, Mother Nature remains a mysterious lady. This shaky scientific footing of medicine all too often means today's medical advice—say, about salt intake and blood pressure—flipflops into tomorrow's no-no. Because medicine cannot be practiced out of a cookbook, good doctors are artists, who must creatively fashion the diagnosis and therapy that best meets the unique needs of each individual.

Even way back then, however, grumblings were heard about the idiosyncratic nature of medical practice. For example, when one study revealed that women in Maine were four times as likely to undergo hysterectomy as those in New Hampshire, a few people concluded that some of the docs up in the back woods were a singularly dumb and greedy lot. They said the solution was clear: Let the smart doctors routinize medicine and tell the timberheads what to do and how to do it. Quality will improve and the costs of health care will come tumbling down. This thinking became one of the cornerstones of today's powerful managed care movement.

The basic contradictions that I observed twenty-five years ago are all the more puzzling when we see them today, in light of the changes that have taken place in virtually every other corner of the American economy.

In the 1970s the problems of the American manufacturing sector were receiving considerable attention. Our once-world-champion manufacturing firms were routinely being beaten up by their German and Japanese competitors. The lumbering giants were simply outclassed. In response, the manufacturing sector abandoned its old motto, "big is beautiful," and gave birth to the focused factory—a leaner enterprise, with a clear, precise agenda. For example, focused steel minimills, once considered economically infeasible because of their size, would compensate for the relative diminutiveness of their scale with the clarity of their vision.

To create focused factories, the vertebrae of large, vertically integrated firms were cleaved, and products that could be more efficiently provided by outsiders were "outsourced." A systems perspective created integration through strategic relationships, rather than ownership. Massive firms—once networked by miles of assembly lines staffed by people who, day after day, performed the same function, never catching a glimpse of the end product—were reorganized into "cells," or tightly knit teams of workers, each focused on a clear output. Transforming workers from automatons into members of a cadre responsible for a clear end product unleashed their creativity and efficiency and simultaneously increased quality and decreased costs. The workers who achieved these goals were supported by considerable training, massive technology investments, new "gainsharing" systems that spread the wealth they created, and exquisitely crafted information systems.

These profound innovations—in organizational structure, in systems perspective, in use of technology, in employee empowerment, and in information—rescued our manufacturing sector. Yet these ideas seem to have eluded much of the health care system. All too many health care providers are instead busily replicating the mistakes of the long-gone manufacturing giants, consolidating a fragmented industry in the belief that "big is beautiful" and implementing top-down directives for the delivery of health care.

At the same time that the manufacturing sector was turning to focused factories, the United States was well on its way to becoming a service-based economy. Service organizations were gaining importance and pioneering ways to provide services that would "delight" customers. To be sure, the goal of pleasing the service customer is hard to accomplish. After all, the demand for services is erratic and hard to predict and is shaped by uncontrollable factors, such as weather for an airline. Then too, service customers are picky—they want quality, convenience, lower cost, and courtesy—and they are assertive—well-informed and time-stressed. Moreover, the "workers" in service organizations—lawyers, teachers, accountants—are an independent lot, as difficult to manage as a herd of cats. Finally, the quality of services is hard to measure. While the tangible physical properties of a manufactured object, like an automobile, can be calculated using familiar units of measure, like inches and pounds, velocity and acceleration, it is hard to measure the quality of something that disappears at the point of delivery. And it's harder to be sure that the qualities of a service delight a customer.

While these challenges were receiving considerable attention from the service-industry pioneers who would later become today's fabled service providers—UPS, Southwest Airlines, McDonald's, Federal Express, and Wal-Mart—they were barely acknowledged by the country's largest service industry, health care. Delighting the customer seemed almost irrelevant to some health care practitioners. Instead of investigating the integrated operating systems that firms like McDonald's painstakingly developed for delivering services, the health care industry focused on altering medical education. But the industry's problems did not originate with doctors, who were a source of its strengths; no, the problems came from the system—or more correctly, from the absence of a system for the delivery of health care services.

By 1986, fifteen years after my initiation into the maddening contradictions of the American health care system, I was convinced that the forces that had revitalized manufacturing and created the astounding American service sector were now ready to reshape the health care system. A revolution was on the way.

The revolution needed generals, sergeants, and foot soldiers— entrepreneurial spirits to guide the forces it would unleash. Unlike many of the other industries created or revived by entrepreneurs, however, the health care sector contained numerous barriers to their entry: complex technology, multiple professional roles, and daunting legal requirements. To help prepare potential managers to enter this challenging arena, I started an MBA course at the Harvard Business School that I call Creating New Health Care Ventures.

The course focuses on the forces that caused the revolution and on the early-stage entrepreneurs who are reshaping the American health care system: those who have responded to the needs of well-informed, busy Americans for convenient, supportive, and informative health care; those who invented and commercialized the technologies that have vastly increased medicine's therapeutic and diagnostic powers; and those who have created integrated, efficient, and focused systems of health care.

Through the Harvard Business School's case study method, my students and I analyze the forces that create opportunities for innovation and the reasons for the entrepreneurs' successes and failures. Answers to questions like the ones that follow help us to draw the map of the emerging system:

- Why did Health Stop, an entrepreneurial provider of convenient health care, fail?

• What accounts for the success of the eyewear sector and of an organization that provides integrated care to cancer victims in giving customers quality, convenience, and control at a good price?

• How did the managers of a successful hospital fumble the ball in their attempts to provide activist women with the kind of birthing experience they wanted?

• Why did Humana, a firm that attempted to increase the productivity of the health care system, succeed as a horizontally integrated hospital chain yet falter as a vertically integrated provider?

• How do biotechnology companies manage to attract vast sums to develop their rocket-science products, and how well have they fared in bringing products to market?

My vantage point as a former member of the board of directors of some of these providers—organizations like Boston's Brigham and Women's Hospital, Salick Health Care, and Wellesley Medical Management (the parent organization of Health Stop), and as a current board member of organizations like Deere and Company—has deepened my understanding of these forces of change and the appropriate responses to them.

The tales of these firms and others, their successes and their failures, are told in this book. I hope that you will find the promise of their endeavors so compelling that you too—as a user, provider, or payer—will join the revolution being created by our market-driven health care system.

ACKNOWLEDGMENTS

Many people have helped me to prepare this book. My husband, lifelong partner, and best friend, George Herzlinger, is chief among them. I most appreciate his knowledge of technology and his help in structuring the book. (He is a Ph.D. physicist with interests in medical technology.) William Mullins compiled the voluminous sources of information this book contains with Susan Weber and Jeff Cronin. The Harvard Business School's research group helped enormously in finding sources of data about topics as disparate as the prices of chickens and angioplasties, including Sarah Erikson, Jane Noonan, Bea Bezmalinovic and other members of the group. My editor, Ellie McCarthy, was always available, always delightful, and always astute in shaping the manuscript into a book. I admire the expertise and am grateful for the support of Bill Patrick, the editorial director at Addison-Wesley, and Bill Leigh, my agent. My able assistant, Jeannette Lurie, kept the ship afloat. Stacy Shore and Aimee Hamel's substantial word-processing skills meticulously transformed my handwritten pages into a typed manuscript and Tom Cameron obtained the needed permissions.

I would also like to thank the people who reviewed earlier versions of this manuscript and generously shared their expertise with me. They include my colleagues at the Harvard Business School: David Bell, Milton Brown, Willis Emmons, Pankaj Ghemawat, Robert Hayes, James Heskett, Thomas McCraw, Malcolm Salter, Bruce Scott, Wickham Skinner; other researchers: John Akula, Gloria Bazzoli, Brad Belt, Lee Benham, Ernest Berndt, Dr. David Eisenberg, Roger Feldman, Stan Finkelstein, Dr. James and Sara Fries, Larry Green, Nancy Kane, Dr. Lucian Leape, Mark Litow, Kate Lorig, Mark Pauly, Dr. Thomas Perls, Dr. Craig Venter, Ken Warner, Arnold Webber; physicians and nurses: Dr. George Battit, Dr. Linda Bennett, Dr. Denton Cooley, Frayda Diamond, Dr. Fred Frigoletto, Dr. Mark Garnick, Dr. Joseph Haas, Dr. Jonathan Kleefeld, Dr. Willem J. Kolff, Dr. Peter Madras, Dr. James Rhea, Dr. Michael Robinson, Dr. Benjamin Sachs, Dr. James Thrall, Fran Ventre, Dr. Gordon Weir; people in various health care sectors: Jack Anderson, Jack Ashby, Mitchell Blutt, Jeremy Brody, Dr. Richard Brubaker, Dr. Richard Cornell, Hugh D'Andrade, Morton J. Davis, Robert Daly, Dr. Daniel Gregorie, John Havens, Susan Herzlinger, Jessie Hixson, David Jones, Susan Kogan, John L. Kordash, Dr. David M. Lawrence, David Lothson, David Matheson, Robert H. McCaffrey, Joanne Nardone, Alan O'Dell, Dr. Stanley Pearle, Michael Plunkett, G. Kirk Raab, Sharon Reich, Peter Rettig, Dr. Bernard Salick, Richard Siegrist, Satish Tyagi, Darryl Urquhart, Steve Wetzell; and the following organizations that reviewed the accuracy of the descriptions of their work: Bread and Circus, BUPA, Citicorp, Deere and Co., Federal

Employees Health Benefits Program, Hambrecht and Quist, Humana, General Motors, Johnson and Johnson, Mayo Clinic, McDonald's, Medtronic, Merck and Co., Morgan Stanley, National Eye Institute, Praxair, Inc., Sears Roebuck, Turner Broadcasting System, The United Network of Organ Sharing.

INTRODUCTION

Why is it that:

- The repair rates for a Toyota model are easy to find, but it would take a massive research effort to find out which heart surgeon's patients in your area had the best survival rates after surgery?

- You can buy just about any product over the phone at midnight, but you have to lose half a day of work just to see a doctor for a minor illness?

- McDonald's can turn out a zillion perfect french fries in a day in more than eleven thousand restaurants all over the United States, but at a hospital someone might take out the wrong kidney or cut off the wrong leg?

- An HMO turned down a dying woman's request for therapy that might have saved her life, yet that year gave one top manager $18 million in a final compensation package when he left?

Are we doomed to have an unsystematic health care system that keeps us waiting, provides all too little information and support, cuts off the one good leg, removes the one healthy kidney, and pays outrageous fees to those who deny us the services we have paid for and need?

Some of the many good people within the system say that we are. Health care is special, they say, turning up their noses at comparisons with McDonald's. We deal with life and death; they deal with french fries. McDonald's business perspective cannot help us. McDonald's may be a miracle of consistency, reliability, courtesy, cleanliness, and low cost—but that has nothing to do with health care. Integrated operating systems, checks and balances, a seven-hundred-page operations manual, long-term relationships with external suppliers, team-building, employee empowerment—all that stuff may be okay for McDonald's, but for health care? No way. As a retired professor of medicine huffily noted in an editorial entitled "Bean Counters Shouldn't Control Doctors," what can managers—or "bean counters" as the article disparagingly labeled them—possibly tell him that he doesn't already know?

Right? Is the health care sector different from the other sectors of the economy? Are there no lessons at all to be learned from the manufacturing and service industries that turned themselves inside out to give the United States back its number-one competitiveness ranking? Do world-class firms like McDonald's that specialize in quick, courteous, consistent, low-cost service really have nothing that the health care sector can emulate? Is there really no role in the health care sector for brilliant entrepreneurs and technologists, like those who created the consumer-responsive Home Depot and the technology leader Microsoft?

The answers to these questions are important. What is at stake is the future of the largest service industry in the United States, whose costs stand at about a trillion dollars a year. Just what is a trillion dollars? Think about it this way: If all the dollars in our GDP were lined up, every seventh one would belong to health care.

Indeed, all aspects of the health care industry are mind-bogglingly large. The system annually delivers 4 million babies; provides 762 million visits to physicians; and enables 539 million days in the hospital. And the industry's strengths are as great as its size: U.S. medical technology is so good that it generates trade surpluses for the country. Our researchers are the Chicago Bulls of the Nobel Prize for Medicine, raking in a disproportionate share of the glory. Our skilled, dedicated practitioners and technology-laden hospitals draw people from around the world. (At a recent visit to the Mayo Clinic, I found the room service card in my hotel, located next to the clinic, printed in four languages.) And if you're old, the United States is a great place to get even older.

But the health care system's problems are of equal magnitude.

Is turning the system over to the know-it-all "doctor knows best" or the managed care crowd the only solution?

No, indeed.

The market forces that have reshaped much of the American economy are now working on our health care system. When they have completed their labors, the system will have lost its fat—inconvenience, lack of information, and high costs—but it will have kept its muscle. A new, market-driven health care system will emerge.

THE TRANSFORMED HEALTH CARE SYSTEM

An earthquake is transforming our health care system. As it rumbles, a new landscape is emerging. If you can't sense it, wake up—this quake is for real. It is caused by primal forces—powerful changes in socio-demographic characteristics, medical technology, and organization structures.

Bam. Gone from the topographical map are the menacing peaks that deny people access: The hour-long waits. The uncommunicative providers. The confusing, fragmented sources of care. The arrogant technocrats who bind consumers and providers alike in miles of red tape, obstructing delivery of the services that people have paid for and that providers want to give. The inconvenient locations. The sky-rocketing costs. A new flat landscape is replacing these mountains with customer-focused, convenient, courteous, reasonably priced, informa-tive, and easy-to-use services and products.

The earthquake is shattering the present health care system—replacing giant providers and huge managed care networks, located in hard-to-reach sites that are open only at inconvenient hours, with what I call "focused factories" (a nomenclature borrowed from the manufac-turing sector) that provide convenient, specialized care for victims of a certain chronic disease, or for those who need a particular form of surgery, or for those who require a diagnosis, checkup, or treatment for a routine problem.

Focused factories will provide overworked Americans with convenient health care, available before and after working hours, in easy-to-reach locations like work sites, shopping malls, homes, and schools. They will offer all the resources required to treat a particular problem—including specialist physicians, primary care doctors, nurses, technicians, pharmaceuticals, supplies, appliances, diagnostic facilities, and easy, integrated access to hospital or home-based care, if it is needed. All of this will be organized not by medical specialty, but for the total needs of the patient with a particular disease or problem. Weary Americans will no longer be forced to stitch fragments of the health care system together into something that can address their problems.

Rays of sunshine, in the form of new sources of information, will illuminate shadowy crevices and enable people to make intelligent, well-considered choices about their health care, in ways that they cannot today. These sources will offer independent evaluations of the quality and cost of care, like those published in *Consumer Reports*, as well as customer evaluations, like those found in the Zagat surveys of restaurant patrons and the J.D. Power compilation of automobile owners' ratings. Focused factories will enable greater comparison shopping; for example, diabetics will readily be able to compare different focused factories for their care, with clear data on price, quality, and customer satisfaction almost impossible to obtain in today's system.

New sources of support will also help Americans to take better care of their own health. For example, focused factories will help asthmatics use the medications that can keep them healthy and out of expensive hospital emergency rooms. Tired Americans, so overworked that they postpone even important preventive health measures like vaccinating their infants and toddlers, will find convenient sources of such services, such as vaccinations provided in the home, school, or work site.

Poof. The miasma that veils health care providers in mysterious vapors disappears. Illuminating rays of sunshine dissipate the mist to reveal their precise cost and quality dimensions. New rivers of support dot the landscape, to nourish people with advice for self-care.

These focused factories and sources of information and support are powerful cost-controllers. First, they keep people healthier, thereby reducing their needs for costly medical interventions. Second, since practice makes perfect, each focused factory will get much more volume in its area of specialization than traditional providers, increasing its quality and lowering its costs. Third, focused factories are intrinsically more efficient than our present system, which is loaded with redundant technology and capacity. Fourth, the clear output of each focused factory will enable payers more easily to compare the costs and quality attributes of different suppliers and thus spur the true competition that generally lowers costs.

Medical technology will continue to reshape the landscape too, helping us to maintain our health and reducing the trauma of therapy when we do get sick. Technological marvels have already emptied out hospitals with clever devices that minimize the damage inflicted by surgery. The traumatic sawing, cutting, and stitching that were once required to repair dysfunctional body parts are going the way of all flesh. Miniaturized instruments are now inserted into natural body openings or small holes, enabling kinder, gentler surgery. Diagnostic and monitoring devices stealthily use natural forms of energy, like sound waves or electromagnetism, to detect our body's innermost secrets, greatly diminishing the need for surgery. Some drugs have substantially limited the damage that diseases inflict, like ulcers and mental illness.

The new sciences incorporated in biotechnology promise to engage Mother Nature, that all-powerful physician, as our healing partner. Biotechnology is unlocking the secrets of our genetic structure, so that sick genes can be repaired before they cause grave damage, while other genes can be ordered to produce naturally occurring compounds in greater or lesser quantity, as needed.

Boom. These dramatic developments in medical technology enable the decentralization of powerful therapeutic, diagnostic, and monitoring services. Services available only at vast, costly, hard-to-reach hospitals will instead be provided by inexpensive, easy-to-access clinics, physicians' offices, ambulances, and helicopters. The most important feature of this newly formed landscape will be better health for all of us.

THE FORCES OF CHANGE

The forces that are creating this earthquake have already reshaped other massive parts of the American economy—the retailing, information, automotive, and manufacturing sectors are among them—

and their fury is far from spent. The changes they will bring are inevitable.

People who are born to work, not to shop, are one such force. Americans today bear an unprecedented burden of work, child care, and elder care responsibilities—all too frequently without another adult to share the weight. The retailing industry has felt their pain and transformed itself to lighten their load. Superstores have been organized to meet their distinct needs, providing a great depth of inventory, like Staples for office equipment and Toys "R" Us for playthings. Their clear focus and the ready availability of their merchandise allow busy consumers to minimize the time they spend shopping. The success of home shopping and the decline of the unfocused, narrow-inventory, general-purpose department store are twin manifestations of the power of this busy consumer.

The well-educated consumers who have caused a boom in outlets for information, especially of the "how-to" variety, are yet another force. Information is empowering: It leads to self-confidence and assertiveness. Today's consumers seek out pragmatic and purposeful information. They go to Home Depot to learn how to install a sink and they read *Consumer Reports* to evaluate nursing homes.

Support services for such mastery-seeking consumers have flourished, ranging from tax preparers and financial advisers to exercise videos and computer-accessible brokerage firms. They enable today's consumers to do for themselves what once was considered the sole province of experts. The clearest evidence of the power of the "do-it-yourself" movement is in automobile sales. Informed consumers have transformed a sleazy deal filled with mysterious options, tawdry haggling, and murky pricing into a straightforward business transaction. Because potential buyers know virtually as much about a car's costs and qualities as the seller, there is no point in fooling around. Let's make a deal and get it over with, consumers seem to say.

The relentless pace of innovation in technology has also reshaped an army of consumer goods sectors, like cars and computers. Technology has made these products better and relatively cheaper than they were before.

The pressures of competition constitute yet another powerful force that has caused our once-sprawling corporate giants to shed distracting side businesses and excess capacity as eagerly as a snake sheds its skin. They have focused, focused, focused. In the 1990s the venerable Eastman Kodak discovered its true inner child, after it spun off some massive chemical and pharmaceutical businesses. It found—surprise, surprise—the photography business that dwelled within.

The powerful organizations that emerged have substituted muscle for fat—replacing three-hundred-acre factories and miles of production lines with small, tightly knit teams focused on a single, clear objective. McDonald's, the ubiquitous hamburger purveyor that feeds 7 percent of the U.S. population daily, epitomizes the qualities of the service-focused factory: consistency, reliability, courtesy, low cost, cleanliness, and fast service. You don't like fast food? Forget about that—the principles of McDonald's management are what interest us, not its french fries.

These powerful forces of change are already cracking the thick crust of the health care establishment. But change is hard to implement. If it were easy, Woolworth's would be doing a better job of catering to convenience- and mastery-seeking consumers. If it were easy, the medical device company U.S. Surgical would not have lost billions of dollars in market value in one devastating year-and-a-half period. If it were easy, a variety of innovators—including seasoned Silicon Valley venture capitalists, experienced health care entrepreneurs, and well-intentioned hospitals—would not have failed in the early-stage ventures that tried to fulfill the promise of this revolution.

WINNERS AND LOSERS

The new health care system will have many winners but also some powerful losers.

Well-informed, overworked Americans will be winners, reveling in the convenience and support that the new health care system will provide and in the efficacy of its technology. The transformed system will make them healthier and more productive and will open up their limited free time.

Those who are presently crushed by our health care system's gargantuan appetite for money will like the new landscape too—the elderly; the employers whose health care costs exceed their profits; the federal government, whose tax revenues were vastly outstripped by health care cost increases; the very sick; and the uninsured. For one thing, healthier people require less medical care. For another, the new health care system will be intrinsically more efficient than the old one.

Dedicated, talented providers of health care will also admire this new system. No longer will they be reviled as greedy bloodsuckers or pushed around by bottom-line-oriented managed care insurers. Indeed, they are likely to lead the new system, replacing the managed care technocrats in this role.

Finally, the new American cowboys and cowgirls—the adventurous, brilliant technologists and entrepreneurs, like those who created our great new enterprises, from Turner Broadcasting, to Microsoft, to Wal-Mart—will find the new health care system a welcoming arena for their many talents.

But the new system will create plenty of losers as well—powerful entities that will be flattened by the earthquake.

The health care providers who believe that patients must be patient won't be pleased with the new emphasis on customer convenience. Although most physicians believe in a shared doctor-patient relationship, the physician who wrote the article, "Why I Let Patients Tell Me What Treatments They Need," surely won't enjoy his customers' assertiveness. His patients consult multiple sources of health care information, he complains, and do not revere his opinion. (I know how he feels: When I first started teaching MBAs a quarter-century ago, they addressed me respectfully as Professor Herzlinger, although I was their age. Now, when I am twice their age, I am called Regi.) But wake up and smell the decaf, light cappuccino, Doctor. Well-informed, mastery-seeking Americans are no longer going to put you or anybody else up on a pedestal. Make them your partner, not your enemy, in the health care process.

The technocrats who believe that they can reduce health care costs with a "just say no" cure won't enjoy having their supremacy stripped away. And the strategists who constructed the giant, vertically integrated systems of health care will be horrified when, like the French soldiers who built the Maginot line, they find that big is not beautiful.

WHAT LIES AHEAD

So powerful is this earthquake that it will have its way no matter what. The rapidity of its transformative powers will be accelerated by savvy entrepreneurs who can clear managerial hurdles as easily as Olympians clear the hurdles on the track and by a federal government that defuses legal and tax barriers that hinder the rate of change.

This book examines thought-leader companies and models of governance to learn the secrets of their success and the forces that propel them. In Part 1 we will review the lessons to be learned from the businesses that give their customers the convenience and mastery they want—like Home Depot, Charles Schwab, and the eyewear sector. In Part 2, we will analyze why two proposed remedies for the health care system—downsizing, or managed care, and upsizing, or "big is beautiful"—will fail in most cases, drawing from the sobering experiences of the media, airline, and banking industries and other health care enterprises that tried them. In Part 3, we will apply two successful productivity-enhancing concepts to the provision of health care: the focused factory, as exemplified by McDonald's, and technology, and we will analyze the lessons for the health care system inherent in Deere and Company's revitalization through the application of these concepts. An effective market needs consumers, as well as providers—demand, as well as supply. In Part 4, we will discuss how to create an effective voice for consumers in the health care system and how to provide managers with the tools they need. These will help health care consumers, providers, and payers to advance the new market-driven health care system.

To your health!

PART I

What Consumers Want: Convenience and Mastery

CHAPTER I

The Consumer Revolution

Susan's voice on the telephone had a familiar, urgent tone. I knew my friend had news. She is the busy executive vice-president of a growing business, with two teenage children and an equally busy husband. She is usually the first to find new things, and like a good friend, is always eager to share her discoveries.

"Did you hear about Quick Pharm," she asked, "the new drugstore on School Street? Your doctor calls in your prescription, and they deliver it to you, at your convenience. They will try to renew it if you ask them to. This drugstore is good and fast, and costs no more than the usual one. They work on my schedule, not theirs.

"You know how busy I am, with my job and the kids, and we all need drugs—the kids for their acne, Larry for his allergies, and me for my arthritis. And now my mother has developed Parkinson's, and I have to deal with that too. This drugstore gives me an extra hour a week to spend with my family and my mom. What a find!"

Many people are like my friend Susan: they know what they want, they want it fast, and they want it when they want it. Well informed, overworked, and overburdened with child and elder care responsibilities, they are a new breed of consumer, and their demands for convenience and control have caused many American businesses to greatly enhance their quality and control their costs.

These consumer revolutionaries are now affecting the health care system too. Because they have stopped smoking, moderated their alcohol intake, increased their exercising, and eliminated some of the fat from their diets, their illness and death rates from many diseases caused by poor health habits, like heart disease, have plummeted. But these changes are not enough. The consumer revolutionaries want their health care system to provide them with the same kinds of convenience and mastery they've found with Home Depot, *Consumer Reports,* and NordicTrack, so that their health status and costs will improve even further.

But unlike many of the industries that have understood the importance of responding to consumer demands—retailing, information, and automobiles, for example—much of the American health care system remains unmoved. Patients must continue to be patient and be flat on their backs, passive and acquiescent. The inconvenience of the system causes busy Americans to defer needed medical care, such as immunizations for their children, and waste considerable time and money in waiting for care or finding an appropriate source of it. All too many of those saddled with life-sapping personal habits get all too little help in reversing them. Health care providers' slow pace in responding to Americans' needs for convenience and support in eliminating persistent, destructive habits and in caring for chronic diseases or problems needlessly reduce health status, increase health care costs, and limit national productivity.

A few fissures of entrepreneurial innovation have cracked the thick crust. While most of the system appears to regard convenience as a frivolous luxury, like pop-tops on beverage cans, and efforts to reverse health-destroying habits as an afterthought, these innovators have stepped out of the pack. One focused factory has organized the fragmented providers of cancer treatments into a convenient, integrated system. A disease-management program empowers victims to care for their disease themselves. An information company enables subscribers to accurately track their health status. An entire health care sector provides consumers with the choice, information, and control they seek.

Americans' health and productivity will greatly benefit as the health care system learns from these leaders and changes in the same ways that the other sectors of the economy have changed.

Part 1 of this book describes how these further transformations will be achieved. It first explains how consumer revolutionaries have reshaped the massive information, automobile, and retailing sectors to meet their demands for convenience and mastery. It then examines how consumer needs have affected the health care system and analyzes why various entrepreneurial health care ventures have succeeded or failed to meet these needs. It concludes with a description of how the future health care system will better meet the needs of these revolutionaries.

THE BIRTH OF THE CONSUMER REVOLUTIONARY

A new generation of hardworking, well-informed Americans have turned many industries inside out. Who are these consumer revolutionaries, and what changes have they wrought?

Born to Shop

Back in the 1950s, my mother viewed shopping as a social event and a theatrical experience rolled into one. She spent most mornings shopping for food, picking and sorting among the wares of the hundreds of stores lining Utica Avenue in Brooklyn. She carried a vast data bank about their prices and quality in her mind: some ripe peaches here, a nice tomato there, and of course fresh bread, freshly ground coffee, and fresh meat daily. She emerged triumphant from these expeditions, victorious over the hordes of other dedicated shoppers and over shopkeepers hoping to palm off stale merchandise on her.

In the afternoons she and her best friend would descend on the Fulton Street department stores. Their knowledge of the stores' merchandise was encyclopedic: "Want a nice black silk blouse, drastically underpriced? Try May's, third floor, in the rear, near the ladies' room. A real leather bag to match? A steal at $9.99, only a little scratch on it, at the Abraham and Strauss clearance table." For my mother and her friends, shopping was so much fun, they spent most of their ample free time doing it.

Born to Work

But for my friend Susan, for me, and for millions of other consumer revolutionaries, shopping is a nuisance. It robs us of our precious free time—the social and entertainment time we would like to spend with our families and friends, or on ourselves.

Modern-day Americans are no longer "born to shop." Instead, they are "born to work." The number of people who work for pay has increased substantially. In 1960 only 60 percent of the population was in the labor force and only 38 percent of women were employed. By 1993 the percentage of labor force participation had risen to 66 percent and that of working women to 58 percent. While in 1960 only 32 percent of married women worked, by 1993 that rate had nearly doubled. Even teenagers now work. Some two-thirds of high school students in suburban schools hold part-time jobs, according to the *Wall Street Journal.* Describing a young girl who in another era might have "captained the cheerleading squad or hit the books after school," the *Journal* notes that while the wages from her work help to pay for her car, "she's tired. When she awakens each morning, her first thought is of bedtime that night."

The child care picture has changed too. In 1960 only 28 percent of married women with children under the age of 18 were working, but by 1993 that percentage had increased to 68 percent, and for widowed, divorced, or separated women with children, the percentage had risen to 72. Finding quality child care remains a major problem for working parents. Many of them want child care but cannot find acceptable arrangements.

Americans also work harder today. Over 6 percent of those employed have more than one job. Full-time workers spent 138 hours more a year working in 1989 than in 1969. In 1992 the average worker spent 45 hours working and commuting, and 27 hours in chores and care for children during the work week, and an additional 26 hours on nonwork days. Meanwhile, between 1970 and 1993 the number of people aged 75 or more who lived alone rose by 2.8 million. The Census Bureau estimates that in the future 80 percent of the long-term care needs of those 85 and older will be provided by families. The 7 percent of workers who already care for disabled elderly loved ones spend from 12 (men) to 20 (women) hours a week in providing this care. (Although I write primarily about the United States, these trends also occur beyond our boundaries. For example, in the United Kingdom the number of people with second jobs increased by 70 percent between 1984 and 1994. A majority of them were women.)

When you add up all these responsibilities, it is no wonder that people are exhausted. Today's workers with employed spouses and children have only 1.4 hours to care for themselves on any given weekday. Understandably, most of them complain that they do not have enough time with their children or their partners.

The Smart Consumer

People with so little free time can no longer shop as my mother did. But lack of convenience is not their only complaint. While my mother enjoyed playing her daily game of wits with the local food merchants, today's generation has no wish to spar with retailers. Their intellects are sufficiently challenged at work, thank you. Instead they want good prices, many choices, top quality, fast delivery, and excellent service—all the time. They do not want to play games. A furniture retailer notes that American shoppers say, "I want it the way I want it and when I want it—and I want it instantly."

This assertive behavior is fueled by the self-confidence that years of education provide. After all, education is empowering. It urges us to critique the work of world-class minds and to access the information that can make us self-sufficient. Knowledge is power. And the current generation of middle-aged shoppers proved their unprecedented power early on, in their twenties, when they toppled two presidents, Johnson and Nixon.

The rise in both level of education and number of educated people in the United States is astonishing. In 1960 only 41 percent of the population had a high school education or more. By 1993 that percentage had doubled, and the percentage of college graduates had nearly tripled. Even 50 percent of those 75 and older had at least graduated from a high school, and a majority of those under 44 had at least some college education. And yet the public's appetite for learning apparently remains unsatisfied. Fifty-seven million people participated in adult education in 1990–1991, including at least a third of all people aged 25 to 54, and 12 million who themselves paid for work-related training.

Although many observers believe that these educational phenomena lack substance, a review of standardized educational test scores says otherwise. Yes, the average Scholastic Aptitude Test scores for college entrance declined somewhat, but not substantially considering the surge in the number of people taking the exam. The students in the top

60 percent of their high school class actually raised their average SAT scores a bit between 1980 and 1993, and American College Testing program composite scores increased between 1967 and 1993. The proficiency scores of elementary and secondary school students also held steady between 1977 and 1990. The increases in average educational levels in the United States thus represent genuine advances in educational attainment. The average 1990 American consumer is smarter than ever before.

RETAILERS RESPOND TO CONSUMER DEMANDS FOR CONVENIENCE

Today's well-informed Americans demand convenience. To fill this demand, retailers have radically redefined the very process of shopping. Merchandise that was once available only by going to a shop is now available at home, through mail order catalogs, the computer, or television. In 1992, 102 million people made at least one purchase from a catalog. While retail sales levels in shopping centers fell between 1988 and 1992, consumer purchases from the home, paid for by check or credit card, grew by 30 percent. Although the wares presently available on TV resemble those in a flea market, powerful catalog vendors like J. C. Penney and established stores like Saks Fifth Avenue and Nordstrom are experimenting with convenient television shopping. When their merchandising skills are applied to interactive TV, convenient home shopping will become a colossus.

For those who still want to touch the merchandise—a group that spent $1 trillion in 1992—savvy merchandisers have also increased convenience. A large variety of shopping sites are newly available, ranging from neighborhood stores, which stress service and minimize travel; to shopping malls, anchored by huge discount stores with a vast array of merchandise; to malls located in office buildings and transportation terminals, where busy people work and travel.

Retailers have also reorganized their stores' contents to increase shoppers' convenience. Instead of providing the jumbled array of merchandise that once required my mother's cartographical skills to navigate, many stores now replicate her efforts to match items. Stores are clearly organized around lifestyles and provide coordinated looks. Women's clothing stores such as The Limited are clearly targeted at young adults, Ann Taylor at young careerists, and Chanel at successful older women. Stores that sell linens, like Pacific Linen, feature thirty to fifty bedroom settings that display coordinated bed, table, and window coverings. No wonder Sears dumped its big general catalog but kept its thriving specialty-item catalogs alive.

Superstores enhance convenience by providing an abundance of merchandise and choice in one location, such as Toys "R" Us for playthings, Staples for office equipment, and Home Depot for building supplies. Superstores are particularly popular with time-stressed, dual-career couples because they enhance the productivity of the shopping experience. Some superstores not only offer more merchandise but cater to their educated customers' desire for mastery by encouraging them to experiment with their wares. For example, SuperSports stores offer test-play areas, including a half-size basketball court, a computerized golf course and tennis court, and an in-line skating area. "We developed the format because the consumer asked for it," notes the company's CEO. Superstores also clearly understand their customers' need for comfort. Aisles are wider, not crowded with merchandise, and some stores offer in-store rest and relaxation areas.

Retailers in successful stores accentuate service by training employees in new, clearly defined roles. McDonald's, for example, carefully engineers the job of each employee, then trains, monitors, and rewards them to enhance their speed and courtesy. And stores like the venerable Sears, hard hit by declining sales, no longer require their salespeople to restock merchandise—now they can concentrate on serving the customer. Catalog sales employees are also trained in telephone skills. Telephone Doctor, a consulting service that provides telephone etiquette training services, finds its business booming with video offerings such as *How to Treat Every Caller as a Welcome Guest* and *How to Handle the Irate, Angry, Rude, Unhappy, and Sometimes Abrasive Caller.*

Has enhanced convenience raised prices? Apparently not. The prices of the ubiquitous Wal-Mart are as much as 15 percent lower than those in local stores. Notes an observer of a local Wal-Mart, "As advertised, [it] is a discount store with helpful personnel—and incredibly low prices." The prices of the three consumer items he purchased there were 32 percent lower than in a local store. No wonder sales revenues at discount stores increasingly outstrip those at traditional department stores. To further enhance convenience, Wal-Mart's concept of everyday low prices has freed customers from the need to hunt for special sale days. Many other stores have adopted this new form of pricing. One superstore executive notes, "Time is a big factor. Consumers compare prices by looking at newspaper ads. Once they are in our store, they see . . . the sharp pricing. They know they do not have to go elsewhere."

Accomplishing such changes in the mammoth retailing industry is like turning a battleship around in a small lake. And yet to meet customers' needs for convenience and mastery, retailers have changed shopping sites, reorganized merchandise to meet lifestyle needs, and trained and motivated employees to emphasize service. To calibrate the difficulty of making these changes, consider the $30 billion Kmart chain. Here, change after change has met with disappointment and evaporating profits. Its CEO was dismissed in 1995 after an expensive modernization strategy and new merchandising failed to reverse the slide.

Yet while Kmart floundered, other retailers, like Wal-Mart, achieved fabulous success. From its inception in the early 1960s, it grew to a $55.5-billion-in-sales retailing giant in 1992. How did Wal-Mart do it? With vast stores, smart buying, well-trained and motivated employees, and endless attention to the details that enhance customers' convenience. Wal-Mart's obsessive attention to its customers' needs extends even to this minor detail: elderly Wal-Mart shoppers find large price labels that they can read without bifocals. Other successful retailers also enhance customers' convenience by giving attention to details. The mall in Menlo Park, New Jersey, provides strollers, wheelchairs, diaper kits, and even a mall-walkers' club, whose members walk around the mall for exercise before the stores open.

INDUSTRY RESPONDS TO THE
MASTERY-SEEKING CONSUMER

Charles Schwab, founder of the discount brokerage firm that bears his name, caught this wave early on. As far back as 1982, he introduced twenty-four-hour, seven-day-a-week order entry for stock trades. Schwab's brokers offer assistance, not advice, to their informed, mastery-seeking clients. If you want them to page you when your favorite stock hits fifty dollars a share, they will do so; but unlike most other brokerage firms, they leave the research to you. Schwab figured that his customers would turn to other data sources, like the Internet, for information, and increasingly Americans have validated his hunch. Motley Fool, a computer service that offers advice and a forum on personal finance, is one of the most successful America Online sites.

To capture the "do-it-yourself" set, Schwab offers those who enter their orders directly on a telephone keypad a 10 percent discount. They now account for 20 to 25 percent of the firm's trades. Notes Rose Wunder, a sales representative for Pitney Bowes and a typical Schwab customer, "I don't need a broker. I don't want to talk to a real person. I don't have the time."

The boom in information outlets is the clearest evidence of the market's response to the informed consumer's desire for mastery. Consumers like their information straight—no hyperbole, no pressure, just the facts. And they want their information helpful—the kind that cuts to the heart of the matter and helps them achieve their goals.

Education is a prime source of this kind of information. Once the exclusive province of those under 30, education has now been redefined as lifelong. Adult education is available everywhere: at the employment site, in extension schools, through books and videotapes, and in computer, television, and radio programs. These sources of information cover a vast range of topics, but a large proportion focus on how to master aspects of life once abdicated to professionals or neglected because of their complexity. No wonder Ted Turner, the visionary businessman who pioneered around-the-clock television news, studs his programs with snippets of "how-to" information on business, health, and fashion.

Tens of millions of Americans can now easily access information about how to manage their own legal affairs (wills and divorces); finances (investments and taxes); home construction, landscaping, and gardening; and of course, cooking. The latter perhaps best exemplifies the evolution of the desire for mastery. Beginning with Julia Child's then-revolutionary 1960s co-authored book, *Mastering the Art of French Cooking*, which enabled untrained home cooks to create a reasonable semblance of French cuisine, the how-to-cook field now covers virtually all ethnic styles of cookery techniques, preparation, and ingredients. Hankerings for vegetarian Thai entrees and multilayered

Austrian marzipan confections can be satisfied with the authoritative instructions available in the local bookstore and daily cable television programs.

Retailers have abetted "how-to" information by providing helpful advice at sale sites. Home Depot fueled its spectacular growth by providing its "do-it-yourself" customers not only with wood, nails, and paint but also with support about "how to" use these materials. It even provides contractors to install appliances, kitchens, and bathrooms.

Nevertheless, information that enables consumers to "do it themselves" does not fulfill all the desires of those who seek mastery. They also want to find the "best"—the best restaurant, the best store, the best coffee bar, the best car, the best you name it. This desire for the "best" is natural for people who for many years have received detailed evaluations of their own performance from teachers and employers. In addition to the venerable *Consumer Reports,* hundreds of services and magazines have sprung up to evaluate the goods and services that educated consumers want.

Looking for the best car? *Consumer Reports* conducts and compiles tests that complement government safety, economy, and air pollution evaluations. The polls of J.D. Power and Associates, an independent firm, present car owners' assessments of quality. Ratings in various magazines enable buffs to evaluate a car's pizzazz. Price information is readily available too; the *Blue Book* lists used car prices, while *Consumer Reports* gives detailed itemizations of the dealers' costs for most car models and various available options.

Looking for the best restaurant? Every newspaper's restaurant critic will readily provide his or her opinion. Michelin, Mobil, and AAA guides will chime in with their preferences. Zagat's will report customers' reviews. Need an evaluation of a new computer program? No problem—every large newspaper carries evaluations written by a computer-program tester, and the electronic bulletin boards are filled with users' evaluations. Want to find out if your customers can pay their bills? Dun and Bradstreet will provide you with their credit ratings.

The consumer revolutionaries' desire for mastery, and the information boom it created, has completely reshaped many industries. The mighty American automobile industry, for example, nearly collapsed from the repeated negative evaluations that, conversely, caused the

Japanese and German car industries to boom. For years its cars were almost universally rated as clunkier and less reliable than their foreign counterparts. Finally the industry restructured itself to produce vehicles whose quality and cost stand up to foreign competition. Ironically, today's American car ads proudly trumpet the results of the same surveys that once nearly caused their demise. "Ranked best in its class," states one Buick ad, citing a J.D. Power and Associates survey.

Indeed, some American car manufacturers are now sleeping with their former enemy—the quality evaluating firms. After a J.D. Power survey revealed that car owners encountered relatively many problems in Chrysler's cars in their first ninety days of ownership, Chrysler's chairman assembled the company's top six hundred officers and bluntly informed them that "clearly, we need to put more focus" on quality. The company hired a consulting firm for the sole purpose of converting its internal quality audits to the criteria used in the J.D. Power survey of perceptions of quality.

Restructuring the automobile industry to increase its quality did not even increase its relative costs. To the contrary, while family income in current dollars increased by 33 percent between 1985 and 1992, the price index of new vehicles purchased increased by only 22 percent.

Well-informed consumers have also changed their relationships with automobile dealers. Increasingly, dealers now quote a flat price rather than haggling about the prices of various options over a pro-tracted period. Haggling has become pointless because the customer knows virtually as much about the car's cost as the dealer. A *Business Week* cover says it all: It features a caricature of a sleazy, cigar-smoking car salesman, with an oily gleam on his chin and a greasy slick in his hair. "This Guy Is History!" proclaims the cover. Inside, Lonnie Reeder, a freelance video producer who had recently bought a car, explains why. Instead of a salesperson, Reeder had tuned in to Auto Vantage, a forty-nine-dollar-membership-fee buying service on America Online that reports on all aspects of automobiles and offers firm, discounted prices from two thousand dealers. By the time Reeder went to the dealer to pick up her car, the purchase was all set. "It was done within a half an hour and we figure we saved several thousand dollars," she notes.

The activist 1960s and 1970s generation that toppled Presidents Johnson and Nixon is well versed in using the legal system to accomplish its aims. "Lemon" laws, environmental standards, and mandatory recall requirements were enacted to insure the integrity of automobile manufacturers. To insure dealers' integrity, truth-in-lending and other disclosure rules that minimize misleading or flat-out fraudulent information were introduced. All the legislation was enforced by well-funded government agencies, overseen by consumer-advocate sharp-shooters like Ralph Nader.

These laws have had a profound impact on the automobile industry. As a result of Florida's lemon law, for example, a list of the models that produced the most complaints as a percentage of sales was published in 1994. (*Lemons* are defined as cars with chronic defects that are hard to repair.) Among the list's bottom ten were the once-vaunted German cars produced by Porsche and Volkswagen and Daimler-Benz's Mercedes. Most of the manufacturers conceded that "quality is an issue we are addressing." Both Porsche and Volkswagen subsequently redesigned their cars, partially in response to such surveys.

It is no accident that cars and many other retail items have become cheaper, of better quality, and available in greater variety. A mass consumer revolutionary movement that demanded convenience and mastery propelled these changes.

KEYS TO THE BIRTH OF A REVOLUTION

Responding to consumers' desires for convenience and mastery requires more than money alone. Woolworth's, the retailing giant with over $9 billion in sales, has tried for years to effectively respond to the consumer revolutionary, yet its profits continue to tumble. In the second quarter of its 1994 fiscal year, the company lost $42 million, more than four times its prior year's loss. Nor is professionalism the only key. Faltering retail store chains are filled with experts in merchandising and purchasing. Genius, too, is not necessarily the answer. Although Sam Walton, the founder of Wal-Mart, was undoubtedly a business genius, his intellect could have produced nothing had it not been accompanied by energy, discipline, people skills, a flair for marketing, a passion for control, generosity, and frugality. No single factor explains the success of Wal-Mart, but thousands of details are crucial, including its choice to locate in rural America; the precise information systems that enabled virtually instantaneous restocking of inventory; the revolutionary contracts that forced suppliers to meet Wal-Mart's own stringent quality and price terms in order to obtain its huge volume of business; and the training programs and generous profit-sharing plans that made millionaires of many Wal-Mart store personnel.

Predicting whose venture will succeed is exceedingly difficult. Before he started the Wal-Mart chain, his résumé did not show Sam Walton to be an obviously natural winner. After all, he had been only a local Arkansas store owner and could easily have been taken for a hick, whereas the managers of his retail store competitors had long experience in running big businesses. Similarly, Ted Turner, the pioneering provider of CNN's around-the-clock cable television news, had the kind of dilettantish résumé that is usually scorned by those seeking leaders for large-scale businesses. His most notable accomplishment before creating CNN was winning the America's Cup yacht race.

The key to the successful transformation of the retailing, automobile, and information industries has been consumer supremacy. The American economic system automatically sorts out winners from losers by permitting the customers to pick their favorites. Consumers vote with their dollars, choosing the retailers, cars, and information services that best meet their needs for convenience and mastery. The system encourages courageous entrepreneurs as well, handsomely rewarding those who succeed. Those rewards are well earned—after all, the innovators take tremendous risks to ferret out the best ways to satisfy demanding, assertive consumers. Responding to the needs of the consumer revolutionary requires a daring, visionary businessperson, not a bureaucrat or a social engineer. But entrepreneurs do not pick their customers' pockets to earn these handsome rewards. Their ventures are crafted without wild increases in cost and, more usually, with decreased costs.

Affirming the sovereignty of the consumer and rewarding skilled, visionary risk-takers is the key to successful transformations in the economy. Can such a revolution be accomplished in the health care sector? Can Americans obtain better and lower-cost health care? As the remaining chapters in Part 1 demonstrate, the answer is a resounding yes.

CHAPTER 2

When Patients Won't Remain Patient

Americans really do crave convenience—yet the health care system just doesn't seem to get it. After all, an industry that labels its consumers "patients" is clearly off to a bad start in factoring in convenience as a prime attribute of its services.

Some health care providers will no doubt shrug their collective, massive shoulders: "Big deal! So what if it's inconvenient?" To them, convenience is a frivolous characteristic—more appropriate for minor products such as facials or frozen dinners. Health care folks do important things—they save lives and ease pain. And they do them very well. So, how can we demand something as trivial as convenience?

The answer is that the inconvenience of our health care system packs a deadly double punch. Not only does it rob people of their time, it prevents them from obtaining important preventive medical care. Inconvenience, in fact, substantially reduces people's health status and needlessly inflates costs.

According to a recent analysis, only 45 percent of the two-year-old children of employees of Johnson and Johnson, the large medical device and pharmaceutical company, were up-to-date on their required immunizations. The relatively low rate was surprising in this affluent population, in which virtually all children were insured. The statistic was worrisome too, because since 1989 inadequate childhood immunization rates in the United States as a whole have contributed to a startling uptick in the number of measles cases and deaths. In general, fewer preschool children now in the United States are adequately immunized against many childhood diseases.

Why did these middle-class parents fail to adequately immunize their children? A detailed analysis revealed two primary reasons: lack of convenience and lack of knowledge. "Difficulty in leaving work to take the child to the physician" and "difficulty in getting an appointment" were the two main convenience factors; "awareness that immunization should begin at about two months" and "fathers graduating from college" were the two main indicators of knowledge. Neither lack of insurance nor cost was an important factor.

INCONVENIENCE INCARNATE

I recently accompanied a friend to a hospital-based ambulatory surgical center, where she was to undergo foot surgery. Ironically, the ambulatory center—literally, a site for health care for the patient who can walk—was located at the end of a maze of corridors on the eighth floor of the hospital (a long journey for someone with a foot problem). The waiting room, filled with grim-faced, long-suffering patients and their companions, resembled a holding pen. A sign on the desk announced, "Call this number when you enter this room." After a number of her calls went unanswered, my frustrated friend entered the surgical suite to announce her arrival. It turned out that the nurse assigned to answer the phone was also supervising the surgical floor. Rube Goldberg, have you come back to life as a hospital systems designer?

Hospitals are hardly the only source of inconvenience in our health care system. Although Americans hold their doctors in high regard, they grouse about long waits for appointments and long waits in the appropriately named waiting room. "Have you ever had the first appointment and still waited?" asked a friend. They consider physicians' office locations to be inconvenient as well.

Is anybody home? Doctors seem oblivious to the convenience revolution. During the years when the convenience revolution was in full swing, from 1983 to 1991, the waiting time for an appointment with a doctor increased by 40 percent. Even big cheeses have to wait. When G. Kirk Raab, the then-CEO of the fabled biotechnology company Genentech, slammed his thumb in his car trunk, he spent ninety minutes waiting in agony to see a noted hand surgeon. "I almost blew my cork," notes Raab, with admirable restraint.

Many people expand their concept of inconvenience even further after encountering the health insurance system. Finding the right person to respond to an inquiry requires yeoman labor. Convincing the person to discuss the query is yeoman level two. Obtaining resolution of the problem is yeoman level ten. People find inconvenience problems particularly acute in health maintenance organizations and other managed care organizations.

Consider the case of Susan C. Rosenfeld, a health care lawyer with breast cancer. Rosenfeld wanted to switch from her fee-for-service insurance policy, which usually requires relatively little red tape to see a specialist, to an HMO. She attempted to evaluate six major New York City HMOs:

> The first problem was just finding the right person to talk to. Multiple calls were necessary at each plan; at one, I never could find anybody knowledgeable to take my call. I tried to find out when I could expect to get permission [to have her case followed by a breast cancer specialist]. [Only one] would give me any indication. The others said they couldn't answer the question. . . . I also learned that a cancer specialist, if I got to one, might not be making the final decision about treatment. [One HMO] required my primary care physician's authorization for all specialist-recommended care. [Two] require that the primary care physician authorize all chemotherapy. [One] requires the plan's approval. [One] requires the primary care physician [to] authorize all nonemergency hospital services. [And the last requires that] nonemergency hospitalizations must be approved by the plan as well.

When Rosenfeld tried to find out which HMO physicians had experience in treating breast cancer, only two of the six HMOs provided her with their names. Nor could she find out which drugs the plans covered. Indeed, the descriptions they gave her of the services they provided were so general that she could not understand what was covered. One HMO representative told her, "You don't know what services are covered until you actually hand in that claim form."

When Rosenfeld asked each HMO for a copy of the contract that would govern the relationship between her and the HMO, only one complied after a single request. One required six calls; two refused to send the contract to her (Oxford and Healthnet); and one sent her the wrong contract. She did not succeed in finding anyone to take her call at the last HMO. Aetna, Oxford, and PruCare "even require a check for the first premium with the application form, although at that point the applicant has not seen the contract."

Notes Rosenfeld, "I can only imagine what it must be like for other people—those who aren't lawyers with health care expertise." Adds *Consumer Reports* in "Are HMOs the Answer?": "Only one thing is really certain in the brave new world of managed care. . . . It puts additional burdens on sick people."

But the inconvenience of doctors, hospitals, and health insurers is a mere quibble compared with the inconvenience of the health care system as a whole. It is simply not organized to provide convenient care for patients with chronic diseases like cancer, arthritis, or allergy, or for those who need surgery. A 1995 *Journal of the American Medical Association* study found that the overwhelming reason that people with chronic diseases use expensive hospitals inappropriately as a source of care is the absence of other, better sites. The system is organized according to the physician's specialty and the patient's requirement either for inpatient surgery (provided in a hospital) or for outpatient surgery (provided in an ambulatory surgery center or a doctor's office). Frequently, sick, debilitated patients themselves must integrate these resources to obtain all the care they require. In much of today's health care system, obtaining appropriate medical care for a chronic disease is like eating in a restaurant where you must bring your own bread, entrée, vegetables, dessert, and wine.

The absence of sites that provide disease-focused or procedure-based care is all the more surprising because of the magnitude of the need for it. For example, the 30 million people who have arthritis and the 591,000 women who had hysterectomies in 1991 each represents at least a $10 billion market. These needs could be relatively easily met because they are so concentrated. In 1987, for example, five diagnostic categories accounted for 50 percent of the costs (cardiovascular, injuries, cancer, genitourinary, and birth-related). In any other sector of the economy, a consumer in such a huge market could easily find all the resources needed to treat the problem in one convenient location. Retailers, for example, created superstores to meet the needs of much smaller markets. But most of the health care system is organized around the needs of its providers, doctors, and hospitals, not around the needs of consumers.

Nevertheless, a few innovators have responded to Americans' needs for convenience. Some, like the eyewear sector and a chain of cancer centers, have succeeded; others, like the chain called Health Stop, failed. In this chapter, I will describe how the rest of the health care system can replicate the successes and avoid the failures of these innovators.

WHY MY FRIEND'S FEET STILL HURT— A SOLEFUL STORY

Clearly, the inconvenience of health care sites, hours, and organizational structure places substantial burdens on the patient. My friend with the foot problem is a good example. After her foot had swelled to the shape of a football, she first consulted her internist, a member of the HMO to which she belonged. He referred her to a radiologist, who took a picture of the foot after she had waited for three hours. She then went back to the internist—when he was available, a few days later. He looked at the films and referred her to a podiatrist. When she finally was able to see him another few weeks later, he said, "You have arthritis. You have a bone spur. I want to do a resection on one of your foot bones—cut out a wedge, pin back that area, and remove the bone spur. I then want to scrape the bone to create a new cartilagelike growth to replace the cartilage that the arthritis destroyed." (Cartilage acts like a sponge, softening the bone-on-bone interactions in a joint.) He added, "We must do this immediately." My busy friend blanched at the grim prospect of surgery. She returned to her internist and asked him for a referral to another specialist for a second opinion. He agreed and suggested a blood test "while we're at it," handing her a form to take to the laboratory.

By this time the swelling in my friend's foot had deflated some-what, but it was still very painful. She had consulted three different doctors and spent a week of her personal time, mostly in arranging visits to them. She had not found relief: even the pain pills her internist prescribed produced such a zombie-like state that she stopped taking them. But she did start to educate herself on the problem, through the excellent *The Arthritis Help Book.* There she learned that osteoarthritis, the wearing down of joints, is a ubiquitous disease in middle age. Much more frightening are rheumatoid arthritis and gout, diseases that lead to debilitating malformations of the joints and systemic effects. These two diseases, she learned, leave markers, clues to their existence that can be found in a blood test.

Although her HMO physician pooh-poohed the need for a blood test, after he gave her the form to take to the laboratory, she surreptitiously checked off the blocks for the factors that indicate rheumatoid arthritis or gout. She then went to the hospital-based orthopedic surgeon for a second opinion. Because the hospital's director was a personal friend, she was given "special" treatment: She had to wait only a week for an appoint-ment, and the orthopedic surgeon was only an hour late for it. "No doubt about it," he said after examining the X rays, "you have gout. It looks like gout and intelligent women like you are prone to the disease." Meanwhile, the internist, alarmed by the blood test results, which showed a marker for rheumatoid arthritis, referred her to a hematologist, a blood specialist. After a two-week wait for an appointment and a two-hour wait after the scheduled time, he appeared. His reading? Yes, the markers were elevated, but because my friend showed no other symptoms of this dread disease, he really did not know what to think.

At this point, two months had passed, my friend had visited five different doctors in three different locations, and her foot still hurt. In desperation, she asked a physician friend if he could recommend some-body who specialized in treating feet. Two weeks later she found herself in yet another hospital, waiting for a podiatrist who treated primarily diabetic patients. During the hours I sat with her in his waiting room, she told me that she nevertheless counted herself lucky. Her co-waiters had terribly malformed feet. Many had lost their toes and foot bones.

After a five-minute examination of her feet and X rays, the podia-trist was frank and effective, my friend told me afterward. "I do not know the cause of your problems," the doctor had said, "but I think I know how to enable you to cope with them. The word is *orthotics*— inserts to your shoes that are molded to your feet and greatly reduce the stress placed on them. By the way, gout is totally out of the question. Gout affects the foot bones in a totally different way from that shown on your X rays. You clearly have arthritis." Two more visits to the orthotics maker (who lost her shoes at one point), and she was on the road to recovery. She could walk without pain once again.

But the story does not end here. Although the second podiatrist was excellent, my friend simply could not afford to spend the time he required—the hour-long waits for scheduled appointments. Nor could she tolerate the sloppiness of his office practices—some of the time her medical records or most recent X rays were missing. By asking many people "Do you know a good one?" she finally found yet another podiatrist who honored his appointments, kept good files, and pre-scribed exercises to strengthen the ankle and other changes. But finding him required five years, hundreds of wasted hours, and thousands of misspent dollars.

As my friend recounted the many episodes of her story to me, I wondered why a "foot center" to treat needs like hers does not exist. As I conceived of it, a foot center would be staffed by a multidisciplinary team of providers, equipped with on-site laboratory and X-ray centers, and prepared to provide foot inserts, shoes, and exercises. Every patient would be treated by a team of professionals with different expertise to bring to the diagnosis and treatment of a problem. The market for such a foot center would be vast. More than 30 million people suffer from arthritis, and many millions more suffer from foot problems; one examination of elderly people found that 22 percent complained of foot pain when standing, and those who suffered from other foot conditions (65 percent had corns or calluses) had a much higher incidence of foot pain. Foot pain is quite debilitating; in the study, it was significantly related to inability to perform everyday tasks like shopping or walking four hundred meters.

In business terms a foot center would serve a market that is not only huge but is filled with repeat customers—many foot problems are chronic. A dream of a business! Customers would flock to the center because of its convenience. And it would likely provide better care too.

The doctor who misdiagnosed my friend's condition as gout and the one who wanted to operate immediately would likely not survive in this environment because their peers—the other professionals on the foot center team—would critique their judgment. Such doctors would either shape up or be shipped out.

A foot center would certainly reduce the cost of visits to doctors and other medical professionals. As my friend noted, "With some of the doctors, I felt that they were learning on my foot and that I knew as much about my problem—honestly, more—than they did. Think of all the money I wasted with professionals who really didn't know all that much about feet. But when I finally found the real foot specialists— wow! They made the correct diagnosis and prescribed the right cure like a shot." In addition the foot center would save her employer—and the U.S. economy—all that time she wasted waiting for scheduled appointments. Because many of their patients would have similar problems, foot center schedulers should be able accurately to predict the appropriate length of visits and to minimize the lengthy waits caused by appointments that run over. The foot center would be a clear winner—the business would be good for its customers and good for the economy. But despite its clear appeal it does not exist. Why not?

SO WHAT IF IT IS INCONVENIENT?

Inconvenience denies many Americans the health care services they need. A nationwide survey of childhood immunization levels confirmed the findings of the Johnson and Johnson study. While immunization levels were inadequate in all the cities surveyed, there was considerable variation among cities. Why? Cleveland and Philadelphia—cities with low levels of immunizations for two-year-olds—were found to have substantial convenience barriers, such as lack of weekend sessions, long waiting periods, and appointment-only schedules. But Cleveland, with fewer such barriers, achieved higher immunization rates.

A more systematic analysis reached similar conclusions. A study based on the federal government's 1987 National Medical Expenditure Survey found that the number of children's visits to the doctor were negatively affected by the amount of time required for the visit—the time spent in travel, waiting time, and contact time. Improvements in convenience, however, substantially raised the number of visits. The presence of a convenient source of care—for example, a provider who is available on weekends or evenings—increased the number of visits by 16 percent. The financial characteristics of the visit were far less important than these convenience-related variables in explaining the number of visits.

Similarly, an analysis of 803 families found that single-parent families had a higher rate of "needing care but not obtaining it" than two-parent families. Other studies found that the children in single-parent families received fewer preventive and other health care services than those in two-parent families. The lack of social support in single-parent families likely influenced these results. More women in the single-parent families reported that "fewer than two persons [were] available for help in times of need."

Indeed, inconvenience is probably one reason for the puzzling failure of many well-intended efforts to improve the health care of the children in single-parent families and the rates of immunization of poor urban infants. Although well-intentioned observers believed that these shortcomings were caused by the costs of the services, providing free vaccinations and health insurance did not significantly improve the problem. An intensive analysis of the efficacy of a free vaccine program concluded, "In this sample of poor urban infants . . . free vaccines did not guarantee immunization." Similarly, an analysis of the disparate levels of preventive care in single-parent and two-parent families concluded that "differences in the probability of preventive care use between types of families remain regardless of insurance coverage." Lower-income people may suffer more from inconvenience than higher-income ones, even when they have complete health insurance. For example, lower-income Scottish women used a free osteoporosis screening program less than higher-income ones because, unlike salaried higher-income women, they were more likely to be paid by the hour, and thus, were compelled to give up wages to access the screening.

Inconvenience robs children, and probably many adults, of the prompt health care they need. Working parents find it difficult to bring their children to doctors' offices during work hours, and single parents lack the support mechanisms they need to obtain care. But deferred or denied health care is not the only consequence of the inconvenience of our system. Americans also waste untold amounts of time in wending their way through it.

The costs to our economy of these losses cannot be readily computed because the necessary data are unavailable. So alien is the idea that inconvenience diminishes our national health and productivity that the information needed to calculate its impact systematically is generally not collected. Indeed, few estimates exist of the effect of inadequate health care on productivity. Most analyses focus only on the direct costs of treating the problem and not on the ripple effect on our economy.

One early-stage analysis of this issue did attempt to estimate the productivity losses associated with certain illnesses. In one 1995 article the authors estimated that in 1990 the total cost of the mental illness depression was $44 billion. They attributed only 28 percent of this figure to the cost of direct care; the bulk of it was caused by productivity losses due to absenteeism ($11.7 billion) and low productivity ($12.1 billion). Many of these expenses could have been avoided because "80 to 90 percent of [those] suffering from a major depressive disorder can be treated successfully," but only one-third of its victims seek care.

The rise in absenteeism in the American economy is also likely related to the inconvenience of our health care system. Overall absenteeism increased by 14.1 percent between 1992 and 1995. The 1995 absenteeism level of 2.78 percent means that the average employee was paid for 2.78 hours of unproductive sick time in every 100 hours of paid time. The average annual costs of sick time were substantial—they ranged from $335 to $505 per employee. Most of the absenteeism was caused by three factors, all of which are associated with the inconvenience of the health care system: personal illness, family issues, and personal needs.

If the data needed to demonstrate the linkage between inconvenience and productivity losses do not exist, some suggestive analyses can still be performed. For example, if inconvenience accounts for only 10 percent of undertreated depression, its 1990 toll on productivity amounted to $2.4 billion. Similarly, if each of the 704 million physician visits in 1990 required a wait of "only" thirty minutes, then the loss to our economy equaled 176,000 *years* of productive work. At a conservative value of $20,000 per year lost, doctors' waiting rooms contain $3.5 billion in annual lost productivity.

These losses represent only the tip of the iceberg of productivity lost because of inconvenience. The impact of inconvenience on our health status, as exemplified by the deferral of childhood vaccinations, can only be imagined but is surely highly significant.

INCONVENIENCE IN OTHER COUNTRIES

Have other countries solved the inconvenience problem? Not at all. Consider Costa Rica, a haven of calm in a roiling sea of discontent—the Switzerland of Central America. After its visionary president, José Figueres, disbanded its military, the country invested the funds it saved in government-run systems for health care and education. As a result, Costa Rica is broadly middle-class today, with excellent health statistics for a country of its level of wealth.

When I addressed Costa Rican health practitioners about the shortcomings of the American health care system, however, my interpreter told me: "You do not know how bad things are here. The system is so inconvenient that we have to hire people to stand in line for us when we need to see a doctor. The government clinics keep their costs low by refusing to schedule appointments. Their 'first come, first serve' philosophy causes waiting lines to start forming at two A.M. Those who cannot afford the time to wait, hire somebody else to wait on line for them."

Lack of convenience is not restricted to Costa Rica. In Japan similar queues require patients to come back the next day. And in both Japan and Canada, whose national health care systems pay physicians for each patient visit, patients are required to visit their physicians much more frequently than in the United States—perhaps because physicians break up a visit into ever smaller pieces to increase their income. (Although the United States has many fewer sick days than other countries, this difference is probably heavily influenced by the generous sick day allowances available elsewhere and not only by the inconvenience of other health care systems.)

CONVENIENCE INNOVATIONS THAT RESPOND TO HEALTH INSURANCE INCENTIVES

Some American health care providers seem unaware of the impact of inconvenience on health care usage. For example, a recent article that speculated about why American women have low rates of mammograms—only 39 percent of women in their fifties had a mammogram in 1990—did not even contemplate that inconvenience might be a major factor. Yet if a mammography unit is not readily available at her doctor's office, the woman must make an additional trip to another site and probably face a lengthy wait once she gets there. Many women simply do not have time to do all this.

Instead of considering the impact of such inconvenience, the article hypothesized that the women who do not get mammograms are not knowledgeable. After all, early detection of breast cancer increases the cure rate and lessens its trauma. Knowledgeable people would surely not take the risk of missing a mammogram. Or perhaps they were lazy. Or maybe they were fearful of the pain (breasts are flattened to the extent possible during the procedure to maximize their exposure to the camera's lens), or of the high cost, or of the radiation. Put another way, the medical professionals who authored this article speculated that ignorance, laziness, and irrationality were the reasons for the low mammogram rate. Although they also gave a slap on the wrist to doctors who did not recommend the test, they answered the question "who's to blame?" by squarely blaming the victim.

The few convenience-enhancing innovations that have been made in the health care system, such as home infusion services, were created primarily for reasons other than convenience. Infusion services pump nutrients through tubes into the bodies of people who cannot swallow or digest foods and drugs but require massive amounts of them, such as those suffering from cancer. Infusion services delivered at home with the aid of smart pumps and a visiting nurse, rather than at the hospital, greatly increase the patient's convenience. But the primary motive for establishing home infusion was simply to reduce the cost of hospitalization. Because of their lower costs, the volume of home health services increased dramatically, from $100 million in 1970 to $10.3 billion in 1992.

But the focus on cost reduction in home health services is problematic. For one thing, the patient's level of satisfaction with the service is generally unknown. Are the nurses gentle or brutal when they insert the needle into the frail patient's vein? Are the people who deliver the infusions surly or courteous? Prompt or laggardly? Neat or messy? The answers to such important questions are not known because they are usually not asked. After all, the primary purpose of the innovation is not to increase customers' convenience but to reduce costs. The health insurance companies that primarily pay for home health services are much more interested in controlling their costs than in the patients' satisfaction.

Providers of home health services lavish attention on those who can raise their revenues: the doctors and hospitals who refer their patients to them. The providers' interest in these referral sources has caused allegations of corrupt and unethical practices in the industry. Some providers of home infusion services have been accused of bribing sources of referral or engaging in more subtle but equally unethical practices to induce referrals. For example, one federal grand jury charged a doctor with receiving $134,600 in alleged kickbacks from Caremark International, the country's largest provider of home health care, for referring patients to the company. Because the physician did not provide any services to the company, the grand jury viewed these payments as a bribe. Similarly, T^2 Medical Inc., a home-infusion company, agreed to pay a $500,000 penalty and to cease many of its physician payment patterns as part of its settlement of federal fraud charges.

CONVENIENCE INNOVATIONS WHEN THE HEALTH CARE CONSUMER IS SOVEREIGN

In contrast to health care sectors whose revenues are derived primarily from insurance companies and that remain, by and large, inconvenient, the convenience revolution has most dramatically affected those parts of the health care system in which consumers pay for services directly out of their own pockets, such as eyewear and some dental services. Because these providers are usually paid by the consumer and not by the insurance company, they have designed their services to meet consumers' needs for convenience. They have increased the variety and quality of their services, made useful information freely available, and sold the services in easy-to-reach places. Further, they have increased their prices at only moderate rates, comparable to other industries that seek to meet customers' needs. Problems of corruption generally do not exist in these ventures. After all, why bribe a doctor for patient referrals when customers are free to choose?

High quality, low cost, convenience, choice—how do they do it?

The Secret of That Sparkling Smile

The Mid America Dental, Hearing, and Vision Center in Mount Vernon, Missouri, offers exceptional low-cost, same-day service for dentures. (Customers are sensitive to the costs of dental care because only 55 percent of all insurance companies offered dental insurance in 1991, and the coverage was frequently incomplete.) The center draws customers from all over the United States. Notes an administrator, "We had a woman fly down from Alaska last spring. She had a lot of crown and bridge work. It was going to cost her $12,000. It was $4,500 here. So she flew down for two visits and still saved money." The prices of Mid America and those of providers of similar services differ substantially. For example, while the center's lowest-priced set of dentures sells for $195, a comparable set is sold by a dentist in the area for $1,000 (although the dentist's price includes some services for which the center charges extra).

How does Mid America keep its prices so low and its service so fast? Volume and focus. The center owns its own laboratory, so that it can produce the dentures rapidly, and it spreads its costs over an unusually large number of customers, typically a hundred each day. Apparently, it is not a reduction in quality that keeps prices low. Notes the ex-head of the Missouri Dental Board, "I would say the number of complaints generated per number of visits is probably lower for them than it is for the average dental population." He adds, "People do realize they get what they pay for." To maintain quality, the center offers free denture adjustments in the first ninety days and carefully monitors customer feedback. As a result of the favorable perception of its quality and costs, 80 percent of its customers are referred through word-of-mouth.

The Eyes Have It

Another example of convenient health care is the eyewear sector, as I discovered when I myself went shopping for eyeglasses and contact lenses. I found the experience even more convenient than shopping for a business suit in the revamped retailing system and vastly more convenient than shopping for most other forms of health care.

I began by referring to a *Consumer Reports* article on "Buying Glasses." The article explained clearly the different materials used in contact lenses and glasses, their prices, and their pros and cons, among other things. Although I could have chosen from many different providers—including one-stop stores that provide examinations and eyewear in one visit—I chose to see my doctor, an ophthalmologist (a physician who performs surgery as well as more routine eye procedures). He examined my eyes and explained why I could no longer see things that were either far away or very close, then gave me a prescription for eyeglasses and contact lenses. He explained how I could fill my contact lens prescription by mail.

Off I went to buy eyeglasses. Here too I found the *Consumer Reports* article helpful. It told me what to look for in the fitting of eyeglasses and the prices charged by different optical shops. Armed with this information, I went off to a store in the local mall that was open for business at night and on weekends, surrounded by acres of parking.

A friendly optician helped me select, from the hundreds of available choices, the eyeglass frames that were most flattering to my face and best suited to my lifestyle. (Opticians cannot assess eye conditions, but they can fit eyeglasses. In the past they shaped and ground the glass lenses. Today, however, prescription lenses are mostly supplied by centralized laboratories and shipped to the opticians, who then grind them to fit the opening in the eyeglass frame.) The variety of prices was as wide as that of the styles—ranging from $50 for a store-brand frame to more than $200 for an Armani design.

Although opticians are not required to have much formal education, this one had considerable on-the-job experience. Her skills were evident as she carefully fitted the eyeglasses to my face. Many of the frames are delivered quickly, complete with lenses, because the store has its own machine to grind eyeglass lens blanks. The optician explained that my prescription took "so long" to fill (one day) because of its unusual nature. Normally, the glasses would have been ready in an hour. The store would even have given me a beeper, so that I could leave to do whatever I liked. The beeper would have notified me when my glasses were ready to be picked up.

Meanwhile, my teenage son went to a neighborhood optometrist (a graduate of a four-year college of optometry, who can examine eyes and prescribe corrective measures, including, in many states, drugs, but who cannot perform surgery) for his contact lenses. I knew that wearing contact lenses is tricky and requires considerable education and training. This optometrist's convenient location, less than a mile from our house, made her an ideal choice for my son's needs. Because she is a member of my community whom I see often, I thought she would want to succeed with my son's lenses as much as I. Her work did not disappoint me. She was informed, supportive, and effective in fitting him for lenses and educating him in how to wear them.

What a difference between this experience and the care my friend received for her arthritic foot. Unlike her, I experienced convenience: wide choices in materials, styles, and prices, no waits, convenient locations, and expert, friendly service. And I had my pick of sites and types of professionals—no hassles, no need for referrals. When I checked the price history of eyewear versus that of the hospitals and doctors my friend used, my eyes really popped. Eyewear prices had inflated at a rate comparable to that of the general economy, while hospitals' and doctors' prices had inflated at rates double or triple the economy.

Eyewear products are reasonably priced and convenient, while foot care is outrageously high priced and inconvenient. Why?

Two factors clearly distinguish the two types of health services: the consumer and the sources of supply. As a consumer of eyewear, I chose my own suppliers and paid for their services mostly out of my own pocket. My friend, in contrast, was told who to see and was almost fully insured for the care. In eye care three different types of professionals provide overlapping services, while in foot care each professional has his or her own narrow niche.

These two factors cause providers of eyewear products and services to compete ferociously for clients. Both ophthalmologists and optometrists can assess visual acuity, and they, along with opticians, can sell eyewear. No single one of them is the sole provider of a particular service (except for ophthalmologists, who are the sole providers for surgical services). More important, they must appeal directly to the customers, who pay directly for most of their services. Because the consumer is very interested in price, the different suppliers compete on this basis. *Consumer Reports* found that the most satisfied customers were those who bought from the eyewear chain stores that charged the least. The price information is readily available, pasted right on the eyeglass frames themselves or in advertisements.

Eyewear chain stores clearly have a cost advantage over the local optometrist or optician who works independently. For example, the hundreds of stores owned by Lenscrafters and Pearle Vision, the two largest optical retail chain stores in the United States, can extract price concessions from their suppliers in exchange for the large volume of their purchases. My local, independent optometrist probably could not obtain comparable price reductions from her suppliers.

But customers value other aspects of service besides price, and the different eyewear stores compete in these dimensions as well. The *Consumer Reports* survey found that for all types of stores, location and choice of frames were more important to respondents than price. Those who shopped in independent stores valued service quality much more than those who shopped at chain stores. Price was rated as a major attraction by only 6 percent of the respondents who bought at private stores, compared with 32 percent of those who shopped at chain stores. But same-day service was much more important to chain store shoppers than to those who shopped at a private store.

The competitive dimensions are clear. Local, independent optometrists and opticians compete by offering what consumers perceive as better quality of service, while the chain store operations offer lower prices, better hours, and more rapid service. Both offer good locations and choices of frames. No wonder the overall satisfaction of the respondents to the survey was so high!

Competition in the eyewear sector not only lowers price, it enhances the quality of the product and continually lowers its costs. The thick, Coke-bottle lenses of yesterday have been supplanted by thin glass or lightweight, impact-resistant plastic ones. The first hard contact lenses, which required weeks of training to acclimate the eye to the presence of a piece of plastic, were succeeded by soft plastic lenses, which are more comfortable than hard ones, and by gas-permeable rigid lenses that provide better visual acuity than the soft ones. Competition motivates suppliers continually to innovate the materials and instrumentation used to produce contact lenses. Johnson and Johnson, for example, recently invested millions in a technology to produce clear, disposable, soft contact lenses at low cost to the consumer. Managerial innovations lower costs too. Ultimately, mail-order houses will no doubt fulfill the desire of 80 percent of patients who want to receive their lenses by mail, thereby eliminating the need for many retail stores.

Direct payment by the consumer also plays a key role in explaining the difference in the "shopping" experiences for foot care and eye care. The only exception to the generally modest price increases for eye care is with the ophthalmologists. Their incomes have inflated from $120,000 in 1990 to $162,000 in 1994, at twice the rate of inflation. It is surely no coincidence that ophthalmologists are the only providers of eye care whose services are primarily paid for by someone other than the user. (In 1990 97 percent of the private companies that offered vision coverage paid for eye examinations, but only 68 percent paid for eyeglasses.) Indeed, when I used my ophthalmologist's service, I had no idea what he charged, because my insurance company was paying the bill. Similarly, my friend did not know the cost of the many doctors she visited in her lengthy foot-healing journey. All of their fees too, except for a modest copayment, were covered by her health insurance policy.

Conversely, the orthotics that help support painful feet are generally not paid for by insurance. Their prices are very reasonable—only $150 to $250, including the doctor's fee, for custom-made devices. Their cost is kept down by competition with mass merchandisers of orthotics. I found mass-manufactured orthotics for only $15 a pair at my local drugstore. The fact that the patients pay directly for orthotics out of their own pockets also helps keep their prices down.

BARRIERS TO CONVENIENT VENTURES

When consumers pay directly for health care, the services they receive are economical and convenient. But the success of convenient health care ventures is not guaranteed. Two factors distinguish successful convenience innovators from unsuccessful ones: the ability to overcome legal barriers to innovations, and the presence of the relevant managerial skills.

Legal Barriers

The competitive environment in today's eyewear sector was not easy to create. In the 1970s three major barriers to such competition existed. First, customers frequently could not obtain a copy of their prescriptions. In many states the eye specialist could legally refuse to release it, even if requested to do so by the customer. Secondly, advertising was prohibited in many areas, so that even when customers had the prescription, they could not easily compare prices among different suppliers. Providers justified both laws as necessary for the protection of patients, who were portrayed as naifs, easily dazzled by misleading advertising and seduced into buying eyewear ill-suited to their needs. Third, in many states optometrists were prohibited from working for opticians or for a chain eyewear store. They were to be "independent," working only for themselves in their own offices. State laws frowned on practices in which an optometrist or optician owned a number of stores, staffed by other salaried optometrists.

These laws considerably hampered competition. Patients who could not obtain their prescriptions were virtually forced to buy their eyewear from the prescribing optometrist. And with advertising prohibited, price competition was virtually impossible. Last, if an optometrist could not open multiple offices, then he or she could not make the large volume of purchases that could reduce the costs of supplies.

These anticompetitive laws were most often promulgated by state boards for optometrists, which defined the standards that optometrists had to follow for state licensing. Frequently the state boards were staffed by independent optometrists whose interests inevitably involved self-preservation. Not surprisingly, they created some standards that protected them from competition. The extensive testimony compiled during Senate hearings on restrictive and anticompetitive practices in the eyeglass industry explains and refutes these self-protective laws, as illustrated by the following exchanges:

> Mr. Gordon [staff economist to the select committee on small business, subcommittee on monopoly and anticompetitive activities]: What are the arguments generally advanced to justify [these] State laws . . . ?

> Ms. Smith [acting director, Bureau of Consumer Protection, Federal Trade Commission]: One is that . . . abolition of the ad ban . . . will result in false and deceptive practices. We do not take that very seriously, because one of our functions is to prevent false and deceptive advertising. We think that [without advertising] . . . it would be very difficult to find out where to purchase items and what they cost. Another argument . . . is that the quality of service will deteriorate, that eye

care will become a commercial operation, as opposed to a professional operation. We think that argument can be easily answered. The quality of care depends a great deal on the individual practitioner. There is no way that advertising bans should affect the quality of care. . . .

Mr. Gordon: What does that mean . . . [professionalism]?

Ms. Smith: That is the term that has been used by all of the professions to distinguish themselves from commercial occupations. Advertising bans have been considered by all professions as a way of preserving professionalism.

Senator Haskell [Colorado]: I could put it a different way. Of course, professionals are interested in making money and for that reason they do not want to advertise, and if they advertise, then they would be lowering themselves in the money-making department.

The Federal Trade Commission's staff testified that it found no evidence to indicate that advertising lowers the quality of care. It did, however, find substantial evidence that advertising lowers price. A study conducted by Lee Benham and Alexandra Benham demonstrated that the prices in states with high degrees of control by boards of optometry were 25 to 40 percent higher than elsewhere. In states with higher prices, 25 to 40 percent fewer people obtained eyeglasses. Less well-educated people were more adversely affected by these restrictions. Here was a vicious cycle: the lack of advertising needlessly increased prices, and the resulting artificially high prices reduced the purchase of eyeglasses, particularly by those who were less well-educated.

Ultimately, the bans on advertising and some of the other anti-competitive practices were overturned. But progress was slow. Dr. Stanley Pearle of Dallas, the pioneering optometrist who founded Pearle Vision Centers, recollects that he opened his first stores in Georgia, although he lives in Texas, because Texas laws prohibited corporate ownership of multiple sites by an optometrist. Nevertheless, Dr. Pearle and other entrepreneurs persisted, overcame the profession's self-protective laws, and ultimately transformed the eyewear sector into the consumer-friendly one I recently encountered.

Dr. Pearle explains its evolution: "Extended hours of services have been demanded by consumers, and we met this need by providing convenient locations, evening hours, and recently even Sunday afternoon service." Noted an associate of Dr. Pearle's, "Increased volume plus more visible locations changed the traditional merchandising of eyewear to a more open concept with self-service and walk-up displays. The full service laboratory, rapid fabrication, and deep inventory of frames, lenses, and contact lenses made for one-stop, competitive delivery of total eyecare."

The competition among providers of eyewear continues to be ferocious. For example, For Eyes, an eyewear chain known for its rock-bottom prices, has grown explosively. Its prices have been rated 40 percent lower than those of most competitors by a nonprofit group that surveyed eyewear stores in San Francisco and Washington, D.C. Additionally, notes the publisher of *Consumers' Checkbook,* a nonprofit magazine that has evaluated Washington-area retail and service outlets, "their presence in the market does keep prices down."

Managerial Barriers

Even in the absence of legal barriers, convenience-enhancing health care ventures can still fail. The saga of Health Stop illustrates the managerial deficits that can cause such failures.

WHY HEALTH STOP STOPPED "Mommy, Mommy!" screamed the little boy's voice in the radio commercial. "I have a bad cut! Help me, help me."

"No problem, Billy," replied a calm, matronly voice, "We're going to Health Stop. Your cut will be cared for in a few minutes."

The ad sounded good to me. It implied that Health Stop offered quick, convenient, competent health care services. But a few years after this commercial first aired, Health Stop folded. Why? Because the company encountered unexpected requirements in the convenience-enhancing health care sector that it lacked the skills to manage.

Health Stop was created to meet the needs of consumers for convenient physician care. It targeted two different types of consumers: the 24 percent of the public who did not have a regular source of care, and those whose regular source of care was not immediately available and who needed care for minor emergencies, like Billy's. A substantial amount of this type of care is paid for directly by the consumer.

Health Stop's aim was to serve these customers quickly in convenient neighborhood locations. Over time it hoped to build a loyal base of regular customers, supplemented by those who used it for emergency care. Its CEO, a well-regarded business consultant, chose its locations carefully, selecting middle-class communities that were underserved by private physicians. He placed his centers in shopping malls and kept them open from 7 A.M. to 9 P.M. on weekdays and during daytime hours on Saturdays and Sundays. The Health Stops were always staffed with a doctor, a nurse, and a receptionist and were equipped with laboratory and X-ray facilities. The centers provided convenience in four ways: location, hours, a "no appointment needed" policy, and immediately available laboratory and X-ray services.

The Health Stop concept was similar to that of a supermarket. Indeed, its name was chosen because the centers were initially planned as physical extensions of the Stop and Shop supermarket chain—easy to reach and easy to use. The patient would walk in, with no appointment needed; sit down, but not for long; receive quick service; pay the bill; and leave. Health Stop's charges were similar to those of neighborhood private physicians and substantially lower than those of the hospital emergency room. It monitored quality carefully too, making double readings of X-ray films and external reviews of medical records and systematically informing physicians of developments that were likely to affect their patients, such as local flu epidemics.

Health Stop thus offered greater convenience, a wider range of services, and better review of quality than most individual physicians could offer. For a while, the company prospered. Buoyed by a massive investment from Hambrecht and Quist, a San Francisco venture capital firm with a good reputation for investing in technology ventures, the company, at its peak, earned revenues in excess of $100 million. But it was rarely profitable, and after a long period Hambrecht and Quist pulled the plug. Bereft of that nourishing flow of cash, the company folded.

What went wrong? Like the eyewear chains, Health Stop faced

formidable pressure from existing providers. The managers of hospital emergency rooms complained that Health Stops, and other organizations like them, were unfairly taking away their "best patients"—that is, those with minor emergencies—and leaving the hospitals with only serious emergencies. Although self-preserving complaints from existing providers against innovators should come as no surprise, the nature of the complaint was somewhat odd. After all, isn't a hospital supposed to care for serious emergencies? And aren't minor emergencies best treated in the community? Why clog up a hospital emergency room with patients like Billy? (Ironically, some centers that were owned by Health Stop are now owned by the very sorts of nonprofit hospitals that once complained about them.)

But the basic reason for the demise of Health Stop was that it could not adequately fulfill its promise of convenience. Yes, the centers were conveniently located—but the service was frequently as slow as cold molasses. The physicians were paid a fixed salary and therefore had little incentive to see the customers quickly or to delegate work to the nurses to speed up the process. They earned the same income whether they saw patients quickly or not. And because many of the physicians were moonlighters—that is, they had full-time jobs elsewhere and worked at Health Stop for only a short period of time— they felt little loyalty to the organization or to its patients. So if a patient was angry over having to wait three hours to see Dr. X, the doctor was not too upset: after all, he or she was very unlikely ever to see that patient again.

Why did Health Stop not pay its physicians on a fee-for-service basis, as private physicians are paid? Because if the physicians were to be paid on a fee-for-service basis, they might as well be in business for themselves, as independent practitioners. And they might prefer that status because as independent practitioners they would not have to defend themselves against charges of providing "unfair competition" by the medical and hospital establishment.

So Health Stop's management was between a rock and a hard place. Fee-for-service payment would enhance the patient convenience, but the physicians wanted the safety of a fixed salary; yet while the fixed-salary policy insured the physicians' presence at Health Stop, it did not offer incentives to provide efficient, convenient service.

Was the problem unsolvable? Not really. After all, many service organizations, such as restaurants and hotels, have figured out how to motivate their salaried employees to provide efficient service. The medical professionals in the eyewear industry certainly know how to do it. Although providers of health services cannot control their patients' needs, nor select who they will serve and when, numerous techniques have proven successful in minimizing waits and delays. Even a busy hospital emergency department reduced its median waiting time by 22 percent through the application of simple changes: providing separate processes for short-duration and routine visits, using the waiting time to provide information and counseling to the patient, affiliating with a primary care group to which patients were referred, establishing guidelines for response time and monitoring them, and analyzing historical data to estimate future demand patterns. But the venture capitalists from Silicon Valley who knew how to motivate engineers to etch ever more circuitry into tiny pieces of silicon were not nearly as conversant in how to motivate doctors. They were also unfamiliar with the public-relations hardball of the medical-hospital establishment. After Health Stop was tarred as a profit-gouger and spurned by its potential customers, Hambrecht and Quist gave up the battle, despite last minute modifications to the physicians' incentive program.

Health Stop's management was hardly incompetent. But they lacked the experience needed to successfully enhance convenience for health care customers. It can be done, but it is not easy. The Salick Health Care centers present one way to do it.

SALICK HEALTH CARE On a sunny Sunday afternoon, Dr. Bernard Salick, a California nephrologist, watched his teenage daughter gamely mount her horse. She found it a bit difficult because one of her legs had been amputated to halt the spread of a ravenous cancer tumor in her leg bone. But once mounted, she rode with the best of them.

"She probably would not be alive today," Dr. Salick notes, "if I hadn't sought out the services of that wonderful doctor in New York. He saved her life with his method for treating cancer. Her tumor was so rare that most doctors might treat only one per year; but he treated hundreds of them. Nobody out here was willing to do it his way. In fact, most of the other doctors hadn't even heard of his treatment protocols. But when I saw that their way was not going to work and faced the prospect of my daughter's death, I searched the medical literature for an approach that made sense to me.

"When I read the reports on his work and learned of his vast experience," Dr. Salick continues, "I hopped on a plane to New York with my wife, my daughter, and two other children. He saved her life. But even there, as in California, the hospital service was not satisfactory. First of all, the diagnostic radiology and radiation therapy sites were usually miles from her room, buried in a dark, lead-sheathed suite in the basement. The poor weak kid had to travel endlessly, up and down long hallways and freight elevators, to reach them. And her room wasn't much better: ugly, small, with no place for us to stay to give her support while she was being slowly infused with the toxic chemicals used to kill cancer cells. Sometimes treatments would take twenty hours. We had to squeeze ourselves in there.

"It was very important for us to be with her. After all, cancer is a deadly disease, she was only a child, and the treatment is painful and debilitating. She needed our support, especially because the hospital offered few emotional support services to her and virtually none to us. I hired a psycho-oncologist (a therapist who understands cancer, the side effects of its drugs, and pain management and who deals with the dynamics of the disease and the response of the family to it) to work with us. Don't get me wrong—we're not a dysfunctional family. But one of us was in the throes of a deadly disease and all of us needed help in coping with all the feelings her illness created in us.

"And although the nurses were wonderful, hardworking, and devoted, they really knew all too little about cancer. How could they? They were working in a hospital that treated so many other health care problems that they couldn't know very much about hers. But my daughter needed special care. Cancer is different.

"The worst part of the hospital's services was the emergency room. Whenever she had an unexpected complication, we would drive out to the hospital. The first problem was finding a parking space. So here's my young daughter with an emergency; my wife is sick with worry and has two other young children to care for; and I have to desert them to try to find a place to park in the hospital's cramped garage. The next problem was the emergency room itself. We were usually there next to people bleeding profusely from gunshot wounds, suffering from heart attacks, or suffocating from an asthma seizure. It was a madhouse. Trying to obtain prompt, courteous treatment for my young daughter in that environment was a challenge.

"I synthesized the problems we encountered into two types. First, the health care professionals who treated cancer patients frequently felt overwhelmed. The doctors didn't have a large enough pool of professional colleagues to cross-fertilize each other with their takes on the latest cancer developments. And the general hospital environment was not well suited to their needs. One doctor after another complained to me about the difficulty in obtaining the medical equipment, drugs, and supplies they needed. The hospital administrators had so many different demands to deal with that they could not focus clearly and effectively on the special needs of the oncologist. Because cancer treatment changes so rapidly and because there are so many different kinds of cancers, the administrators' slow response could create a real problem for the quality of care. And of course, billing for these doctors' services was a constant hassle. The billing staff was no more specialized than anybody else in the administration. They didn't know the difference between EPO and EPA. [EPO is an expensive biotechnology product used to treat the anemia caused by cancer therapy, while the EPA is a federal government agency.] So they made many mistakes, which the doctors had to spend much time to correct. The nurses had the same kinds of complaints.

"All of the medical professionals felt the need for more social services for their patients. All diseases affect the mind and the heart just as much as other parts of the body, but the medical staff could offer little mind and heart support. Again, the emotional problems created by cancer are different from those created by other diseases. After all, your own cells are running amok, eating up healthy parts of your body. Other diseases are different—and they all require different kinds of emotional therapies. But virtually none were proffered. Medical professionals themselves need support for dealing with the intense effect of this disease on their own emotions.

"The second problem I noted," Dr. Salick continues, "was that of physical design. Miles and miles of corridor separated one thing from another. Everything was ugly—designed for ease of maintenance and not for visual beauty. The patient rooms were too cramped for visitors, and the visitors' rooms were cramped and ugly too. The hospital was designed to suit the doctor and those who donated buildings, not the patient. For example, all the radiologists were in the basement, the only site that could support the weight of the heavy lead sheathing their equipment requires. But nobody else wanted to be down in the basement. So Dr. X, the oncologist, has his office in the fifth floor of the doctors' office building, next door to the hospital. The operating suites are tucked away in yet another building constructed before World War II and miles away. One kind donor gave the hospital a few million dollars to build new rooms for the patients, but because no space was left on the hospital's present grounds, the new rooms were built on top of an existing ten-story building. What a mess!

"These problems were widespread. After all, over a million people in the United States get cancer every year. Most of them encounter similar problems. Serious as they were, my problems weren't so bad because I'm a doctor myself; but what about other people? The problems of lack of focus on the disease and on the patient must be an even worse burden for them than they were for me."

At the time of his daughter's cancer treatment, Dr. Salick, an entrepreneur, had recently sold his chain of kidney dialysis centers to a large national corporation. Because of his business skills and experience, he could respond to the problems he had observed in delivery of cancer services by creating a better way of providing them. Presently eleven new cancer centers exist under the umbrella of Dr. Salick's company, Salick Health Care.

Shortly after his daughter's recovery, Dr. Salick designed and implemented a way of delivering cancer services so that other patients could avoid the difficulties he encountered.

First, to insure that all their personnel are well trained and totally focused on the treatment of cancer, the cancer centers treat only cancer patients. Although the centers are located on the grounds of major hospitals, they are self-contained facilities, equipped with all the medical technology needed to treat ambulatory cancer patients. Next, the centers were designed with the comfort of the patients and their loved ones in mind. The patient rooms are lovely and cozy; the infusion rooms are stocked with interesting distractions; there are playrooms for young children, along with play therapists; and social support is always available from trained therapists. Patients pay a flat rate for a visit and the use of the facility and therapists are not billed as extras to encourage their use. Companions are welcome; both in the patients' infusion rooms, with their inviting armchairs, or in the waiting areas, stocked with reading materials and plentiful, free food and beverages. The oncologists and other medical specialists who staff the centers learn from each other and from the experiences of the many other Salick centers, a cross-fertilization difficult to attain in a multiple-purpose hospital.

The ambience in the centers is familial. When I toured one with Dr. Salick, he greeted a patient who was receiving infusion therapy. "Hey, doc," said the patient, "will I be able to play the violin when this is all over?" "Of course," replied Dr. Salick. "Wow, this place is wonderful," said the patient. "I can't play the violin now!" An old joke, of course, but it captures the friendly environment. Perhaps the most telling point that distinguishes Salick centers from other sources of cancer care is a detail—twenty-four-hour valets greet weary cancer patients and their companions and relieve them of the need to park their cars.

The Salick Health Care centers have clearly increased the quality of care, from both the patients' and the providers' point of view. Notes one oncologist, "I have so much more time to practice good medicine here. The administrative hassles that once consumed so much of my time—the billing corrections and the endless justifications for the support I needed—have all evaporated."

Like other disease- or procedure-centered providers of health care, such as the so-called "cataract factories" that offer only cataract-removal operations, the costs of these cancer centers are likely lower than those of most other cancer care providers. (The reasons for the lower costs are discussed in Part 3 of this book). But unlike many other disease- or procedure-based providers, the major innovation of the Salick centers is in their convenience. They are easy to find, easy to enter, and easy to use. They organize all the disparate elements of care so that patients can focus on the healing process. Notes the *Economist*, "Salick has . . . become the world's first full-service disease management firm."

The word *convenience* perhaps trivializes the importance of these innovations, because it is so often connected with products like plastic wrap. But Salick's centers represent significant change in the context of the vastly inconvenient health care system. Most health care service sites are designed with the providers' ease in mind. These cancer centers, in contrast, are designed primarily to make life easy for the patient. It's a revolutionary concept indeed.

KEYS TO CONVENIENCE-ENHANCING VENTURES

If convenience improves the quality of medical care *and* increases the productivity of the economy, why don't more convenient health care services exist? The reason is that substantial regulatory and managerial barriers stand in the way.

The founders of Health Stop understood the importance of convenience. They had the right idea, and they invested substantial amounts of money to translate the idea into a reality. But money and a good idea were not enough. Implementing the concept successfully required managerial skills: human resource management skills to recruit and motivate the right doctors; operations management skills to schedule and staff the offices to minimize the patients' wait; marketing skills to understand the customers' needs and their satisfaction with the services; and regulatory skills to counteract the sniper attacks of established health care providers.

Stanley Pearle and Bernard Salick, the founders of Pearle Vision and Salick Health Care, had good ideas too. But unlike Health Stop's managers, they also possessed the requisite managerial skills. Dr. Pearle understood how to grapple with the substantial regulatory barriers created by independent optometrists, who viewed optical chains as a threat. And Dr. Salick understood well the process of delivering medical care—after all, he was a doctor himself—and he deeply understood the patients' needs too, because of his daughter's bout with cancer.

Drs. Pearle and Salick are happy accidents—health care professionals with a knack for business. But we cannot rely on people like them to create successful convenience-enhancing health care ventures. Their combination of skills is too rare. Instead, experienced service-providing managers who have the requisite skills should find the health care industry an inviting setting. People with experience in the retailing and service industries, in which the consumer is sovereign, know well the lessons that eluded Health Stop's managers. They understand how to provide quick service, even when a rush occurs (think of McDonald's), and they know how to manage unavoidable waits; for example, understanding that "unexplained waits are longer than explained waits," they take care to apologize to their customers when a scheduled appointment has been delayed.

Presently, two barriers dissuade experienced service managers from entering the health care industry. First, the market for convenience-enhancing ventures is relatively small, because most parts of the health system whose costs are paid directly by the consumer are already convenient. Moreover, the health care services paid for by an insurer or by government are unlikely to reflect consumers' desires for convenience. The Registry of Motor Vehicles is an example of a governmental notion of convenience. And insurers want to control their costs, rather than to enhance productivity. To them, inconvenience is costless.

Considerable regulatory barriers also hobble innovation. Licensing requirements needlessly restrict managers' ability to select appropriate personnel, while various legal roadblocks against the union of medical and business skills are in place. For example, within their area of competence, physician assistants (PAs), cost-effective complements to physicians, can provide care of a quality virtually indistinguishable from a doctor's, at much lower pay. Yet some insurance-reimbursement laws require a physician's on-site supervision of the PA, even when it is unnecessary or when the PA is providing care in rural areas that have no physicians. Restrictions on the rights of PAs to prescribe medication also hamper their ability to deliver care in the isolated rural areas that need them. Such legal restrictions are likely guided by the desire to protect consumers from unqualified and greedy practitioners. But whatever the intention, they clearly also protect physicians' turf from raids by PAs, their potentially cost-effective competitors.

Weary Americans want convenience from their health care system, and a few early-stage innovators have demonstrated how to provide it. Ultimately the public will get its way, as it should; after all, people pay a considerable price, in lost time and health status, for the system's inconvenience. But until consumers can more directly voice their needs and until self-serving regulatory barriers are overturned, the convenience revolution that has transformed the retailing industry will be slowed and Americans' health and productivity will continue to be held hostage to the inconvenience of their health system.

CHAPTER 3

Give Me Mastery or Give Me Death: The New Health Care Activist

The success of businesses that provide customers with information, choices, and a sense of control—what I call mastery—is clear. From *Consumer Reports* to Home Depot, people want to control their fate. Does meeting this demand for mastery work in health care? You bet it does.

DO YOU KNOW A GOOD ONE?

I was on a long flight back from Europe with two acquaintances, when Stella asked, "Do you know a good gynecologist? I need one to help me deal with menopause. My doctor gave me hormones to overcome the flushing and night sweats, but the pills have all sorts of side effects. They cause bleeding and I feel bloated. Anyway, I don't like taking pills, especially hormones.

"I looked up the menopause treatment options in my *Merck Manual.* The estrogen patch it described sounded much better than the pills to me. But my doctor won't discuss options with me. She's a little dictator. She tells me what to do, instead of discussing different solutions with me. And when I have questions, she's hard to reach on the phone and gives brusque responses.

"I don't want a doctor who is a dictator. I don't want lectures. I want someone who will work with me in dealing with my symptoms.

"Do you know a good one?"

The dynamic that Stella expresses is a subtle one: she wants information and support—but she wants to do it herself too. As one advertising executive notes, "What you're seeing is a real sea change in the way people interact with the marketplace. You've got a much smarter, much more seasoned consumer. These are people who go to a [provider] and say, 'Together let's figure out how I can do this myself.'"

So what happens when people "do it themselves" in health care? A lot of good things, as Sam's story illustrates.

Sam's usually smiling face looked pinched and clouded that day in 1980. "You all better be nice to me now, 'cause I will be gone pretty soon," he said. "Us Johnson men and women have bad heart genes. Our hearts just give up and die prematurely. I'm fifty-five now, and I see the Grim Reaper lookin' over my shoulder. I know I'll be gone soon."

At his sixty-fifth birthday party, I reminded Sam of this statement. "I guess I outfoxed those bad genes," he said. "What's your secret, Sam?" I asked. "No secret," he responded. "All that stuff in the papers about fat, smoking, binge drinking, and exercising got to me. I went to the doctor, and she got me some help in getting off the sauce. I joined a support group. She gave me a nicotine patch to help me stop smoking and a pep talk every once in a while. All in all, I did just like everybody else. I got boring. No more rib roasts and bacon, no more tobacco, just a little bourbon to take the edge off, and lots of horseback ridin' and sleep. And I feel great."

Between 1968 and 1976 the lives of 630,000 Americans, like Sam, were saved from ischemic heart disease (a disease in which the heart's blood-pumping function is impaired because the heart is deprived of oxygen). During that period the death rate from the disease declined by 21 percent. Between 1980 and 1990 it plunged still further, by 22 percent. In 1980, the year Sam made his prediction, 544 years of potential life were lost before the age of 65 per 100,000 people. By 1991, the year of his sixty-fifth birthday, the number of years needlessly lost because of ischemic heart disease had dropped to 344 per 100,000 people.

A careful analysis has concluded that lifestyle changes caused 54 percent of the reduction in the 1968–1976 period—30 percent was attributed to the decline in blood cholesterol levels, and 24 percent to reductions in smoking. During that period these lifestyle modifications saved an estimated 340,000 lives. Medical innovations helped too. The new devices that unplugged clogged arteries to the heart, the drugs that controlled high blood pressure, and the coronary care units that treated injured hearts saved an estimated 249,000 lives. But while these medical interventions were important, none of them reduced death rates as significantly as either of the two lifestyle modifications alone. It is important to note that the total impact of the medical interventions was less significant than that of the lifestyle modifications because medical interventions are expensive; in 1993 they accounted for a considerable portion of the $122 billion cost of treating heart disease. Lifestyle modifications, like smoking cessation and diet modification, on the other hand, are not nearly so costly.

Sam's story has been replicated by tens of millions of Americans who changed their destructive health habits, frequently with the support of the health care system but always with the support of themselves. Their mastery has saved the system a ton of money and enhanced the country's productivity too. But plenty of costly, life-draining habits remain. This chapter describes new ventures that have helped us to take care of ourselves and those that failed to do so and then analyzes how the rest of the health care sector can learn from their experiences.

THE HEALTH CARE ACTIVIST

Rising levels of education and feelings of mastery have created the many health care activists, like Sam, who use information and support to seize responsibility for their health status.

In a 1987 report of the American Board of Family Practice, 39 percent of Americans surveyed described themselves as "working at staying healthy," the group the pollsters identified as *health care activists*. Another 40 percent were partially activist, and only the last 21 percent were complacent about their health.

While a 1994 survey of 800 households confirmed these general categories, it unearthed a new subcategory, a group I will call *contrarian activists* after the class of Wall Street investors who bet against prevailing financial advice. Health care contrarians not only reject the "doctor knows best" dictum, they think they know better than the doctor. The members of this large group, 23 percent of the respondents, have higher representation in the $60,000-plus income category than the others and are better educated. Last, the survey identified a group of passive *apathetics,* the 22 percent who avoid seeking medical care and even "thinking about" health issues. They were less well educated than the average and were more likely to be male.

A "healthy lifestyle" survey of 5,464 people confirmed these categories. Passive lifestyles involved 25 percent of those surveyed; activist lifestyles accounted for 35 percent; and contrarian and self-destructive lifestyles accounted for the rest. (Although 23 percent were heavy smokers and/or drinkers, nearly a third of them exercised.)

Clearly the passive "doctor knows best" group is in the minority today. Most Americans are no longer willing to cede control of their health status to another person.

T. George Harris, the founder of *Psychology Today* and *American Health,* how-to-take-care-of-yourself magazines squarely aimed at the activists, provides a vivid illustration of this transformation: "I published a painting by a famous illustrator of medical textbooks on the cover of the second issue of *American Health.* But when the magazine was actually in print, I knew it was all wrong. Although the painterly qualities were great, its message was exactly backward. It showed a patient lying down on an examination table, looking up at the doctor. My readers did not want to look up to anybody. They were not passive and lying down. No, they were aggressive, upright health care activists."

Tales of health care activists' exploits fill the media. Janine Jacinto Sharkey, in *Town and Country,* told how she custom-designed the types of incisions that removed her breast cancer tumor, faxed questions that arose from her research about breast cancer to her surgeons, and even selected the classical music to be played in the operating room. Notes Sharkey, "I'm not the kind of person to sit there and allow someone else to dictate to me. I question. I'm involved. I want to know what's going on with my body." The *Wall Street Journal* weighs in with a tale of a mother who made a hundred-dollar payment to MedCetera, a firm that searches databases for medical articles. As a result, she replaced the surgeon initially scheduled to operate on her nine-year-old son with a more experienced one who suggested a much less invasive procedure. This woman is hardly alone: Human Responsibility Systems, an America Online service that offers a database of medical articles, logged more than a million requests between October 1995 and February 1996.

Some activists disregard even medication instructions. Louis Ullman, a 67-year-old retired engineer, substituted a seven-dollar-a-month aspirin order for the $144-a-month anti-inflammatory drug that his doctor had prescribed for his arthritis. Notes Ullman, "Don't get me wrong. I like doctors. But we all need to rely more on ourselves and our knowledge. My philosophy is that I'm paying the doctor to be an expert; and if I don't at least listen, I'm wasting my money and time. But I have no problem . . . deciding myself what to do with the results."

Andy Grove, the CEO of Intel, the semiconductor company, wrote an article on his battle with prostate cancer, concluding:

> There is no good gatekeeper. . . . Your general internist is not; the field of prostate cancer is a . . . specialty. Neither is a urologist; [they] have a natural preference toward surgery, perhaps because urologists are surgeons and surgery is what they know best. Any other treatment is deemed experimental even if it has just as much data associated with it.
>
> The whole thing reminds me of the uncomfortable feeling I experienced when I first sought out investment advice. After a while, it dawned on me that financial advisors . . . were all favoring their own . . . instruments. I concluded that I had to undertake the generalist's job myself. . . . Similarly . . . that's the only viable choice any patient has. If you look after your investments . . . you should look after your life as well. Investigate things, come to your own conclusions, don't take any one recommendation as gospel.

These examples of activism should come as no surprise to those who followed Hillary Rodham Clinton's failed attempt to reform the health care system. Americans value their freedom of choice and their control over their health care so much that they have always rejected proposals that would increase government control, including Mrs. Clinton's well-intentioned plans. In the heat of her health reform effort, 65 percent of the 1,000 respondents said "being able to choose the medical services you want" was more important than "controlling your costs for health care." Two-thirds were unwilling to permit their doctors to choose their medical services.

The Fruits of Mastery

In the quest for good health, Americans have modified their lifestyles enormously. No longer does the family sit down to dinners consisting of huge, tender, fat-streaked steaks, accompanied by a baked potato slathered with butter. Between 1970 and 1992 the per-capita consumption of beef and butter dipped by 21 percent. In their place Americans substituted fish and chicken: the chicken consumed per person grew by 65 percent over the same period. And in 1992 the average American consumed 4.3 pounds of yogurt, a food virtually unknown in 1970, because of its reported low-fat, high-calcium, and easy-to-digest properties.

Once disdained for their "from my lips to my hips" qualities, the 1992 consumption of grains increased by 38 percent from their 1970 levels, up to 187 pounds per person. Oat bran was thought to be a cholesterol absorber, and in general grains were almost devoid of the dreaded f-word—*fat*. The pounds of low-calorie sweeteners eaten per person increased from 5.8 in 1970 to 24.3 in 1991, while the consumption of fresh fruits and vegetables grew by at least 24 percent between 1970 and 1992. The consumption of foods known for their medicinal value grew especially fast. Despite President Bush's disdain, the consumption of broccoli jumped by 335 percent, fueled by its purported anticancer characteristics and high calcium content. Carrot-eating grew by 23 percent, as vitamin A and beta-carotene were said to be important anticancer agents. Americans have quaffed bottled water at 185 percent greater rates than ten years ago: they have found it not only chic but also possibly purer than tap water.

All in all, health activists have transformed the way Americans look at food, celebrating its nutritive properties more than its flavor. Even high cuisine, with its delicious cream, egg, and butter-laden dishes, became *nouvelle:* stripped of fat, with vastly decreased portion sizes, and more notable for artistry of presentation than for flavor. Alcohol consumption habits changed too. From 1983 to 1993 the percentage of drivers who claimed they don't drink either while driving or at all increased from 68 to 83 percent.

Health activists now control not only the food they put into their bodies but also their shape. Joggers, speed walkers, bikers, and Roller-bladers can be found in large numbers in virtually any middle-class street or park. In 1990 over 40 percent of Americans said they exercised regularly, and the number who claim to exercise strenuously three or more times a week—52 percent, in 1996—increased from the 45 percent who did so in 1993. Busy Americans exercise because they know that aerobic exercise enhances endurance, protects against heart disease, and enables fit people to exert themselves strongly without stressing their hearts.

Surprisingly, the very word *aerobics* did not even exist in 1968. Dr. Kenneth H. Cooper invented it when he was looking for a catchy word for endurance types of exercise, like biking and running, for a book. He notes, "The publisher thought, 'That's unique—let's call the book *Aerobics.*' That was twenty-five years ago." Today knowledge of exercise techniques is so pervasive that a typical newspaper, like *USA Today,* can carry a "Yoga Videos" headline without concern that its readers will be mystified about the story's contents. Indeed, *Billboard* magazine, which tracks music hits, has a separate chart for health and fitness videos. In 1996, 23 percent of Americans claim that they regularly do yoga or other stress-reducing activities.

Americans have also improved their health care by breaking the boundaries between patient and doctor. Many now actively monitor their own health status. The market for home diagnosis and monitoring products is expected to triple to $3.5 billion by the year 2000. These products monitor pregnancy and ovulation for women; glucose levels for diabetics; blood cholesterol and blood pressure for those with levels that warrant concern; and of course, temperature. Others ingested substances that had the efficacy of drugs but were available without a prescription. The value of the vitamin, mineral, and other nutritional supplements they used clocked in at $3.5 billion in 1992. Nor are Americans afraid to use powerful medicines, when they become available without a doctor's prescription. The 18 million women using Monistat 7, a vaginal yeast infection product newly available over the counter, represent a 50 percent increase from the number who used it when it was available only with a prescription.

Perhaps the most dramatic change is in the number of people who have stopped smoking. Although many addiction experts rate withdrawal from cigarettes virtually as difficult as withdrawal from heroin, cocaine, and caffeine, the percentage of adults smoking decreased by 40 percent between 1965 and 1993. Their concern about the relationship of smoking to heart disease, cancer, respiratory and circulatory problems, and birth defects convinced them to accomplish this enormously difficult task.

These changes have not only caused substantial declines in age-adjusted death rates for problems linked to lifestyle—such as heart disease, motor vehicle accidents, pneumonia, diabetes, and ulcers—they have also saved money. A dramatic example, the Steelcase firm, which manufactures office equipment, found that its low-risk employees, who did not smoke, were not overweight, and who exercised, incurred far lower medical costs ($638) than did the high-risk ones ($1,155).

An Army of Elders?

When I lecture about the health care system, members of the audience sometimes voice fears that all this activism will merely create an avalanche of old people who will deplete our economy with their needs for expensive health care.

Although health care for the elderly is expensive, it is not nearly as expensive as many people think. Indeed, Medicare—our health insurance for the elderly and some other needy groups—accounted for only approximately 17 percent of total health care spending in 1993. The 5 percent of national health care expenditures that was used in 1988 for the elderly in their last year of life has held steady over time. And it is difficult to avoid these expenses: the last year of life is largely unpredictable. One study estimated that avoiding heroic attempts to rescue an elderly dying person, by issuing advanced directives not to resuscitate a patient, for example, can save at most only 3.3 percent of total national health expenditures.

Why are these relatively modest expenditures so wildly inflated in the minds of many otherwise knowledgeable and thoughtful people? I suspect the reason is that most of us think of death, when we do, as an unnatural event preceded by a vast array of medical interventions. We picture a frail old person breathing laboriously through a mask or tube hooked up to a machine that pumps air into weakened lungs. Other tubes puncture the skin, bringing or removing fluids from various body parts that no longer function properly. The patient is struggling to recover from the major surgery that was performed to correct a problem that fundamentally cannot be corrected. In this commonly held view, death is inevitably accompanied by serious and expensive physical and mental deterioration.

But an alternative view of aging and death may be entirely appropriate. Like all other living beings, some of us will die because we have reached the end of our naturally destined life cycle. We will not die because of disease and disability. We will die simply because nature designed our lives to end at some point.

The enormous beech tree in my front lawn is likely more than a hundred years old. Every year it loses some of the branches on its mammoth limbs and grows fewer leaves. At some point the tree will produce so few leaves that it will not be able to obtain the nutrition it needs. Then it will die. My family and I do not think of the tree as sick. We view its death as inevitable, and we acknowledge that we cannot prolong its life, although we can try to avoid its premature death from neglect.

The condition of the so-called "oldest old," people in their late nineties or older, illustrate that aging is not inevitably accompanied by serious deterioration. To dramatize their robust health, a January 1995 *Scientific American* article pictured a youthful-looking 100-year-old swimmer, who also throws the javelin and shot put, bowls, and plays golf. Dr. Thomas T. Perls, the author of the article, notes that the oldest old do not usually die from "long-standing lethal conditions." Rather, "the available information suggests that the usual causes are acute illnesses, such as pneumonia."

Further, although health care expenditures clearly do increase sharply with age, James Fries, a Stanford University professor of medicine, argues that this pattern need not hold in the future. In Fries's view our current expenditures on medical care for older people are caused in large part by chronic diseases, such as heart disease and respiratory failure, that could have been avoided with adequate preventive measures, such as smoking cessation. As today's health care activists age, the rates of preventable chronic disease will decrease, and so will real health expenses, compared with the current elderly. When the health care activists reach 70, their health care expenses may be lower than those of the current 70-year-olds, in real dollars, because they likely will have fewer debilitating chronic illnesses than our present elderly population. Absent new diseases that strike the elderly selectively, Fries predicts that the real costs of caring for them will decrease over time.

Fries's hypothesis is supported by a study that demonstrated that a 26.4% increase in the number of people 65 years of age or older would result in a slight decline in net Medicare expenditures, if the increase in the number of elderly was caused primarily by health promoting activities. A 1996 Dutch study refined these views. It found that elimination of nonfatal diseases, such as arthritis, increases both life expectancy and the percentage of life free of disability. On the other hand, elimination of fatal diseases, such as cancer, *decreased* the percentage of life spent free of disabilities because it increased life span and thus left people vulnerable to other disabilities in their later years of life.

Because his views are controversial, Fries has conducted considerable research to test them. With a colleague, Fries demonstrated that the 1988–89 health care costs for retirees who practiced good habits were from $372 to $598 a year lower than for other retirees. His view is also supported by the decrease in the prevalence of heart conditions and high blood pressure that occurred between 1987 and 1993, for those under 74. Smoking reductions and technological improvements are likely factors in these decreases. (Note that because cardiac conditions usually strike people in their forties or older, the decrease in their prevalence among the 20-year-olds who stopped smoking in 1980 will not appear until they are in their mid-forties, in 2005 or so.) Conversely, the prevalence of these conditions in people aged 75 or more increased between 1987 and 1993. Following Fries's logic, this increase occurred because this elderly group did not participate in the advances in health care and self-management.

The new self-help techniques for managing chronic diseases also likely substantially help reduce treatment costs. For example, one inexpensive health promotion program that provided a group of retirees with regular individualized health-risk appraisals and personalized recommendations decreased the costs of their care by 11 percent. Similarly, a self-help program for arthritis reduced the four-year costs for a rheumatoid arthritis patient by $648 and for an osteoarthritis patient by $189. To assess the importance of these results, consider that in 1993 there were 31 million Americans over 65 and that 15 million of them suffered from arthritis.

So while the aged currently do require a disproportionate share of our health care expenses, and their numbers will certainly increase, the rate of health care cost increases for them may well be lower than the increase in their numbers.

The Spoils of Excess

Despite these activist successes and the promise of more to come, the benefits of better health care are not equally distributed. The poor rate themselves in worse health status than other income groups, blacks experience significantly higher death rates than whites, and men fare less well than women. And many measures of poor health have changed not a whit. For example, the incidence of cancer has increased, and many unhealthy practices persist: Over a quarter of the population still smoke, and despite new food fads, between 1980 and 1991 the percentage of overweight Americans increased by 31 percent.

Destructive personal habits like these are correlated with many diseases. Poor nutrition—too much fat and cholesterol in the diet; too few fresh fruits and vegetables; too little calcium; and excessive food— and low exercise rates are linked to various cancers, heart disease, diabetes, and deterioration of the bones and joints. Excessive consumption of alcohol and illicit drugs is clearly associated with accidents, violence, cirrhosis of the liver, digestive diseases, and mental illness. After a careful analysis the eminent public health specialists J. Michael McGinnis and William H. Foege concluded that in 1990 tobacco caused 19 percent of all deaths; poor nutrition and lack of exercise, 14 percent; alcohol, 5 percent; lack of vaccination for infectious diseases, 4 percent; firearms, 2 percent; and unprotected sexual behavior, poor motor vehicle control, and use of illicit drugs, 1 percent each. In total these lifestyle choices caused over one million deaths in 1990. Some experts claim that eliminating these habits would greatly reduce the harm they cause. For example, smokers who stop before the age of 35, they contend, can add from 4.47 (men) to 6.66 (women) years to their lives in avoidance of coronary heart disease alone.

Destructive habits also exact substantial tolls on economic productivity. Tobacco, for example, accounted for 13 percent of all potential years of life lost by death before the age of 65, and alcohol 15 percent. In a 1989 study the MIT economist and physician Jeffrey S. Harris demonstrated that a hypothetical ten-thousand-employee corporation would lose over 13,000 years of useful employee work prematurely because of destructive lifestyle habits. For male employees under 35, the main causes of premature death that this study found were sedentary lifestyle and nonuse of seatbelts. While refusal to "buckle up" was a major risk factor for women as well, the second highest controllable cause of premature death among women was smoking. For both sexes, alcohol use and high blood pressure were also major risk factors. The Health Insurance Association of America estimated in 1994 that health care attributable to unhealthy lifestyles required $188 billion of expenditures.

The failure to eliminate life-destroying and costly health habits is not the only shortcoming of health activism. A surprisingly large number of people with serious chronic diseases, like asthma and diabetes, fail to comply with the health care protocols that could help them. Notes one physician, "Compliance with asthma meds is at best 30 percent to 50 percent." Adds a pharmacist, "A lot of patients just don't understand their asthma or their medications." Similarly, many experts feel that as many as half of all diabetes-related complications, including blindness, gangrene, and kidney disease, could be prevented if patients adhered to the admittedly challenging protocols for managing this deadly disease.

HAS HEALTH ACTIVISM FAILED?

Why have increasingly activist Americans failed to eliminate so many of the deadly habits that continue to destroy people's lives and the economy? Why do people with chronic diseases so often fail to comply with regimens that could ease their suffering?

There are many possible hypotheses. First, the health care system may not as yet be providing health activists with the assistance they need to "do it themselves." Second, the large population of contrarian activists may simply disbelieve or disregard conventional medical advice about the causes of deadly diseases. Third, many lack the incentives or education needed to become activists. Last, the absence of health insurance stops people from improving their own health. I will explore the validity of each of these hypotheses. This analysis provides the basis for the recommendations about how to increase activism that conclude this chapter.

Support for "Doing It Yourself"

A number of national studies have revealed that doctors simply do not provide Americans with enough support to eliminate their deadly habits or manage their chronic diseases on their own. One study found, no doubt to the surprise of the many parents, that some doctors did not check to see if the children they examined during well-baby visits were up to date on their immunizations. Other studies showed that some doctors did not follow the protocols strongly recommended for maintenance of their diabetic patients; did not provide their patients with enough information about how to manage their asthma; and did not even ask their patients the most basic questions about their functioning and well-being.

But is all this just yuppie whining? Do patients really need support to eliminate bad habits or comply with protocols? Can't they just do it themselves? After all, information about health self-care is everywhere. Americans can obtain it from the 3,428,000-circulation *Prevention* magazine, available right next to the *National Enquirer* at the supermarket checkout, squarely aimed at the blue-collar reader. They can get it from the regular features on virtually every TV newscast, like the HealthBeat feature on a local Boston station. They can get it from videotapes, computer networks, CDs, and books. Virtually every medium advances a considerable number of health-promoting messages. Americans can even get information on nutritional content from food packages, be they Snickers bars or boxes of cereal.

Apparently, however, information alone is not enough. Considerable evidence exists that support mechanisms are important. Even brief periods of physician advice and follow-up, when combined with self-help materials, increase smoking cessation rates by up to a third, compared with the rates achieved by only a nicotine patch and self-help materials. A twenty-four-hour telephone health service, staffed by nurses, was found to help callers better manage their chronic diseases. Computer-generated calls that remind parents of appointments for immunizations have increased the kept appointments by 183 percent.

An asthma management program has significantly reduced the symptoms of severe asthma. As one spokesperson notes, "The key is to improve physician familiarity with the guidelines and then give patients the tools and knowledge to treat themselves." Finally, a six-year follow-up study of the 3,597 students who had participated in a drug-abuse prevention program and periodic "booster" sessions found up to 44 percent fewer drug users among these students than among those who received more conventional instruction.

Why is support so important? A program that successfully taught arthritics how to cope with the disease suggests an answer. Arthritis, a disease with no cure, strikes millions of Americans, causing them considerable pain, lack of mobility, and sometimes paralyzing depression. Kate Lorig of Stanford University, a nurse who also holds a doctorate in public health, has devised a program that helps victims of chronic arthritis to better manage their health. Her Arthritis Self-Management Program, conducted in six weekly two-hour sessions by pairs of trained lay leaders, teaches participants about the origins and symptoms of the disease and ways to attain the most effective control over diseased joints, pain, and communication with the doctor. The course encourages interaction and experimentation with techniques for self-care. All participants receive a self-care book co-authored by Lorig, *The Arthritis Help Book.*

When Lorig studied the outcome of the program, she found that participants had substantial reductions in pain and depression, increased physical activity, and 40 percent fewer physician visits. After deducting the program's cost of $54 per participant, she found that the program created potential four-year savings of $648 for each victim of rheumatoid arthritis and $189 for each victim of osteoarthritis. If only 5 million victims of arthritis participated in such a program, a savings estimated modestly at $200 per participant could amount to $1 billion over a four-year period.

What aspects of the program caused these dramatic results? Much to Lorig's surprise, the information it presented was not the main factor. Rather, the changes were caused primarily by the growth in the participants' self-confidence that they could manage their disease. In scholarly parlance, the program increased perceptions of self-efficacy, "a person's belief in his or her own ability to effect a change in, or achieve the goal of, the behavior." In this program the combination of support and information, what we normally call education, proved to be empowering. It gave people the self-confidence to manage their own health.

Not surprisingly, because this program had fundamentally altered the participants' approach to their disease, follow-up sessions proved unnecessary. Empowered adults do not need periodic booster shots. The results have been replicated in other populations including the indigenous inhabitants of British Columbia.

How Education Affects Health Care Practices

Can education of the sort offered in Lorig's program help to reduce the prevalence of destructive habits and thus improve people's health? The relationship between education and health seems beyond dispute. For one, the connection is an intrinsically appealing one. People who understand the relationship between their own behavior and their health are better prepared to manage their health. For example, women in Thailand with elementary school education are 30 percent more likely to treat children who have diarrhea with some form of rehydration than are those with no education. (Young children may die of dehydration if their diarrhea is left untreated.) Secondly, education is empowering—it relieves people of the need to consult "experts" and gives them the self-confidence and the knowledge to direct themselves. Last, as Leonard Sagan points out in his thoughtful book, *The Health of Nations,* education enables people to cope better with events that may cause them stress—that is, to recognize sources of stress and develop strategies to relieve them. Such critical life skills are provided through the process of education because it requires students to develop and implement effective strategies for learning.

Evidence of the correlation between education level and health status is compelling. Educated people live longer and feel better. Although death rates have declined substantially for everyone, the decline has been more substantial for men and women with high education than for those with low education. Between 1960 and 1986, for example, the death rate for highly educated men declined from 5.8 to 2.9 per 1,000, while for men of low education the decline was much smaller, from 9.0 to 7.6. And educated people are more likely to rate their health status as excellent than are those with lower levels of education. The relationship between education level and feelings of excellent health is invariably progressive. Only 17 to 27 percent of those with no education rate their health as excellent; 27 to 42 percent of those with 9 to 11 years of education give themselves that rating; and 51 to 62 percent of those with 16 years and more of education do so.

Income undoubtedly also affects perceptions of health status, and income and education are correlated, but a detailed analysis of the variables that affect perceived health status found that within each income category education has the primary effect. Similarly, although race also affects health status, and race and education levels are correlated, within each racial category the prevalence of risk factors varies inversely with education level.

Better educated people manage their health in different ways from others. Fundamentally, they demonstrate greater control over their lives— they exercise more, they smoke less, they are more likely to use seatbelts and obtain prenatal care, and they are more deliberate in their choices of food and use of alcohol. None of these practices is easy to master. Acquiring good health practices or unlearning bad ones is hard work.

The effect of education on the health choices that people make is universal. For example, in the United Kingdom, 50 percent of the most educated smokers stopped during the period 1958–1975, but virtually none of the least educated did so; in the United States the highest educated smokers gave it up at a rate nine times faster than the least educated ones. In Pôrto Alegre, Brazil, in 1987, approximately 73 percent of those who had no schooling still smoked, while only 48 percent of those with postsecondary education did so. In the United States smoking prevalence is inversely related to education. The highest rate is among males with less than a high school education. Similarly, while 44 percent of college-educated Americans claimed to exercise strenuously three or more days a week in a 1992 survey, only 38 percent of those who did not graduate from high school made that claim. A similar pattern prevails in Pôrto Alegre: the World Bank estimates that 90 percent of those with no schooling show lack of exercise as a risk factor for poor health, as compared with only 75 percent of those with postsecondary education.

Or Does It All Come Down to Health Insurance?
Some people may feel that ascribing such importance to education underplays the key role played by health insurance. Many experts feel that people who are insured are healthier because they can buy more

health care. Because education and the prevalence of health insurance are related—educated people generally are more likely to have a health insurance policy—these experts attribute health status in some measure to the access to health care resources provided by health insurance.

The clearest evidence of the role played by health insurance in health status can be found in countries with a long history of universal health insurance, such as the United Kingdom, France, and Finland. All of them removed the economic barriers to obtaining health care long ago: their citizens enjoy equal access to health care resources regardless of income. For example, a number of studies in the United Kingdom have concluded that all social classes have equal access to medical and social resources and make appropriate uses of them. Differences in the availability of health care resources in high- and low-income regions were not significant: per-capita expenditures for health care differed by less than 10 percent between the richest and poorest regions. If health insurance were the key to health status, U.K. residents would enjoy roughly equal health status, as evidenced by their death rates and incidence of chronic diseases. But they don't.

In these European countries the death rates of less educated people are substantially higher than those of better-educated ones. In the United Kingdom the death rates for adult males in social classes IV and V were twice as high as for those in classes I and II. (The British use straightforward, albeit insensitive, social classifications. Classes I and II are professionals and intermediate workers, such as managers, nurses, and schoolteachers. Class III includes skilled nonmanual and manual workers. Classes IV and V include partly skilled workers, such as postmen, and unskilled workers.) Although the differences in death rates are undoubtedly influenced by occupational patterns, the incidence of differences in death caused by lifestyles such as digestive problems, accidents, poisonings, and violence among the classes were unusually high. All these causes of death are clearly linked to behavior patterns, such as nutrition, exercise, alcohol and drug use, and ability to handle stress.

Similar patterns prevailed in France and Finland. Although both countries have universal health insurance, in France in 1968 the death rate of men aged 45–64 who were in the "higher cadres" was less than half that of "qualified workers." Similarly, the Finnish category I workers had an age-adjusted mortality rate of 78 per 10,000, while the category IV workers were at 148. The incidence of chronic illnesses in such countries exhibited similar patterns. The lowest social groups had higher rates of chronic illness in Britain, Norway, Denmark, France, and Hungary.

All in all, a study of the relationship of health status to education level in six European countries in the 1970s and 1980s, for people 35–54, found that "death rates . . . decline with increasing years of education with a remarkably similar pattern in all six countries."

THE ROLE OF PRIVATE SECTOR INNOVATORS

The private sector has helped people to modify their habits by offering a wide variety of easy-to-obtain aids. After the connection between dietary calcium and the bone-thinning disease osteoporosis was identified, a wide variety of calcium sources appeared—ranging from the venerable "Tums for the Tummy," to pills and capsules, to calcium-enriched drinks, to milk products without the allergens that had stopped many people from drinking them. My local drugstore has more than twenty different varieties and brands of calcium for sale. Similarly, foods low in cholesterol have proliferated. Salad dressings, bakery products, and frozen dinners, among many others, all carry the ubiquitous "no cholesterol" or "low cholesterol" label. And Americans have apparently found it easy enough to reduce their consumption of butter, eggs, and red meat—the most common sources of cholesterol and saturated fat, the other dietary no-no—and substitute readily available chicken and unsaturated fats. Frank Perdue is a happy and wealthy man. He and other poultry processors have been rewarded for making chicken ever more appealing by offering it in easy-to-prepare ways and in great variety.

Health clubs and at-home exercise aids have proliferated to simplify the process of exercising. Health club membership hit an all-time high of 20 million in 1994, up 22 percent from 1990. Aerobic exercise equipment was newly designed for the home, ranging from low-cost trampolines and jump ropes to costly, high-tech StairMasters, rowing machines, and NordicTracks. All in all, sales of athletic clothing, shoes, and equipment blossomed to $30 billion in 1991.

Innovators continually found new ways to provide support for change. James Fries is a notable example. As co-author of the best-selling 1989 medical handbook, *Take Care of Yourself: A Consumer's Guide to Medical Care*, Fries distilled and clearly presented information that could help people care for themselves. And as a medical researcher, he provided evidence to counter the objection that health promotion is not cost-effective.

Still, Fries felt that he should do more to spur people to change their destructive habits. With Sarah Fries, his wife, he founded Healthtrac, a Menlo Park, California, firm that provides personalized advice on how to improve health and assesses the risks caused by a person's life habits. The risk assessments and advice are based on a lifestyle questionnaire that is periodically completed by those enrolled in the program. In a test of the efficacy of this approach, a large group of Bank of America retirees who were enrolled in the program was split into two. Both groups were asked to complete the lifestyle questionnaire each year, but one group was also provided with personalized recommendations on how to improve their health, a risk assessment for their present lifestyle, and a copy of a self-care book. A comparison of the differences in behavior of these two groups enabled Fries to evaluate the effects of providing self-care information in this supportive environment.

The results? Over the course of a year, even this modestly supportive provision of health information significantly lowered sick days and the total costs of illness. The group receiving the additional material experienced savings of $598 in total medical costs per participant. These individual savings may appear modest, but consider their potential: If the Healthtrac program were used by tens of millions of elderly Americans, it could save billions of dollars a year. Similarly, the Aetna insurance company achieved such dramatic results from distributing a self-care book that it launched a telephone program that gives people considerable amounts of health information at their request.

How does self-care information work? Consider a common problem like hemorrhoids, or swollen veins in the rectum that may cause pain and bleeding. About half of the population over 50 has them—they are "one of the most common complaints a physician can evaluate," according to Dr. Lee E. Smith, director of colon and rectal surgery at the George Washington University Medical Center in Washington, D.C.

Many hemorrhoids can be treated with self-care. A high-fiber diet, with plenty of liquids, hot baths, and the many preparations sold in drug-stores help relieve the pain hemorrhoids cause. Professional interventions are called for primarily when the hemorrhoids show dark red bleeding.

I learned all this from the information sent to me by Mark Haverland, a former MBA student of mine who is the founder of Consumer Health Information, in Ankeny, Iowa. Mark sells information on virtually any health topic to employers, currently over the Internet, so that their employees can quickly access it. If I were an employee in one of Mark's client firms and suffered from hemorrhoids, I would eagerly read this easily-available information.

Other innovators provide similar support. For example, Access Health was the leading provider of personal health management products and services in 1996. The firm was formed in 1987 by Ken Plumlee. The company's stock price increased from $6 a share in September 1992 to $55 a share in May 1996.

What fueled this spectacular growth? The company is currently the leading provider of a variety of services: PHA, or personal health adviser, enables managed care patients to telephone a registered nurse and ask her questions about their health care, around the clock. Ask-A-Nurse enables hospitals to provide similar services. And Cancer HelpLink provides cancer information and referral services to victims through registered nurses who are specially trained in cancer care. Customers can also access individually researched information on issues like pregnancy and a library of recorded information on self-care for various problems and receive printed information as well. Not surprisingly, 90 percent of the PHA users report that the service increases their satisfaction with their health plan. By 1995 the company had 6 million members enrolled in the PHA.

The support offered by the nurses is key to the success of Access Health. It ranges from advice on whether to see a physician or treat a problem at home to support for victims of serious illnesses. Notes a *Fortune* magazine article on the company, "Access is midwife to a new birth in health care, the rise of the educated consumer."

The creativity and energy of innovators like Kate Lorig and the Frieses have been important in helping Americans to change their habits. The aids they have provided are of such a wide variety and so easily accessible that many people can find something to help them.

CARROTS AND STICKS

Eliminating substance abuse, quitting smoking, and maintaining appropriate weight are apparently much more difficult tasks to accomplish, despite the widespread availability of private sector aids. Until recently, smokers who quit did it mostly by themselves, cold turkey. As an ex-smoker, I know how painful this process is. After sixteen years of trying, I finally quit when I noticed my baby daughter's interest in the ritual surrounding cigarette smoking. She was clearly fascinated by the flame when I lit a match, by the glowing tip of the lit cigarette, and by the plumes of smoke it created. Maintaining a cigarette-free state is almost as difficult as quitting: Twenty-two years after I first quit, I still long for a cigarette virtually every day, as do many other former smokers.

More recently, however, two innovations have helped smokers quit more easily. One is a carrot, the other a stick. The carrot is the nicotine patch. This medically prescribed source of nicotine has been available in the United States since 1991, and it helps smokers to wean themselves of the habit. The sticks are the prohibition of smoking in public spaces and the taxes that increase the cost of smoking cigarettes.

The nicotine patch has been found to be effective. When compared with a placebo patch, one that did not contain nicotine, the nicotine patch was twice as effective in helping smoking cessation. Average abstinence rates six months after the patch were 22 percent. Yet despite their efficacy, nicotine patches have had only limited use because until recently they were available only with a doctor's prescription. One analyst notes that when nicotine patches were made available in drug-stores in Europe, sales took off.

The efficacy of the two sticks is only partially known. Gary Becker, the 1992 Nobel Prize winner in economics, writing with Michael Grossman, a colleague, estimated that each 10 percent price increase in a pack of cigarettes causes a per-capita decline in cigarette consumption of about 8 percent. But the economists predict that if prices were further increased through tax hikes, eventually an active black market would form to undercut these prices. (Becker and his colleague view the practice of banning smoking in public places because of the injurious effect of secondhand smoke as controversial, judging the scientific evidence on this issue to be "very weak." Nevertheless, an editorial in the *Journal of the American Medical Association* concluded that "evidence continues to accumulate that environmental tobacco smoke is not innocuous." The effect on smoking cessation of this ban is as yet unknown.)

Despite these disclaimers, the combination of the carrot and the stick in helping people to modify hard-to-change habits appears to hold great promise. The carrot is a medical intervention that eases the pain of the transition, and the stick is a price increase that forces people to contemplate the costs of the medical treatment their behavior will likely cause. In 1993 the medical costs of treating smoking-related illnesses amounted to at least $50 billion. Presently these costs are shared by smokers and nonsmokers alike, because their health insurance premiums usually cost the same. If treatment costs were incorporated in the price of smokers' health insurance premiums, however, smokers would confront more closely the costs of their habits. Because the rate of smoking is sensitive to price, this price-increasing stick may decrease smoking.

A similar strategy holds promise in motivating people with other, seemingly intractable, destructive lifestyle habits that are not genetic in origin to change their behavior. Consider the problem of overweight. Those who are more than double their ideal body weight are not merely plump or chubby. In the cruelly descriptive medical terminology, they are called "morbidly obese" because their weight is killing them. They are much more prone to heart disease, to diseases of the respiratory and muscular-skeletal systems, and to diabetes than people of more normal weight. Once they become sick, their treatment costs are much higher because of the additional problems that their extreme weight poses. For them, the carrot would consist of a new class of drugs that effectively depressed appetite; the stick would be a health insurance premium that appropriately reflected their likely health care costs.

The life insurance industry is a model of insurance pricing that reflects the risk characteristics of the applicant. Before an individual's life insurance rate is determined, a doctor's confidential examination verifies the applicant's health status. For health insurance applicants, a doctor could confirm weight, smoking, and alcohol-drinking habits, among other attributes. The price of their health insurance policies would reflect these characteristics. Enrollees who felt that their health status was incorrectly assessed or that they were unfairly penalized for problems that were genetic in origin would have access to other sources of opinion, and the entire process would remain confidential.

In a 1995 survey a surprisingly large percentage of the respondents backed health insurance policies with differential premiums. Approximately 75 percent of those with health-active lifestyles preferred policies that provided incentives for good health practices; even 57 percent of the "inactives" approved of such a policy. Lower-income respondents (under $25,000), were as likely to prefer these policies as higher-income ones.

Are the treatment costs of those with unhealthy lifestyle habits sufficiently higher to warrant higher health insurance premiums? That unhealthy lifestyle habits have a substantial impact on health care costs is illustrated by an analysis of six thousand life-years of data of Chrysler employees. Smokers and substantially overweight employees increased average claims costs by more than 30 percent. Another analysis confirmed these findings; it established that heavy drinking increased average annual costs per employee by $398.

ALTERNATIVE THERAPIES

Some people decline to modify their lifestyle habits because they do not entirely accept the conventional medical explanations for disease. These contrarians make up around one-quarter of the American public. Their skepticism about the efficacy of conventional medicine is surprisingly widespread. In 1990, Americans made 425 million visits to providers of unconventional therapies, such as chiropractors and massage therapists, exceeding the 388 million visits to conventional physicians who provide primary care.

Alternative therapists do not follow traditional medical theories of cause and effect. Acupuncturists, for example, believe that they can heal by exciting nerve bundles with electrically stimulated needles. Chiropractors rely on bone manipulation to relieve symptoms. Homeopaths

cure with medicines that consist of vastly diluted amounts of the substance they believe to have caused the problem. These practices are not
widely accepted by conventional physicians. Nevertheless, Americans
not only use alternative therapists frequently, they tend to pay for them
directly out of their own pockets, since health insurance covers few
alternative treatments (although acupuncture and chiropractors are
gaining insurance coverage). In 1990 users' out-of-pocket costs for
alternative therapy exceeded $10 billion. Those who used diet supple-
ments spent an additional $1.2 billion, or $228 per person.

Who uses alternative therapies? Educated, high-income people are
more likely to use them. And they use these treatments largely for chronic
problems, such as backaches, allergies, and arthritis. Because most of
them have also consulted a medical doctor for these problems, they are
likely seeking other sources of help because the traditional medicine did
not work. For example, 41 percent of the patients who saw a medical
doctor for treatment of obesity also sought out alternative sources of help.
Additionally, a third of those using an alternative therapy used it not to
treat disease, but probably for promotion of their health.

The alternative health movement is not limited to the United
States. In France, for example, sales of medicinal herbs have doubled in
less than ten years, and in Paris one of five households now uses them.
Notes the president of the National Association of Pharmacists, "Now
there's a return to plants because . . . they act more gently and may be
less invasive than chemically based medicines." A 1994 Fair of Alternative Medicine in Paris drew 50,000 visitors.

A few medical providers do not seem to get the interest in alternative therapies any more than they accept the need for convenience. They
may find the skepticism about traditional medicine so unsettling that
they choose to ignore this powerful movement. Although visits to
alternative practitioners exceeded those to conventional primary care
doctors, the medical professionals who sympathetically discussed the
subject in the *New England Journal of Medicine* still referred to it as
"unconventional" medicine. They seemed shocked by the number of
visits to alternative practitioners and concerned by the finding that fewer
than 30 percent of their patients even told them about their use of
alternative therapies. They classed these people as "unsupervised" and
editorialized that "the use of unconventional therapy, especially if it is

totally unsupervised, may be harmful." Although some traditional doctors do not seem to understand that health activists who visit alternative practitioners view themselves as the "supervisor" of their health status, others do. Dr. David Eisenberg, for example, an assistant professor at Harvard's Medical School, heads the Center for Alternative Medical Research in Boston.

Like it or not, contrarian activists simply do not share some physicians' view of themselves as the fountain of health information.

MEDICINE: ART OR SCIENCE?

Clearly, many health activists do not believe that traditional medicine provides definitive healing or that the conventional medical doctor is the sole source of health information. Instead, they control the health-creating process themselves.

Surprisingly, a number of traditional physicians would likely concede the wisdom of their judgment. The late Lewis Thomas, the eminent essayist, oncologist, and leader of the renowned Sloan-Kettering Cancer Center in New York City, labeled medicine "the youngest science." In his wonderful book of the same title, Thomas explains how in their day his parents—a physician and a nurse—could give their patients little more than tender loving care. Better therapies were simply not available. But the discovery of antibiotics, and later of the structure of DNA, made medicine more of a science: like other sciences, it could now conduct experiments that tested hypotheses about disease-causing agents, such as the polio virus, and their curative interventions, such as the polio vaccine. Nevertheless, medicine remained a young science.

Yes, modern medicine possesses awesome powers to treat diseases that once caused considerable pain or premature death. Procedures that unclog the circulatory pathways to the heart now enable people to live without the viselike chest pain they once endured. Artificial hips give mobility to those who would once have been confined to a wheelchair. Various drugs permit epileptics, formerly disabled by violent seizures, to lead more normal lives. But, the "science" of medicine contains all too little understanding of cause and effect. You think that taking stomach-acid-reducing drugs like Zantac, once the world's largest-selling drug, is the best way to deal with an ulcer? Think again. It turns out that ubiquitous bacteria, *H. pylori,* cause most stomach ulcers. The cure? Plain old Pepto-Bismol and antibiotics. You think margarine and antioxidant vitamins that reduce the aging effects of "free radicals" are just dandy? Think again. They may well be bad for you. You think leaky breast implants cause autoimmune diseases of the connective tissue? In fact, breast implants may well not affect these diseases. All too often, today's sage medical advice flipflops into tomorrow's no-no.

Because the link between cause and effect in medicine is so weak, different physicians treat patients with similar symptoms in widely different ways. A study of 20,000 patients showed that the probability of their hospitalization was significantly influenced by factors other than their needs, such as the physician's specialty, how the physician was paid, and whether they were solo practitioners or members of a large physician group.

Not surprisingly, different modes of medical interventions are followed in different countries. French medicine relies heavily on the view that many ailments originate in the digestive tract and can be cured with digestive interventions like enemas. American medicine, in contrast, relies more heavily on systemic, massive interventions, like surgery and drugs. The styles of medical practice in these two countries clearly reflect other cultural attitudes, such as the French focus on food and wine and the American love of technology.

Unlike medicine, the laws of physics are independent of cultural attitudes. Apples fall from trees, obeying the law of gravity, in both France and the United States. E equals mc² everywhere. But medicine has few such powerful, universal laws. Other than "laws" about the effect of bacteria and viruses in causing some diseases, doctors may not agree on the etiology and treatment of many illnesses.

Dogma or Science?

Because medicine is such a young science, with few empirical underpinnings, some of today's medical advice may be dogma rather than science, based on beliefs about the relationship between cause and effect rather than on facts. Although Galen is honored as the father of Western medicine because he urged physicians to examine empirical evidence rather than accepting unsupported theories and interventions, a few ignore his advice. For example, some question the "peer review" process—which subjects proposals for most publicly funded medical research to an evaluation by scientists of attainments equal to the applicant's—because they feel that peer review is all too often tainted by group-think. In such cases, "peers" are those who think alike and who seek to perpetuate their view of cause and effect. As a result, creators of legitimate medical advances may find their ideas rejected if they deviate too far from the accepted norm.

The problem of dogma in medicine is one of long standing. The history of medicine is shamefully studded with stories of men of great insight who committed suicide or were driven to insanity because of the intransigent hostility of the conventional medical community to their views. For example, two of those who contributed to bringing anesthesia and antiseptics into hospitals, thus revolutionizing surgical practice, were driven mad—in part because they received so little recognition for their work. As Brian Inglis recounts in his excellent book, *A History of Medicine,* W.T.G. Morton, a dentist, was asked to prove the efficacy of an anesthetic agent before a dubious audience at the Massachusetts General Hospital in 1846. When Morton failed to arrive on time, a sarcastic surgeon, John Collins Warren, said, "I presume he is otherwise engaged." Morton finally arrived and performed a procedure from which the patient felt no pain. Warren then noted to his colleagues, "Gentlemen, this is no humbug." Nevertheless, Morton failed to receive the kudos he felt he was owed. He died shortly after attempting suicide.

The medical establishment's longtime reluctance to accept antiseptic practices is even more disturbing. In earlier eras surgeons did not wash their hands or clothes. As Inglis recounts, some surgeons' operating gowns had so much blood caked on them that they could stand up on their own. One observant obstetrician thought that unwashed physicians' hands might be spreading puerperal fever, and he urged the doctors in his ward to wash their hands in an antiseptic solution before examining a new patient. The obstetrician, Ignaz Semmelweis, was dismissed from his post and derided. He died insane.

The problem of dogma in medical science persists to this day. When an Australian researcher first proposed that ulcers are caused by bacteria, according to the *Harvard Health Letter,* gastroenterologists "guffawed." Stung by the lack of support for his thesis, the lead researcher finally infected himself with the bacteria to demonstrate his point.

Yet physicians themselves clearly acknowledge that medicine is a young science. Notes an editorial in the *Journal of the American Medical Association,* "At present there are only modest empirical data to support many of the clinical guidelines being promulgated for various clinical problems." Although a few such guidelines have been developed by the Agency for Health Care Policy and Research through a "consensus conference" method, physicians have not eagerly incorporated them into their practices. They are likely well aware of the dogma and cronyism that pervade "peer reviews" and "consensus conferences" and shy away from the advice they yield. One physician said, of a recent consensus panel recommendation that ulcer patients be treated with antibiotics, "they were so dogmatic. . . . It does not leave any room for clinical judgment. If this business is wrong and people rebleed, they can die, particularly frail elderly patient[s]."

To be sure, the problem of dogma is hardly unique to medicine. It is present in all "sciences," particularly the social sciences, whose theoretical underpinnings are so weak that confirmatory tests of the theories cannot be conducted. Take marketing science, for example, whose purpose is to predict consumer behavior. To test whether the $2.4 billion marketing research industry could accurately predict events—the ultimate test of any theory—one researcher asked high school students, marketing academics, and practitioners to predict how consumers would behave in certain situations. None of the groups gave predictions better than those that could have been obtained by a flip of a coin. In other words, this experiment could not provide evidence of any "science" in marketing science. There is all too little science in economics as well. In 1965, when Congress passed the legislation creating the Medicare health insurance program for the elderly, the costs of the program were forecasted to be $9 billion in 1990—a figure that fell short of actual 1990 costs by some $58 billion.

Effects of the Lack of Science

In most sciences practitioners are frustrated by the lack of predictive ability. We all crave certainty, the comforting feeling that because we understand "how things work," we can shape events to our liking. Intellectuals particularly long to crack the code between cause and effect. Sometimes they may delude themselves into believing that they have done so, but their neat explanations ignore inconvenient facts and do not lead to effective remedies.

Although modern medicine is equipped with a powerful arsenal to treat many problems, the exact cause of many ailments remains unknown. As a result, the "cure" for a particular disease is likely much more traumatic than it would be if the etiology of the disease were better understood. For example, cancer patients, whose malignant cells are eradicated with a bombardment of X rays and toxic chemicals, frequently find that this therapy perniciously affects the rest of the body. Present cancer therapy may well be supplanted eventually, by gentler treatment that eliminates mutant genes or other yet-unknown causes of the disease. For some diseases no cure exists because their cause is unknown. For example, because the origins of common, chronic problems, like arthritis or pain, are largely unknown, no effective cure exists.

Some people may harbor nagging doubts about the etiology claimed for many ailments because of data that do not comfortably fit into established explanations of cause and effect. For example, although the connection between smoking and heart disease appears incontrovertible, French and Japanese people, who smoke nearly as much as Americans, nevertheless incur much lower rates of heart disease. As some epidemiologists acknowledge, heart disease follows a "web of causation" model in which smoking may be only one factor causing heart disease.

Despite the lack of knowledge about the causes of and consistently effective cures for many ailments, especially chronic ones, medical advice is sometimes couched in dogmatic language, whose certainty of tone vastly exceeds the certainty of knowledge. Savvy Americans deal with this dogmatism in two ways: They either ignore the advice, or they seek out alternative treatments.

The American public seems quite capable of distinguishing between dogma and science in many fields. For example, despite the massive amounts of money spent to advertise brand-name products and despite the extensive market research that underlies the advertising, private-label brands that do not advertise do very well. As exemplified by the high-quality President's Choice private-label products sold in many supermarkets, private-label managers use the money they save on advertising to enhance their product's quality. The many savvy consumers who buy these products recognize quality even without advertising.

Sometimes the public is way ahead of the experts. For example, the efficacy of drinking cranberry juice to ease urinary tract infections, an old folklore remedy, was confirmed in a recent medical study.

BARRIERS TO THE CREATION OF MASTERY-ENHANCING VENTURES

While self-control of health-destroying habits and self-care of chronic diseases have already substantially improved Americans' health status and created major reductions in costs, the promise of health activism remains only partially fulfilled.

There are several possible reasons. Some Americans are likely unaware of the connection between their own behavior and their health. Education is probably the single most important factor in creating good health. Others may find their health-destroying behavior impossible to change in the absence of encouragement to do so or disincentives for failure. And still others are skeptical that behavior and health status are connected in the ways they are told.

For all these groups, the private sector is key to improving mastery of health. Private companies like Healthtrac and the Rodale Press (which publishes *Prevention*) provide much of the information and support on which health activists rely. And private sector innovators provide the wide variety of aids that activists use, ranging from calcium supplements and exercise machines to novel self-care programs for chronic diseases.

But creating effective mastery-enhancing health care ventures is enormously difficult, as the initial problems of the North Shore Birth Center exemplify. Nevertheless, these managerial challenges can be successfully addressed as the details of the service system of the Bread and Circus supermarkets will illustrate.

The North Shore Birth Center

Birth centers—devoted solely to a normal, unmedicated birthing process—were developed for parents who wanted greater control over giving birth. Notes Fran Ventre, a nurse-midwife who is one of the pioneers in the birth center movement, "My interest . . . started with the birth of my own children. I felt ripped off . . . because during the birth I wasn't in control." (Nurse-midwives are registered nurses who receive additional education in childbirth for an average of eighteen months to two years.)

The history of birth centers mirrors the changing role of consumers in the health care system. Initially, childbirth was a social event controlled by the mother, in which she was surrounded by friends and relatives. At the beginning of the twentieth century, over 95 percent of all deliveries took place in the home. But with advances in anesthesia, the site of the birth changed from the home to the hospital, and the prime source of support changed from the nurse-midwife to the doctor. Although these changes enhanced the safety of both the mother and her baby and greatly reduced the excruciating pain that frequently accompanies childbirth, they required women to abdicate a large degree of control over the process. While the death rate of mothers in childbirth plummeted by 90 percent between 1950 and 1987, the warm, supportive environment of the home was supplanted by the depersonalized environment of the hospital.

The growth of the medical model of childbirth, however, caused new concerns. Cesarean births, in which the baby is removed from the womb through a large opening cut into the uterus rather than being expelled through the vagina, became increasingly common. Cesarean section is now the most frequently performed operation in the United States, accounting for almost one of every four births, up from one of every twenty in 1970. The rise was worrisome because cesareans are much more invasive to the body than a normal vaginal birth and are more costly to boot. Although the "right" number of cesareans is not known, the National Center for Health Statistics has concluded that $1 billion a year in physician and hospital charges would be saved if cesareans were performed at the "optimal" rate of 15 percent of births.

Some of the nurse-midwives who innovated birthing centers feel that the birthing process has been overmedicalized and depersonalized. Noted the president of the American College of Nurse-Midwives, "We view pregnancy and birth as a normal life process rather than a medical event." Observes Dorothy Kuell, a nurse involved with the formation of the North Shore Birth Center, "At a birth center . . . a mother [is] not confined. . . . She [can] walk outside, sit in the living room, rest in the bedroom, or take a bath. She [can] deliver squatting, lying, or sitting.

There [is] no limit on visiting hours or on the number of family and friends attending the birth." Birth centers have other advantages too. Because the nurse-midwives there work in teams with the mother and her partner from the early stages of her pregnancy, the mother in labor is surrounded by familiar, supportive people, no matter what time of day or night the birth takes place. Finally, birth centers cost less than hospital births.

Small wonder, then, that after the Childbearing Center, a birthing center demonstration project, began operations in New York City in 1975, the number of birth centers grew to 130 by 1994. Women who use nurse-midwives for maternity care are so satisfied with their services that they often return to them for other health care needs as well.

As with the eyewear innovators, however, the path of the innovative nurse-midwives was not smooth. By the 1970s the occupation of nurse-midwifery had fallen from its previous high level of regard. Many health insurers would not pay for a birth at a birth center, despite the lower cost.

But a subtler barrier slowed the development of birth centers: the hierarchical management style of some hospital administrators. In its early days, in the 1980s, the North Shore Birth Center, in Beverly, Massachusetts, collided with its well-intentioned parent organization, the Beverly Hospital, in just this way. The hospital managers were uncomfortable with the full implications of customer mastery. On the other hand, the nurse-midwives were uncomfortable with the traditional, hierarchical model of hospital management, in which one person supervises others and strict protocols guide organizational relationships. Instead, they created a flat, fluid organizational model in which all the nurses are equal and free to respond to the mother's needs, whatever they might be. The nurse-midwives wanted the independence and teamwork that characterized their professional work to be mirrored in their organizational structure. A flat organizational structure was their ideal.

Noted the budget director of the Beverly Hospital, "The midwives . . . had difficulty accommodating to institutional policies. When they were asked to choose a director, they resisted, saying, 'No, we are all equals.' They also resisted the idea of [individual] merit evaluations. They made statements to the press without consulting the hospital's public relations staff. . . . I've spent a lot of time teaching them about administration." Apparently the lessons did not take. Despite its good intentions of serving mastery-craving women, the Beverly Hospital received considerable adverse publicity after one of its key nurse-midwives resigned to protest what she viewed as the hospital's oppressive insistence on bureaucracy rather than independence, and on hierarchy rather than teamwork.

As the case of the North Shore Birth Center shows, managerial barriers can complicate the creation of organizations that truly support customer mastery. Lip service to the notion of consumer mastery is easily paid, but actually putting the consumer in charge is a cultural sea-change that some old-line health care providers find immensely difficult to accomplish.

Bread and Circus: How To Do It Right

Late one Sunday morning I opened my door to find my fifteen-year-old son on the doorstep, somewhat sheepishly holding a large bag of groceries. A bunch of flowers was sticking prominently out of the bag. "Did you buy these for me?" I asked, amazed. "Well, yes and no," he answered. "They're yours, but I didn't buy them. I got them, and this bag of groceries, for winning the gold medal in the Bagging Olympics at the Bread and Circus Supermarket. At our team meeting this morning, they lined up all of us baggers and judged how well we put the groceries in a bag. Were the eggs on the top or the bottom? Did we tape shut the deli containers? Stuff like that. And I got twenty bucks too!"

"How do you feel about all this?" I asked. "It is great to have the twenty bucks," he said. "Enjoy the flowers."

Bread and Circus, a Whole Foods supermarket, is another organization whose purpose is to help the health activist achieve mastery. But unlike the North Shore Birth Center, it has succeeded in doing so. The Bagging Olympics is just one of the many techniques its management uses to train and motivate employees to serve this challenging customer. In what follows, my purpose is not to promote "health food," which may or may not produce good health, but rather to present a model of a management that serves health care activists well.

Bread and Circus has got its customers' needs nailed and makes sure that its employees get the message loud and clear. A good example of how to support the mastery-seeking customer is its "Walking the Talk" technique, as described in its *Team Member General Information Guidebook:* "In directing customers to something on the shelf, we should *walk with them.* . . . We should also talk to them as we walk if we can. When we get there, it is best to remain there until we are sure the customer is satisfied." Appropriately, employees are strongly warned against preaching to the knowledgeable customer. Notes the guidebook, "People come . . . looking for high quality food, not dogma. . . . On the other hand, always try to supply as much product information as any customer may require. If you don't know the answer . . . this is why we have an Information Team." You want information and support? Bread and Circus knows how to deliver them.

As my son explained to me after the first orientation meeting, which he was paid to attend: "They told us that their customer is strong-minded. So we have to provide excellent service. The customer is always right."

"Well, what do you think about this new job of yours?" I asked.

"I really don't have a job," he answered, "until my team leader recommends me as a customer service team member. All the other members of the team will then vote on this recommendation about a month or so after I start working. If they think I carry my fair share, they'll vote me on the team; if not, I hit the beach."

Paid training sessions, contests to dignify even the most mundane job, a focus on teamwork—just what kind of supermarket is this? I wondered.

Even before my son started working there, I had noticed that Bread and Circus differed from other supermarkets. On my first visit, when I asked a young man who was stocking shelves where I could find bulgur wheat, he not only knew what it was, he actually accompanied me to its location. The contrast between his knowledge and that of the typical young supermarket cashier, who will pick up an unfamiliar vegetable— say, a turnip—and ask me, "Whaddya call this?" was startling.

Even more startling was the sheer beauty of the market's food displays: gorgeous, crisp red-leaf lettuces sitting in pristine crushed ice beds; ravishing carrots arranged in a sunburst pattern, cleverly reflected in an angled overhead mirror; pyramids of polished apples radiating light. The fish and meat counters too were mosaics of color and texture, displaying their firm-fleshed and obviously fresh wares. Even the pre-pared food line was stunning. I had come to laugh at the veggie burgers, and yes, they were there. But so were glistening, crisp roasted chickens; wonderful melted cheese-oozing pizzas, quiches, and pasta; and dozens of delicious salads. There was fresh-brewed dark roasted coffee too, along with the chicory and carob drinks. The beauty, choice, and quality of the merchandise was like manna from heaven to the picky health activist customer.

A very skilled management must be in back of all this, I thought. I had often visited health food stores, but I had never returned to any of them until I shopped at Bread and Circus. Many are dirty and dark, and they smell bad too. (What *is* that natural food store smell?) And some do not display a good understanding of their mastery-seeking customers. Those who ask customers to bring their own grocery bags and bag their own groceries, for example, eliminate a large number of convenience-seeking consumers. Others do not train their service personnel ade-quately, thus repelling the activist customers who consider themselves very knowledgeable. The message of this type of health food store is clear: You must suffer for good health.

By contrast, Bread and Circus's managers not only clearly under-stand the controlled lifestyle and convenience that their customers want, they are able to deliver it. Not surprisingly, the company does well. By August of 1996, its stock price had more than tripled in a year.

Clearly, Bread and Circus understands how to please health activ-ists. What is its secret? My son's experiences can help us answer the question. Although he was the lowest man on the corporate totem pole, the summer bagger, he was paid to attend monthly team sessions, in which he also learned how to display food, clean the store, and attend to various customer needs. Unlike the North Shore Birth Center, which discouraged teams and encouraged hierarchy, the emphasis here was on a team that focused clearly on the customer.

Still, all is not sweetness and light, or tofu and wheatgrass juice, at Bread and Circus. Steely-eyed business motivation and control practices are used as well. An innocuously named Customer Snapshot is provided by a mystery shopper who inspects every store and rates it. In Gainshar-ing employees can receive a sizable fraction of the gains they create when they beat their budgets. And to insure that employees understand their financial results, all team meetings contain extensive discussions of each department's performance against its own budget and in comparison to other stores. So detailed is the review that my then-fifteen-year-old son asked me a question usually asked by first-year MBAs: "What does *gross margin* mean?"

So you don't believe in natural food? You think the Bread and Circus customers are elitist whiners? Forget about that. My point is to extol the Bread and Circus management, not its products. The details of their service model—paying attention to the customer, training, teamwork, flexibility, measurement, and rewards—can and should be replicated in other ventures that seek to serve activist consumers. Because of health activists, health food is now a $6.2 billion industry and is growing at four times the rate of food expenditures in the United States. Savvy companies like Bread and Circus will help to increase even this explosive growth rate.

KEYS TO MASTERY-ENHANCING VENTURES

While a specific health practice like taking antioxidant supplements may or may not promote better health, the health activists who think about and master these practices do make a difference. Having already mastered various aspects of their health, they now enjoy better health status, lead more productive lives, and incur fewer health care costs than others. Those who eliminated destructive lifestyle habits reduce death rates from diseases like cancer and heart disease. Many health activists who care for their chronic diseases themselves reduce the costs of medical treatment and at the same time improve their health status, such as the participants in Healthtrac and in the Arthritis Self-Management Program. And those who play a major role in the process of health care, like mothers who deliver their babies in a birth center, also reduce costs while enhancing their feelings of well-being.

What encourages people to master their health? Education is a key factor, and the primary source of health education for Americans is the innovators. Aids like calcium tablets and home exercise equipment play an important role too. These too are primarily provided by the private sector. Last, continual innovation and research are key, because medicine is a young science and many savvy Americans doubt established medical explanations of cause and effect.

Role of Entrepreneurs

American health activists want a wide variety of innovations that can help them to further master their own health care. Because creating such innovations is difficult and risky, entrepreneurs of vision are necessary. The "Doctor knows best" system is unlikely to create the mastery-enhancing ventures that health activists demand. Such ventures are more likely to originate with outsiders who have experience in industries where the consumer reigns supreme, such as retailing and information.

The success of Bread and Circus and the early struggles of the North Shore Birth Center illustrate the powerful effect that business people can have in creating new health care ventures that respond to consumers' needs. The successful organization, Bread and Circus, is led by retailing experts. Its organizational structure puts consumers at the top and then provides a tightly knit unit to meet their needs. Team members understand that no matter what their individual jobs may be, their primary focus must be on helping the customer and they are trained to fulfill multiple roles. The shelf-stocker who stopped his work to accompany me to the wheat is an example of this focus. Bread and Circus employees are trained, evaluated, and rewarded primarily for service to the customer.

The instincts of the nurse-midwives at the North Shore Birth Center were to do exactly the same. They too wanted to place the mother at the top and create a team to meet her needs. But the managers of the traditional, hierarchical hospital stand in their way. Despite their good intentions, the hospital's management has difficulty accepting the "customer is queen" model and the flat, flexible team structure it requires.

Currently, outside entrepreneurs are surely put off by the substantial barriers to creating mastery-enhancing innovations in the health care system. The monumental effort required of the nurse-midwives to have the modern birth-center movement credentialed by established hospitals and reimbursed by traditional health insurers might well cause entrepreneurs to say, "No, thanks! I think I'll go into some other industry, one I can enter without one hand tied behind my back." Until the playing field is leveled, so that new players can enter the game as easily as existing ones, new ventures that could successfully reduce costs and enhance health by emphasizing the primacy of the consumers will not easily develop.

Role of Consumers

Because insurers and government payers do not value mastery and control as much as consumers, the reimbursement problems experienced by the nurse-midwives do not occur when the consumer pays directly. The innovators who provide self-care information and mastery-enhancing aids like vitamins and health food are paid directly by the customers who value these qualities. They do not need to convince a reluctant health insurance company to pay for their services. Not surprisingly, innovations that enhance health mastery are much more common in those sectors where consumers pay directly than in those where a health insurance company is the primary payer.

When consumers pay directly, innovators respond to their needs—that's how a market works. But when a health insurance company pays, innovators are not nearly so likely to respond to consumers' needs. It is difficult for health insurers to know what consumers want. Most health insurance is purchased by the employer or the government, not the user. In the absence of direct feedback from consumers, traditional providers heavily influence health insurance companies' selection of the services for which they will pay. And as we have seen, some traditional medical practices are based more on dogma than on science. And however well intended, traditional providers are not likely fully to reflect consumers' demand for mastery.

Until such barriers to innovation are removed, the entrepreneurs who are key to increasing health mastery will likely invest their considerable skills in other, more inviting sectors.

CHAPTER 4

The Health Care System That Provides Convenience and Mastery

Picture how our future health care system will function:

> Early one Monday morning, a ten-year-old boy returns from a week at camp with alarming sores on his arms and legs. The family's regular doctor is not yet available, so his horror-stricken mother sits down at her computer to evaluate whether she should take her son to the hospital emergency room or the local twenty-four-hour doctors' offices. She calls up her Doctor system and types in a description of the lesions. The system asks her some detailed questions about the size of the sores and their number, and whether the boy has a fever or is excreting brownish urine. After a few seconds, a message appears on the computer screen. "Seems like impetigo to me," says the Doctor system. "My reasoning is described on the next page. Listed below are the medications and treatments recommended for impetigo. If you want more information, use our Call-a-Nurse number, or punch 5 for an impetigo video. If the lesions do not improve promptly, see your doctor."
>
> The reassured mother e-mails the Doctor's output to her own real doctor, along with some pictures of the sores. Soon

thereafter the doctor alerts her that a prescription for medication has been sent to a local pharmacy, and he recommends some self-care ointments. The mother e-mails the pharmacy to indicate her approval of the order. Shortly thereafter the medication and ointments arrive at her doorstep.

The total elapsed time? Two hours. The total cost? Twenty dollars for the doctor's time and fifteen dollars for the medication. The total time spent by the mother? Thirty minutes.

To provide further help if the sores do not clear up, the computer-based system prints out a list of nearby providers who could treat them, their location, and their hours, as well as records of consumer complaints, quality ratings, and prices. The list includes a doctor's office in the center of their suburban town, a physician group located in the office complex in the technology park where the mother works, and a skin-care center in the nearest shopping mall, which specializes in the treatment of acne and other skin diseases. The skin-care center and the local doctor are available on Saturdays and Sundays and before and after work, while the group physicians are available during work hours.

The mother calls her friend Nancy, whose psoriasis is treated at the skin-care center. Psoriasis is a complex chronic disease from which she has suffered since college days. Nancy sings the praises of the center. "The skin-care center's great team of doctors and nurses helps me manage the physical and psychological causes of the disease, and their aestheticians advise me about how best to present it," Nancy says. "The team members initially met with me as a group to hear about my symptoms all at once. I did not have to repeat them over and over for each separate provider. I don't have to travel from one to the other for my care. They are all present, right there at the mall. When I develop a problem related to my disease, say an infection, the skin center has professionals on its staff who specialize in treating related problems. Because they treat so many people with skin problems, they have experts in almost every related problem too. And the center provides all the medications, bandages, ointments, and cosmetics I need right in the office. Whenever a new development in the management of psoriasis comes up, they send me a fax about it that includes an order or an appointment form, if I want to follow up on it. They have a great library too, which I can easily search and download on my computer, and I belong to a support group they formed.

"I also like the way they price the service," Nancy continues. "They charge a flat price that covers everything I might need, except for the cosmetics. I know the price is good because I've compared it to the prices charged by competitive skin-care centers for the same service. And the flat price gives the center's providers a financial incentive to take good care of me, so I don't come back all the time for minor problems. After all, the more frequently I come back, the less money they make; but on the other hand, if they provide me with too little care and I feel that I'm not getting a good value for the money I spend, I can easily go to one of the many other skin-care centers. The quality ratings of skin-care centers are regularly published in our local newspaper, and I can access them on the QualMed system. That makes it easy for me to evaluate how other people perceive the quality and the prices of different sources of skin-care."

Are these examples of a convenient, mastery-providing, competitively priced health care system a pipe dream? I think not. The convenience of the eyewear sector; the customer focus of Salick Health Care; the empowerment provided by Healthtrac, by birth centers, and by the Arthritis Self-Management Program; and the support mechanisms of Access Health are but the first waves of what will become an avalanche of new ventures to increase convenience and mastery in health care. The consumer revolutionary movement and its cause—better health, lower cost—are too powerful to resist.

Patients Must Be Patient; Doctor Knows Best

As yet, however, the hardworking, overburdened, educated consumer revolutionaries who transformed other industries have had all too little impact on the health care sector. The system remains inconvenient, hard to reach, harder to use, and obscure, failing to provide the fundamental information and the support they require.

The absence of convenience and mastery needlessly diminishes Americans' health and drains our economy. As we have seen, hardworking people put off important measures like immunizations, and they spend too much time waiting for or traveling to providers. Victims of ubiquitous chronic diseases like arthritis are particularly hard hit, as they awkwardly wend their way through a medical maze organized according to physician specialty instead of to their needs. The "patients must be patient" dictum exacts a considerable toll. The absence of support diminishes Americans' ability to eliminate destructive habits and care for chronic diseases. The deadly duo of inconvenience and lack of mastery sap our health, our time, and our productivity.

By contrast, the skin-care system described above is extremely convenient and rich in support. The skin-care center provides a team of specialists, the services of nonmedical professionals, and drugs and supplies all in one site. Its services are organized around consumers' needs for skin care, rather than around the specialties of dermatologists, allergists, neurologists, surgeons, and psychiatrists. The center is conveniently located in a shopping mall, and it provides services during nonworking hours. The consumer could choose from many other service sites and hours as well, ranging from a local physician's office to a medical group located at his or her work site. The availability of self-care information and the convenience of services like the delivery of pharmaceuticals reduce the time consumers now waste.

Self-care information and support, as well as data about the quality and prices of providers, also increase convenience and mastery. The use of flat prices for a bundle of services and the availability of quality measures enhance the consumer's ability to compare different providers, and it provides an incentive for the providers appropriately to balance their financial needs with the customer's welfare. Some are concerned that the use of information will be limited to educated elites, but extensive marketing research indicates that new products eventually diffuse to most potential users regardless of their level of education. Typically the process of using an innovation such as health care information is first adopted by "innovators" who usually account for 2.5 percent of the total users. The innovators are frequently well-educated and higher-income individuals. They then influence the "early adopter" group (13.5 percent of the total users), the key opinion leaders within their communities who have the greatest impact on other consumers. The opinion leaders, in turn, influence the "early majority" (34 percent of the total), whose dominant characteristic is deliberateness. The "late majority" (34 percent of the total) are people of below average income and education. The market is nearing maturity when this group begins to use the product. The "laggards" (16 percent of the total) rate the lowest on these social characteristics and tend to be socially isolated. The health activists who seek out information and products that enhance their health are likely the first sign of the early adopters.

For all its virtues, however, this convenient, information-rich, efficient system does not exist in health care.

Convenience and Mastery

How do we get from here to there?

First, we must identify the parts of the health care system that are convenient, reasonably priced, and filled to the gills with helpful information. These rays of sunshine can be found where health care products are paid for directly by consumers, such as eyewear or information on self care. Eyewear is available in convenient locations—in shopping malls or local stores; it is available at convenient times—after working hours and on weekends; and it is available in a vast array of eyewear materials and styles from which to choose. The prices inflate at normal rates; service for customized products is fast; considerable information on prices is available directly in the store or from advertisements; and evaluations of quality can be had from consumer watchdogs like *Consumer Reports*.

By contrast, a typical doctor's office is open only from nine to five, requires long waits, and offers all-too-little control. (Although health service providers have far less control over the service process than optical stores—after all, they cannot limit their patients' needs—numerous techniques exist that effectively reduce patient waiting time and delays. Indeed, Boston's Institute for Healthcare Improvement 1996 National Congress on the topic of reducing delays and waiting time contained many examples of such techniques.) Price information is hard to get, and quality evaluations are rarely available. My former assistant, a temporary worker whose agency did not offer health insurance, had typical difficulties in getting a checkup before she entered law school.

She called the physicians whose offices were located nearest to her home, according to the telephone directory, to determine their prices for a routine checkup. A few were so flabbergasted by her request that they could not even respond. The prices quoted by the others ranged from $40 to $150. Although she chose the lowest-priced doctor, she was worried because, for all her energy and ingenuity, she could not obtain any information about his quality.

What makes eyewear so different? The eyewear sector is consumer-friendly because consumers pay for its products and services directly. The connection between convenience, information, and the source of payment is remarkably consistent. When people pay for health care services directly from their own pockets, those services are invariably convenient and helpful information is readily available. When people pay only partly out of their own pockets, as is common in the United States, the services are inconvenient and consumer-oriented information is largely unavailable. What little information does exist ignores the consumer's point of view, like studies of the cost of diseases that do not consider their effect on our national productivity. And when no health care services are paid for directly by consumers, inconvenience and obscurity reach new heights, as demonstrated by the long queues for care in countries where health care is paid for by the government.

But then, most of us cannot afford to pay for expensive health care services, like a birth or a heart transplant, out of our own pockets. We rely on health insurance to protect us against such catastrophic expenses. In a sense our insurers do our health care shopping for us and try to provide us with the features we would choose for ourselves.

Here's the rub: The insurers do not know what we want because we have no means of communicating our preferences to them. Diabetics have no way to communicate to an insurer that they want a doctor who has evening and weekend hours, who lives within ten miles of their home, who keeps appointments on time, who has high ratings from patients for empathy and communication, and who adheres to the monitoring and therapeutic protocols recommended by experts. Diabetics cannot communicate these preferences, because virtually none of this information exists. And until this information is compiled and made available, insurers cannot possibly reflect our preferences for convenience and mastery even if they want to do so.

The Wasteland of Health Information

Some types of health information are available in abundance, but information about costs and quality is notable for its absence. Ironically, while consumers who pay directly for their health care find no shortage of such information, the employers and insurers who spend hundreds of billions of dollars on health care each year find little. Ratings of items like eyeglasses, contact lenses, calcium supplements, and aerobics videos are readily available, but those who buy much more substantial amounts of health care are literally flying blind. As a special April 1996 issue of *Medical Benefits* noted, "The fundamental failing in employer-sponsored health care today is that employers generally have not become informed purchasers."

A few years ago, I asked the vice-president for human resources of a large company renowned for the quality of its health benefit information to provide me with data about the company's average cost per employee for different health insurance plans, including a few HMOs and the company's self-insured health care plan. So far, so good. Next, I asked what I did not intend to be a trick question: Could she explain why the average cost of one health insurance plan was so much higher than the others? Were a greater number of families or older people enrolled? To my surprise, she was stumped. The vice-president for human resources simply did not have information about the age or the family size of the employees covered under the different plans, nor could she easily obtain it.

This firm spends hundreds of millions of dollars on health care, yet it lacks even the most elementary information to evaluate its spending. It would be like buying a bag of nails without knowing how many nails the bag contains nor their length. As for quality, few employers are aware of the quality of the medical care their employees receive. Was it appropriate? Was it convenient? Was it well done? Answers are rarely given.

Such information shortages are inconceivable in any other setting. Do you know what you bought when you last went shopping? I bet you do. Does General Motors know how much steel, and of what type and quality, it purchased last quarter? You bet it does. Does my half-day-a-week gardener know the lowest price for mulch? Unquestionably. So why do those who purchased $205 billion of health care in 1991 know so little about what they bought?

A simple answer is that health care cost inflation snuck in on employers and they are still unprepared to manage it fully. In 1965, for example, private businesses paid only $6 billion for health care; although expenses had increased tenfold by 1980, they were still modest—"only" $64 billion. By 1991, however, expenses had tripled, standing at a record-breaking $205 billion. In the period 1984 to 1991, the average cost of an annual health insurance plan per employee more than doubled, from $1,645 to $3,605. Neither prices nor profits grew nearly so fast. By 1990 medically related expenses had become the single largest benefit category clocking in at 7.4 percent of payroll.

If you repeatedly hit a stubborn donkey with a two-by-four, you will ultimately get his attention. Slowly, like the donkey, the business community has awakened to the burden that growing health care costs are placing on its profitability. CEOs who once carelessly joked about the managed care alphabet soup—HMO, PPO, IPA, POS—are now surprisingly conversant with these techniques of health care cost control.

Yet another obstacle stands in the way of health care information: the people in corporations who are charged with purchasing health care. Most corporate purchases are executed by a purchasing department, staffed by steely-eyed, assertive cost accountants and engineers who haggle over every nickel and evaluate every item. Cost and quality information is like mother's milk to them. They love data—the more, the better. But these denizens of accounting and technical manuals do not purchase health care. As a "benefit," health care is purchased by human resource managers. Now, don't get me wrong—some of my best friends are human resource managers. But the orientation of human resource managers is toward benefits, not toward costs. Their interests are more toward expanding the coverage of employees than in constraining its costs. And rightly or wrongly, they are generally out of the mainstream of the corporation—a side function whose purpose is to keep the employees happy. Even after years in which human resource managers were charged to control, not expand, health care costs, a 1995 survey revealed that only 55 percent of CEOs thought of benefits in a "strategic way." In other words, the benefits managers were not yet true equals in the corporate ladder with strategy-formulating managers.

The users of health care, for their part, did not oversee costs because they had little personal responsibility for them. People whose employers provide them with health insurance usually pay very little for the services they receive. Since somebody other than themselves is paying, they perceive these services as "costless." Although most insured employees must pay a deductible out of their own pocket before their health insurance kicks in and many must pay a co-payment every time they use insured services, the amounts are usually minimal. In 1992 per-capita out-of-pocket spending equaled only $58 for hospitals and $100 for doctors. In 1993 most Americans spent more out of their own pockets on entertainment, apparel, and services than they did on health care.

The Future Is on Its Way

Spurred by the magnitude and enormity of the problem, some employers have finally banded together to obtain some of the information necessary for intelligent health care purchasing and to pressure their providers—hospitals, doctors, and health insurance companies—to compile it. The Cleveland Health Quality Choice Group, for example, a voluntary association consisting of employers, hospitals, and physicians, developed and published measures of patient outcomes and satisfaction for eleven hospital services in twenty-nine area hospitals. The group evaluates "quality" partially by predicting how a hospital should have performed, given the severity of a patient's illness, and comparing that prediction with its actual performance. (Performance is measured by death rates.) Similar data are published in New York, Pennsylvania, and Missouri at the behest of the state governments.

Some health insurance plans, such as HMOs and hospitals, now issue "report cards" in which they judge themselves on criteria such as rates of childhood immunization. In various states community efforts are building data systems that track every health care transaction. Eventually such systems may enable detailed cost and output analyses.

Industry standard-setting groups are rushing in to control this process. In Chicago, for example, the Joint Commission on Accreditation of Healthcare Organizations developed a rating system for public disclosure of the results of its accreditation process. And the National Committee for Quality Assurance in Washington has developed a "report card" that will compare the results of different health plans, using a system called HEDIS. The independent Health Outcomes Institute in

Bloomington, Minnesota, was created in 1993 "to encourage the development and dissemination of public domain tools and techniques for measuring the effectiveness of health care through assessment of functional outcomes and satisfaction."

Each of these groups hopes that its measurement system will become the gold standard in evaluating health care. Indeed, so substantial is the promise of "gold" that many entrepreneurial firms have rushed into the breach. Currently estimated at $10 to $15 billion, the health information industry is expected to double or triple in size in the next decade. Small wonder that, in 1996, the stock prices of health information companies like HBOC were so high! The growth prospects for firms providing health information in the current wasteland are enormous.

The Westborough, Massachusetts, firm MediQual is a typical such entrepreneurial venture. Backed by a substantial venture-capital investment, it provides the elaborate computer modeling that the Pennsylvania Health Care Cost Containment Council in Harrisburg uses to measure the severity of illness of the patients treated by different hospitals and physicians and to predict their associated death rates. Actual death rates are then compared with the predicted ones for each procedure, by physician and by hospital. Producing these data is an extremely costly process, because most doctors and hospitals lack computerized patient records. All the information required for assessing the patient's severity of illness must be laboriously picked out from the fat, messy folders stuffed with hand-scribbled notes that are dignified with the title "patient record."

Despite these laudable efforts, however, health "information" presently remains a misnomer. The costs and quality of most of the activities in today's health care system remain unmeasured and are therefore uncontrolled. What little cost and quality information does exist is often completely unaudited. Because much of it is produced by the providers themselves, the fox is guarding this chicken coop.

Further, the providers' focus rarely reflects the consumers' point of view. Some dimensions of consumer satisfaction are generally ignored in providers' measures of quality, including convenience, comfort, and perceptions of service quality. The health care equivalent of the surveys of consumer perceptions, like the Zagat's survey of restaurants and the J.D. Powers surveys of automobile quality, has yet to appear. Notes an unusually tart review, in the *Journal of the American Medical Association,* of various systems that measure quality of life, "Because quality of life is a uniquely personal perception . . . [it] can be suitably measured only by determining the opinions of patients and by supplementing (or replacing) the instruments developed by experts."

A Glimpse of the Future

The future of health information is nonetheless promising. Consumers can easily access the abundant clinical health information available on the Internet. National magazines like *U.S. News and World Report* publish annual lists of the "best hospitals," while local outlets rate the "best doctors." And to avoid undue reliance on provider-produced data, national purchasers of health care compute their own measures of quality and cost. For example, GTE Corporation employs five experts who evaluate each of the 125 managed care organizations with which the company contracts and produce a "report card" of the HMOs. In cases where the company was not satisfied with the results, it has set up its own clinics.

The demand for health information is so great that Jeremy Brody, a former student of mine who now works in the health information sector, wrote to me, "Over the past year, a day doesn't go by in which I don't hear about another company in this market." A reassuring public squabble has broken out about the quality of health information. A consumer watchdog group faulted the "cozy relationship between the accrediting body and the hospital industry." It cited internal accreditation documents in which more than a third of the hospitals surveyed in 1992 received poor or "nonconforming" scores, while public reports accredited 99 percent of all hospitals. The system for rating HMOs has also been battered by critics. Employers point out the conflict of interest inherent in the HMOs' involvement in designing and paying for the reports and the lack of auditing of the data. In the August 1996 issue, *Consumer Reports* warns its readers that the HMO accreditation procedure does not look at results, but only at the processes for providing care. It found that accreditation was not well-correlated with its surveys of user satisfaction. The magazine was so dissatisfied with the system that it devised its own measures for rating HMOs.

In light of the public's interest in obtaining accurate, relevant information with which to evaluate providers, savvy politicians have hopped on the bandwagon. Massachusetts Governor William Weld in 1996 signed a Physician Profile Bill that allows consumers to review information on doctors' education, training, disciplinary actions, malpractice settlements, and criminal records via a CD Rom or the Internet. "Choosing a doctor is one of the most personal and important decisions a person can make, yet up until today, consumers have had little information on which to base their decision," noted Weld when he signed the bill. Providers also understand the importance of information. Notes the CEO of the country's largest hospital corporation, "The future belongs to whoever best measures quality of care. . . . Whoever does it will absolutely control the market, and everybody else who doesn't will disappear."

PART 2

What Payers Want:
Quality and Lower Costs

CHAPTER 5

Options for the Productivity Revolution

Senator Joseph Biden sat in his elegant office in the Russell Building. Although he looked fit, the picture of health, he pointed to a scar on his head. "The doctors gave me back my life," he said. "They repaired aneurysms in the artery leading to my brain that would have either killed or impaired me. And I know how valiantly they worked to restore my sons' health after they were involved in a serious automobile accident as children. No doubt about it, for this and many other reasons, the U.S. health care system is wonderful. Sure it costs a lot, and of course we must help those who don't have enough health insurance. But I don't want to destroy this great system in the process.

"How do we keep what's good about our health care system and yet make it cheaper? If we knew the answer to that question, we could bring the many Americans who don't have health insurance into the mainstream, without breaking our economy's back or ruining our system."

The question Senator Biden raised is a complicated one. He does not want merely to shrink health care costs. Rather, he wants to maintain the quality of the system while controlling those costs. In the language of Economics 101, he wishes to increase productivity—the amount of output achieved per dollar spent. Fortunately, many firms in the U.S. business sector provide examples of how to succeed in doing just that.

Answering the senator's question is the topic of Parts 2 and 3 of this book. The win-win solution offered will trim the system's fat, not its muscle. The solution can be learned from the American corporations who transformed themselves from yesterday's overweight stumblebums, easily defeated by their German and Japanese opponents, to today's lean, mean fighting machines. It can be summarized in two words: *focus* and *technology*. In the 1980s American firms focused: They shed considerable excess baggage, ridding themselves of distracting side businesses and concentrating on their core competencies. And they invested heavily in the technology and operational systems that have since increased their productivity. These firms did not succeed by becoming larger or smaller. They stayed the course by getting better, substantially increasing their productivity in the process.

Applying this lesson to the health care system will radically transform it, from a confusing jumble of multipurpose providers to a range of lean enterprises that are clearly focused on single health care objectives, smartened up with technology, and smoothed out with integrated operating systems.

Say good-bye to the general-purpose health care provider. Say hello to the focused health care factory.

Say good-bye to outrageous health care costs. Say hello to the new health care system.

THE LITTLE GIRL WITH THE LITTLE CURL

The American public generally shares Senator Biden's sentiments about the health care system. Despite its inconvenience and lack of support, they applaud our health care system more strongly than the citizens of other countries applaud theirs. Americans believe their health care system offers a higher quality of care than can be found anywhere else in the world and that its aggressive, inclusive style offers the possibility of a longer, more productive life. But like the senator most Americans also believe the system costs too much. And like him too, many would like to see health insurance extended to those who lack sufficient coverage, if it can be done without bankrupting the economy.

When It Is Good, It Is Very Very Good

The American health care system gives its users more of what they want—advanced medical technology, choice, control, and greater convenience—than the systems in some other developed countries. In one large-scale survey, more Americans said they were "very satisfied" with their health care system than did people in Germany, the United Kingdom, and Japan. They were more content with many crucial aspects of the system: their perceptions of control, their waiting time for an appointment or for elective surgery, and their ability to access advanced drugs, procedures, and other high-tech options.

The differences in satisfaction between Americans and the residents of other developed countries represent more than a statistical ripple. Americans were two to three times more likely to be satisfied with these important aspects than were Germans, English, and Japanese. Even Canadians, second only to Americans in their fondness for these aspects of their health care system, expressed some grave doubts about their system. For example, fewer Canadians than Americans were very satisfied with their system's responsiveness to the need for elective surgery. A 1996 report found that 50 percent more Canadians and Germans could not obtain an appointment without a long wait and that Canadians with significant health problems were more likely to complain of inadequate choices of specialists.

Americans also support advanced medical technology and its use in treating patients who are terminally ill. While they generally feel that current spending for these purposes is adequate—only about 20 percent stated that it was too low—between 25 and 58 percent of the European respondents felt too little was spent in their countries for terminally ill patients and advanced medical technology. More than half the British respondents bemoaned the U.K.'s stingy budgets for these purposes.

Fans of the American health care system do not live only in the United States. The international admirers show their affection the old-fashioned way—with money, and lots of it. In 1994, pharmaceutical firms exported $26.2 billion of goods, generating a trade surplus of $500 million. The medical device industry exported $9.2 billion in products in 1994, creating a $4.2 billion trade surplus in the process. In a pleasant reversal from the situation of many other American industries, Japan was the largest customer for U.S. devices: It imported $1.4 billion worth in 1994. Even our health care services command export markets. For example, Caremark International, a provider of a variety of managed care services, claims to have had a 45 percent growth internationally in three years. A company official explained its appeal: "With our extensive expertise in HIV, for instance, we knew who to talk to, how to create a clinical model and have leading-edge physicians to help introduce new concepts."

Substantial American investments in medical research support this enviable record. For example, in 1989, the U.S. government spent 13 percent of its research and development funds in health, while the next leading country, the U.K., expended only 5 percent of its funds for this purpose. In that year American R&D spending roughly equaled the *combined* spending of Japan, West Germany, and the U.K., when measured in constant 1982 dollars.

These monies appear to yield handsome rewards, not only in commerce but in basic knowledge. Testimonials to the excellence of American medical research abound. Between 1985 and 1990 nearly 80 percent of the Nobel Prize winners in medicine were Americans. The average U.S. drug patent garners substantially more citations than do German, Japanese, British, and French patents. In a 1993 *Business Week* "Patent Scoreboard," the health care industry led twelve other industries in its links to science and technology. Many of the listed U.S. companies scored substantially above the group's composite rankings, including Merck and Bristol-Myers Squibb. While some foreign firms scored high as well—especially Roche Holdings, whose quality of scientific research is nearly legendary—many of the others did not, including large English, German, and Japanese pharmaceutical firms.

The American public strongly supports our country's investment in medical research. Respondents to a 1991 survey were more interested in new medical discoveries than in any of the other listed issues, including pollution, new inventions, and economic and business conditions. Indeed, in 1990, 72 percent of Americans felt that too little was being spent on medical research activities to improve and protect health. (While 68 percent of Americans were "very interested" in new medical discoveries, only 41 percent of European respondents shared that sentiment.)

If the American health care system is typified by excellence in medical research, by easy access to the advances it yields, by compassion in treating those with life-threatening illnesses, and by positive trade balances—what is the problem?

But When It Is Bad, It Is Horrid

The American public knows the system's weak points all too well. Survey respondents overwhelmingly say that too much is spent on hospitalizations and physicians: physicians earn too much and hospitals waste too much. Inefficiency, greed, and waste are their watchwords. In contrast, the citizens of Canada, Britain, Germany, and Sweden are more likely to feel that spending on hospitals and physicians in their countries is either too low—74 percent of U.K. respondents felt that way about hospitalizations—or about right.

International comparisons of health care spending buttress the perception that the American system is a fatty. In 1992 total *per capita* health expenses in this country clocked in at $3,086; our nearest competitor for this dubious honor was Switzerland, whose *per capita* expenses were $1,000 less. The United States spent substantially more of its GDP on health care (13.6 percent) than did Canada (10.3 percent), Germany (8.7 percent), Japan (6.9 percent), or the U.K. (7.1 percent).

Since 1982 health care price increases in the United States have considerably outstripped increases in the prices of food, clothing, housing, and even energy. These increases have taken big bites out of the American economy. The corporate sector was particularly hard hit. In 1989 American corporations' profit after taxes almost equaled their health care expenses. Because for many corporations health care costs inflated more rapidly than profits, their rapid increase ultimately constricted the wealth of those who owned stock in these businesses through their pension funds or personal investments. Government budgets were hard hit by health care costs too. The federal and state government budgets that pay for health care for the elderly (Medicare) and the poor (Medicaid) were spun out of control by these mammoth expenditures. Medicare and Medicaid payments per person served jumped 8 percent in one year alone, outstripping increases in inflation and tax revenues.

Individual Americans were also pummeled by these health care cost increases. Increasingly, American workers are paid with health insurance, not with salary. While the wages and salaries of workers in private industry rose by only a dollar per hour between 1991 and 1994, or 9 percent, their compensation in the form of health insurance rose by 24 percent. The percentage of health care costs for which Americans pay out of their own pockets has plummeted, from 88.4 percent in 1929 to 20.1 percent in 1993, but some expensive items, such as nursing home care and drugs, still require considerable individual payment. The elderly and chronically ill who consume considerable amounts of these resources may face particularly large health care bills; for example, in 1993 the average person 75 years or older spent about 17 percent of income before taxes on health care. And the 35.3 percent of the uninsured who in 1993 had family incomes of $14,000 or less surely had a hard time paying for their health care needs. Small wonder that the uninsured feel much less positive about our health care system than do the insured. They feel they have far less control over decisions affecting their health care and they are much more likely to be discouraged from seeking medical treatment.

Although the growth of health expenditures in the United States has slowed since 1990, and in 1994 we incurred the second smallest increase since 1960, these statistics provide no cause for celebration. National health expenditures have continued to outpace the growth of GDP throughout this period. This growth appeared to slow recently primarily because of decreases in the general inflation rate in our economy. The factors within the industry that have fueled its growth in the past—population, medical inflation, and others—have continued to grow at their historical rates. No wonder that in a 1996 report, health care costs headed the list of employers' human resource concerns.

THREE DIETS

So how do we keep what is good about our health care system—choice, technology, control, and convenience—and discard what is horrid—its high costs, which hurt corporations, governments, the old, the very sick, and the uninsured? How do we increase productivity so that we get more output from every dollar spent?

Essentially, only three diets are available—downsizing, or the "just say no" diet; upsizing, or the "big is beautiful" diet; and resizing, or the "trade fat for muscle" diet. These three diets apply to any fatty entity—

be it an overweight person, a flabby corporation, an obese government, or the jumbo American health care system.

Downsizing—The "Just Say No" Diet

Downsizing is a stringent diet that slims down by "just saying no"—"no" to overconsumption of food, in the case of a person; "no" to excessive numbers and pay levels for employees and other resources, in the case of a corporation; and "no" to profligate use of or payments for resources, in the case of the health care system.

In the 1980s many American corporations tried this particular diet. They got skinny by laying off employees or reducing their compensation and slashing other costs. Managed care organizations represent the health care equivalent of the same diet. They promise to reduce costs by saying no to unnecessary calories. The junk food that they say they will purge from the health care system consists of unneeded visits to expensive specialists; imprudent use of medical technology; overlong hospital stays; and extravagant payments to doctors, hospitals, and other providers. Apparently many believed these promises. The many types of managed care organizations increasingly dominate the United States, enrolling 21 percent of the health care market, or 55 million Americans, in 1994.

Upsizing—The "Big Is Beautiful" Diet

Upsizing takes just the opposite tack from downsizing. Its premise is that "big is beautiful."

The premise has a good tradition. "Big is beautiful" was the hallmark of the middle stages of industrialization, in which firms increased their efficiency by increasing their size. General Motors, in its earlier incarnation, typified the "big is beautiful" approach. It became the dominant American automobile company by gobbling up not only other automobile makers but many of its suppliers too. As GM grew wider (producing more and more brands of automobiles) and taller (encompassing all the facets of production), it also got leaner. After all, as the number of the cars it manufactured increased, some of its costs remained the same; for example, big or small, it needed just one CEO, and the more cars it produced, the smaller the fraction of the CEO's salary each one carried.

Health care organizations enthusiastically embraced the "big is beautiful" approach. In 1995 the number of large hospital mergers and acquisitions jumped by 44 percent from the previous year. Remarkable as these numbers are, however, hospitals were pikers compared with physician groups, whose merger volume increased by nearly 60 percent over the same time period. All told, 623 mergers and other "big is beautiful" integrations occurred in 1995—a 20 percent jump from the heady level reached in 1994. The rate of vertical integration increased as well. The number of integrated health networks nearly doubled to 504 between 1994 and 1996.

Resizing—The "Trade Fat for Muscle" Diet

The diet that substitutes muscle for fat is more subtle. Because muscle tissue burns more calories than do fat cells, this diet creates more efficient organisms, ones that obtain more output from the food they ingest. While the "just say no" diet slims down the whole body, the "fat for muscle" diet resculpts the anatomy, so that a more efficient calorie-burning person emerges.

Corporations that resize attempt to enhance their productivity by intelligently pruning away nonessential functions and building up the muscle of those that remain. Two key activities are common to many of them. First, they focus on their core competencies and "outsource" an increasing number of the goods and services they once produced in-house. Second, they invest heavily in technology and integrated operating systems that enable them to work smarter, not just harder. The importance of organizational changes in increasing productivity is frequently overlooked, but as *Business Week* stated, "The real breakthrough . . . [is in] the sweeping changes in management and organizational structure that are redefining how work gets done. . . . Often, this means breaking down the old functional fiefdoms—in marketing, engineering, manufacturing, and finance, for instance—and redeploying workers in multidisciplinary teams that concentrate on getting the right products and services to the customer."

SELECTING THE RIGHT DIET

Many observers of the American health care system believe that the best choice of diet is obviously the first one. The system clearly needs rationing, they believe—less food, less technology, and less money. Put it on the financial equivalent of a 1,200-calorie-a-day diet, and a skinny system will emerge from its cocoon of fat. Others believe the correct diet is obviously the second one: to them, the key to increased productivity is to get big, not to get small.

Meanwhile, the public is not so sure of the wisdom of either diet. Americans may worry that either downsizing or upsizing would deplete the things they most admire about the system—high technology, choice, and control. They may worry that neither diet attacks what they believe to be the root cause of the cost problem—the rampant inefficiency of the system. They want the "trade fat for muscle" diet that would resculpt the corpulent anatomy of the health care system.

In what follows, I will review all three of these models for slimming down our health care system, citing evidence from both the corporate and health care organizations that have attempted to implement them. The conclusion is clear: As detailed in Part 3, resculpted organizations that substitute muscle for fat are the best bets to maintain or increase quality while reducing costs.

Is big beautiful? Is downsizing the future? Don't bet on it.

CHAPTER 6

Downsizing: The "Just Say No" Diet

In "Slashed and Burned," the *Wall Street Journal* nailed the lid on the coffin of downsizing. In downsizing, noted the *Journal,* "many companies ... make flawed decisions—hasty, across-the-board cuts, that come back to haunt them, on the bottom line, in public relations, in strained relations with customers and suppliers, and in demoralized employees." A systematic analysis of the factors commonly claimed to have increased American productivity also pooh-poohs the impact of downsizing. Although American firms shrank their labor force substantially, cutting their permanent staffs by over 400,000 workers in the period July 1992 to June 1995, two-thirds of the downsized firms in a recent survey reported unchanged or lower productivity. In other words, the downsized organizations got smaller, but most of them did not improve their output produced per unit of input.

In retrospect, the results are not surprising. A diet that shrinks the entire body is as likely to snip away muscle as fat.

The results are worrisome for the health care system. After all, the ever-more-prevalent managed care organizations essentially use a downsizing approach to shrink the health care system. Like the corporations that downsized, they believe they can do more with less.

HOW THE HEALTH MAINTENANCE ORGANIZATION GOT ITS NAME

Health maintenance organizations derived their name from their initial purpose—to maintain the health of enrollees. Early-stage HMOs, such as Kaiser Permanente, founded in 1945, which first provided prepaid health services to a group of construction workers employed by industrialist Henry Kaiser, emphasized just this aspect of the name. They typically contracted for services with a group of physicians for a prepaid sum. Unlike other physicians, who were paid on a fee-for-service basis, the early-stage HMOs' physicians were financially motivated to maintain health rather than to treat illness. And the physicians who practiced in these HMOs believed in their mission of health maintenance, devoting their entire professional careers to achieving it. Not surprisingly, most of these early HMOs were top-ranked in preventive care in 1996 evaluations of HMOs in both *Consumer Reports* and *Newsweek.*

The image of health maintenance organizations was transformed in the 1970s, when they came to be extolled for their cost-controlling properties. An influential 1984 article accelerated this transformation by demonstrating that the Group Health Cooperative of Puget Sound achieved hospitalization rates 40 percent lower than rates for a control group that used a fee-for-service health insurance plan. Although the study was excellent, the generalizability of its findings was dubious—after all, this HMO, unlike most others, was a cooperative with a relatively long history of provider and consumer involvement. Yet the article's abstract asserted that the study demonstrated that "the style of medicine at prepaid group practices is markedly less . . . expensive"—an assertion akin to stating that Wal-Mart's success can be replicated by all discount stores—and the article continues to be cited as an example of the cost-controlling prowess of *all* HMOs.

Simultaneous research findings demonstrated regional variations in treatment that were ascribed primarily to the number of physicians in an area and their practice style, rather than to the health needs of the patients. These findings were widely accepted. For example, one essay cited the "extensive evidence of inappropriate and ineffective care" as the basis for its complaint that "all developed countries but the United States had reached the end" [of the] "expansionary enthusiasm" for medical care. But, as discussed in Chapter 3, medicine is a relatively young science, in which determinations of appropriateness are not easy to make. Nevertheless, the combination of these two streams of research seemed to indicate substantial promise for the cost-reducing potential of HMOs—so much so that the number of Americans enrolled in HMOs grew from 9.1 million in 1980 to 42.2 million in 1994.

New types of HMOs accounted for much of this growth. Instead of employing salaried physicians, in a staff model HMO like the Harvard Community Health Plan, or forming exclusive arrangements with a group of physicians, as in the so-called group model HMOs, the new HMOs were more likely to contract with individual or groups of physicians who operated in a variety of settings. This model of HMO required neither the substantial up-front costs of the group or staff models nor the risk that the capacity of the employed physicians or affiliated groups would not be fully utilized, and it could still control the costs of the health care system in a number of ways. After all, if inappropriate variations in medical care treatment patterns were pervasive, they could be corrected just by saying no to providers of medical care.

HOW MANAGED CARE CAN "JUST SAY NO"

Managed care organizations have many mechanisms that enable them to say no. Some of them require both providers and enrollees to obtain permission before using the system. That is, before I can use a hospital emergency room, when my physician is not available, on weekends or in the evenings, I must obtain permission from my HMO representative. And before my primary care physician can refer me to some expensive specialists or diagnostic tests, he too must obtain permission. Other managed care ventures pay physicians a flat rate, called a capitation, for providing their patients' health care needs. Capitation payments typically take the form of X dollars, per member, per month. Capitated physicians know that when they say no to their patients, their take-home pay will increase. In twenty metropolitan areas, the pay of as many as 74 percent of the providers is adjusted by their utilization or cost patterns. The staff and group models of HMOs can also say no simply by limiting the number of expensive specialists they employ. A two-month wait for an appointment with a dermatologist or neurologist is just another way of saying no. Last, managed care organizations can say no to the questionable expensive, potentially life-saving procedures. This strategy is seductive because the expenses of a relatively small number of very sick people account for a large fraction of the health care costs of any insurer and some question the effectiveness of their care. But the strategy is worrisome too. After all people buy health insurance primarily to protect themselves against the costs of treating cancer, not as payment for the cost of treating a cold.

THE INTELLECTUAL BASIS FOR MANAGED CARE

These "just say no" mechanisms may have gained legitimacy because they are intellectually linked to systems analysis, a widely accepted and useful set of mathematical techniques that analyze the impact of individual actions in the context of a collective system. Just as the techniques of managed care enable a group of experts to oversee and override the decisions of individual doctors, the techniques of systems analysis enabled a group of economists to oversee the military's conduct of our war in Vietnam. Alain Enthoven, a distinguished Rhodes Scholar and PhD economist who was the assistant secretary of defense charged with this type of analysis during some of the Vietnam War, is one of the most visible advocates of managed care today.

Modern-day systems analysis was first used in Great Britain, prior to World War II, to install radar devices. At one time individual radar devices were installed in locations that minimized their chances of being jammed. The systems analysts, in contrast, successfully designed an installation process that minimized the probability of jamming the whole system. After this early triumph, systems analysts were entrusted with ever-larger problems, beginning with the development of a construction schedule for a weapons system, progressing to the analysis of specific tactical strategies, and culminating in a plan for major military operations.

So successful were these applications that the techniques of systems analysis were brought to the U.S. Department of Defense in the 1960s by its then secretary, Robert McNamara, a brilliant Harvard MBA who in his younger days had taught accounting in the business school. As recounted by David Halberstam in his Pulitzer Prize winning book, *The Best and the Brightest,* McNamara wanted to reshape the flaccid

Pentagon, with its sloppy, unsystematic military decision-making, by using his disciplined mathematical approach.

In the heyday of systems analysis, brilliant, young, politically appointed economists suddenly wielded enormous power. As one observer of the Defense Department notes, "The revolutionary manner in which McNamara made his decisions transformed the 'expert' (military) career bureaucrat into the 'novice' and the 'inexperienced' appointee into the 'professional.' " Precisely because the analysts were trained in economics and were not professional soldiers, they were presumed to be free of the military's parochial interests and able to attend to the best interests of the public.

The application of systems analysis was not limited to military problems. Soon its use spread to other government organizations. In 1967 President Lyndon Johnson ordered all the agencies of the federal government to adopt them. Many state and local governments fell into line too. New York City's Mayor John Lindsay, one of its many advocates, boasted in a large 1970 recruiting ad that his staff, along with McKinsey and Company consultants, were "creatively utilizing quantitative analysis and computer technology. But all the problems are not [yet] solved and we need more talented individuals." Yet within the decade, the city teetered on the brink of bankruptcy.

Many academics, entranced by the newfound power of systems analysts, became true believers too. Programs in public policy analysis to train the acolytes in the field flourished in schools of government, public health, education, and social service. As McNamara's assistant secretary of defense, an economist, noted in *The Economics of Defense in the Nuclear Age*, a widely read primer on systems analysis, "we regard all military problems as . . . problems in the efficient allocation and use of resources." And who could solve such problems better than the systems analyst?

Enthoven, now a professor at Stanford University, came to view managed care as the preferred method for delivering health care. The intellectual basis of the attraction is clear: Managed care organizations place decision-making experts in the center of power to determine patients' care. The *New York Times* notes that "the fact that an HMO has a management structure . . . appealed to Enthoven's passion for rational systems." A consultant to Kaiser Permanente, Enthoven frequently presents that giant as an example of the efficacy of managed care. He particularly admires its "set of documented practice protocols." Its triage system, which permits primary care physicians to treat most illnesses, appealed to him too because in his opinion the number of specialist physicians in the United States could be reduced by 67 percent.

With 6.9 million enrollees the fabled Kaiser Permanente system is one of the country's largest health care systems. Kaiser operates its own hospitals and sells its own health insurance. Enrollees can obtain virtually all their health care from one source—the Kaiser Permanente organization, in which *Kaiser* represents the business side and *Permanente* the medical side. For many years Kaiser charged the lowest premiums in its California market. Its customers seemed to like it too, as evidenced by the substantial growth in its enrollment from its inception in the 1930s.

Kaiser's success seemed directly linked to its vertical integration. Because it owns its hospitals in its home base of California and does not pay its physicians on a fee-for-service basis, neither the hospitals nor the doctors are tempted to increase their revenues—and the organization's costs—by prescribing medically unnecessary procedures. Kaiser's large size, moreover, makes it a natural laboratory in which the firm can study innovation. It can identify "best practice" procedures that bubble up in one site and replicate them elsewhere in the organization. Kaiser's managers can also balance shortages in one part of their vast empire with excessive capacity elsewhere, so that the whole organization remains efficient. Finally, because of its vertical integration, Kaiser can avoid paying the profit margins that independent providers would normally command.

MANAGED CARE: A DOWNSIZING SUCCESS STORY?

With these distinguished antecedents, is downsizing health care immune to the problems of downsizing in corporations? Does it increase the amount of health care delivered per dollar spent? Or does it merely shrink the system without improving its productivity? If the latter, will the qualities that Americans treasure about their health care system disappear in the shrinking process?

On one level, managed care appears to be the health care cost-control success story of the 1990s—one that simultaneously offers attractive features and controls costs.

Many managed care organizations contain appealing health care options. For one thing, they offer convenience: some people find that having a limited choice of practitioners simplifies the physician selection process. Moreover, staff and group HMOs usually "bundle" their physicians and related diagnostic services in one site that is relatively accessible to their enrollees. In theory managed care organizations can also easily provide an organized system of care for treatment of chronic diseases. (But as the story of my friend with the sore foot illustrates, they don't necessarily pull it off well in practice.) And unlike other insurance policies, managed care frequently covers well-child visits and preventive, diagnostic procedures for adults. I personally find these characteristics so attractive that I have belonged to managed care organizations for virtually all my adult life.

Despite all these extras, managed care costs less. One study showed that 1995 monthly family HMO premiums of $447 were nearly 10 percent lower than the $493 premiums for a traditional health insurance plan, called an indemnity policy. The recent decline in cost increases has paralleled the growth in market share of managed care organizations. A front-page headline, "Health Plan Cost Remaining Stable, Managed Care Key to Control," in the trade newspaper *Business Insurance* offers but one instance of the common assumption that a causal relationship exists between our increasing control of health care costs and the greater market presence of managed care. In a thoughtful analysis, two economists, Jack Zwanziger and Glenn Melnick, find that areas with a large managed care presence have tended to have much lower increases in their costs. (Following common usage, I will use the terms *HMO* and *managed care* interchangeably in what follows.)

Rational or Rationing?

Is managed care really the miracle cure for health care costs that it appears to be?

The answer to this question should take into consideration the ways in which managed care organizations achieve their lower premiums. After all, if they do it by *rationing*—denying people the health care services they need or discriminating against sick people—they are clearly not an appropriate solution. They may create another set of problems if sick people cannot obtain the health care services or insurance they need. On the other hand, if managed care lowers costs *rationally*, by intelligently selecting cost-effective health care providers and practices, reducing bloated physician and hospital receipts, or by restructuring inefficient organizational relationships, then it represents an attractive solution to the productivity dilemma.

The economics of managed care make the need for an answer all the more compelling. After all, managing other people's health care does not come cheaply. Managed care requires a legion of well-paid administrators to oversee and sometimes override the decisions of health care practitioners and their patients. CEOs of some managed care organizations are particularly well paid. A 1996 report by Graef S. Crystal, an analyst and critic of CEO compensation practices, noted that the CEO of Foundation Health Corporation received a whopping $3,255,000 in annual pay. All told, the managed care companies Crystal studied paid their CEOs 62 percent more in total compensation than did comparable-sized firms in other businesses and 35 percent more than the organization's size and stockholder performance warranted.

But these lavish incomes are a mere trickle when compared to the large bite of the premium dollar that the other administrative expenses and profits of managed care firms take. The marketing and administrative expenses of one million-member plan, Oxford Health Plans, for example, averaged 18.7 percent, and its pretax profits 5.3 percent of revenues, in 1995. These hefty expenses left only 77.5 cents of every premium dollar to pay for the services of doctors, hospitals, and other health care providers. (In managed care terminology the expenses of paying for medical care are tellingly called the "medical-*loss* ratio," as if expenditures on health care were a "loss.") Nonprofit managed care organizations exhibit economic characteristics similar to those of the for-profits; for example, the nonprofit Harvard Community Health Plan's administrative expense ratio was 14.2 percent in 1994, while in the same year the ostensibly nonprofit Kaiser Permanente earned a 6.7 percent profit rate, a profit percentage comparable to that of most corporations.

These big profits have created huge cash balances. In 1994 many managed care organizations showed in excess of a billion dollars in cash on their balance sheets. United Healthcare Corporation, for example, had a $2.6 billion cash balance, while Kaiser Permanente's cash clocked in at $1.3 billion. According to the *Wall Street Journal*, most of this cash could be freely used, for any purpose.

In contrast, the insurance companies that offer indemnity policies and do not manage care present a substantially different economic profile. They spend a much greater percentage of their premiums on health care. Their average 1994 expense ratio was only 6.9 percent, in contrast to the HMOs' average ratio of 10 percent. And while HMOs earned an 8.3 percent profit on every dollar of premiums, indemnity insurers earned only a 3.7 percent profit margin on their premium dollar.

In plain English, indemnity insurers spent a lot more of every premium dollar on health care and a lot less on administration and profits. Managed care requires that a hefty fraction of insurance premiums be spent for the nonmedical purposes of managing the care the user receives and for their profits.

Downsizing via Managed Care

These statistics dictate a clear algebraic conclusion: Managed care organizations spend proportionately less on providing medical care per premium dollar than do indemnity insurance payers. Put another way, managed care organizations lower the costs of health insurance premiums but they may provide fewer health care resources, per premium dollar, than do other insurers.

Many studies bear this conclusion out. A 1995 Congressional Budget Office study concluded that managed care organizations reduce the use of health care services by 8 percent, when compared with a typical indemnity plan. HMO members generally experience lower hospital admission rates and lengths of stay, leading to significantly fewer hospital days per HMO enrollee than for those enrolled in indemnity plans. HMO members also use fewer expensive ancillary procedures. For example, one study revealed that the average managed care patient spent two fewer days in the intensive care unit and five fewer days in the hospital than did the average patient enrolled in an indemnity insurance policy. The financial impact of these differences exceeded $4,000 for the average patient. Finally, managed care organizations generally use fewer specialist resources, through a combination of reduced use and payment fees for specialists. A University of Michigan Medical School study revealed that if the university's specialist services were provided solely to HMO members, the university faculty required in many specialties would be reduced by more than 50 percent.

Impact of Managed Care on Quality

These statistics still beg the key question of rational or rationing. Does managed care reduce costs by reducing the quality of care? Do HMOs' lower hospital admission rates result from callous disregard for needed stays or from prudent elimination of unnecessary stays? Do the shorter stay lengths result from throwing patients out of the hospital prematurely or from intelligently replacing expensive in-patient services with home health care and other nonhospital services? Is the reduced use of ancillary procedures the result of denying sick people diagnostic specificity and therapeutic efficacy or the pruning away of unjustified costs? Does replacing specialists with primary care physicians and other health personnel hamper the quality of care?

A mountain of anecdotal evidence seems to affirm that managed care organizations reduce costs by reducing the quality of care. Numerous front-page stories have recounted the sagas of deadly-ill HMO enrollees who could not obtain the medical treatments that might have saved their lives. The tragic victims of breast cancer who were denied potentially life-saving, costly bone marrow transplantations by their managed care organizations have been the subject of many such tales. A 1996 cover story in *Time* magazine, for example, juxtaposed the tale of a desperate schoolteacher trying to raise the $92,000 needed for his wife's bone marrow transplant with that of the $18.1 million in a final compensation package that her managed care organization paid a departing executive. After the woman's death, an arbitration panel ruled in favor of the family in their case against the HMO, concluding that its administrators had actively interfered with the patient-doctor relationship and had attempted to "influence or intimidate" the hospital and doctors who had recommended a transplant. Nevertheless, the HMO's medical director still contends, "I'm sorry the panel didn't see that [the HMO] was doing what was best for the patient, which was to deny the treatment as investigational."

Is the use of bone marrow transplants for breast cancer experimental? Although the jury is still out on their efficacy, some oncologists are enthusiastic about the procedure. Notes a spokesman for New York's famed Sloan-Kettering Cancer Center, "It's absurd to refuse to pay on grounds that these procedures are 'experimental.' Extensive research shows this to be the best therapy for women with an otherwise hopeless condition." Sloan-Kettering doctors worry that the label "experimental" will be applied to all promising but expensive therapies. A former medical reviewer for three managed care companies reinforces the validity of their concerns. "If there was any way at all to claim that something requested was experimental or nonstandard we took it. We looked for ways *not* to cover treatment," she notes.

Fundamentally, if insurers refuse to pay for procedures that might save lives, what *is* the purpose of health insurance? Most people buy it to protect themselves against the expenses of catastrophic illnesses. If they are refused payment for such treatment, why do they need health insurance?

But, HMOs are not the only insurers that are likely to deny coverage for experimental procedures. A 1994 survey revealed that 76 percent of the certified employee benefit specialists who responded noted exclusions of experimental treatments in their largest health plans. Insurers like Blue Cross Blue Shield take considerable care to evaluate the effectiveness of experimental treatments. As Dr. Richard Cornell, a medical director of Blue Cross and Blue Shield sincerely notes, "The whole issue must be dealt with in as rational and humanistic a way as possible."

Restrictions on coverage can affect the quality of care in more subtle ways too. For example, *Forbes* reports that victims of heart rhythm abnormalities who want automatic defibrillators implanted in their bodies to shock their sometimes arrhythmic heartbeats back into a smooth pattern may find that their HMO prefers that they use drugs instead. The economics of the situation are clear: Drugs cost about $1,500 a year, while implanting a defibrillator costs about $47,000. The medical consequences are also pretty clear: The drugs work about half as well as the medical device and have unpleasant side effects to boot. Although HMOs do not admit denying needed defibrillators, cardiologists, hospital administrators, and the device manufacturers strongly disagree.

Some doctors also worry about the effect of managed care's restrictions on patients' choice of providers. A panel convened by the National Cancer Institute to evaluate roadblocks to treating cancer noted that the "freedom to choose the most appropriate provider" was "especially critical in managed care plans, since the most effective treatments for a patient's problem may be available only from [a] . . . provider outside the plan." A study of the results of breast cancer surgery found that survival rates were "significantly worse at HMO hospitals than at large or small community hospitals."

Some studies indicate that substituting general physicians for specialists can compromise the quality of care and others do not. A Duke University study of more than 200,000 subjects found that elderly heart attack patients who were immediately treated by a cardiologist were 15 percent less likely to die within a year than those treated by a family doctor. On the other hand, a large-scale, multiyear study of the outcomes achieved for diabetics and people with high blood pressure found that specialists' patients fared no better than those treated by general practitioners (although diabetics received far more foot-care attention from the specialists). But a telling study by the RAND Corporation found that general doctors provide a low quality of care for depressed patients. Still, even the patients who were treated by psychiatrists did not always experience positive outcomes. Their outcomes differed according to payment plan: those who were enrolled in managed care functioned "more poorly over time," while those in indemnity care did not. The study's co-author noted, "as a psychiatrist, I am concerned that the sickest patients in the [managed care] system evidently aren't getting enough extended care."

Other studies of the impact of managed care on quality also provide conflicting evidence. One analysis of 10,000 Medicare beneficiaries with joint or chest pain found that HMO enrollees used fewer resources than indemnity policy members. Although there were no significant differences between the two groups among those who were no longer experiencing pain, the improvement in symptoms for those reporting joint pain was significantly lower in the HMO group. (Many prior studies of Medicare, and one of Medicaid, have found no difference in outcomes between HMO participants and others. But some of these results are suspect because they were based on demonstration projects. The study cited, in contrast, focused on an ongoing program.)

Virtually all reviewers, however, agree that HMOs provide as much diagnostic, preventive care as, if not more than, indemnity programs. Thus, for example, elderly HMO enrollees are likely to have their cancer detected earlier. A 1995 California "report card" found that the HMOs performed about the same in all the categories of preventive care in which they were rated. But a recent medical outcome study noted, "Little evidence exists to show that the successes of prepaid care in relatively healthy populations can be replicated among sicker patients." Thus, excellence in diagnosis of the healthy does not necessarily mean excellence in treatment of the sick.

Undoubtedly, the public perceives that HMOs deny care. One survey of sick people found that those enrolled in managed care were more likely to complain of difficulties in obtaining necessary treatment, diagnostic tests, and referrals to specialists than were those enrolled in indemnity policies. A 1996 report also found significantly higher dissatisfaction among sick enrollees in limited choice managed care than among those enrolled in fee-for-service plans in the wait for an appointment and the doctor's interest in the case. Even the industry's lobbying group concedes that it has a bad image. As for doctors, Dr. Warren S. Francis undoubtedly spoke for many of his peers when he wrote, "Managed care and rationed care are synonymous."

No Sick Need Apply?

Do HMOs achieve lower costs by discriminating against the sick?

The design of managed care policies virtually guarantees that newly insured healthier people will prefer them to traditional insurance policies and that sick people will try to avoid them. Sick people who have already established relationships with health care providers will likely find managed care to be an unattractive option. They may fear that managed care overseers will interfere with and hamper their existing relationships. Healthy young people, on the other hand, will probably prefer HMOs to other insurance policies because they cost less. Those who have few health problems are likely to opt for the cheapest policies. Further, because most managed care plans offer "free" well-baby and child care, in contrast to other types of health insurance, they are likely to attract healthy young parents as enrollees.

Two studies support this reasoning. A Congressional Budget Office analysis of the 1992 National Health Interview Survey data found that many people who are planning to have a baby insure with an HMO and an analysis of 1987 National Medical Expenditure Survey data determined that HMOs tend to enroll a younger population. To be sure, the latter analysis and another one did conclude that the indemnity-insurance policy-holders are not sicker than HMO enrollees and do not appear to have a consistently greater incidence of chronic diseases. But, their conclusions contradict the 1988 and 1994 findings of two economists, Harold S. Luft and Robert Miller. In both studies Luft and Miller found "favorable selection bias"—that is, healthier people—in HMOs. Similarly, a detailed analysis concluded that "individuals who consume large amounts of health resources are often unwilling to sever their ties with their health care providers and to enroll in organizations that limit their choice of provider." The General Accounting Office has also documented that a healthier population enrolls in Medicare's HMO program.

How to reconcile these conflicting conclusions? A financial analyst noted for his coverage of HMOs, David J. Lothson of Paine-Webber, openly states the whispered secret: "HMOs have been financially successful [in] courting below-average and average-risk patients whose health care costs fell well below the premium paid annually—avoiding high cost patients is a strategy practiced by nearly every HMO."

Does Managed Care Reduce Costs?

Do managed care organizations lower the costs of health care by reducing the bloated expenses of some hospitals and the inflated incomes of some physicians? Anecdotal evidence suggests that they do: They pay lower fees than indemnity carriers for selected procedures. One three-area study revealed that managed care organizations pay from 50 to 58 percent less for mammograms than do indemnity insurers. More systematic evidence is sparse, but another study indicates that in California between 1982 and 1988, a substantial increase in HMO market share reduced the rate of increase of hospital costs per admission. These results have been confirmed elsewhere, using data through 1990. Managed care may also have played a role in the decline of the median 1994 net income of private-practice, office-based physicians to $148,890 from their 1992 income of $153,620. (Their gross revenues, or the value of the bills they sent out, fell even more substantially. Some physicians, such as radiologists, psychiatrists, and orthopedic surgeons, compensated for their shortfall in gross revenues only by increasing the efficiency of their practices.)

While the impact of the increased penetration of HMOs on controlling hospital expenses and physician incomes thus appears positive, so-called "any willing provider" legislation will likely lessen it. This legislation prohibits the most popular models of managed care from excluding a provider who is willing to meet their terms for participation. It thus weakens the ability of HMOs to lower the prices paid to certain providers in exchange for bringing them a large volume of patients. In November 1994 thirty-one states had enacted or were contemplating some form of this legislation.

That this legislation would likely have a favorable impact on providers is indicated by the strong support it has received from state medical societies. But providers are not the only ones supporting "any willing provider" legislation—consumer groups likely advocate it too. Americans clearly place great value on freedom of choice. Survey after survey has found substantial patient dissatisfaction with the aspects of managed care that limit control or convenience, such as the choice of physicians, access to specialty care, availability of emergency care, and waiting time for appointments.

A large medical outcomes study found that patients were significantly less satisfied with "staff model" HMOs, which pay physicians on a salaried basis, than with indemnity insurance. These HMOs received particularly low ratings in terms of appointment waits, time spent with the patient, providers' personal skills, and the ease of telephone access. *Newsweek*'s 1996 HMO evaluations revealed, for example, that the otherwise highly rated staff model Harvard Community Health Plan had a high customer complaint ratio and relatively lower levels of satisfied customers. The study also found that the "group model" of HMOs, which employs a physician group rather than individual providers, did not fare particularly well either.

Small wonder, then, that staff and group model HMOs lost market share, while the looser forms of managed care, which permit their enrollees a greater choice of provider, boomed. In the period 1992 to 1994, the loosest model's enrollment increased from roughly 39 percent to approximately 50 percent of the market. In June 1994 staff and group model HMOs held only 22.3 percent of the market, while the others controlled 77.7 percent. This shift in market share is not likely to be reversed, and many managed care organizations are now retreating from the staff model. In 1995, for example, FHP, a major California-based provider, announced that it was relinquishing its fifty-seven staff model

HMO medical centers because "there was too much competition from HMOs that give their enrollees a much broader choice of providers." A systematic analysis found that HMOs that face more competition are more likely to offer an "open" version that maintains the consumer's freedom of choice.

The shift is noteworthy because most analysts consider group and staff model HMOs to be the most effective cost reducers in the managed care panoply. The Congressional Budget Office, for example, estimates that they reduce the use of resources by nearly 20 percent, while the most popular, least restrictive model of managed care effects an almost imperceptible reduction in use. The "any willing provider" legislation may extinguish further the cost-control potential of managed care.

KAISER: A GIANT QUAKES

The once-mighty Kaiser system reflects the impact of these forces. Kaiser has lost market share in California. It is not always the lowest-priced provider in the California market and it has faltered in its attempts to replicate itself outside California, losing membership in 1995 in two of its twelve regions and suffering low growth elsewhere, while the general managed care market boomed. Although the *Newsweek* and *Consumer Reports* surveys show high enrollee satisfaction, a union representative testified that internal surveys show significant dissatisfaction even among its California enrollees. Kaiser "members' responses seriously lagged those of its competitors . . . in three key measures—time on the phone needed to make an appointment, days wait for routine tests and exam," and most significantly, "ability to get care when needed."

Some of Kaiser's physicians are unhappy too. When the company implemented programs to reduce its costs per enrollee by 5 percent a year for the next five years, its northern California physicians protested on their electronic bulletin board and leaked the story to the *San Francisco Chronicle*. "Physicians are facing increasing scrutiny of every decision we make," they complained, noting the "drastic cuts" that affect "the caregiver-patient relationship." A union-sponsored state-ballot initiative aims to curb such "medical rationing" at Kaiser and other managed care organizations.

Nor are the unions that once enthusiastically backed the Kaiser system quite so rapturous about it any longer. To the contrary, some now view Kaiser as part of an unresponsive establishment. The president of the Los Angeles chapter of the powerful Service Employees International Union has argued against the use of the Kaiser system as a national model for health care reform. In testimony before Congress, he criticized Kaiser's reduced service levels to its enrollees, its substantial layoffs of key workers, its wasteful capital spending, its reluctance to provide services to the poor, and its outlandish profits.

What is the problem? Kaiser's massive investments in buildings and physicians may have caused organizational inertia and resistance to innovation. Nimbler competitors, unsaddled with this infrastructure, could take advantage of Kaiser's rigidity, like the elf who dances between the giant's legs. In one of Kaiser's markets, a successful nonintegrated insurance competitor routed its enrollees to seven different hospitals, while Kaiser's patients were required to travel only to the two Kaiser-owned hospitals in the area.

As we saw in Part 1, today's busy consumers no longer accede to restrictions in their freedom to select providers. Patients will not be patient. They prefer insurers that do not severely limit the hospitals and physicians that they may use. Even as overall membership in managed care organizations has soared, the market share of plans that offer limited access to physicians has diminished. Kaiser, however, cannot easily respond to such preferences in some of its markets. After all, its stock in trade is the hospitals it owns and the physicians with whom it has serious relationships. So while rival insurers can offer their enrollees considerable choice in service sites, Kaiser's enrollees are forced to use only the sites the company controls.

FHP, the California-based rival to Kaiser that once emulated its vertical integration and is now hastily dismantling it, found that enrollees prefer insurance plans that offer a freedom of choice of physicians to those that offer a limited choice of salaried ones. "Our membership for the [salaried physician portion] has been flat, whereas the [free to choose] side of the business has really taken off," notes a company spokeswoman. National data support this appraisal. FHP also notes that contracting with independent hospitals is less expensive than owning them.

In response, Kaiser too is exploring different models of managed care. Its North Carolina region now offers its enrollees insurance policies that enable them to use physicians with whom Kaiser does not have an exclusive relationship. So tumultuous is the environment, that to help guide its way, this vast distinguished organization has called in a corporate psychiatrist—the McKinsey consulting firm, which holds the hands of *Fortune* 500 firms as they go through their midlife crises. Although this eminent organization will undoubtedly, once again, triumph as a health care provider, presently, Kaiser is not a model for the health care productivity revolution.

MANAGED CARE: "MORE MONEY, LESS CARE" OR "LESS MONEY, MORE CARE"?

Have you ever found a television commercial lodged in your mind, despite your best efforts to purge it? A particularly heinous commercial for "lite" beer did this to me. The ad depicted two groups of beer drinkers repeatedly chanting the phrases "less filling" and "tastes great." Like many advertisements, the catchy phrases caught on, and I must confess I found them readily applicable to my area of study. The managed care incarnation of the commercial might ask: Does managed care require "less money" and provide "more health care," or the reverse— "more money" and "less care?"

Ideally, objective data should enable us to weigh the pros and cons of managed care. The pros are indeed plentiful: Good managed care organizations provide an organized system of care, cover preventive activities, and carefully select providers for their quality and prudence. They can also rescue their enrollees from unneeded and potentially harmful medical interventions. But the cons abound too: Overly aggressive managed care organizations may deny their enrollees needed access to specialists, hospitals, drugs, and high-technology devices. And managed care organizations are intrinsically expensive to operate. Thus as the competition for the business of cost-conscious employers progresses, managed care organizations will be forced to cut their medical expenses even more.

Unfortunately, to date, objective data that would permit us to weigh the pros and cons have not yet been compiled. As a result, the impact of managed care on the American health care system remains unclear. Even a comparison of the premiums charged by managed care and indemnity policies provides little information. Although managed care premiums may appear to be lower, any comparison is confounded by the fact that managed care organizations offer more benefits than indemnity insurance but enroll healthier people. An accurate comparison of premiums should adjust for the opposite effects of these factors on costs. Similarly, managed care organizations undoubtedly reduce their costs through prudent selection of practitioners and practices (rational reduction) and through diminished quality of care (rationing reduction); but the respective effects of rationing and rational reduction on HMO costs is unknown.

Casting doubt on the possibilities for "rational" is the fact that the science of medicine is not as rational and objective as it seems. Martin Feldstein, the economist who once chaired the President's Council of Economic Advisers, notes in a review of nearly thirty years of his research that "I now recognize the fundamental importance of the uncertainty of health care technology . . . although doctors know a great deal, uncertainty is ubiquitous in health care. . . . Even after diagnosis and treatment, uncertainty remains . . . even the . . . relation between behavior and outcomes is itself often very uncertain." But medical judgments are generally expressed in a forceful way that brooks no dissent. Warns Dr. Sherwin Nuland, a Yale School of Medicine clinical professor of surgery, "Better watch out or the pendulum swing of medical dogma will bash your head in. It swings back and forth far more often than most people realize and with far greater velocity. Thirty years ago patients with inflammation of . . . the colon were routinely treated with a diet low in roughage. There was no uncertainty about this course of action . . . and yet, a few years later, medical opinion reversed: decreased roughage was found not to be a panacea but a cause of the disease. This new medical discovery was announced in the same assuredness and supported by just as much evidence as had been used for precisely the opposite viewpoint. . . . Clinical theory and decision making are a mix of science, experience, contemporary culture, . . . and even emotion."

Even the seemingly dispassionate, ultrascientific world of medical research is permeated with fads and emotions. All too many researchers who have made world-class discoveries were initially denied recognition by envious, self-seeking, or stubborn peers. In "The Philosophical Basis of Peer Review and the Suppression of Innovation," David F. Horrobin provides a depressingly long list of Nobel Prize work that was initially rejected for publication or that received no research support after its initial publication because "peers" rejected the researcher's request for grant financing; important clinical research that was funded out of the researcher's own pockets; restrictive peer review criteria that forced scientists to disguise the true nature of their inquiries in their grant applications; and the suppression of rebuttals to conventionally accepted dogma. Says Horrobin, "The most distinguished of scientists may display behavior that can only be described as pathological. . . . many scientists are against innovation unless it's *their* innovation."

THE MANAGED CARE STORY

All in all, I belong to HMOs because I believe they might well standardize medical practice, driving out outrageously inefficient or expensive providers and provide more preventive care. But managed care might also unduly limit choice and the quality of care.

Stringent managed care organizations, such as group and staff model HMOs, could potentially reduce extravagant physician incomes and hospital budgets. But many health activist Americans dislike the restrictions these models place on their freedom of choice. Activists have already teamed up with providers to enact legislation that undercuts the ability of HMOs to reduce provider costs, like the "any willing provider" laws, and they are likely to continue to do so in the future. In early 1996 other legislation to enlarge patients' freedom of choice and access was enacted in at least ten states and was pending in twenty-two others.

All told, while managed care organizations have succeeded in downsizing the American health care system, their impact on the quality of care and their receptivity to sick people remains unclear. The public has made up its mind about these issues, however: The activists among them have enlisted the legislative system to protect them from further downsizing. The legal restrictions they have created; the limited appeal of the most stringent but most effective HMO models; and the high costs of administering the managed care system cast doubt that the "just say no" diet will be able to control the costs of the American health care system. As PaineWebber's David Lothson says of HMOs, "The industry has demonstrated its marketing acumen, but [it] is not nearly as good at managing health care costs as . . . it had believed."

CHAPTER 7

Upsizing—The "Big Is Beautiful" Diet

When Henry Ford completed his first massive automobile factory in 1914, it resoundingly demonstrated the efficiencies inherent in the "big is beautiful" strategy. In one fell swoop the labor hours required for a Model T declined by 90 percent, from 12.5 to 1.5 hours. By 1921 Ford paid the nation's highest wages, charged much less for his Model T than his closest competitor, and amassed a huge personal fortune. The economies of scale endemic to mass production seemed to create the ultimate American success story: high wages, low prices, and sizable rewards for their brilliant innovator.

Ford's triumph inspired generations of managers, including those who now think they can wring the inefficiency out of the health care system through economies of scale. Their managerial solution does not require rationing. Instead, like Henry Ford's, their solution is to get big.

"Big is more efficient."

"Big is better."

"BIG IS BEAUTIFUL"

Bigness has become the all-American solution to any problem. Need office space? Find a skyscraper. Need a meal? Eat a Double Whopper. Need a site for sports? Build a megaplex. From the Mile High Apple Pie to our giant corporations, Americans fervently believe that big is beautiful.

Did not Alfred Sloan prove that it is when he cobbled together General Motors out of many separate automobile companies? It is General Motors' size that got it to where it is today. Size gave it substantial economies of scale; for example, it can spread the cost of retooling for a new design over hundreds of thousands of cars. And because GM produces many of the components used in its cars—such as chassis and electrical systems—it can avoid paying independent firms for them.

GM got big through both horizontal and vertical integration. Its mammoth horizontal integration, through which it sells a number of different brands of vehicles, and its vertical integration, in which it manufactures many of the components used in its cars, have greatly reduced its costs and enabled it continually to improve the quality of its cars.

Or so the story goes.

The Urge to Merge

Apparently the American health care system believes the story. The urge to merge is zooming like an electrical current through the sector, reshaping virtually overnight a fragmented cottage industry of hundreds of thousands of individual providers into a sleek, horizontally integrated system of giants. In 1994, for example, 650 hospitals merged, whereas in 1993 only 18 did so. Managed care organizations merged at such a furious rate that in 1996 seven HMOs accounted for 74 percent of all the enrollments in the country. Producers of medical technology also integrated horizontally. For example, Glaxo Holdings spent a record $14 billion in 1995 to purchase Burroughs Wellcome. Other providers formed large vertically integrated organizations, stitching together hospitals, doctors, and insurers into new networks. And three pharmaceutical companies spent $13 billion to buy pharmaceutical benefit managers, which provide mail-order distribution and managed care for drug purchases.

"Big is better." "Big is cheaper." "Big is beautiful."

Or so they say.

A careful analysis of the effects of integration paints a different picture. Big firms are often clumsy and slow to innovate. They are hard to manage, requiring a torrent of nourishing cash to keep them alive and massive managerial efforts to keep them networked. Worst of all, big firms may be bad firms, acting to suppress competition. The experiences of some early pioneers present a sobering picture of the feasibility of upsizing in the health sector.

Big may not be beautiful, when it comes to our health care system. In years to come we may well find that we have created a costly and unresponsive monster rather than the lean, mean, fighting machine we sought.

HORIZONTAL INTEGRATION

Today, managers who believe that big is beautiful are rushing to integrate the fragmented health care system. Many of the stand-alone providers that characterize the sector have been cobbled together into chains of horizontally integrated hospitals, nursing homes, home health providers, and physicians' practices, among others.

Huge companies emerged rapidly, virtually overnight. From its inception in 1987, Columbia Health Care Corporation, a chain of 326 hospitals, grew to earn revenues of $17.6 billion in 1995. It claims already to have reaped the benefits of horizontal integration. For example, it boasts of having reduced its multimillion-dollar supply purchases by 28 percent. "We're now a bigger buyer of medical supplies than anybody else in the world," says Columbia's CEO. "Without size, you have no ability to direct volume to suppliers, where they would be interested in giving you a better price." As an example of Columbia's bidding process, consider the response when it asked various suppliers to place bids for its business in products ranging from gowns to sutures. After selecting the best bidders for each product, the hospital system asked them to go through a new round of bidding and submit price quotations for these products in bundled form. This process saved the company $60 to $65 million. The large volume of its purchases, $220 million, commanded the vendors' close attention. Columbia's strategy of horizontal integration also aims to eliminate excessive hospital capacity. In El Paso, Texas, the company bought three hospitals and closed one of them, not only reducing the total number of beds in the area by 16 percent but boosting the occupancy of Columbia's remaining hospitals. In 1995, it closed twelve hospitals with 2,131 beds. Five of the closed hospitals were in Houston and three in South Florida. In the opinion of a J. P. Morgan analyst, these hospital consolidations will improve future earnings by lowering costs.

Other early success stories also buttress the virtues of horizontal integration. When similar types of organizations merge, for example, they frequently find many duplicated expenses that can be eliminated. The merger of two large home health care companies led to expected annual cost savings of $40 to $50 million. Horizontally integrated firms can also identify the "best demonstrated practices" among their many sites and replicate them throughout the system. No wonder that Medical Care America, an ambulatory surgery company with over ninety centers, could maintain a relatively flat average price per case, over a three-year period, while increasing its profitability. The economies of horizontal integration were likely making their presence felt when this firm applied the lessons of excellence it had discovered in individual centers throughout the ninety-center organization.

More systematic analyses, however, provide scant support for the cost-reducing promises of recent horizontal integrations. A 1995 comparison of the 1988 performance of independent and system-based hospitals in California concluded that "systems were no more able to exploit scale economies . . . than independent hospitals." The authors found that the benefits of a horizontally integrated hospital system accrue more in the ability of the systems to market themselves than in the economies they achieve. A 1996 analysis of the short-run performance of ninety-two hospital mergers in the period from 1982 to 1989 did not find dramatic improvements in operating efficiencies, although "trends toward inefficiency were arrested somewhat after the merger." A 1995 analysis that traced a group of hospitals that were financially distressed from 1983 to 1985 found that 91.2 percent had survived through the end of 1990, and only 3.2 percent were acquired through mergers. If the hospitals' poor financial situation had resulted from inefficiencies that could be cured with mergers, they should have been integrated or closed, but in most instances, neither event occurred. As for HMOs, their horizontal integration did not appear to result in reduced premiums either.

VERTICAL INTEGRATION

Other managers are even more ambitious than the horizontal integrators. Not content with mere size, they are trying to reorganize the entire health care system so that Americans can obtain all the services they need from just one integrated system. *Seamless* is the adjective of the day. Expert health care tailors aim to stitch together the many different parts of the system—doctors, hospitals, nursing homes, surgery centers, even insurers—into a fluid garment, one so expertly sewn that the patient will not be able to feel its seams.

Vertical integration of this sort could confer two benefits. First, it would provide patients with a ready source of care, no matter what their needs. Second, it would lower costs. After all, a vertically integrated system does not pay for the profits earned by its component parts. And patients are not needlessly kept in one expensive part of the system because capacity is not available elsewhere. In a vertically integrated system, patients can be readily transferred from one site to the next.

In Minneapolis the business community stepped up to the plate to exploit the virtues of vertical integration. Spurred by big firms like General Mills, 3M, and Honeywell, it decided that Minneapolis would become a test site for the "big is beautiful" thesis. To induce the formation of large vertically integrated providers, many separate companies in the area decided to join forces and become a megabuyer of health care. By 1994 one business-based buying group controlled over half a billion dollars in health care purchasing power—a substantial amount in one geographic site. When the group announced that it would award all its business to one provider of health care, the lure of such a large contract proved irresistible to Minneapolis's health care providers. They integrated. By 1994 the city's health insurance market was dominated by two vertically integrated firms and a large insurer that has contractual arrangements with providers; two of them were so large that their revenues exceeded $800 million in that year. The rest of the provider community was also remarkably consolidated; about 95 percent of the area's physicians worked in groups, compared with 31 percent of the physicians in the U.S.

The Birth of Giants

Emboldened by the example of Kaiser and heartened by early tales of Minnesota's success, other providers have rushed to form large, vertically integrated systems. Some providers created physician-hospital organizations, or PHOs, which meld a variety of providers to provide health care services for insurance companies and employers. By 1996, 10 percent of all medical groups with more than fifty physicians were owned by hospitals. A 1994 survey found that nearly 75 percent of the PHOs were young—only twenty-five months old—and half were under a year. By 1994, 88 percent of all American hospitals were involved in integrated health systems. But hospitals were not alone in forming integrated groups: 69 percent of physician groups, 62 percent of home health agencies, 55 percent of managed care organizations, and 46 percent of skilled nursing facilities accompanied them. The pharmaceutical industry also integrated vertically. Three of these giant companies have bought distributors, called pharmaceutical benefit managers, since 1993.

The horizontally integrated Columbia/HCA is also integrating vertically. Its 1994 plans included opening 38 skilled nursing units, 11 sites for psychiatric care, and 21 home health service outlets. In 1996 Michigan's vertically integrated Henry Ford Health System included a 903-bed high-tech hospital, two community hospitals, a psychiatric hospital, a 1,000-physician-member group practice, a home health and dialysis unit, two nursing homes, and a 500,000-member managed care plan.

Like a stack of dominoes, as one part of the health care system integrates, other parts fall. Physicians are increasingly joining forces to operate in group practices rather than as solo practitioners. Between 1980 and 1991 the number of physicians in specialty group practices more than doubled, and those in multispecialty group practices increased by over 50 percent. The size of the average physician group has also increased. Many physicians feel that these jumbo groups can better bargain with large integrated hospitals and insurers; a large physician group could more easily resist the demands of a hospital for exclusive affiliation, for example, than could a solo-practice physician.

Big buyers, big suppliers, big success.

Or is it?

THE BIG CHILL
IN MINNEAPOLIS

The proponents of integration appear to have a good formula: "Big is beautiful. Long live integration." Nevertheless, any reader of the daily papers would have some nagging doubts about upsizing. If vertical integration is so foolproof, then why did vertically integrated IBM stumble in the marketplace and shed more than 100,000 workers, not to speak of internal divisions, in an attempt to cure its problems? And why is General Motors, another prime model of vertical integration, now assessing the merits of owning the parts of its business that are not central to its mission?

General Motors, like other automobile companies, now carefully evaluates whether its own internal suppliers can match the quality and innovation that outside suppliers can provide. A *Business Week* article explains another attraction of devolution: "Just as a light bulb wastes electricity to produce unwanted heat, a traditional corporation expends a tremendous amount of energy running its own internal machinery— managing relations among departments or providing information up and down the hierarchy, for example." To minimize waste, many corporations have resized themselves. A 1994 survey reported that 56 percent of the larger American manufacturing companies are now experimenting with "cells," or small teams that produce a complete product, in lieu of traditional techniques of mass production. Opel, the German car manufacturer, reduced its inventories and space requirements by at least 30 percent by forming many small, five-to-eight-member teams out of its two thousand employees.

Well okay, proponents of upsizing may hedge, maybe big is not beautiful for the *Fortune* 500. But the thesis is good enough for the health care sector. After all, the vertically integrated Minneapolis providers are ample evidence of its power, aren't they?

Perhaps not. Lately, the Minneapolis group is changing strategies. Its actions raise serious questions about the wisdom of prescribing the "big is beautiful" diet for other parts of the health care system.

The buying group in Minneapolis is backpedaling from the "big is beautiful" thesis because too few benefits, it feels, have emerged from the large vertically integrated providers. For one thing, ferocious price competition has yet to materialize. True, cost increases have moderated, but they have still not approached the low levels achieved elsewhere or even the rate of general inflation. One report revealed that in 1995 the hospital costs in the Minneapolis/St. Paul area increased by 2.3 percent while those in other similar high-managed-care penetration areas decreased by .27 percent. Nor has the product differentiation that characterizes real competition emerged. The three giants share many of the same physicians, with an overlap as great as 70 percent. How can competition take place when the Taurus looks like the Escort and the Special K tastes like Raisin Bran? Finally, the big firms seem indifferent to innovation. In one case, a physician group stationed one of its doctors in each hospital so that all its member doctors could avoid making a daily trip to visit their hospitalized patients. This cost-reducing innovation was greeted with a yawn by the big three buyers.

Why Vertical Integration Falters

Economists would not be surprised by these results. Most economics textbooks sternly warn of the dangers inherent in markets dominated by excessively large firms: little price competition and extensive use of marketing to gain competitive advantage. To these economists, the benefits of competition occur only in "perfect" markets. You or I may find perfection in a child's rosy cheek or a Matisse painting, but economists find "perfection" when information and an abundance of suppliers enable buyers readily to pick and choose from among many competing products and when new providers can easily enter the market. In such a perfect market, if one firm becomes too fat and lazy, offering overpriced and/or low-quality products, its competitors can lure its customers away with cheaper, better goods. The resulting dynamics of competition induce continual improvement in the price and/or quality of goods and services.

Small, innovative firms are key to the workings of such a perfect market. Their role in promoting price competition is illustrated by one hospital executive's experiences: "When purchasing pharmaceuticals . . . I witnessed how the small drug companies that produced generic drugs played a key role [in] reducing the cost of pharmaceuticals. The larger drug companies were constantly pushing purchasing agreements which bundled their products into a package, offering discounts on the whole package if we bought the full product line from them. However, we felt that we could do better in the long run by continuing to buy individual drugs from whatever company offered the best price. . . . The flexibility to change vendors freely . . . promotes . . . a free market."

In contrast, large providers can distort perfect markets. Big firms that dominate a market may decide implicitly to avoid price competition and instead to compete on the basis of nonprice characteristics such as marketing. Large firms that own substantial infrastructures are notoriously wary of price competition, fearing that price wars may leave them with their big fixed costs uncovered. And big providers are hardly renowned for their willingness to innovate. For example, both General Motors and IBM lost enormous market shares to smaller, more innovative suppliers.

But wait—if big is not beautiful, then why did the health care cost increases of the Minneapolis buying group moderate? Two possible explanations exist. First, the health care system is so corpulent that decreasing its costs by a small amount is not a difficult challenge. The cost reductions in Minneapolis may be compared to the loss of five pounds in a five-hundred-pound person. A five-pound loss is good, but it's not sufficient in a person who must lose three hundred pounds. The question the Minneapolis buying group faced was whether the "big is beautiful" diet could cause the loss of the next three hundred pounds. A Minnesota consumer group offers the second possible explanation. The price concessions gained by the big business buyers, it claims, were charged to other buyers of health care in the state. The big providers did not reduce health care costs—they merely shifted them away from large powerful buyers to weak, helpless ones. As evidence, the group cites the fact that Minnesota's health care costs continue to exceed national averages.

After its flirtation with upsizing was over, the Minneapolis buying group decided to break with the vertically-integrated provider giants and to contract with provider groups directly. Although providers are free to hire insurers to help them, the buyers no longer deal directly with them. By contracting with provider groups and eliminating the middleman, the Minneapolis buying group hopes to motivate innovation and reward product differentiation. By dealing directly with providers, the group is implicitly betting that the smaller provider groups will be more sensitive to innovation, more willing to compete on real differences in services, and more likely to engage in sharp price competition. For their part, some of the providers have decided to bypass the HMOs and offer their services directly to employers. They reason that employers will reward them for the cost-savings they create, while HMOs will keep the savings for themselves.

OTHER TROUBLED VERTICALLY INTEGRATED VENTURES

Other vertically integrated health care ventures are already experiencing disappointing results. *Modern Healthcare* reports that hospitals that purchased physician practices usually lost money. A 1995 survey showed that only 17 percent achieved a positive return on their purchases. And by mid-1996, several systems were selling either total or partial interests in their HMOs. A 1996 *Modern Healthcare* analysis of thirty-seven HMOs owned by vertically integrated systems showed that ten had posted losses and eight experienced declines in net income.

The vertically integrated systems usually attributed their problems to a lack of relevant managerial skills. Notes an executive of UniHealth, a large integrated health system that established its medical group operations as a separate division in 1994, "What we failed to recognize is, being a hospital and being a physician group are fundamentally different businesses." Similarly, a consultant noted that health systems failed to develop their HMOs "because they did not develop the risk management [skills] needed to succeed."

A study of twelve health care organizations that were at an early stage of vertical integration also found discouraging results, especially "low levels of physician system integration and clinical integration." Generally, the corporate managers who headed these organizations expressed more optimism about the extent of integration achieved than those who actually managed the operations. The authors of the study tactfully suggest that the corporate managers' unduly rosy view of their systems may result from their "having less detailed . . . operational knowledge . . . regarding how integration is really 'playing out' in the field, resulting in somewhat 'inflated' responses on the part of corporate respondents."

Two observant writers explain the failures of integration this way: "Because many of the organizations considering vertical integration are acute hospital systems, expertise may be lacking at both the corporate and institutional levels. Yet, expertise—in evaluating and negotiating . . . and in managing new services—is often the single most important ingredient in success."

Hospital CEOs echo these concerns. In a 1993 survey fewer than half agreed that the majority of hospital CEOs possess what it takes to lead their organizations in today's competitive environment.

The pharmaceutical companies that attempted vertical integration strategies in 1993 have yet to find a "payoff," in the opinion of some experts. For some, the market share gains they sought for their drugs by buying drug distribution companies have not, as yet, occurred. In 1996 a *Wall Street Journal* article speculated that disappointing results would force Eli Lilly to reduce the value on its books of its $4.1 billion acquisition of a pharmaceutical benefit manager by as much as $3 billion. Nevertheless, some of the firms may yet succeed. Morgan Stanley's Paul Brooke contends that Merck's $6.6 billion purchase of Medco, a pharmaceutical benefit manager, has already increased Merck's market share and will ultimately, profoundly, and beneficially reshape the culture of the company. Notes Brooke, "We would argue that basic research may not be as much of a core competency for Merck as many investors believe. Its capability may be more focused on 1) competitive product judgments, 2) aggressive development of clinical compounds based on competitors' discoveries, 3) [clinical] studies to develop and capture markets, and 4) innovation in [financing and managed care]."

The Case for Vertical Integration

Why did these problems occur so rapidly in so many vertically integrated health care ventures?

To answer this question, we should reexamine the rationale for vertical integration. After all, most economists agree with the noted Oliver Williamson's assessment that "product markets have remarkable coordinating properties." So if markets can coordinate without ownership of the resources of production, why is vertical integration necessary? Couldn't purchasers of health care goods and services practice "virtual" integration and merely buy the products they need from independent producers? What is the value added by a vertically integrated system that owns these independent producers?

The literature for vertical integration suggests that in the health care sector there are four reasons for vertical integration. First, the independent producers may possess such unusual resources that they could "hold up" the purchasers for outrageously high prices if they weren't acquired. Physicians with a large loyal patient following exemplify such resources. If the hospital does not purchase their practices, they may "hold it up" with requests for high payments for patient services. Of course these physicians can still hold up the acquirer by insisting on a high price for the acquisition of their practice. Second, the environment may be so uncertain that purchase of resources assures the acquirer of access to them regardless of environmental changes. Given the abundant supply of health care resources, this is a dubious rationale for integration. Third, the acquirer may be innovating some intellectual capital that can be better developed with acquired resources; for example, hospitals may be able to develop integrated medical record systems best when they own physician practices and HMOs. Last, the "transaction costs"—that is, the expenses of coordinating the separate resources—may be lower when the resources are owned.

The fourth reason for vertical integration is often viewed as the most compelling. As the Pulitzer Prize winning business historian Alfred Chandler wrote, the modern business enterprise "began and expanded by internalizing activities and transactions previously carried out by a number of separate businesses. It emerges at the point when the businesses or units could be operated more profitably through a centralized hierarchy than by means of decentralized market mechanisms." Yet, the automobile industry whose development Chandler described so thoroughly did not totally vertically integrate. Instead, the industry chose to integrate primarily in specific circumstances where it acquired specific technical know-how, rather than specific assets, and at points in its history when product innovation had matured and economies of scale could be obtained with acquired firms through improvements in the process of production and marketing. The industry was likely well aware that purchase of another firm is a double-edge sword: it might well decrease the productivity of the acquired firm, while it increased the internal communication efficiencies of the acquirer.

As it does in other industries, the vertical integration of health care imposes daunting requirements for coordination of the acquired firms. One integration scorecard lists the six areas required for effective clinical integration; the eight areas required for integration of key functions, such as financial management; and the four areas needed for physician-system integration. A 1994 report of the extent of integration in these areas in a number of vertically integrated systems found only 42 percent of the functions standardized; low levels of physician integration across operating units; and low to moderate levels of clinical integration. These results are not surprising in light of the substantial organizational barriers to effective integration. They include the merger of different cultures (for example, of physicians, hospital, and insurers); the reconciliation of different types of personalities; the development of new payment methods for the acquired units; and the creation of a mutually agreeable business plan.

DAVID JONES AND THE HUMANA EMPIRE

Vertical integration has clearly yet to fulfill its promise. It is not likely to be the diet that will finally slim down our health care system.

To understand why, we must examine the saga of Humana, a firm managed by David Jones, one of health care's great visionaries. The entrepreneurial Jones succeeded in building a large, well-managed, horizontally integrated hospital chain, but he could not create a successful vertically integrated one. Examining his efforts will enable us better to understand the managerial difficulties in fulfilling the promise of integration.

David Jones

David Jones is a visionary who always saw way ahead of the curve. Long ago, in the 1960s, he diagnosed the health care system as corpulent and co-founded Humana to slim it down.

Jones's special combination of intellectual and personal qualities were apparent at an early age, when he left his native Kentucky to attend Yale University and its law school, picking up a CPA title along the way for good measure. After graduation, he and his lifelong business partner looked around for problems that needed smart young people to solve them. Pretty soon they found a big one—the hospital sector. Even in the 1960s it was apparent that hospitals were a problem: There were already too many of them, and they cost too much. Jones figured that he could help solve this problem in two ways. First, he could run a hospital better than its present managers, by bringing the discipline of good accounting to the information-starved hospital sector. Second, if Wall Street would give him enough money to buy a large number of hospitals, he would lower their costs with economies of scale.

To the business-minded Jones, economies of scale were primarily administrative in nature. Humana ultimately developed a world-class information system that measured the costs and outputs of every separate part of the hospital, from the laundry to the nursing station. The system was so enormously expensive to design and implement that few stand-alone hospitals could contemplate it, but it was affordable when its costs were spread over many hospitals.

Jones's skill and energy caught Wall Street's eye, and it did give him the money to go on a spending spree. At one point the company owned more than ninety hospitals. Jones operated them so efficiently that between 1973 and 1985 the market value of Humana's stock increased by $3.5 billion. Like many entrepreneurs, especially those with a financial orientation, Jones liked to steer the ship. As most observers agreed, he kept tight rein on his hospitals with masterfully detailed measurement and incentive systems. On a one-to-ten scale of decentralization to centralization, Humana defined the outer boundary of ten.

Jones, no wallflower, played the local-boy-makes-good role to perfection. He engaged a world-famous architect to design Humana's spectacular headquarters in Louisville, and he sponsored many cultural and humanitarian events there. Media coverage flowed.

Still, his outside activities did not keep him from noticing the handwriting on the wall: it was all over for hospitals. Occupancy was already dropping because of technological progress and the desire of busy consumers to either shorten or eliminate their hospital stays. Meanwhile, hospital prices were coming under increased scrutiny. Jones squarely faced the danger that his jewel—his prized collection of hospitals—would soon become an albatross.

Lord, Give Me Patients

Jones devised a new strategy to keep his hospitals afloat, one that is now emulated by many other hospital chains. His strategy was to form new businesses—a health insurance company and a physician network—that would send patients to the Humana hospitals. He would integrate these businesses with the hospitals.

The economic cornerstone of this strategy lay in a hospital's cost structure. A hospital's total costs barely increase or decrease with occupancy. After all, it must be prepared to provide services, food, and maintenance no matter how many patients show up on a given day. Hospitals are like airplanes: The cost of running them remains much the same whether they are full or empty. Such firms are called high fixed-cost businesses, because their costs remain largely constant despite wide variations in volume. For such businesses every additional customer brings considerable additional revenues but few additional expenses. An additional hospital patient may require only small incremental expenses for food, linen, and medical supplies, but he or she will bring in a much larger sum in revenues. Thus, the name of the hospital game is occupancy: Patients. Patients. Patients.

Jones reasoned that his newly created insurance company would attract enrollees because its prices were lower than its competitors'. It could afford to charge lower prices because it would use the highly efficient Humana hospitals. And the more patients a hospital got, the lower its average costs and, in a sustainable downward price spiral, the lower the prices of his insurance policies. But the visionary Jones understood, even then, that people do not want limited choices. Thus, his insurance policy came with a twist: Enrollees would pay no additional charges if they agreed to enter a Humana hospital, but they were required to pay some out-of-pocket charges at the time of admission if they chose a non-Humana facility.

Jones's newly formed physician network, composed of doctors carefully selected for their efficiency, was part and parcel of the insurance package. The enrollees in Humana's insurance policies who visited these doctors paid no additional charges, but those who chose non-Humana physicians did. Humana selected only a small number of physicians for its network, choosing primarily those who were prudent users of health care resources. After all, if its insurance company were to cover the expenses of profligate doctors, its costs would explode and its low-price competitive advantage would disappear.

Finally, to help enrollees who lived in areas that lacked primary care physicians, Jones created new centers and staffed them with salaried doctors. He located the centers in convenient, easy-to-reach sites and kept them open on the weekends and in the evenings. Patients were welcomed at these centers whether they were Humana health insurance enrollees or not. Those who required specialist care or hospitalization would be referred to other components of the Humana system.

In this way, Jones created an early-stage vertically integrated health care system, complete with primary care doctors, specialists, hospitals, and an insurance company. His system could fulfill most health care needs at lower costs than its competitors. After all, every part of the Humana system was as trim as it could be: The hospitals were notably efficient, the specialists were selected for their prudence, and the salaried primary care doctors worked for Humana and would follow its guidelines about the use of resources.

Humana's insurance policy was certain to be low-cost because it utilized these low-cost components. Surely its success was a foregone conclusion. After all, it was competing against a fragmented bunch of small town hospitals, small doctor groups, and ivory-tower academic medical centers.

What could possibly go wrong?

Problems Encountered by Humana

As it turned out, lots and lots of things went wrong. In the end Jones sold the primary care physician centers and spun off all of the hospitals to a new hospital corporation. He retained only the health insurance business and the corporate name Humana.

If the bright, battle-tested David Jones failed to implement a vertical integration strategy, backed by the money and brain power of Wall Street and years of experience in running a large number of hospitals, how can the many stand-alone hospitals that are now attempting this strategy hope to succeed? Unless thousands of hospitals learn the lessons of Humana's mishaps, we may be doomed to lose tens, if not hundreds, of billions of dollars as they try to replicate it.

So what went wrong?

The first problem is that in their economic objectives the health insurance business and the health care–providing business are intrinsically at loggerheads. The purpose of a health insurance company is to sell insurance policies by keeping its premium prices low. The best way it can control its expenses is to minimize its customers' use of health care services. In contrast, health care providers have exactly the opposite purpose. They want to give their patients the best and most of everything, under conditions convenient to the providers. In this way, they maximize their patients' welfare and their own.

As David Jones discovered, it is very difficult to put the economic interests of these two groups in accord, so that both do what is best for the company and the patients, despite their own opposite interests. Indeed, coordinating the interests of separate divisions so that they act to maximize the corporation's welfare is a problem so well-known to the many large vertically integrated manufacturing firms of yesteryear that it is a standard topic in introductory managerial accounting courses today.

Suppose for example, that a car company wants its own internal manufacturer of automatic wiring systems to keep its costs down in its efforts to improve product quality. (Note that this problem would not occur if the internal supplier were an independent company. After all, as an independent, it would be forced to keep its costs and quality in line with those of its competitors. If it failed to do so, it would be out of business. But as part of a larger firm, the internal supplier is protected from the ravages of competition by its parent's wealth and size.)

How does the car company keep its internal company as efficient as it would be as a stand-alone company? It creates an artificial income statement that credits the internal division for the revenues it would have earned if it had charged its internal customers the market price. From these revenues, the division's actual expenses are deducted. If the expenses are greater than these market-based revenues, it is exposed as a loser—a company that could not make a profit in the real marketplace. On the other hand, if the internal unit makes a profit, it is probably efficiently managed. The market price that the car company uses to compute this income statement is called the *transfer price,* the price at which one division sells its goods and services to another.

Humana used transfer prices to compute the sale of its hospital services to its insurance division. But surprisingly, despite Jones's financial expertise, Humana set the transfer prices for its own hospitals higher than the market prices for the competitive hospitals. As a result, Humana's insurance division preferred to refer its patients to non-Humana hospitals. After all, the hospitals that were not owned by Humana charged the insurance division less. Ironically, the vertically integrated firm was paying to put its patients in competitors' hospitals while beds in its own hospitals lay empty.

Why were the transfer prices of the efficient Humana hospitals set higher than market prices? One reason was that the Humana hospitals' occupancy had dropped, causing their costs to increase. The "profligate" physicians who had been excluded from the Humana insurance division were angry—so angry that they referred their patients to non-Humana hospitals. Humana belatedly welcomed these physicians into the insurance plan, but that created a new problem: Humana had diminished its power to influence physician behavior. After all, Humana's health insurance plan was not a significant factor for these many new doctors, since it covered only a few of their patients, and it therefore had little leverage over them. The physicians' indifference to the success or failure of the Humana health plan meant that the number of hospital days used by Humana enrollees exploded—and many of the days were spent in non-Humana facilities.

Humana hospital costs also grew because the hospital division's management was dispirited. Once the stars of Humana, the hospital team were now its dogs. David Jones had reluctantly started the health insurance division precisely because of the many empty Humana hospital beds. The fabled hospital management team grew dejected. With their loss of morale, Humana hospital costs exploded.

Meanwhile, the salaried physicians in the primary care centers did little to enhance referrals to Humana hospitals. Humana's tightly centralized hospital management had no experience in guiding salaried physician practices and could offer little advice to the physicians. Perhaps because the physicians earned the same salary regardless of the actual number of patients they saw, many of them failed to develop a patient following in their communities. But their presence did serve to irritate the existing primary care physicians with whom they were competing and caused them to spurn Humana hospitals too.

THE LESSONS

Three specific lessons stand out from these experiences:

I. Do Not Own When You Can Rent

Hungry business owners with a great deal of excess capacity often discount their prices ferociously to lure buyers. For example, airline fare wars erupt every so often when there is considerable excess capacity. Hospitals and specialist physicians are the airlines of the health care industry, characterized by considerable excess capacity. Why own these resources when they are so abundantly available? Other options, such as joint ventures and strategic partnerships, should be considered.

As an owner rather than a renter, Humana was forced to pay the full costs of the hospitals and its salaried physicians, whether they were used or not. As a renter, in contrast, Humana would have had the luxury of paying for hospitals only when it needed them, and at bargain rates to boot. Ownership may even reduce productivity; physician practices that are owned by vertically integrated hospitals may not be as efficient as those owned by the physicians themselves because physicians who are salaried by the hospital and have "cashed out" of their practice may lack the financial incentives for productivity.

2. Do Not Integrate Vertically to Protect a Faltering Business

David Jones entered the health insurance business to protect his faltering hospitals from further deterioration. At that time, his primary interest was not in running an insurance company.

This assessment of his motives may appear like pedantic nitpicking, but it is not. A company that is only in the health insurance business will do whatever is required to run itself effectively and efficiently. In contrast, a company that is in the hospital business, even one with a health insurance caboose, will run the business to protect its hospitals. So while the pure health insurer will choose providers on the basis of their merits, the hospital-based insurer will generally favor its own hospital-based providers.

Popular business writers and economists agree: As with Humana, the major problems of vertical integration are favoritism toward in-house suppliers, frequently manifested by transfer pricing systems that do not reflect market prices, and ownership when rental will suffice.

3. Focus, Focus, Focus

Humility is probably the most important lesson to emerge from Humana's experience. Even the smartest among us can rarely accomplish more than one thing very well.

When Humana vertically integrated, it entered a number of new businesses: primary care offices, physician networks, and health insurance. Managing any one of these businesses would represent a large challenge; for example, health insurance companies traditionally lose money every so often, even those that have been in the business for a long period. Humana not only entered many new businesses, it simultaneously attempted to integrate them with its existing one. Not even David Jones and his crack management team could learn and integrate all of these businesses, all at the same time.

LESSONS FROM OTHER INDUSTRIES

The problems of vertical integration experienced by Humana, the early integrated health systems, and the pharmaceutical companies are not unique. Many other vertically integrated health care ventures are also likely to experience them. Analyses of vertical integration in other industries support the conclusion that it confers benefits only in special circumstances.

Vertical integration has beneficial results primarily for firms that integrate to secure rare or erratic sources of supply, such as forest products or mining firms that acquire their own timber or ore sources. But even in such firms vertical integration has drawbacks in times of surplus supply. In the oil industry, for example, as one analyst notes, "forcing market bosses to buy from one company's refineries removes their freedom to shop around for the cheapest petrol." And the health care industry is hardly suffering from shortages in any of its resources.

Vertical integration can also succeed when a company has had a long history of alliances with the firm it acquires and substantial experience in managing that kind of business. When Pepsi-Cola bought some of its independent bottlers, for example, it already had considerable experience in managing its own bottling operations. It used this experience to improve the inefficient operations of the bottlers it purchased and to reduce retail prices. But such extensive experience and knowledge of acquirees' operations are generally absent among health care vertical integraters.

The Siren Song of Vertical Integration

In the end, in a mature industry, vertical integration fails primarily for one reason: It is very hard to implement. As a staff paper from the McKinsey consulting firm notes, "Vertical integration is a highly important strategy lever, but it is notoriously difficult to set, easy to get wrong, and—when a company does get it wrong—very costly to fix."

Nevertheless, despite its notorious difficulties, the list of companies seduced and abandoned by the siren song of vertical integration contains some of the biggest in the United States: IBM, General Motors, United Air Lines, Time Warner, and Citicorp are among them.

A firm that is in the process of redefining its corporate identity is one that is likely to fall for the lure of vertical integration. When Citicorp redefined its business from banking to information, it bought Quotron so it could offer up-to-the minute data about securities. Eight years later Citicorp decided to go back to the banking business. Quotron Systems had lost money consistently since its acquisition.

Similarly, when United Air Lines decided that it was not merely an airline but also a one-stop shopping center for the business traveler, it acquired a number of hotels and the Hertz vehicle rental company to help implement the new concept. The United Air Lines reservation system was to be the brains of the outfit, the glue that held all these pieces together. A dubious Wall Street did not share United's enthusiasm for its new identity, and ultimately all the nonairline assets were sold off. Other airlines that tried this "one-stop shopper" strategy also got scorched.

When the Time publishing firm merged with the Warner entertainment company, it too developed a new view of its identity. The company was no longer merely a publisher; it was now a media company. So what happened? In the opinion of the *Economist*, Time Warner has become such "a collection of feuding, and often ill-defined baronies ... it is hard to spot the synergies." Notes another observer, "This isn't one company. . . . This is five companies."

Not surprisingly, many vertically integrated companies have been forced to divest themselves of once-cherished holdings. Ford, for example, no longer makes its own steel, and General Motors has been evaluating for years whether to shrink the size of its in-house components manufacturers. A 1996 study demonstrated that GM's reliance on its own internal parts manufacturers added as much as $598 to its costs per vehicle, compared with the costs of its less vertically integrated rivals, Ford and Chrysler. "GM's managers would like nothing better than to wake up tomorrow with an in-house supplier providing [many fewer] of their parts," notes one industry expert. And IBM, which once made its own chips, wrote its own software, manufactured its own hardware, and sold through its own sales force, has been forced to retrench after a thorough trouncing in the market and by Wall Street.

The Lesson: Focus, Focus, Focus

One lesson stands out from all these ill-fated ventures: *Focus, focus, focus.* Most of us are very lucky if we can do only one thing very well; a lucky few may be able to do several things very well. But no one can do many things well. Even Olympic heptathlon gold medalists may not excel in any of the seven specific sports in those events. In this respect companies do not differ from human beings. When they stray out of their area of core competence, they falter.

The reasons for the failures of vertical integration are simple: A free-standing unit that focuses on only one function—whether it is making batteries, renting cars, or writing software—is likely to perform better because it is not hidden within the bowels of a parent and protected from competition. Thus, while an automobile company may indulgently tolerate the inefficiencies of its internal component manufacturers and subsidize them with profits earned elsewhere in its business, free-standing component manufacturers must pay their own way and earn their own profits. Moreover, internal units are less eager to innovate. Quotron, for example, was slow to move to PCs, perhaps because its insulated position within Citicorp sheltered it from competition. Its independent, more innovative competitors, on the other hand, had no choice but to adopt new technology.

Historically, companies may have integrated vertically because they feared that the market was incapable of supplying them with some critically needed resources. Probably for this reason Ford once manufactured its own steel and General Motors its own batteries. But in today's dynamic marketplace, this rationale for vertical integration has by and large disappeared. There is no shortage of suppliers for batteries, records, magazines, hotels, or software. You name it, you can get it. All you need do is ask.

DOES HORIZONTAL INTEGRATION REDUCE COMPETITION?

Horizontal integration does not pose as many managerial challenges as vertical integration. Yet its desirability is another question. Horizontally integrated organizations may well reduce costs, although they have not appeared to do so as yet, but the possibility of anti-competitive effects caused by their domination of a market raises serious concerns.

Effect on Prices

The leading industry journal, *Modern Healthcare,* has extensively documented that merged hospital facilities raise prices at increased rates, especially in small areas. The reason, according to *Modern Healthcare,* is that nobody is in a position to step forward to stop them. After all, in such areas the merged hospital is frequently the only source of care, and it takes a lot of capital to start a new competitor hospital. For example, after the two hospitals in rural Ottumwa, Iowa, merged, Deere and Company, a major employer in the area, experienced 20 percent health care cost increases. Small wonder that Deere executives were key government witnesses in a Justice Department suit to block the consolidation of the only two hospitals in Dubuque, Iowa. Deere is Dubuque's largest employer, and as one of its executives testified, "We think a merger like this causes a monopoly. We didn't take a stand in Ottumwa, and now it's one of our highest-cost areas. We are very concerned and want to keep hospital costs in line."

A 1994 *Modern Healthcare* analysis of eighteen merged hospitals found that they increased prices faster after their merger than before. It notes that in three out of four small-market areas, hospital prices increased at higher rates after a merger. Nor did mergers prevent the hospitals from investing in medical technology that was readily available elsewhere. To the contrary, such investment sometimes increased after a merger. Merged facilities may prefer to purchase new equipment so that they can offer more comprehensive care.

There is inconclusive evidence about whether merged hospitals reduce costs by eliminating duplicative services. In a 1992 survey *Modern Healthcare* found that only four of its responding merged hospitals eliminated services, while thirteen added them. As one hospital executive commented, "What you basically have are hospitals trying to acquire, maintain, or expand markets. It has very little to do with community need."

In this era of vigilant managed care organizations, how can merged hospitals continue to raise their prices and increase their expenses? Explains one researcher: "When the markets were less consolidated, the mergers delivered some utilization efficiencies, as financially stressed hospitals with higher expenses were merged into other hospitals. But as markets became more concentrated . . . hospitals were able to extract higher payment from payers. That means [that in the more concentrated or less competitive markets] some of the competitive advantages of market competition were thwarted."

Numerous researchers warn of the dangers of excessive concentration of providers in the hospital field. For example, one study showing that the large presence of managed care organizations in California had caused hospitals to lower their prices and costs sharply warned that their continued effectiveness was "highly dependent on there being sufficient competition in the market. It is, therefore, incumbent upon both . . . payers . . . and government agencies . . . to ensure that market conditions remain competitive."

Indeed, an extensive study conducted by the research arm of the American Hospital Association concluded that the most effective way to contain hospital costs is to increase consumer awareness of prices through health insurance reform. HMOs did not limit hospitals' cost growth, the study found; since HMOs must respond to the consumer preference for a wide choice of hospitals, they cannot obtain significant price concessions from hospitals. They simply do not have enough clout with any single hospital. The researchers' recommendation was that "health insurance reform, rather than maintaining or increasing hospital competition, is likely to be a more successful strategy in containing hospital costs."

Other aspects of horizontal hospital integration also raise questions. What will be the effects of nationwide integration in a service that is fundamentally local in character? Notes David Weldon, a physician who is also a congressman: "Our patients are our neighbors, they are our friends. They play with our children, they go to the same churches we go to. We therefore have a vested interest in making sure that these businesses in our community are able to have access to quality health care at a reasonable cost so that they can be competitive in the emerging global marketplace. Today, we have corporations making decisions about health care for folks in our communities. . . . If I were a patient, I'd rather that decisions about my health care were made by someone in my own community, rather than in a corporate office in another state." Echoes a senior health insurance official, "We haven't yet seen a hospital provider that's national in scope yet consistently has the best track record in every local community." A *Business Week* article that applauds the giant Columbia/HCA's financial success nevertheless worries, "Will doctors, patients, and those who pay the bills do as well?"

Perhaps more worrisome are the effects of horizontal integration on the practice of medicine. Concentrated market power of hospitals and health insurers may adversely affect physicians in a number of ways. For example, twenty-three physicians filed a lawsuit to prohibit the sale of a physician practice with a large number of primary care physicians to the Intermountain Health Care hospital chain. The plaintiffs claimed that the sale would make it difficult for a second hospital, which they preferred, to enter the area, because the physicians in the purchased practice would refer their patients only to the Intermountain hospitals. Another group of doctors claimed that the large health insurer Aetna employed coercive practices to force them to join the company's HMO. They allege in their suit that Aetna threatened to drop the hospitals in which these doctors practiced from its HMO if the physicians did not sign up with Aetna too.

Although the federal government has vigorously prosecuted anticompetitive mergers its reasons sometimes appear unclear to members of the legal community. For example, when the Federal Trade Commission permitted the huge Columbia hospital chain to merge with a large rival hospital chain, some lawyers noted the apparent conflict with the FTC's prior decisions to block smaller hospital mergers. And in 1994, when the FTC blocked the merger of two hospitals in Pueblo, Colorado, the defendants noted that they found the FTC's position "very confusing," since only a week before the Department of Justice had approved a merger in another two-hospital town.

One health care lawyer sheds light on these puzzling actions when he notes that the government legislation enacted to break up the cartels and trusts of yore "did not contemplate the level of activity or the types of activities that we see today." A 1995 study found that the 1992 government merger guidelines do not adequately predict when a given merger will be challenged. Although these conclusions were vigorously contested by a U.S. Department of Justice representative, both that department and the FTC are currently attempting to distinguish more clearly the integrations they view as enhancing efficiency from those they view as attempts to restrain trade. The two agencies issued clarifying policy statements in 1993, and again in 1994, and the FTC provided yet additional guidance in 1996.

Despite this admirable effort, however, it is doubtful that the federal government will successfully outwit all health care integraters that have anticompetitive agendas. Our limited ability to forecast the future and the large number of institutions involved and the rapidity with which they can alter their corporate identity may significantly limit the possibilities for effective government intervention.

THE VOICE OF EXPERIENCE SPEAKS: BIG IS NOT BEAUTIFUL

John Hickey, a consultant, speaks for many when he notes, "I don't think the most efficient organizations are the biggest. You can get almost too big, and I think some of these companies have gone beyond that." Even if the promised efficiencies do materialize, some may scoff at the possibility that they will be passed on to the consumer in the form of lower prices.

Seasoned business observers also caution that big may not be beautiful. The distinguished economic historian Charles Kindleberger reminds us that the big steel firms were outwitted by nimbler minimills. The fearsome antitrust lawyer and former mayor of San Francisco, Joseph Alioto, notes that "[t]he idea that all of these potential competitors are allowed to eliminate competition has dramatic effects," such as slower innovation and, perhaps, higher prices. Felix Rohatyn, a legendary old hand at integration activities as a partner in an investment bank, nevertheless warns that in the health care sector, "people are making big bets on big unknowns." The importance of their cautionary words is amplified by the inability of government action to control fully the anticompetitive effects of health care integration.

Will the "big is beautiful" diet preserve the attractive qualities of our health care system, while controlling its costs? Don't bet on it.

PART 3

What Works:
Health Care Focused Factories
and Medical Technology

CHAPTER 8

Resizing—the "Trade Fat for Muscle" Diet

Managed care and integration once promised to be the diets that would reshape the American health care system. Although managed care held costs in check, its most effective models proved unpopular and its most effective methods proved questionable. The integration movement may prove infeasible and create unwarranted risks of monopolies in some areas.

If neither downsizing nor upsizing can solve the health care sector's productivity problems, perhaps resizing will work. Resizing, however, is the hardest diet to follow, because it relies not on a simplistic change in size but on a fundamental, dramatic change in the body's composition: trading fat for muscle.

Let us begin to examine this issue with a peek into the large ballroom of a Toronto hotel. It is filled to capacity with noisy revelers. Sounds of merriment echo in the halls. Are they celebrating New Year's Eve? A promotion? A wedding or birth? No, these celebrants are "alumni" commemorating the repair of their abdominal hernias at Toronto's famed Shouldice Hospital.

It is difficult to imagine another hospital attracting so many alumni (with the possible exception of a transplant facility that restores life to its patients). What is so special about the Shouldice? Two words: *focused factory*. The Shouldice Hospital, which performs *only* abdominal hernia operations, is so good at what it does, so successful in creating a social experience for its patients, and so relatively inexpensive that former patients celebrate the repair of their hernias there.

The Shouldice Hospital represents the answer to Senator Biden's question (see Chapter 5). It contains the win-win solution he is looking for—high-quality health care at lower costs.

The American health care industry is filled with opportunities to establish focused factories, ranging from those that perform only one procedure, like cataract surgery, to those that provide the full panoply of care for a disease like cancer. To fulfill the promise of focused factories, however, the industry will have to resize—that is, replace its unfocused multipurpose providers and redundant, underutilized technology with muscular focused factories, loaded with cost-saving, quality-enhancing medical technology.

In itself, the mere concept of a focused factory will not guarantee success. The details of its execution will make the difference between success and failure. In this chapter, I will explore the details of execution that make a focused factory work, using the example of the Shouldice Hospital. And as an example of a service system taken to an art form, we'll look at one of the most prominent success stories among focused factories—the redoubtable McDonald's Corporation. Why McDonald's? Because week after week, year after year, it demonstrates how to attain exactly the qualities the health care system needs—consistency, reliability, clear standards, and low costs—in each of its twenty thousand restaurants all around the world. In the next chapter, I will discuss the key role that technology plays in the resizing diet.

Can our mammoth trillion-dollar health care system go on a resizing diet? The same question was asked in other organizations, in a different context—usually, how a company near the end of its rope, with high costs, a shrinking market, and huge losses, can turn its situation around, start to make money, *and* increase wages, *and* deal with severe foreign and domestic competition, *and* ship a high-quality product. Something has to drastically change for the better—but what and how?

Deere and Company is a good example of such a firm. It resized itself under the most difficult of circumstances—it had aggressive competitors, assertive unions, huge losses, and more than a century of corporate history. Yet Deere returned to triumphant profitability. It accomplished this feat by increasing its productivity, not by raising its prices, reducing its employees' wages, or compromising the quality of its outstanding products. Chapter 10 discusses how to apply the profound lessons offered by the Deere case to the health care system.

THE SHOULDICE HOSPITAL: A MODEL OF THE FOCUSED FACTORY

Let's go back to the ballroom filled with merry Shouldice Hospital alumni.

What makes the Shouldice experience such a positive one? Thousands of details differentiate it from other hospitals. But the overwhelming reason for its success is its clear focus on only one surgical procedure. This limited agenda concentrates the talents and energies of Shouldice's staff on one clear goal. The hospital has staunchly resisted many lures to expand its array. With elegant simplicity its administrator firmly notes, "We are good at what we do, and we do not want to do anything else."

General purpose hospitals, in contrast, cannot duplicate the intensity and quality of this attention, because their staff's focus is diffused over a wider range of services. (The typical hospital provides procedures ranging from appendectomies to ultrasound tests.) Nor can they duplicate the depth of experience with one procedure that the Shouldice team has gained. In health care as in everything else in life, practice makes perfect.

Because the Shouldice Hospital has this clear agenda, it handles virtually every part of a patient's stay in a thoughtful, reasoned way. When asked about their protocols, Shouldice administrators generally have a good explanation for why something is done in a particular fashion. A shrugged "that's the way we've always done it" and "it just happens that way" are not among their responses. Nor did its operating procedures grow from habit or convention; they are the products of intense deliberations about patient comfort, convenience, and health status. In management parlance, Shouldice has an *integrated operating system* carefully designed so that each of its activities reinforces the others.

The description of the hospital's alumni reunion might lead one to picture the Shouldice as a luxurious facility that pampers its patients and grants their every conceivable wish. But the hospital is far from extravagant. Although its facilities are attractive and clean and its setting magnificent, the design of the Shouldice's operating system purposefully places considerable demands on the patients. Meals are served only in the dining room, for example, and the patients' rooms lack a television or telephone. Patients even "prep" themselves for the surgery by shaving the area to be operated and are expected to walk from the operating room. Those recovering from their operation are encouraged not to linger in bed either. All staff, including the housekeepers, continually prompt them to exercise. The absence of amenities in their rooms requires them to walk. Recently operated patients instruct new arrivals about what to expect in the surgery. A round of aerobics, led by a tough Scottish nurse, tops off the evening entertainment.

It sounds more like a boot camp than a luxury hotel. So why do the patients love it? Likely they enjoy the self-empowerment created by the Shouldice Hospital's design. The walking not only hastens their recuperation, but also and more importantly, it confirms to the patients that they are in command of their own bodies. Their sense of mastery is reinforced by the self-preparation for the surgery and by their participation in the orientation for the next patients. The Shouldice patient is not a passive lump—he (the surgery is overwhelmingly performed on males) prepares himself for surgery, speeds his own healing, takes care of his own needs, and even helps to prepare others. He is not a patient but an active healer and teacher.

The Shouldice staff plays an important role in its success too. The surgeons are carefully selected. It is not every surgeon who would enjoy, or succeed in, performing only abdominal wall hernia surgeries for the rest of his or her professional life. But the Shouldice surgeons view hernia operations as a continual challenge, and like fine craftspeople, they take great pleasure in performing them consistently and reliably. Notes Dr. Brynes Shouldice, the son of the hospital's founder:

> A hernia is regarded as a relatively simple operation. This is
> quite wrong, as is borne out by the high recurrence rate (when
> it's not handled by a specialist). It is a tricky anatomical area and
> occasionally very complicated, especially to the novice or those

doing very few hernia repairs each year. But at Shouldice Hospital, a surgeon learns the Shouldice technique over a period of a year. He develops a pace and a touch. If he encounters something unusual, he is encouraged to consult immediately with other surgeons. . . . We teach each other. . . . He learns not to take risks to achieve absolute perfection. Excellence is the enemy of good.

Staff members are generously compensated, but surgeons who operate on a patient whose hernia recurs must provide the surgery again at no charge if they were responsible for the recurrence.

Technology also plays an important role in the hospital. Indeed, the Shouldice was created to implement a technological innovation—a new surgical procedure that requires careful separation of the muscles surrounding the herniated area. (In the more usual hernia operation, the surgeon cuts through the muscles around the herniated area and sews them back together, like a seam, after the herniation is presented.) All surgical team members are well-trained in the painstaking Shouldice procedure, which was invented by the physician who founded the hospital. As Professor James Heskett of the Harvard Business School, the author of a case study on the Shouldice Hospital, observes, the presence of twelve surgeons with the same specialty on the staff creates peer group effects in learning and quality. The surgical teams work together in a large number of situations. (The average surgeon performs more than six hundred procedures a year.) As a result of this familiarity, they function smoothly, like a seasoned sports team whose members are well-acquainted with each other's strengths and weaknesses.

These components of the Shouldice system not only create patient satisfaction, they result in lower cost and higher quality (as measured by the need for redos) than do general purpose hospitals that provide hernia procedures. The Shouldice, a privately owned, for-profit facility, charges $2,000 for the procedure; American hospitals demand from $2,400 up to $15,000. Yet the Shouldice recurrence rate is less than 1 percent.

The focused Shouldice concept explains these successes. The large volume of hernia procedures it performs simultaneously not only increases quality but decreases costs. The average general surgeon typically performs fewer than thirty hernia surgeries a year, or 5 percent of the yearly volume performed by a Shouldice surgeon. Surgical team members who continually work together on one procedure work more fluidly and efficiently than do members of teams separately assembled for different procedures, who may stutter and stumble because they do not fully know each other's measure. High-volume teams likely make fewer mistakes too. Moreover, supporting the patients' mastery decreases costs and increases quality—the customers perform much of the work that would normally be done by paid staff. Finally, the early ambulation of the Shouldice patient both speeds healing and further reduces costs.

While its clear focus is essential to the Shouldice's success, however, it does not guarantee it. The thousands of details in Shouldice's integrated operating system—details of recruiting, training, compensation, facility design, and process engineering—provide the key. These thousands of details would be difficult to replicate in a setting that has a broader set of objectives. So while the "focused" part of the focused factory is essential, it is the details of the "factory's" operating system that make the difference between success and failure.

There is substantial potential for focused factories in the American health care system. Units could be established that specialize in any of the millions of high-volume procedures, such as births, cataract surgeries, and bypass operations. Others could provide all the services required to care for the chronic diseases or conditions that account for the bulk of our health care costs, like asthma, diabetes, foot pain, and cancer. These new units could simultaneously improve quality and reduce costs, if they were implemented with operating systems as carefully considered as those of the Shouldice.

Some health care providers find the term "focused factory" off-putting when it is applied to health care. The "factory" aspect of the term makes them think of a large anonymous organization filled with automatons mindlessly working on identical widgets. But the accent should be placed on the "focus" aspect of the term. It is the focus in the focused factories that transforms them from such caricatures of industrial environments to organic, flexible environments that respond with excellence and efficiency to their customers' needs.

Other commonly accepted terms in health care may carry the aura of the focused factories with them in a more acceptable way. The term "centers of excellence" conveys the focus and pride of workmanship of a focused factory. But because these terms have been used for a long period and the organizations they typify may have failed to deliver on their promise, they carry an edge to them—implying more sizzle than steak, more hype than reality. The focused factory, in contrast, is a new term in the health care context and it refers to organizations that have experienced considerable success elsewhere in the economy.

THE HISTORY OF THE FOCUSED FACTORY

A 1974 issue of the *Harvard Business Review* listed an inconspicuously placed article in its table of contents. Written by Wickham Skinner, a professor of production and operations management at the school, the article, "The Focused Factory," presaged the resizing diet that has since revitalized the many companies in the American manufacturing sector.

On the basis of his extensive experience and research, Skinner concluded that "simplicity and repetition breed competence." He argued forcefully that complex and overly ambitious factories were at the heart of the country's productivity crisis:

> A factory that focuses on a narrow product mix for a particular market niche will outperform the conventional plant, which attempts a broader mission. Because its equipment, supporting systems, and procedures can concentrate on a limited task for one set of customers, its costs . . . are likely to be lower than a conventional plant. But, more important, such a plant can become a competitive weapon because its entire apparatus is focused to accomplish the . . . task . . . demanded by the company's overall strategy.
>
> [Despite] their advantages, my research indicates that focused manufacturing plants are surprisingly rare. Instead, the conventional factory produces many products for numerous customers in a variety of markets, thereby demanding the performance of a multiplicity of manufacturing tasks all at once from one set of assets and people. Its rationale is "economy of scale" and lower capital investment.

However, the result, more often than not, is a hodge-podge of compromises, a high overhead, a[n] . . . organization that is constantly in hot water with . . . customers.

To remedy these problems, Skinner recommended:

• Learning to focus each plant on a limited, concise manageable set of products, technologies, volumes, and markets.

• Learning to structure basic manufacturing policies and supporting services so that they focus on one explicit manufacturing [objective] instead of many inconsistent, conflicting, implicit [objectives].

• Seeing the problem as encompassing the efficiency of the entire manufacturing organization, not only the efficiency of the direct labor and work force.

HOW AMERICAN INDUSTRY RESIZED

Fortunately, American industry heeded Skinner's call. Many manufacturing companies resized, continually refining their focus. As part of the focusing process, they outsourced, buying goods they once produced in-house from outside vendors. The outsiders frequently produced better products, at lower costs; for example, automotive safety experts credit the competition among outside suppliers of auto parts for yielding vehicles safer than "anything the world's automakers could have come up with by themselves." Both the slimmed-down firms and their outside vendors are now increasingly likely to be focused factories. The resized, focused factories also reorganized, shifting from a functional structure to a team structure clearly aimed at one output. And they enriched the firm with newly developed operating systems and technology.

George Fisher, the CEO of Eastman Kodak, implemented these changes in his firm. First he "focused" Kodak on its core competencies of photography and film by selling off its pharmaceutical and diagnostics business for $8 billion and spinning off its chemical business. He notes: "The company was trying to do too many things at once and wasn't able to afford to do any one of them well enough." Next, Fisher reorganized what was left into operating units, each with its own profit-and-loss responsibility. Kodak's previous structure had enabled marketing managers to blame manufacturing for their problems and vice versa, with no one unit clearly accountable. Finally, he invested heavily in technology, spending $80 million a year to develop new cameras, for example. The result has been the financial equivalent of trading fat for muscle. Although the sales revenues of the slenderized Kodak slipped by $2.6 billion from 1993, its profits climbed by 63 percent.

The units that are sold or spun off in these resizing diets may well become more productive themselves. Take the firm Praxair, once a relatively small division of the giant Union Carbide. After it was spun off in 1992, Praxair became a tiger—doubling its profits in four years. What changed? As its CEO notes, once Praxair became an independent company, cut from the umbilical cord of its parent, it realized that "it had been underperforming its competitors for many years, but often didn't know it." When Praxair was forced to stand on its own two feet, it looked reality squarely in the face and reinvented itself.

Warren Batts, characterized by the *Wall Street Journal* as the Fred Astaire of the corporate spin-off in his capacity as the senior operating manager of two large businesses and as the director of three others, credits the efficacy of spinning-off to three factors. First, because the managers of spun-off firms are closer to operations, they are forced to focus on pragmatic details. Second, it is easier for spun-off firms to recruit and motivate their employees than it is for those hidden within a large corporate womb. And finally, buried firms may not obtain the level of financial support they require because top management does not really understand their needs.

Resized firms may well outsource to their own spun-off units. After all, outsourcing is a way not only to cut costs but to forge an alliance with a more productive supplier. When asked why they outsourced, one group of businesspeople ranked "improving company focus" and "accessing world-class capabilities" ahead of "reducing costs." The activities they outsourced range from running computer operations to janitorial services. Even high-technology services are increasingly outsourced as companies look for partners that can keep them technologically up-to-date. Notes *Business Week*, "Corporate America can't outsource data centers, computer networks, PC support services, and software development fast enough."

Service Providers as Focused Factories

The focused factory concept is not limited to manufacturing firms. Many successful service organizations are focused factories too, pursuing limited, clearly targeted agendas. In retailing, for example, Peter Drucker observed that "the department store—the success story of the early twentieth century—is slipping everywhere. . . . [T]he new retailers aim at a sharply profiled personality and a clear market niche."

As an example of a focused service factory, consider Jiffy Lube's quick oil-change shops. Jiffy Lube was chosen by Sears, Roebuck and Co. to provide this service to many of the centers in its giant $3.25 billion automotive group because, as a Sears spokesman notes, "we could not do oil changes in as focused and professional way as can Jiffy Lube." Similarly, each of Sears's niched direct response catalogs is produced by a specialist in that category. The home-fashions catalog, for example, is compiled by the leading provider in that field. Although the catalogs carry the Sears name, it is the specialist partners who select the merchandise, mail the catalogs, and fill the orders. Sears's use of outside focused factory vendors has been very successful. When it closed its general catalog operation in 1993, it shrank its staff from 10,000 to 20; but with its focused factory specialty catalog contracts, some 150 million catalogs were mailed to Sears' customer base in 1995.

Today, the focused factory concept is so natural to American businesspeople that when Evelyn Lauder, senior corporate vice-president of the nearly $3 billion Estée Lauder cosmetics empire, founded a breast cancer research foundation, she instinctively conceived it as a focused factory for breast cancer. In her vision the center would not be limited to providing kinds of services offered in more traditional cancer centers. No, her focused factory center would provide "one-stop shopping"—"genetic, nutritional and psychological counseling; a pharmacy," a program for aesthetics—hair, clothes, new bras; physical therapy; and a library. Notes Lauder, "I'm a marketer. . . . I know what women want and I understand what the system lacks."

Lauder's vision places her at the vanguard of American health care. Like the manufacturers and retailers of old, the current health care system is composed primarily of general purpose hospitals, physician groups, and other everything-for-everybody providers. Even the many specialist physicians generally work in multipurpose sites. The few existing focused factories—kidney dialysis centers, home infusion firms, outpatient surgery units—represent the exception rather than the rule.

MCDONALD'S CORPORATION: THE MODEL OF THE SERVICE-FOCUSED FACTORY

Despite their rarity in health care, focused factories are common in other service sectors. The list of "breakthrough service firms" typically includes many focused factories, such as Federal Express, UPS, McDonald's, and the placement specialist Manpower. If we are to apply the focused factory concept to health care, it is important to understand what makes the outstanding service firms tick. Let's focus in on the one name that stands out even in this august company: McDonald's Corporation. This food retailer is noteworthy not only for its quality, consistency, and customer acceptance but also for its continued growth, which outpaced that of the food retailing industry in the period 1983–1988—a feat akin to an adult maintaining the growth rate of a child.

How good is McDonald's? Even the *New York Times* called it "the best restaurateur in America." The article notes,

Each day seven percent of the population of the United States eats at McDonald's. . . . They eat exactly what they like, and it tastes the way it always tastes. . . . They get a lot to eat and feel it was a good deal. They leave happy and come back soon.

They have a lot of expectations. . . . They expect to be served within 60 seconds, to see someone cleaning obsessively, to be smiled at insistently. Mostly they expect that there will be no surprises.

And there will not be. McDonald's makes sure of that.

These unusual qualities intrigue even people like me who do not eat there regularly—at least, not since my children outgrew their fondness for Big Macs. As a matter of professional interest (okay, I confess! I do like the french fries), I try to visit a McDonald's wherever I go to test the consistency of its admirable qualities. From London to rural Arizona, I have rarely been disappointed: The restaurants are generally clean, the service is fast and courteous, and the food of consistent quality. This feat is all the more amazing considering the young age of the average McDonald's worker, its low prices, and the size of the McDonald's enterprise—nearly twenty thousand restaurants with average 1995 revenues of $1.8 million each.

So how does McDonald's do it? On a superficial level, its success appears easy to explain. The simplicity of its agenda is the key. After all, not much can go wrong with a restaurant whose menu is so limited that in 1992 it contained only fifty-five items.

But if McDonald's limited menu were the sole reason for its success, then other limited menu restaurants should be just as successful. But they are not. In 1992, for example, when McDonald's earned an operating profit of 25 percent, its close rival, Pizza Hut, earned 9 percent, and the KFC (code name for the old Kentucky Fried Chicken) chain earned only 8 percent.

While McDonald's clear, limited agenda is essential to its success, it does not fully explain it. The thousands of managerial details that the firm integrates into a cohesive operating system are central to McDonald's functioning. Without them, McDonald's would be just another struggling enterprise. But these details can be implemented most readily in a venture with only modest goals. They would likely disappear in an organization as complex as a hospital, multispecialty physician group, or integrated health care provider.

The details central to McDonald's success fall into four categories: outsourcing, and investments in technology, information, and human beings. Let us review the McDonald's french fry to illustrate these details.

God Is In the Details

Not even Julia Child would turn up her gourmet nose at McDonald's french fries. The long slender sticks of fried potato are always hot, crisp, and frankly delicious.

If you have never fried a potato, you might think these characteristics are easy to attain, but as any experienced cook will testify, such properly fried potatoes are works of art. The difficulties originate with the vegetable itself: Potatoes are weepers that ooze clear liquids and a starchy pulp after they are cut. They are almost impossible to dry. When wet potatoes hit hot oil, large dangerous bubbles form and splatter. As the bubbles break, the oil temperature cools inconsistently over the surface of the cooking pan. Thus, different pieces in the same batch of raw potato sticks can emerge from the frying process either burned or undercooked, and the splatters of hot oil can dangerously scald the chef.

To further complicate the process, not all potatoes are created equal. Bounteous Mother Nature has given us a large variety, ranging from small, glassy-textured, slip-skinned red potatoes to the large, fluffy behemoths produced in Idaho. These different varieties respond in different ways to the frying process. And individual potatoes of the same variety exhibit different characteristics, depending on the climate and soil conditions in which they were grown.

Now imagine that, like McDonald's, you must fry three thousand pounds of potatoes each week in each 11,400 American restaurants. Each batch of potatoes must be identical to the others. The potatoes you fry in Boston must look and taste the same as the ones you fry in Los Angeles and Chicago. Each potato stick within the batch must be perfectly cooked—crisp outside and fluffy inside—no hearts of stone are allowed. The people frying the potatoes do not have Cordon Bleu degrees. The potatoes must be freshly fried; old ones get limp and soggy. And you can sell a small sack of them for only about eighty cents.

The problem confronting McDonald's managers is how to achieve quality, consistency, and low cost on a nationwide scale. Their solutions are noteworthy. First, the company whose low-tech image features a clown turned to technology. With the assistance of their large R&D unit, McDonald's developed a special cooking apparatus that automates the frying process. These superfryers adjust the temperature of the oil so that the potatoes are always cooked perfectly. (McDonald's research had discovered that potatoes are fried perfectly when the oil temperature rises three degrees above the lowest temperature when the raw potato enters the hot oil.)

To insure the consistency of the potatoes, McDonald's developed strict specifications for its suppliers to meet. The ideal McDonald's potato has almost as many specifications as a Nike missile—sugar, starch, and moisture content, shape, and uniformity are but a few of them. To obtain an adequate, steady supply of potatoes, McDonald's turned to external suppliers, including Jack Simplot, an Idaho potato processor who is now one of the wealthiest men in the world.

McDonald's does not begrudge Simplot his millions. The company has no illusions that it can manage potatoes as well as he. To the contrary, instead of integrating vertically, McDonald's outsources—it enters into generous long-range contracts with suppliers who are willing to produce to its specifications. Notes one supplier: "Other chains would walk away from you for half a cent. McDonald's was more concerned with getting quality. They didn't chisel on price and were always concerned with suppliers making their fair profit." Says another, McDonald's "bought a supplier loyalty that the restaurant business had never seen. If you adhered to specifications, and were . . . competitive on price, you could depend on their order." In return, suppliers have provided the firm with many innovations. Simplot, for example, first suggested that McDonald's freeze its potatoes for year-round availability, and he put up the initial production line to test this concept. As a reward, by 1992 the firm asked him to supply about a billion pounds of potatoes.

But not even a smart french-fry-cooking apparatus and a consistent supply of potatoes, bred by loyal, competent suppliers, are enough to produce the perfect french fry. McDonald's must still ensure that its vast army of employees all over the world will remove the potatoes from the oil when they are done to a perfect turn. That they will drain the oil properly. That they will sell the potatoes promptly. That they will discard the old, soggy ones. It ensures that they do by means of extraordinary process engineering and human resource management.

Choreographing the Service Process

The service area of a McDonald's is as well choreographed as a Balanchine ballet. By 1991, the operations manual that documented this choreography had reached 750 pages. It spelled out every aspect of McDonald's operations—the width of a french fry ($\frac{9}{32}$ of an inch), the weight of the onions to be placed on a hamburger bun (a quarter ounce), and how to make everything. Potatoes are to be fried in one of three vats for two minutes and fifty seconds. Each vat is to be shaken after twenty seconds of cooking, as signaled by a beeper. Fried potatoes are to be stored in a hopper for up to seven minutes, and to be bagged with a specially designed scoop.

The techniques of process engineering were used in designing these operational procedures. They are what enable McDonald's to achieve its goal of serving any breakfast product in fifty-nine seconds or less. The system developed uses batch cooking for the separate components of the breakfast meals, which are held in cabinets specially designed to keep them fresh, then assembled as needed.

Human resource management also receives careful attention. McDonald's scrupulously trains its managers. They participate in the extensive training programs offered at Hamburger University in Elk Grove, Illinois, and many stores are equipped with video equipment to show the training materials produced in McDonald's headquarters. McDonald's also listens to its employees. While many of its new menu items and operating procedures are researched at headquarters, McDonald's store owners, franchisees, and managers also create innovations. It was a local California franchisee, for example, that developed the popular Egg McMuffin, an eggs Benedict clone that could be eaten without utensils. McDonald's vast empire of stores are natural laboratories within which such experiments can be conducted. And because of McDonald's integrated operating system, replicating a successful experiment like the Egg McMuffin in all its stores is relatively simple.

Finally, McDonald's is serious about the process of evaluating and promoting employees. It obtains and analyzes reams of performance data and a team of 332 service "consultants" with a checklist of more than five hundred items keeps stores on their toes by evaluating their performance, many times a year. The items the consultants audit range from the cleanliness of the rest rooms to customer service. Employee training focuses on the problems revealed by these and additional in-store audits.

McDonald's first franchisee attributes the firm's success to these operating systems. "All the advertising," he says, "all the gimmicks, all of the new menu items just won't do. It's the day-to-day attention to operations that does it. Well-trained employees, who have an interest and pride in their work, keep the business on a one-to-one basis, between customer and employee." This man has clearly practiced what he preaches. Like other McDonald's franchisees, many of the supervisors in his stores got their start working behind the counter.

Shouldice Hospital and McDonald's: Sisters Under the Skin?

Surprisingly, the Shouldice Hospital and McDonald's share many features in common. Both provide an excellent, consistent product at a relatively low cost; both are loved by their customers; and both accomplish these remarkable results in much the same way.

First, both institutions pursue admirably modest objectives—and they do so with tenacious, obsessive attention to detail. Second, their similarities in implementation are remarkable. Process engineering plays a key role in the operations of both organizations. People, equipment, and physical layout are combined in a deliberate way to create smoothly functioning production. Third, human resource management is thoughtfully and carefully implemented, from the selection of Shouldice's surgeons to the training of McDonald's french fryers. And fourth, technology is carefully considered, from Dr. Shouldice's reconceptualization of the hernia operation to McDonald's automated frying machine.

SYSTEMS FAILURES

The attention that McDonald's showers on its french fries may elicit the response that, as I recall, Terry Thomas, the great comic, got in one memorable movie scene from a nurse who firmly insisted that he strip for a physical examination, despite his strong protestations. After Thomas complied, the nurse scornfully looked down at his groin area and clucked, "All that fuss for such a little thing?"

All That Fuss for Such a Little Thing?

Imagine if all that fuss were made for a big thing—like cancer treatment or open-heart surgery.

Considerable evidence demonstrates that neither the victim of chronic diseases nor the hospitalized patient receives the same deliberate, almost obsessive attention that McDonald's confers on its french fries or the Shouldice its hernias. I do not mean to say that compassionate, competent physicians are callous or stupid—nor do I mean to impugn the many other fine people involved in the delivery of health care. What is wrong is the system, not the people. More precisely, what is wrong is the absence of a system.

Too many people receive inappropriate treatment, or insufficient treatment, for too many diseases and procedures. The reasons for these lapses are clear. First, while the medical care required for many diseases is typically provided over many sites—hospitals, outpatient centers, doctors' offices, the patient's home—frequently no one provider is responsible for coordinating the whole and no integrated operating process exists. In the absence of a coordinator, or a coordinated process, disease victims and their family members are left to put the pieces together—frequently with cursory, poorly understood, and hastily delivered instructions. Second, many providers do not perform any one procedure or treatment in sufficiently large volume that they can develop the fluidity and economy of the Shouldice surgeons or McDonald's service people.

In a nutshell, the absence of focused factories in the health care system needlessly diminishes the quality of care and increases its costs.

Consider diabetes, which afflicts six million Americans and accounts for 15 percent of the total national health care expenses. Caring for diabetes requires scrupulous management of the body's continually shifting glucose and insulin levels. Sustained lapses can cause life-threatening comas, loss of vision, gangrene (leading to leg amputations), reduced tactile sensation, and related diseases such as kidney failure. Yet a careful review of the records of nearly 100,000 elderly patients with diabetes found substantial gaps in the care they received from office-based primary care physicians. Fewer than 55.1 percent of them received the three diagnostic measures that are generally identified as necessary for optimal care of diabetes: Only 16.3 percent received the hemoglobin measure, 45.9 percent the eye examination, and 55.1 percent the total cholesterol measure annually. While the American Diabetes Association's guidelines recommend twice-a-year measures of hemoglobin level, 84 percent of the elderly diabetic patients did not receive even an annual test.

Victims of asthma, whose terrible symptoms include difficulty in breathing, emphysema, and permanent obstructive lung disease, are also victims of system failures. Asthma afflicts many people and causes considerable personal distress. Thirteen million Americans suffer from it, and it is the leading cause of serious chronic disease among children and teenagers. It accounted for 10 million lost school days a year for children and a billion dollars in productivity loss for their caregivers. *Managed Healthcare* estimates the national direct costs of treating the disease at $6.2 billion.

Most informed observers agree that current asthma treatment is far from ideal. When one consultant analyzed a large employer's health care costs, they concluded that 11 percent of its health insurance expenses were spent on asthma and that a number of asthma victims used physicians inappropriately; they saw their physicians when their asthma flared up and not for ongoing management of the disease. The average enrollee with severe asthma experienced more than three emergency room visits and hospitalizations a year, with an average length of stay in the hospital of more than five days. Their use of hospitals and emergency rooms could probably have been substantially reduced with better management of the disease. Practicing physicians concur: Seventy-two percent in one survey said that asthma was treated only symptomatically and not to manage the underlying inflammation.

Patients frequently do not know how to manage their asthma. Compliance with guidelines for the use of inhaled anti-inflammatory corticosteriods was characterized by one analyst as "abysmal," with usual rates of only 10 percent. As he explains, "patients are used to taking their bronchodilators and getting relief right away. The anti-inflammatories have to be used each day whether patients are having symptoms or not. And they won't see much benefit until they've used them regularly for four to six weeks."

Asthma self-care requires an integrated operating system that instructs patients and monitors their progress. Some patients undermanage themselves because their doctors are insufficiently informed about appropriate asthma management; but physicians need not be the sole source of such information—pharmacists and nurses could play an important role in patient education too, because of their knowledge and frequent contact with patients. Yet pharmacists are frequently neither contemplated nor compensated for this role. "Up to 75 percent of patients use their inhalers incorrectly," notes one professor of pharmacy. Pharmacists could instruct and monitor patients' use of the inhaler when they return for refills. Notes another pharmacy professor, "When patients come back . . . they're using the inhaler incorrectly and only get half the dose in their lungs."

System errors are not restricted to complex diseases like asthma, whose treatment is managed in many different settings. Even procedures that occur within one medical setting suffer from them. For example, a study of the hospital stays of 4,031 adults found that approximately 12 percent were victims of clearly or potentially adverse drug events. Of these events, 1 percent were fatal, 12 percent life-threatening, 30 percent serious, and 57 percent significant. Forty-two percent of the life-threatening and serious adverse drug events were judged preventable by the researchers. As for the causes of the errors, three classes of drugs accounted for nearly half of the preventable events and over half of them occurred at the ordering stage. (Wrong dose, choice and frequency were among the most common errors in this stage.)

A study of elderly patients who had been admitted to a hospital for heart attack similarly concluded that all too many received suboptimal care. The study identified the patients who were "ideal candidates" for different kinds of therapies and evaluated the extent to which they had received them. Only 69 to 70 percent of the ideal candidates received clot solvents (thrombolytics) and anticoagulants (heparin) during hospitalization; only 45 percent received beta-blockers at discharge; and only 29 percent of smokers received counseling on smoking cessation. Further, all too few patients were administered thrombolytics within the crucial thirty-minute period after arrival at the hospital that can make the difference between life and death.

Why do these problems occur? One reason may lie in the low volume of a particular service. For example, physicians caring for the elderly diabetics average only 35 such patients in their practice. Because the average physician has a patient load of between 1,000 and 2,500 patients, the 35 elderly diabetics account for only a small percentage of the total. Small wonder the physicians so frequently fail to conduct the recommended tests. Elderly diabetics represent such a small percentage of their patients that the physicians could be unfamiliar with the necessary details of their care. Similarly, the practitioners who cause the adverse drug events probably deal with so many different types of drugs in their general purpose hospitals, and with so many different kinds of patient procedures, that they are unlikely to be familiar with the exact protocols for administering any one drug.

The Problem: Too Little Volume?

Some analysts believe that such system failures can be prevented by limiting the number of health care providers in a given area—a practice called "regionalization"—so that each of the remaining ones handles greater volume and thus achieves better quality and lower costs. Their theory that practice makes perfect appears to be as valid in health care as in every other aspect of life. For example, one study compared areas of the United States whose hospitals perform a large number of open heart operations with those whose hospitals perform relatively few. It found significantly lower death rates in the high-volume areas. Similarly, there were fewer complication rates in angioplasty centers that perform more than four hundred procedures a year than in others.

Substantial improvements in quality and decreases in costs can be attained in high-volume settings. One study estimated that "channeling high-risk [open-heart] patients away from" hospitals with higher-than-expected mortality rates and toward those with better performance "could lower the overall risk-adjusted mortality rate by 54 percent." Another found that high-volume surgeons use fewer hospital resources than lower-volume ones. The per-patient differences in actual versus expected charges were large: $315 per gall bladder operation, for example.

Still, larger volume provides no guarantee of higher quality. Out of the hundreds of major teaching hospitals with more than four hundred beds, only a handful made it onto a carefully developed list of "benchmark" hospitals, and only two of this handful had achieved distinctive quality and costs for three years in a row. Quality outcomes for open heart surgery vary considerably, even though these are high-volume operations in virtually every hospital. Nor does high volume guarantee lower costs: One study found that the volume of hysterectomy procedures actually correlated with increased costs.

Clearly, high volume is not a magic bullet—other factors also play important roles in causing quality and cost differentials. In most industries problems with costs or quality are frequently ascribed to a system failure. But in health care such conclusions are rare. Blame is all too frequently laid at the feet of insufficiently alert or educated people, not at the absence of a system.

One exception is the analysis of system failures that caused the adverse drug events in hospitalized patients. The depressingly long list of problems it found included: errors in communication between personnel from different services; lack of hospitalwide standards for drug doses and frequency of dosage; absence of standardized procedures for storage and distribution of drugs; and ambiguity about who is responsible for the patient. As Dr. Lucian Leape and his colleagues explain in their analysis of the medication errors, "Poor system design creates 'accidents waiting to happen.' The concept of systems failure as the underlying cause of errors has not been widely accepted in the practice of medicine. Rather, technical efforts at error reduction have focused on individuals and episodes, using training, exhortation, rules, and sanctions to improve performance errors.... Error ... experts reject this approach, noting that it is more effective to change the system as a whole."

Contrast these errors in handling drugs with McDonald's scrupulous care in handling potatoes. Contrast the deficiencies in treating desperately ill diabetics and asthmatics with the virtually failproof process the Shouldice Hospital uses in treating hernias. The difference is in the system.

The Cure: Focused Factories

Will implementation of an integrated systems approach solve the problem of system failures? The case of pain management for cancer victims suggests the potential impact of a systems-oriented solution.

Most experts agree that in cancer and other acute conditions, undertreatment of pain is a significant problem. Yet despite decades of effort to convince clinicians of the value of pain relievers, the problem persists. The American Pain Society's Quality of Care Committee has concluded that "the widespread failure ... even in institutions with active analgesic education programs suggests a flaw in the design of local systems for care, rather than lapses by individual clinicians." In response, the committee drafted guidelines for a new system. These guidelines could have been found in the operations manual of any focused factory: They called for recognizing and measuring the problem, guaranteeing the patient that it will be solved, specifying policies to relieve pain, and continually measuring the results. Implementing these guidelines eventually achieved substantial improvements in pain relief in a number of institutions.

Some of the current early-stage attempts to create focused factories in health care demonstrate the power of a systems approach. For example, Denton Cooley, the famed Texas cardiac surgeon who installed the first artificial heart, heads a focused factory at the Texas Heart Institute, which he carefully manages in order to show that he can achieve better and cheaper heart surgery simultaneously. Notes Dr. Cooley, "Of the many firsts with which I have been involved . . . the achievement that may have the greatest impact on health care did not occur in the operating room or research laboratory. It happened . . . when we created the first-ever packaged pricing plan for cardiovascular surgical procedures."

In 1994 Cooley developed a package price of $27,040 for a bypass; the national average price was $43,370. How does he achieve such low costs? First, Cooley himself embodies one of the focused factory attributes—volume. He has led a record number of open-heart procedures—60,000 of them. Notes the *New York Times,* "Watching Dr. Cooley operate . . . is a lesson in economy. No wasted movement, no errant emotion, no extra tools. . . . He [is] ceaselessly modifying and simplifying." Few details are too small to escape his attention. For example, the august surgeon proudly notes that he substituted a $10 plastic disposable tube for one usually costing $75, with no loss in quality.

Other early-stage focused factories reflect the same attentiveness to detail. Duke University's renowned transplant center's systems perspective enables it to provide a bone marrow transplant for $65,000, about a third of the prevailing 1995 rate. After a five-day hospital stay, Duke patients are discharged to a midpriced hotel across the street, where they remain during a course of chemotherapy. The hospital rents a floor of rooms in the hotel and maintains them with antiseptic cleanliness for their patients. The renowned heart-transplant programs at Stanford University and the Cleveland Clinic have reduced their costs by 15 to 20 percent by rethinking details such as the number of sutures used in surgery and the types of diagnostic tests performed.

A large chain of focused factories could improve the results obtained by such stand-alone facilities even further. All of its members would benefit from the innovations that one unit created, just as all the McDonald's restaurants benefited from one store's innovating a new breakfast item. For example, large chains of ambulatory surgical centers typically demonstrate better productivity statistics than ambulatory surgical facilities that are owned by hospitals or are independent. J. P. Morgan calculated that the average chain surgical center has a greater number of cases per procedure room and more procedure rooms per facility. The higher efficiency of the chain centers undoubtedly reflects the impact of shared experiences from all the centers.

Efficiency translates into lower prices, if some of the gains are passed on to the customer. For this reason, one chain of ambulatory surgical centers, Medical Care America, increased its average prices between 1992 and 1994 by only 1 percent, a rate of increase virtually unmatched elsewhere in the health care sector.

HOW FOCUSED FACTORIES DIFFER FROM TRADITIONAL PROVIDERS

Whenever I talk about focused factories to hospital-based physicians, I am inevitably asked, "How can focused factories possibly provide good care? After all, most disease and hospital procedures require inter-disciplinary teams with many different specialties. Would a focused factory contain all these specialties?"

Specialist Practices and Hospitals

The question reflects the traditional organizational structure of hospitals by physician specialty—such as surgery, medicine, and radiology. Many providers find it difficult to conceive of a different structure. But focused factories are not organized by physicians' specialties—they are organized by patients' requirements. They *always* contain *all* the resources needed to provide for a patient. Traditionally in hospitals teams of people are drawn from various specialties to care for a particular case as needed. These made-to-order teams are like sports teams assembled for a pick-up game; a focused factory's team, in contrast, is like the well-seasoned Chicago Bulls.

Because the health care system's traditional organizational structure is so generally accepted, focused factories are sometimes confused with medical practices that consist of specialists for a disease. Some may think, for example, that a cancer-focused factory is equivalent to a medical practice that offers only the services of oncologists. But the purpose of a focused factory is precisely to override such narrow technical orientations. The cancer-focused factory provides *complete* cancer services to its patients. It provides them in many sites, including the hospital, an outpatient center, and the patient's home. And it provides expert specialist care for the other problems that accompany cancer, such as anemia or infections. Its comprehensive menu ranges from the diagnosis, treatment, psychotherapy, and financial counseling provided in its outpatient centers, to the inpatient services offered by hospitals, to services provided directly in the patient's home.

As described in Chapter 2, Salick Health Care has many of the features of such a focused factory. Although its services could, in theory, be replicated in general purpose hospitals, many hospitals would find it difficult to do so. For one thing, the hospital managers may encounter political problems in singling out one service for focused factory status. Then, too, no hospital could possibly replicate the intense attention that Salick's management showers on cancer treatment. While cancer accounts for the bulk of Salick's activities, the typical hospital offers thousands of services, ranging from births to open heart surgery. For these reasons, Salick's managers believe that only thirty centers in the United States provide comparable services, and they are not overly concerned about potential competition from hospitals.

Even if a hospital did succeed in establishing a single cancer center, it could not replicate the benefits Salick derives from owning multiple centers. One of these benefits is information. Salick's uniform data system stores information on 17 million member-months in eleven states, classified into twenty-three cost categories and many types of diseases. This data system enables the company to offer firm, fixed priced contracts for total cancer care to insurers or other large-scale buyers. The company's large size has enabled it to invest millions of dollars in the development of such a database. Its size also enhances its ability to acquire the latest cancer care technology, to disseminate the most up-to-date information about cancer, and to develop advanced protocols for treatment. Further, when the many experiments that occur naturally within its eleven centers give successful results, they can be replicated elsewhere. Few solo flyers can replicate these benefits.

"Carve-Outs" and Disease-Management Programs

A focused factory is thus characterized by a multidisciplinary group of people who work together to achieve a clear, limited objective. As in McDonald's, the team members are guided by thoughtful operating procedures and continually monitor their success in achieving their objectives, using objective, quantitative measures. The large volume of work performed in a focused factory, the harmony and fluidity achieved by its team members, and the attention paid to improving the operational processes result in continual process refinements, quality improvements, and cost reductions.

Early-stage focused factories that superficially share some of their characteristics are the "carve-outs" that increasingly characterize managed care contracts. Carve-outs are usually teams of providers who contract with insurers to provide certain benefits, such as mental health services, at a fixed price. But unlike focused factories, carve-outs are frequently composed of a loose network of providers, who barely interact with each other. The intimate team-learning and improvement that are inherent in the focused factory are, as yet, absent from them, although these features will likely emerge as the carve-out concept matures.

For example, a cardiovascular network has been formed by five hundred cardiologists and heart surgeons in thirty-eight practices all over the United States to provide a total, fixed price for cardiovascular services. It shares a few of the characteristics of a focused factory. In recognition of the importance of volume, member physicians must perform at least 150 bypasses or other invasive coronary procedures in institutions that provide 500 or more such procedures annually. Strict achievement of low mortality rates is required for membership, too, as is the willingness to participate in "peer review." But until carve-outs devote energy and funds comparable to what McDonald's invested in developing their detailed systems, they are unlikely to achieve all the benefits of a focused factory.

A regional program in which practitioners share data and learn from each other's experiences provides an example of the power of team learning in a focused factory. The program involves all the cardio-thoracic surgeons practicing in Maine, New Hampshire, and Vermont. In an organized effort to improve mortality rates from bypass surgery, the participating physicians agree that their individual results will be continually measured and shared with other group members. They receive feedback and training in continuous-improvement techniques, and they visit each other's medical centers for critical site evaluations. Although the outcomes of this experiment are not definitive, they strongly suggest that these components of a focused factory have already resulted in seventy-four fewer deaths than expected.

Disease-management programs are algorithms for a "virtual organization" that provides treatment of a given disease. The practitioners who implement these protocols need not have any physical contact with each other—they are connected primarily by the disease management program. But the shared experiences and learning that characterize teams in focused factories are difficult to replicate with disease management programs.

Clinical Pathways

Clinical paths are treatment plans for a specific condition or problem that emphasize coordination among multidisciplinary members of a team. One recent survey found that more than eighty percent of health care facilities use them in areas such as open-heart surgery, orthopedics, and obstetrics.

Clinical path techniques are not equivalent to focused factories, although they can help to manage focused factories. Clinical paths are used by providers of many services primarily to reduce their costs by decreasing hospital stays, eliminating duplication of services, and utilizing resources more efficiently. Focused factories, in contrast, provide only one service and their purpose is to improve the relationship between cost and output, and not to reduce costs.

Focused factory providers and managers devote all of their energies to attaining this goal. Clinical path team members, in contrast, typically have many other demands on their time and energy. These differences in organizational structure and goals will likely create great differences in outcomes.

Downsizing

The term *downsizing* has gotten a bad smell of late. It implies massive, wanton layoffs that fatten corporate profits and cause human misery. It may sacrifice quality and spirit at the altar of corporate profits.

Such slaughters of the innocent are not what the focused factory is about. Focused factories enhance productivity by releasing the potential inherent in all of us; downsizing, in contrast, aims to enhance productivity by cutting costs. The operative verbs for focused factories are *grow* and *outsource*, while for downsizing they are *cut* and *layoff*.

Small wonder that only 47 percent of companies that downsize increase their profitability. In a recent survey of 1,003 downsized companies, including 51 health care firms, only half experienced the improvements they expected in customer service, and hardly all achieved productivity improvements. Eighty percent of hospitals in a 1995 survey reported cutting their expenses, but it is doubtful that they did so through a restructuring of their operations into focused factories. It is, unfortunately, much more likely that they did so by taking a downsizing approach to their staff.

THE IMPACT OF FOCUSED FACTORIES

Some people worry that focused factories will be difficult to access, because only a few of them will exist. Conversely, others worry that vast numbers of them will be required to meet the American public's needs. Still others wonder if focused factories will eliminate the existing convenient sources for filling everyday health care needs. Last, others are concerned that focused factories will fragment the health care system even more. None of these concerns is merited.

Too Few Focused Factories?

Because constructing a focused factory does not require the massive capital expenditures needed to construct a hospital, they can be inexpensively located in a large number of local satellite units. For example, it would be economically feasible to place the support, regular examination, and therapy services of a focused factory in a community hub, such as a town center or shopping mall, and to provide other services, like nurses' visits and infusions, in patients' homes. A health and information center in a shopping mall cost about $200,000 in 1996, including staff. The services that require substantial capital investment, on the order of tens or hundreds of millions of dollars, such as "open" surgical procedures, would be provided in a focused factory hospital, one distinguished by the large volume of procedures it performs.

In general, the focused factory services that are frequently used by clients—like regular check-ups—will likely be provided in decentralized community sites, while those that are performed only once—like the excision of a tumor—will be conducted in the high-volume hospitals that are also part of the focused factory system of care.

Too Many Focused Factories?

At the other extreme, some worry that the United States would have to be overrun with focused factories. If McDonald's requires 11,400 restaurants to sell only $16 billion of fast food, 700,000 focused factories might be needed to provide services in the trillion-dollar health care system.

But Mother Nature works in mysterious ways. One of her major mysteries is an empirically derived relationship between cause and effect that will greatly reduce the number of focused factories needed to provide better-quality, lower-cost health care services. This relationship, which correlates an activity with its causes, is usually articulated as the 80–20 rule or, more formally, the Pareto rule. (It is named after Vilfredo Pareto, who first derived the curve suggesting that roughly 80 percent of most events can be attributed to approximately 20 percent of their causes.)

Pareto analysis is much beloved by process engineers. As one textbook, *Attaining Manufacturing Excellence,* notes, "The most common descriptive method [for defect analysis] is the Pareto diagram . . . , a simple classification of defects, complaints, or problems by category. The hypothesis in the Pareto rule [is that] 80 percent of the problems come from 20 percent of the sources, so the productive way to attack defects is to attack the cause of the 80 percent." The approximate validity of the Pareto rule can be demonstrated in many ways: For example, 85 percent of the beer consumed in the United States is quaffed by 15 percent of drinkers. I find many examples of the 80–20 rule in my own life, too; 80 percent of the calories I eat in the average day originate from 20 percent of the food items I consume (as I said, I'm fond of McDonald's french fries), and 80 percent of the clothes I wear come from 20 percent of my wardrobe.

If the Pareto rule holds in health care, then focused factories that are aimed at only 20 percent of causes can treat 80 percent of medical conditions. For example, if 20 percent of all diseases account for 80 percent of medical costs, then focused factories targeted at those diseases will help control the bulk of health care expenses and improve the quality of care. And if 20 percent of patients in any one disease category account for 80 percent of the costs of that disease, then focused factories could fruitfully target interventions primarily at those 4 percent of patients who cause 64 percent of American health care costs.

Does the 80–20 rule hold in health care? Although precise data are not available, because the focused factory approach is relatively new in this field, there are many indications that it does hold. For example:

- *Observation:* Ten diagnostic categories accounted for 75 percent of 1987 medical expenditures. Two categories account for 26 percent of the costs (cardiovascular and injuries), and five categories account for 50 percent of expenses (the two above and cancer, genitourinary, and birth-related).
  Conclusion: Focused factories aimed at only five diagnostic categories will control costs and quality for 50 percent of all health care expenses.

- *Observation:* Thirty-three percent of asthma patients accounted for 73 percent of the costs of treating the disease, and 37 percent of patients with chronic obstructive pulmonary disease caused 86 percent of the costs, for one large employer. Similarly, 10 percent of the U.S. population accounted for 72 percent of 1987 health care expenses and 1 percent of the population accounted for 30 percent.
  Conclusion: Focused factories aimed at only 10 to 37 percent of most disease populations can control 72 to 86 percent of costs and quality.

- *Observation:* Infants account for less than 6 percent of the population of children, but they represent more than 24 percent of health care spending on all children (0–18 years of age). Newborns with complications and infants requiring rehospitalization consumed 72 percent of the $12.6 billion spent on infant care in 1987.
  Conclusion: Focused factories aimed at the small number of newborns with complications can control 72 percent of health care costs for infants and 18 percent of all spending on children.

As further evidence of the prevalence of the 80–20 rule, consider that:

- Six types of surgical procedures accounted for 80 percent of all procedures performed at free-standing ambulatory surgical centers in 1991.

- Four conditions account for nearly 50 percent of disabilities in the United States; two of them account for 40 percent (arthritis or rheumatism and back or spine problems).

- Twenty-five diagnostic-episode clusters (DECs) accounted for 76 percent of all the cases treated by primary care physicians in one study. The more severely ill patients in the top twelve of these DECs accounted for only 25 percent of these categories, but the average payments for their care were 3.6 to 14.2 times higher than those for the other patients.

These data overwhelmingly suggest that a relatively small number of focused factories targeted at a handful of high-cost diseases, and at the relatively few severely ill patients within them, could provide enormous benefits.

The Wrong Kinds of Focused Factories?

If the health care system is carved up into focused factories, who will provide diagnostic health care? Once again, the answer is focused factories—in this case, ones that specialize in providing medical diagnostic services.

The world-famous Mayo Clinic is a good model of such a focused factory. Judging by consumer responses, the Mayo model is well worth emulating: Over 80 percent of the 5,500 people who register there weekly arrive of their own volition.

From its earliest days, nearly a century ago, the Mayo Clinic has been characterized by the teamwork and the integrated operating system characteristic of focused factories. The two Mayo brothers who founded the clinic always referred to "my brother and I," perhaps because their father, also a physician, told them, "No man is big enough to be independent of others." As one Mayo physician notes, "The principle implied in the words 'my brother and I' became a cornerstone of this institution. . . . The care of patients is a joint effort of many individuals."

Like the Shouldice Hospital, the Mayo Clinic's physical design is part and parcel of its integrated operation system. All the specialists and diagnostic equipment that a patient may require are available under one roof. Each floor in the main building contains two medical specialties. The center of each floor houses a circular administrative area, from which spokes, containing 88 to 104 examining rooms, radiate. Each room is topped by a vertical line of lights that signal a variety of messages, including whether a patient is waiting to be seen or is being examined by a physician. The attendants at the central desk can thus easily monitor the patient's status in each of the examining rooms by scanning the lights and taking appropriate action if, for example, a patient is unattended for a long period. An internal system of conveyor belts, chutes, and lifts rapidly relays information about the patient from one specialist to the next. The patient's personal physician, from the department of internal medicine, uses the ready availability of specialists and data to coordinate the diagnostic process.

In the future many diagnostic medicine focused factories are likely to follow the Mayo's operating system, right down to the lights over the examination room doors. After all, imitation is the sincerest form of flattery.

Cherry-Picking Focused Factories?

In an effective economic system, some organizations specialize in the tricky, custom work that a few customers require, while most others provide the more standardized products that most of us need. Huge cereal companies produce the products most of us eat for breakfast, but a few companies specialize in producing cereals for people who are allergic to wheat or corn. Chain clothing and shoe stores provide apparel in standard sizes but specialty stores exist to outfit the "big and tall" and those with unusual needs, such as people with deformed feet.

The effective health care system will replicate this structure. Many Shouldice Hospital clones will serve the needs of the ordinary person with a hernia; but a few focused factories will specialize in difficult hernia cases, such as the 500-pound man with diabetes, heart disease, and a hernia. Most focused factories will serve the needs of most of us, but a few will specialize in very complex cases.

A system which separates customers by the uniqueness of their needs makes good economic sense. For example, if a mass market cereal company tried to also serve the needs of the small market that is allergic to their standard products, the effort would likely hurt both product lines. The standard product would receive less of management's attention and the small product line would not receive enough resources or the attention of people who deeply understand that market. Similarly, if McDonald's tried to serve custom grilled burgers made from vegetables, the effort would likely diminish the quality of its standard fare and the vegetarian customers would not be pleased with their McVeggies either.

For these reasons, segmentation of focused factories by the complexity of the customer's needs creates a more efficient health care delivery system. But if every customer pays the same price, regardless of the intensity or uniqueness of the services he requires, focused factories will attempt to cherry-pick. They will do their best to recruit the easiest types of cases and to shun complex, unusual cases elsewhere. The focused factories that concentrate on severe cases will not be created because they will not receive sufficient compensation for their efforts.

To avoid cherry-picking and to insure the availability of focused factories that treat either standard or unusual cases, payments must reflect the severity of the problem.

Uncoordinated Focused Factories?

Some people wonder whether focused factories will further fragment the already fragmented health care delivery system.

Their concerns take two forms. Some wonder how the "co-morbidities" of a disease will be treated in a focused factory, such as the kidney disease that all too often accompanies diabetes. Their concerns are misplaced. An effective focused factory will contain all the resources required to treat all aspects of the customer's needs. Thus, a diabetes-focused factory will provide nephrologists to help manage the diabetic's kidney disease. The focused factory's nephrologists will be more effective than the nephrologists who treat kidney disease elsewhere because they will specialize in treating diabetics with kidney disease. Thus, focused factories will provide better care for co-morbidities than the present system.

Others wonder how a group of focused factories, each specializing in different procedures or diseases, can be strung together to provide all of the customer's possible health care needs. Do we need to create a virtual system that networks all these separate organizations together? The answer is that some customers might prefer this "virtual system" while others might want to create it for themselves. Entrepreneurial managed care organizations or other health insurers will cobble together a system of focused factories that will attend to all possible needs for those who prefer a "virtual system." Other buyers, such as large employers, may prefer to put this system together for themselves.

This system for buying health care is like any other market. I can plan my vacation directly, calling airlines and hotels myself, or I can use a travel agent. If I choose to use the agent, I can select an independent or an agent affiliated with a large travel service. Just as the market system presents me with many different attractive choices for planning vacations, the new market-driven health care system will provide buyers with a range of attractive options for buying health care.

Large companies also "shop" this way. For example, Nike, the world's largest supplier of athletic shoes, buys 100 percent of its shoe production needs from outside focused factories. It retains for itself only production of the technical components of its "Nike Air" system, R&D, marketing, and distribution. It buys everything else from the virtual network of suppliers that it creates.

THE FUTURE OF FOCUSED FACTORIES

So substantial is the promise of focused factories that the prescient financial community has already identified them as the next wave of transformation in health care. In 1993 venture capitalists (companies that provide financial support for early-stage investments) poured $280.8 million into health care service ventures; but in 1995, in recognition of the power of this concept, one such firm alone invested $210 million. Their interest lies primarily in "niched" or focused factory services, especially those that target diabetes, asthma, and congestive heart failure. But they invest in other ventures too, like those that provide care for low-weight babies and children with complicated medical needs.

The Future May Be Now

Focused factories are typically initiated and managed by health care providers, who operate either as a corporation or as members of a corporation led by businesspeople. Insurers and large employers can contract directly with the focused factory for the provision of a limited range of services. With increasing frequency the contract payment takes the form of a capitation, a fixed price for a given procedure or for overall coverage of a certain disease. This arrangement commits the provider to deliver all the services needed for high-quality care, sometimes including pre- and postoperative counseling services.

Procedure-based focused factories are already proliferating. For example, a large majority of the teaching hospitals that have "centers of excellence"—procedural areas for which the hospital has gained particular renown—engage in some form of fixed price arrangements with HMOs. For example, Dallas Medical Resource Foundation (DMR), an alliance of nine Dallas hospitals, offers a number of complicated procedures at a fixed rate. DMR frequently establishes its prices by auditing an employer's health benefits data to determine their past payments. It claims to have saved its clients 20 to 25 percent over what they would otherwise have paid. A typical customer, the three-thousand-employee FINA, also in Dallas, expects that its relationship with DMR will reduce its expenses by hundreds of thousands of dollars each year. Some of FINA's employees are so pleased with the quality of DMR's services that they are willing to travel substantial distances to receive them; one mother traveled three hundred miles for her infant's open heart surgery because of her favorable impression of DMR's pediatric cardiologist. Yet the costs of the surgery were so relatively low that she saved money even after her travel costs were included.

Many physician groups too are forming focused factories, or more frequently their precursor, the specialty carve-out network. They include a seventy-physician oncology network that serves 900,000 managed care patients in southern California, an eighty-five-member network of obstetricians and gynecologists in Chicago, and an ophthalmology network in New England.

These physician-led networks handle their administrative functions in many different ways. Some coordinate with another organization that markets their services; others sell their services, on a capitated basis, directly to managed care organizations; and still others buy the business support services they need from a publicly traded corporation. MedPartners, for example, which provides information and billing services primarily for capitated physician practices, had contracts with 7,250 physicians in 1996, who provided services for 1.5 million patients. In five southern California counties the company's physicians cover 6 percent of the population and 15 percent of the doctors. MedPartners, which had estimated $4.4 billion in 1996 sales revenues, is currently followed in size by PhyCor, with 1995 revenues of $856 million.

Some physician groups have even integrated forward to absorb the risks normally taken by health insurance companies. By eliminating the managed care interface, these groups hope to increase managed care's "medical-loss ratio"—the proportion of funds spent on health care—from only 75 percent to 80 or even 90 percent. They also feel that forming their own insurance companies will restore their lost autonomy. Notes one member of a radiology-focused factory group: "Doctors have almost become indentured [servants] because there is so much control by HMOs."

Physicians' groups that capitate or that fulfill the insurance function can provide an important benefit to the customer. They can eliminate the "gatekeeper," the person from whom many HMO enrollees must request permission for referrals to other sources of care. A survey found that the gatekeeper function was a significant concern to 68 percent of U.S. consumers. The sparse data available to date indicate that capitated or insurance-providing physician groups do not increase the costs of care. Indeed they likely reduce costs by eliminating the gatekeeper function.

The physicians in such groups must balance pressures coming from two directions. Their professional standards push them to provide as many services as are needed, while their economic incentives force them to contemplate the cost-effectiveness of additional expenditures. Yet because they *are* the insurers, these physicians can no longer blame managed care organizations for imposing economic constraints. These groups thus have *both* the responsibility and the ability to deliver cost-effective health care.

The process of forming such an insurance company is expensive, consuming up to $16 million, and considerable legal expenses are necessary to obtain the license that permits physicians to assume insurance risk. As a result, these enterprises are frequently partially financed by outsiders, including venture capitalists and state medical associations. MedPartners' formation of such a group in California prompted one observer to note, "We're going to see larger provider networks develop more experience in managed care and capitation, and they will be negotiating with large health plans to deliver services under capitated payments."

Reasons for Future Success

Focused factories should succeed because of their many advantages. First, they will provide higher quality health care. As a recent issue of the *American Medical News* pointed out, "the concentration of 'intellectual capital' ... is bound to pay off with better outcomes for the patients [and] the tough task for developing clinical standards can be simplified because [they] can draw more readily on a large patient population." Notes the physician who heads a large obstetricians' and gynecologists' specialty network, "We're going to be able to produce clinical outcomes data for payers and the public with almost no limits." And what gets measured, gets done.

Focused factories will also lower costs by reducing the needless proliferation of technology and hospital capital. Presently, many hospitals purchase technology and other capital items as lures to draw big-name physicians to practice there. But when these physicians run focused factories, they will use technology as it should be used—to improve the cost-effectiveness of care—and not as bait. They will shrink the hospital sector too, as they carefully select only the most cost-effective hospitals as their suppliers and limit hospital stays to the number of days needed to provide for patients' care.

Early-stage capitated physician groups have already demonstrated these cost-saving effects. A study of six large capitated medical groups in California revealed that they lowered costs, by reducing the length of hospital stays and through innovation, such as the increased use of physician assistants. Despite a recession in California at the time of the study and the consequent loss of jobs and health insurance, these groups increased their HMO enrollees by 91 percent.

Another reason focused factories will succeed is that their structure makes it possible for patients, administrators, and payers to compare the prices and quality of different providers. Today's multipurpose hospitals and physician practices provide so many services, in so many different settings, for so many different kinds of patients that it is almost impossible to disentangle the costs of the separate elements of care. Even the costs of the country's number-one surgical procedure—a birth—of which there are four million a year, are not routinely available, except from information compiled by special studies.

By contrast, a focused factory price quote generally encompasses the full menu of care required by a patient, and not only in a hospital but in an outpatient facility, the doctor's office, a pharmacy, the home, and other sites. This approach allows payers to compare the prices that different focused factories charge for providing the *full* panoply of care required by a patient. They can certainly evaluate the quality of the care provided by focused factories more readily than that provided by multipurpose providers.

The ease of evaluating the price and quality of care provided by focused factories will cause ferocious competition to break out among them. The competition will provide continual incentives for ingenious entrepreneurs to innovate new operating procedures and technologies that will give their factory a cost or quality advantage.

Finally, focused factories will substantially diminish the unneeded expenditures presently incurred because of the absence of integrated operating systems for treatment of chronic diseases. Focused factories will develop such systems and thus substantially enhance patients' quality of life.

HOW FOCUSED FACTORIES WILL BE COMPENSATED

Imagine the following scenario:

A buyer of health care coverage—let's call her Laura—for a large corporation sits down at her terminal and requests price quotes from all interested providers for complete care for nine diseases or problems and four procedures. She has chosen these items for bidding because the nine diseases and problems—

diabetes, infections, hypertension, heart failure, arthritis, osteoporosis, gastrointestinal difficulties, asthma, and mental health—
account for 73 percent of the health care costs of her corporation. She chose the four procedures—births, reproductive organ
procedures, cardiac catheterizations, and back surgery—because
they represent the most frequently occurring surgeries. Conceiv-
ably, the winning bidders could cover as much as 85 percent of
her corporate health care costs.

Laura requests that each bidder's proposal include a fixed
price quote for providing all the care required for fifty thousand
employees, along with a list of the backgrounds of their providers, the volume of services they have delivered, and their
other qualifications.

The response she receives from Diabetes Management Corporation is typical. DMC is a focused factory whose team members
work only with diabetics. It is owned by its providers, a team
composed of endocrinologists; primary care physicians; ophthalmologists and other eye care professionals; vascular surgeons,
cardiologists, and neurologists; podiatrists and physical therapists; dermatologists; nephrologists; psychiatrists and other
behavioral therapists; nurses; nutritionists; and home health
aides. They can treat all the problems diabetics are likely to encounter, including other related diseases such as kidney or heart
disease. They treat 250,000 diabetics nationwide. DMC also
owns hospitals that specialize in the procedures required by diabetic patients, like vascular surgery for lower extremities and
carotid artery and heart disease; reconstructive surgery; treatment of foot ulcers; and amputations. It also operates dialysis
centers for diabetics.

Because focused factories are not tied to bricks and mortar,
they are not nearly so expensive as hospitals to construct. Indeed,
they proliferate all over the United States. Even rural areas have
access to their services, through diagnostic equipment installed
in vans and helicopters and telemedicine. Like the others, DMC
operates a large number of centers that would provide ready
access to all of Laura's company's employees, even those in
rural areas.

DMC locates its diabetes centers in shopping malls, Laura learns, and they are open after working hours and on Saturdays. It would bring a crew of professionals into the company's work site regularly to examine and educate the diabetic employees.

As new DMC enrollees, the company's diabetic employees would receive a multidisciplinary work-up and be assigned a "team coordinator," who would support them in managing their disease. A home health aide would help them at home, if needed, and a local pharmacist would help them use their glucose test meters. Some of DMC's providers specialize in diabetic children, adolescents, and pregnant women. The diabetics who smoke or are obese can participate in the support groups that DMC sponsors. Its proposal notes that smoking is "devastating to the arteries" of diabetics and that the smoking support group has lowered the members' smoking rate to 10.4 percent, lower than the national average of 25 percent. Diabetic enrollees can also participate in DMC-sponsored "walks" at the local mall and in exercise classes.

DMC has also contracted with Diabetics Monitor, a company whose computer-based program regularly tracks its enrollees' health status and advises them about how to improve it. Diabetics Monitor has produced a video and a handbook that helps diabetics better manage their disease.

DMC studies the Diabetics Monitor reports regularly to insure that its enrollees have received all the required tests. It reports nearly 100 percent compliance with the American Diabetes Association's guidelines for testing. The *Monitor* and the *DMC Newsletter* keep enrollees apprised of the latest developments in diabetes care, such as the new pen-based insulin delivery system, a portable, refillable injection mechanism that many diabetics find easier to use.

The DMC proposal notes that in other corporations it has reduced the treatment costs of its enrollees from $9,500 to $7,500 a year over a five-year period in real dollars and absenteeism rates by 10 percent. Indeed, so confident is DMC of the efficacy of its approach that it is willing to receive part of its payment from the savings it will create. To help corporations monitor their employees' health care costs, DMC maintains information systems that trace them over time.

Laura then dials up her QualMed program to find evaluations of DMC. Her company's nearest competitor, she learns, is very contented with DMC. It has achieved the top ratings from industry quality evaluators, and its users are very satisfied with every aspect of its services. QualMed also reveals that the outcomes of the DMC are exactly as it claims: lower costs and fewer sick days.

Laura is concerned, however, about whether the successful, busy DMC staff can handle the new patient volume that her contract would bring. Moreover, some of the key providers are of relatively advanced age. "I don't want them to retire in midcourse," she thinks. She makes a note to discuss these concerns with DMC's representatives. But she has many choices—she has received responses from twenty other diabetes-focused factories as well.

Within a week she has received more than a thousand bids. With the help of her QualMed program, she checks out the quality evaluations given to each by other buyers, consumers, peers, and independent, focused factory–quality evaluating firms. She finds it easy to compare the costs of the various bidders because each has bid on the cost of providing the complete care the person requires.

Within a few months, Laura signs $120 million in contracts for these services. She supplements them with contracts for diagnostic and primary care providers that have been bid on a similar basis.

At the end of the process, she smiles. Not so long ago, she purchased health insurance and managed care contracts with little idea of what exactly she was buying. Would her employees obtain good care? Would the services be supportive, courteous, expert? She simply could not have answered these questions. All she knew was what the total insurance package cost.

Now, she not only knows exactly what she is buying, but she is paying less for it. And the employees are healthier, too. The diabetics and asthmatics who once needed so much sick time and required such expensive care, for example, are so much better now: healthier, more productive, and less costly. As for the people with cancer and heart disease who once complained bitterly about the inadequate care they were receiving in their managed care organizations, she has not heard from them for a long time. Sure, providers who deny care still exist, but the information in the QualMed program tells her pretty clearly who they are.

Focused factories like the mythical Diabetes Management Corporation are the keys to the renewal in productivity of the American health care system. They will gradually supplant many of the functions of HMOs, which will increasingly act as brokers of a sort, bundling the services of various focused factories into complete packages. And sleek, limber focused factories will likely supplant or absorb parts of those lumbering giants—the vertically integrated health care providers—many of whom will falter in competing against them.

IMPEDIMENTS TO FOCUSED FACTORIES

For all their benefits, however, the interest that insurance companies and employers will take in focused factories is uncertain, especially those for chronic diseases. For example, while Control Diabetes Centers, a diabetes-focused factory, reports that it has contracts with fifteen health plans to provide educational clinics for diabetics, the Wilkerson Group, a consulting firm, speculates that managed care organizations will not invest in a focused factory program that offers intensive management of diabetes because their large membership turnover makes such programs a poor investment. Many managed care organizations have a 20 to 25 percent turnover in membership, Wilkerson asserts, causing them to cast a dubious eye on programs that require intensive efforts in the present to avoid massive future costs.

Further, if managed care organizations—which increasingly dominate the health insurance market—do not wish to attract the chronically ill as enrollees, then they will not implement such programs. Notes an executive at Salick Health Care, "If [an HMO becomes] known as the plan that provides high-quality cancer" HMO executives will worry.

"The last thing they want is to attract more people with these diseases." Indeed, these organizations already reportedly delay referring some of their chronically ill patients to the specialists who can most directly help them. A representative of an asthma victims group notes that parents of asthmatic children enrolled in some managed care plans "end up using their primary care physician much more often . . . and when they finally do get to a qualified allergist who . . . succeeds in getting the child's asthma under control . . . they resent the years they spent seeing a pediatrician."

Large pharmaceutical companies would likely be more willing sponsors for chronic disease–focused factories. Indeed, Zeneca, a large British pharmaceutical firm that puts out a number of cancer remedies, purchased Salick Health Care so it could offer a full array of cancer services. Control Diabetes Centers is owned by the drug firm and major producer of insulin, Eli Lilly. Still, pharmaceutical firms are not ideal sponsors for focused factory programs because their self-interest lies in maximizing the use of drugs that treat chronic diseases. Although drug therapies are frequently cost-effective and deserve a major place in a focused factory's line-up of resources, an appropriate sponsor would be one whose interests lie in increasing total productivity and not primarily in increasing the sale of drugs.

The ideal sponsor—indeed, the only appropriate sponsor—of the provider-controlled chronic disease–focused factory is the user of the factory's services. It is clearly in the interest of diabetics and asthmatics themselves to enroll in a program that will increase their quality of care. If users purchased these services, moreover, they could more effectively evaluate their quality than third-party payers. But our current system, in which insurance pays for the health care services of most employed people, precludes the user from paying for such services directly. In addition, the managed care insurers who should represent the interests of chronic disease victims are unlikely to do so either, if the Wilkerson Group's reasoning is correct.

The focused factory model holds great promise for revolutionizing the delivery of procedures, such as cataract surgery or a CABG (coronary artery bypass graft), and of diagnostic and general medical care. But the concept has "powerful enemies," notes David Lothson of Paine-Webber. "It undermines existing prices and does not protect the marginally competent hospitals and physicians." And the potentially valuable chronic disease–focused factories do not, as yet, have a clear natural home in today's American health care system either. As we have seen, managed care organizations are not likely to favor them.

All in all, the present system for financing health care is unlikely to encourage the organizational innovations of focused factories that will lower costs and improve health. And the consumers who will benefit from these innovations currently lack the financial clout that could accelerate their formation.

Part 4 of this book discusses the impact of different reimbursement systems in encouraging focused factories and the important innovations in technology, convenience, and information that could increase the productivity of the U.S. economy by improving our health status and reducing our health care costs.

CHAPTER 9

Resizing and the Role of Technology

Quick: Consider the goods and services that most Americans use on a daily basis. Which one do you think most consider the best value for their money?

Okay, time is up. Did you guess cars? They are way up on the list, but they are not number one. How about TV sets? You're getting closer. But the all-time champion in value for the money is . . . poultry. Poultry was ranked number one in 1989, number one in 1992, and number one in 1994, by the 6,500 households responding to a regular consumer survey.

Now, what do you think is the worst value in the eyes of the American public? The undisputed king of the bottom dwellers is . . . hospital charges. They were rated dead last for those same three years. To judge the ignominity of this ranking, consider that even lawyers' fees were ranked slightly better than hospital charges. Other low value-for-the-money ratings were awarded to health insurance and doctors' charges. (The highest-rated medical care products were prescription drugs and eyeglasses.)

What makes chicken so special in the eyes of the American consumer and hospital charges so bad? The answer in both cases is technology. Innovations in technology have made chickens and health care better and cheaper, but because medical technology is overbought, it helps to increase hospital costs to the point that consumers rate their charges as the worst value for the money.

This chapter explores the impact of technology on health care—the good, the bad, and the ugly—in greater detail.

CHICKENS, CARS, AND COMPUTERS: CHEAPER AND BETTER

The Cheaper Cheeper

Why has poultry attained its number-one status? The reasons are several. Chicken is relatively cheap, versatile, and tasty. It is not the dreaded red meat. And it can be easily purchased at virtually all food stores. But chicken was not always the tender, readily available, relatively inexpensive morsel that it is today. It was technology that made it cheaper and better.

At one time, finding a tender chicken required such expertise that chicken-buying expeditions sharpened the shopping skills even of my "born to shop" mother. In her day, most of the birds sold were either old, grizzled, egg-laying veterans or unappetizing, fatty, neutered roosters, called capons. In search of the elusive tender chicken, my mother would grill recalcitrant butchers about the chicken's lineage and most frequently—absent a birth certificate to testify to the chicken's age—demand to see the live bird, in the flesh. Nevertheless, despite her valiant efforts, the chicken she brought home was more often than not too tough to sauté and was suitable only for the tenderizing vapors of the stew pot.

As Frank Perdue says, "it takes a tough man to make a tender chicken," or more correctly, it takes some bright scientists. Chicken breeders ultimately perfected tender chickens grown with such uniformity that they could be processed with automated equipment. The automation of processing and distribution substantially lowered costs. As a result, between 1980 and 1991 the average price that farmers received for their chickens decreased, while quality, as measured in tenderness and flavor, improved. Americans liked these chickens so much that their per capita consumption grew from 28 pounds per year in 1970 to 46 pounds in 1992.

The Cheaper and Better Car

Technology has had positive effects on the other highly rated value-for-the-money items too. Take automobiles, for example—technology has also made them relatively cheaper and better.

To judge the "better" aspects of 1996 automobiles, let's review a *Consumer Reports* comparison of their characteristics to those of the 1966 cars. *Fuel efficiency* was 27.5 miles per gallon in 1996 but 13 miles per gallon in 1966. *Tailpipe emissions* were reduced by 90 percent. *Safety equipment* was virtually nonexistent in 1966, but antilock brakes and dual air bags were nearly standard in 1996. *Ease of starting* was low in cold weather in 1966 but high in 1996. *Engine wear and tear* was also improved—1966 cars needed replacement of piston rings and valves, but these parts rarely require replacement in 1996 cars. Finally, the car's *length of life* was double in 1996 what it was in 1966.

Technological innovations have been pivotal in these improvements. A staggering cornucopia of inventions have increased cars' fuel economy. Styling improvements that reduced drag have increased their efficiency. New materials and better design of space have shrunk a car's weight without squeezing its passenger space. And computer-based sensors and microprocessors have relieved engine friction (which accounts for about half of fuel use), tightened the adjustment of the valve intake and exhaust processes, and created a more efficient relationship between the transmission and the engine. Technological innovations have also decreased the relative cost of cars. Thus, while in 1960–61 vehicle purchase expenses accounted for almost 14 percent of the average family's expenditures for current consumption, by 1987 they had dropped to 8 percent of the average. As cars became cheaper and better, automobile ownership grew from 34 cars per 100 people in 1960 to 56 in 1993.

The Better and "Chipper" Computer

In my own lifetime I have personally witnessed the dramatic impact of technology on lowering the costs of and improving the quality of computers.

When I graduated from college in the 1960s, computers were large holy icons. They required special air-conditioned sanctuaries to house them and specially trained acolytes to service them. I spent seemingly endless dull hours punching data onto cards that served as the computer's nourishment. Yet the sanctified object's performance seemed hardly worth the effort. At that time computers were capable mostly of mundane, number-crunching applications—accounting, payroll records, and relatively trivial programs. They were expensive too—so costly that only large corporations and institutions could afford them. The PDP-1, introduced by DEC in 1959 and hailed as a revolutionary advance that made computers available to smaller companies, had only four kilobytes of memory and cost $120,000.

Fast forward to 1994. With the relentless pace of innovation, the costs of data processing have plunged. In 1982 Intel's 286 microprocessor could handle a million instructions per minute at a cost of $360. Eleven years later its Pentium chip cost more, $950, but it could handle a hundred times as many instructions per minute as the 1964 model. And today's computers have even bigger and cheaper memories. Most 1996 personal computers are outfitted with about 18 megabytes of memory. The wholesale cost of 8 megabytes dropped from $425 in 1990 to $100 in the first quarter of 1996.

Today the sanctuaries, acolytes, and punchcards that I knew as a student have completely disappeared. Computers are now household objects. In 1995 Intel's Pentium Pro microprocessor virtually completed the computer's transformation from icon to everyday object. Today's PCs are as powerful as once-expensive workstations. With their soaring powers and decreasing costs, it is small wonder that personal computer ownership increased from 7 percent of households in 1983 to an estimated 37 percent in 1994.

THE COST-REDUCING EFFECTS OF MEDICAL TECHNOLOGIES

In contrast to the cost-reducing impact of technology on chickens, cars, and computers, most health policy experts firmly believe that medical technologies are the root cause of excessive health care costs. Some cite the greater abundance of technology in the United States than in other developed countries or argue that medical technology innovations are so inherently cost-increasing that they will cause health care costs to continue climbing even after all the waste and inefficiency has been wrung out of the system.

This view of the cost-increasing impact of technology in the health care sector contradicts the experience of most other modern industries, where technology has reduced relative costs or, more precisely, increased incomes more than costs. Indeed, the Industrial Revolution, which lifted the ancestors of many readers and certainly the ancestors of the author of this book out of poverty and into a huge, new middle class, was fueled by technological innovations. Even today we benefit from continued inventions that diminish the amount of labor needed to produce goods and services, vastly increase their availability, and reduce the ratio of their costs to our income. Why would medical technology differ from other technologies in its impact? If chickens, cars, and computers are better, relatively cheaper, and much more available largely because of technology, why has technology failed to replicate these results in the health care sector?

The answer is that while many new medical technologies have reduced health care costs, they have been so pervasively purchased by health care institutions—some of which use them very little—that they have increased costs as well. Imagine, for example, that PCs were so widely owned that every person in the United States had a few of them. The new PCs would still deliver more bit for the byte than in the past, but their newly widespread ownership would considerably dull their cost-reducing impact.

Then, too, analyses that purport to measure the *costs* of medical technology frequently base their conclusions on the *prices* of the technology. The cost data needed for such analyses are not available in most health care institutions. In most industries interchanging costs and prices would not be a severe problem, because prices ultimately reflect costs. In price-competitive industries, when prices are set much higher than costs, the large profit margins that result attract new providers, who then discount the price to compete for customers. This Economics 101 competition, in most industries, ultimately makes prices reflect costs. But because the health care industry did not compete primarily on the basis of price, analyses that have concluded that medical technology raises *costs* may actually be demonstrating that in an industry that is not price-competitive, new technology enables providers to raise their *prices*.

I will discuss these separate aspects of the cost impact of medical technology—the intrinsic cost-effectiveness of some medical technology; the impact of its needless proliferation; and how health care providers use technology to raise their prices—below.

MINIMALLY INVASIVE SURGERIES (MIS)

It's Not Nice to Fool With Mother Nature

Do you remember the late-1960s clip of President Lyndon Johnson pulling up his shirt to display the scar left on his ample belly from his gall bladder operation? President Johnson was as justly proud of his scar as the other survivors of the grueling surgical procedures of that time. Perhaps your elderly relatives had vivid and lengthy recollections of their own "operations."

Why did they all find operations so traumatic?

Most surgery is performed to remove a diseased, unnatural, or debilitated part of the body—an inflamed appendix, a malfunctioning kidney, the stretched-out part of a blood vessel, or the calcified section of a joint. Sometimes its purpose is to insert a replacement part—an artificial hip, a new heart valve, an elastic tube or piece of a blood vessel, or a new organ. President Johnson and your kin found surgery traumatic because clever Mother Nature designed our bodies to foil invaders like surgeons. To protect us from disease-carrying injuries, she buried the key parts of our anatomy deep inside the body and covered them with a sturdy sheath of skin, muscle, connective tissue, and bone, then a cushioning layer of fat. She even laid in an alarm system, our nerves, that cause us to scream with pain whenever the security of this protective sheath is breached.

Mother Nature does not take kindly to violations of her defenses. When deft inventors developed anesthetics to knock out the body's alarm system, Mother Nature retaliated: early anesthetics induced virulent responses, ranging from nausea to death. She built in many other defenses against invaders too. She punished patients who permitted surgeons to probe inside their bodies by making sure that the doctors left daunting mementos of their visit: trauma to surrounding tissues, infections of the open cavities, and ugly scars. Patients who endured operations thus learned painfully that it is not nice to fool with Mother Nature.

No wonder President Johnson was so proud of his scar. Even the removal of a gall bladder was a big deal in those days. Nor was the cost of such procedures a minor matter. In 1984 a surgeon charged $1,000 for a gall bladder operation, to which the hospital would likely add $2,000 to $4,000 for the use of the operating theater and a semi-private room. The resulting expenditure of up to $5,000 equaled about a fourth of the median income of American households in that year. Not only was surgery expensive, it required lengthy hospital stays that busy and burdened consumers found increasingly difficult to manage.

The New Technologies

Nevertheless, for many years people endured traumatic and expensive "operations." After all, frequently the only alternative to surgery was death, debilitation, or pain. But recent technological innovations dramatically changed all that, greatly reducing the trauma of surgery, the time needed for recuperation, and its cost.

LIGHTS, CAMERA, ACTION The key innovation came from a most unexpected source—the plastic industry, the same one we laughed at in the film *The Graduate*, when the boorish businessman advises Dustin Hoffman that the future lies in plastic.

Looking back over some thirty years, it appears that the businessman was prescient. Plastics revolutionized surgery with small plastic rods, that are inserted through catheters (tubes) into natural body cavities—such as the mouth, penis, vagina, and nose—or into small holes punched into the body. These rods are fiberoptic light sources that illuminate the surgical site for the miniature cameras (endoscopes) and small surgical instruments that are also inserted through catheters. When these lights and cameras reach the surgical site, the surgeon can spring into action, using small instruments to operate, while watching the image of the site on a screen.

The plastic tubes that enabled these minimally invasive surgeries were as revolutionary as the canals that ushered in the Industrial Revolution. They facilitated the distribution of needed products through existing modes of transportation and created a revolution in the process.

NONINVASIVE DIAGNOSTICS AND THERAPY Other technological innovations also helped to reduce the trauma and costs of surgery. Computer technology automated not only the tiny camera sent down the catheter but many other devices that can diagnose or monitor the body's functioning without violently breaching its defenses.

New diagnostic instruments produce clear, crisp pictures of the soft tissue buried deep within the body that once could be seen only during exploratory surgery. Powerful computers reconstruct the information produced by the different forms of energy sent into the body to diagnose its contents. Sonar instruments image the heart and distinguish a malignant tumor from a harmless growth, a healthy embryo from a malformed one. CT (pronounced *cat*, an abbreviation for computerized axial tomography) scanners use X rays to detect subtle differences in tissue densities. And magnetic resonance imagers (MRIs) use electromagnetism (or more precisely, the interaction between external electromagnetic fields and those of the atomic nuclei of body tissues) to image tissues. Small chips and other electronic instruments power miniaturized monitoring devices, such as the noninvasive pulse-oximeters that can monitor the patient's blood oxygenation without puncturing the skin.

These computer-based devices have eliminated not only many exploratory surgeries but some of the world's worst diagnostic procedures. For example, the late, unlamented pneumoencephalogram was a particularly gruesome procedure that was used to detect masses growing in the brain. The procedure began with an injection of a gas into the patient's spine. The patient was then strapped into a chair and catapulted into various positions that caused the gas to flow into the normally fluid-filled cavities in the brain. The gas-filled cavities were then visualized. As Dr. James Rhea, an associate professor of radiology at the Harvard Medical School vividly puts it, this "procedure almost inevitably resulted in the mother of all headaches." It has been completely replaced by MRI and CT techniques.

Dr. Jonathan Kleefield, an associate professor of radiology at the Harvard Medical School and director of neuroradiology at Boston's Beth Israel Hospital, recalls the terrors of the cerebral angiography procedure that was once exclusively used to diagnose brain blood vessel abnormalities. The procedure relied on a catheter that was inserted through a puncture in an artery in the groin and then navigated through the body to its destination near the brain. For many of those who required the procedure, this trip through the circulatory system was laden with hazards because of atherosclerosis, a disease that deposits plaques onto artery walls. As the catheter snaked its way to its destination, it might inadvertently dislodge the plaque, causing a blockage of the circulatory system and a potentially lethal stroke.

Because MRIs have diminished the need for this procedure, Dr. Kleefield observes "with pride and a certain amount of relief" that "virtually none of the procedures that I learned to perform twenty years ago are used in my practice today. We now have tools that provide far more information with considerably less patient risk. The great diagnostic sensitivity and specificity of these examinations significantly diminishes the number of tests necessary to arrive at a precise diagnosis, with attendant cost reduction."

THE SELECTIVE PAINKILLERS Yet another technological advance that has significantly lessened the trauma of surgery is the anesthesia agents that selectively desensitize parts of the body that are likely to feel pain, replacing the general anesthesia that required sedation of the whole corpus, especially the brain.

Selective or regional anesthesia confers many benefits. General anesthesia is like a knock-out punch that sedates not only the body's nervous system but other vital systems, such as the circulatory, respiratory, and digestive systems. When these important systems are slowed, the patient can develop emboli—blood clots that can choke off circulation—or cardiac or breathing difficulties. The constipation that sometimes accompanies anesthesia because of the sedation of the digestive system is a minor difficulty compared with these much more serious problems.

Regional anesthesia significantly diminishes some of these life-threatening dangers associated with general anesthesia because it selectively targets the knock-out sites. Various regional anesthesia agents relieve constipation associated with abdominal surgery and may reduce the severity of pulmonary complications; diminish death from heart problems, when used after an operation; and may well deter thrombi and the deterioration of mental functions that sometimes accompany general anesthesia. Regional anesthesia can also be used for virtually pain-free recovery, precluding the use of opiates and sedatives which infirm patients poorly tolerate. It thus leads to faster, less complicated recovery.

A Tale of Cabbages and Angioplasties:
An Example of Catheter-Based Surgery

New forms of surgery were made possible by fiber optics, computer-based and miniaturized instruments, and regional anesthetics. Once some of these marvels were developed, MIS techniques rapidly supplanted many older invasive ("open") procedures. The pace of the change was staggering. For example, 80 to 90 percent of all gall bladder removals are now performed laparascopically.

Because MIS procedures do not require long periods of recuperation, they are typically performed in sites other than the in-patient section of a hospital. Of the estimated 29 million surgeries in 1994, 65 percent were completed outside the hospital walls, reversing the ratio that held a mere decade earlier. An increasing number of these out-of-the-hospital surgeries are conducted in doctors' offices or in free-standing facilities that are not affiliated with a hospital. In 1994 more than 5 million surgical procedures were performed in these sites. The top fifteen outpatient surgeries include cataract removal, inguinal hernia repair, and knee arthroscopy for the Medicare population.

Why has MIS diffused so quickly and widely? Because it has greatly reduced the trauma, cost, and recuperation time of surgery. Its appeal can be clearly illustrated by comparing two procedures to unclog coronary arteries and enhance the flow of blood to the heart: an old open procedure and one performed with a catheter.

People with blocked-up, compromised coronary arteries (the arteries that supply the heart muscle itself with oxygenated blood) typically endure symptoms ranging from shortness of breath to acute pain, as if their chest were caught in a vise. If these symptoms are not relieved, they may well die. The open procedure to bypass the blockage, called a CABG (for coronary artery bypass graft) and pronounced *cabbage,* bypasses the clogged-up portion of the artery with a section of a healthier blood vessel, taken from a vein in the leg or an artery beneath the breastbone.

If the leg vein is used to bypass the coronary artery, one surgical team opens the leg, from the groin to the ankle, to remove the vein, hands it to the operating team, and then carefully closes the long incision. Meanwhile, another surgical team exposes the heart by cutting through the fat, muscle, and skin of the chest wall and sawing through the large breastbone that protects the heart. Retractors forcibly hold the chest open as the gunked-up portion of the coronary artery is bypassed with segments snipped from the leg vein. The surgeon completes the procedure by closing up the chest and applying a dressing. Because the vibration of a beating heart does not permit the surgeon to perform the exquisitely careful snipping and stitching that this procedure requires, the patient's heart is usually stopped for the duration and an external heart-lung machine takes over its function. After the procedure is completed, the stilled heart is spurred back into action with warming or electrical shock.

CABG patients typically display two badges of their courage: a scar on their leg and another on their chest. They sometimes may also carry a third memento: a scar on their throat, which marks the site where a ventilator tube was inserted to help them breathe after the operation. A CABG usually requires three to four hours in the operating room; a minimum of four to five days of recuperation in the hospital; a surgical team consisting of a heart surgeon and resident, anesthesiologists, a nurse anesthetist, a perfusionist to oversee the heart-lung machine, and at least two other nurses or technologists; and recovery in an intensive care unit staffed with highly trained nurses and cardiologists. Small wonder the 1992 hospital charge for a CABG was $40,800.

Let us contrast the CABG with a catheter-based procedure, also used to improve blood flow through the coronary arteries, called coronary angioplasty (also called PTCA, or percutaneous transluminal coronary angioplasty). In this procedure a radiologist or cardiologist snakes a catheter through a tiny opening, made in the artery in the groin, up to the coronary artery. Contrast media enable the physician to watch the catheter's progress through the vascular system to its destination. When the catheter reaches the gunked-up portion of the coronary artery, a collapsed balloon, cleverly furled along the catheter, is positioned so that it straddles the blocked-up section of the vessel. *Poof*—the balloon is then inflated to distend the artery at the plaque. It is then deflated and removed along with the catheter.

The total time required for an angioplasty ranges from one to two hours. It is typically performed on an outpatient basis and requires only mild sedation and local anesthesia.

Because angioplasties are so much easier on the patient than CABG procedures, their use exploded shortly after their introduction. Their rapid growth raised many concerns of inappropriate use, but a 1993 series of articles in the *Journal of the American Medical Association* showed that the rates of inappropriate and uncertain use of both CABGs and angioplasties were very low.

The cost differentials between CABGs and angioplasties are significant, if somewhat eroded by the reclogging of the artery that sometimes follows angioplasty and, less frequently, CABG procedures. The reclogging requires additional procedures. But if price provides a surrogate for cost, in the worst of cases, even with repeated procedures, the total price charged for angioplasty is only 75 percent of that for a CABG. This significant cost differential is likely replicated for many other surgeries. After all, many MIS procedures require fewer resources than open ones: less time in the hospital, less time for recuperation, a smaller team of assistants, and an outpatient setting for several procedures.

But the diminished resources are not the sole economic difference between the two types of procedures. More important, procedures like angioplasties enhance national productivity because they enable people to return to work more quickly. In a sample of 72 patients, the median angioplasty patient returned to work in 18 days, whereas those who had a CABG recuperated for 54 days before returning to work. More recently, Dr. Peter Madras, a vascular surgeon and associate professor at the Harvard Medical School, noted that in his experience patients fortunate enough to be candidates for angioplasty typically remain in the hospital overnight and can return to work in a matter of days.

Minimally Invasive Surgery and the Quality of Care

When MIS and other new technologies were introduced, some physicians worried about the poor quality of these procedures. At that time, legitimate grounds for concern existed. After all, MIS obligates physicians to learn new ways of performing their work, and some of the MIS techniques are tricky to master. Surgeons have to learn to operate while looking up at a two-dimensional screen rather than down into a three-dimensional body opening. The small openings that characterize minimally invasive surgery add further difficulties: They restrict surgeons' mobility and their ability to gauge the pressure they are applying and the resistance they are encountering.

Clearly, physicians who have performed hundreds of these new procedures are likely to be much more proficient than those who have performed only a few of them. As with any other new technology, quality concerns are nearly inevitable just after their introduction, but they generally abate as the technology diffuses and the users' expertise increases. Indeed, after reviewing the records of nearly 39,000 patients, authoritative Mayo Clinic researchers concluded that the overall death and complication rates from ambulatory surgery and innovative anesthesia techniques were very low.

Impact on Costs

Although MIS procedures are generally of high quality and reduce trauma and recuperation time, one concern about their prevalence has proved valid. In certain cases, the ease of an MIS procedure has substantially increased its use. For example, one health insurer discovered that its total charges for treatment of gall bladder disease had increased after MIS techniques were introduced. Although the MIS technique itself cost less per surgery because it reduced the hospital stay significantly, the insurer's total charges increased because of the substantial increase in the number of procedures performed. In a five-year period its total medical expenditures for gall bladder disease actually inflated by 11.4 percent. Yet this HMO's charges for other MIS procedures, such as hernia procedures and appendectomies, either did not increase or increased only moderately.

Why was the growth in charges restricted to gall bladder operations? Likely the new procedure increased the desirability of the operation to patients, who in the past had suffered in silence. To envision what "suffering in silence" means, consider that gall bladder disease can occur when gallstones develop in the gall bladder and may also get trapped in the narrow ducts that lead from the gall bladder. The trapped stones can cause severe pain, either from spasms or from infection. One well-known symptom is pain that becomes a midnight visitor. In unusually severe cases the infection caused by the trapped stones can cause the gall bladder to perforate, spewing its poisonous contents into other parts of the body.

Many people endured this awful pain in silence, however, because the classic open surgery was so onerous. It required a five- to eight-inch slit through which the gall bladder was removed, a five-to-seven-day hospital stay, and four to six weeks of recuperation. Patients who lacked health insurance had to pay a $10,000 fee too. An MIS gall bladder procedure, in contrast, requires a shorter stay, far smaller incisions, and only one to two weeks of recuperation. And the likelihood of death is reduced by 59 percent.

MIS innovations likely increase the volume of surgery primarily in cases where the new procedure is so much quicker and less traumatic than its predecessor that patients who once would have preferred to live in pain will elect to have it. So does MIS increase or decrease costs?

The MIS procedure did appear to increase the HMO's payments for treatment of gall bladder disease after it was introduced. The lower *price* per procedure was apparently overwhelmed by the increased *volume*. But total *costs* do not necessarily increase as a result of increased volume. Although the *prices* paid by the HMO for the treatment of gall bladder disease increased with the MIS technique, *prices* measure only the hospital's best guess about the amount the insurer is willing to pay for the procedure. *Costs*, by contrast, measure the real economic value of the additional resources consumed to provide the service. From a societal perspective we should be concerned with health care *costs* and not only with the *prices* that providers charge.

How do hospitals price their MIS procedures? Administrators probably peg them at only slightly lower prices than those they charged for their open surgical counterparts. MIS procedures are highly preferred by patients, the administrators may reason, so why should we charge less than for an open procedure? After all, the insurer, not the patient, will pay for the surgery, so patients will demand the MIS procedure regardless of our price.

Even if the *price* of an MIS procedure is about the same as the price of an open procedure it supplanted, the incremental *costs* may be lower, or higher, or the same. My evaluation of the resources they use suggests that MIS procedures cost substantially less. A review of the scant available hospital cost data indicates that *total* hospital costs would increase only if the number of MIS procedures increase by 67 percent over the invasive ones.*

But the volume increase in gall bladder procedures that the HMO experienced did not approach this level. If its experiences can be generalized, the likely impact of MIS has been to *reduce* total hospital costs. Of course, it also enhances national productivity by shortening recuperation times significantly.

THE COST-REDUCING EFFECTS OF VACCINES AND DRUGS

Vaccines and pharmaceuticals have also played a major role in reducing health care costs. Some of these products have virtually eliminated deadly, expensive diseases. Vaccines have almost completely wiped out polio—the last case of polio in the Americas was in Peru in 1991—and they decreased the rates of diphtheria, whooping cough, and measles to their lowest level in the United States in 1993. Drugs have greatly reduced the pain and trauma of many diseases. In the 1920s syphilis and various respiratory illnesses, like pneumonia and tuberculosis, accounted for a substantial proportion of deaths. But antibiotics have greatly diminished the damage these diseases cause. After the discovery of antibiotics, their prevalence and impact dropped; for example, antibiotics helped the the death rate from syphilis to plummet from 17 deaths per 100,000 people in 1920 to 1 in 1980.

More recently developed pharmaceuticals abate the damage caused by hardening of the arteries, high blood pressure, emphysema,

---

* In 1993 hospitals incurred an average of 30 cents in direct expenses for each dollar of surgical charges. These direct expenses represent the cost of those resources that are clearly used for surgical purposes; the remaining monies are used to cover the general expenses of administering the hospital and to provide profits. The ratio of the direct expenses of inpatient surgery to revenues was 40 percent and of ambulatory surgery 24 percent. Using these data, and the assumption that prices for MIS equal those of inpatient surgery, the total direct cost of MIS will exceed those of open surgeries when the volume of minimally-invasive surgeries rises by 67 percent [1.67 = (.40)/(.24).] (American Hospital Association. *Monitrend II Data.* Chicago, Ill.: American Hospital Association, 1993.)

My analysis of the cost data for open and MIS gallbladder surgeries provided by Richard Siegrist of Healthcare Decision Technology in Acton, Massachusetts confirmed these ratios. In some hospitals, his data showed that MIS costs were as low as forty percent of open surgical procedure costs. (Rick Siegrist, letter to author, July 26, 1996.)

and ulcers. A new class of ulcer medications, introduced in 1977, reduced the number of operations from 97,000 to a mere 19,000 ten years later and even fewer now. The drugs clocked in at a cost of $900 per patient, while ulcer surgery costs about $30,000. Lipid-lowering drugs can reduce and may even reverse coronary artery disease, according to an analysis of ten studies involving 2,095 patients. At a cost of between $1,300 and $4,000, these drugs may prove more cost-effective than CABGs and coronary angioplasties. Finally, a drug that helps schizophrenics reduced the average cost of their care by $23,000 a year. The recently developed drug enables them to stay out of the hospitals in which they once occupied 25 percent of all psychiatric beds.

Some states have restricted their Medicaid participants' access to drugs, with results that testify to the cost-effectiveness of pharmaceuticals. One extensive analysis demonstrated that such restrictions caused a 28.7 percent increase in physician expenditures and a 39 percent increase in inpatient mental hospital expenses. (Many of the states limit drugs that enable outpatient treatment of mental illness). The authors concluded that "the adoption of a policy [that restricts access to drugs] might actually increase overall Medicaid expenditures." Another study of the effects of limiting schizophrenics' access to drugs found that the increases in the costs of mental health services exceeded the savings in drug expenditures by a factor of more than seventeen.

THE PREVALENCE OF MEDICAL TECHNOLOGY

If medical technologies reduce health care costs, why does the American public rate hospital charges as the worst value for the money? Why hasn't technology affected their perceptions in the same way as it has for chickens and cars?

Some may point to the high costs of our health care system as the answer. Despite its high costs, our system superficially resembles those of other countries whose citizens think too little is spent on their health care system. Indeed, in some ways, Americans have access to fewer health care resources and use them less than do citizens of other developed countries. One might conjecture that our health care costs are so high because we use more of its most expensive component, the hospital, or because we have more hospital capacity than other developed countries. But *au contraire,* fewer beds were available per 1,000 population in the United States than in many other countries, and Americans were admitted to hospitals at lower rates than Germans and British.

Hospitalized Americans were discharged much more quickly than hospital patients elsewhere too. In 1987, for example, the number of days in the typical stay in British, Canadian, and German hospitals was in the mid-teens, while the American length of stay has been in single digits since 1964. In the 1990s the average American spent fewer than half as many days in the hospital as people in other developed countries.

Nor do Americans see their doctors more frequently than do Europeans and Japanese. To the contrary, in 1990 U.S. physician visits per person were substantially lower than those in Germany and somewhat lower than in Canada and France. The ratio of physicians to the population is lower in the United States than in most European countries except for the U.K. and Austria.

Lose–Lose?

Are we to conclude, then, that Americans complain about high hospital charges because we have the worst of all possible cases—a health care system that costs more and yet delivers fewer services than its leaner neighbors?

Apparently the American public does not think it delivers fewer services. To the contrary, despite their qualms about hospital charges, the public perceives that their health care system intrinsically delivers more than the European, Canadian, and Japanese systems—that it has more advanced technology, more convenience, and more care for the very sick. People in most other countries corroborate this perception. They find that their countries spend too little money for these important purposes, and they want more spent for hospitalizations, more for advanced medical technology, and more for the terminally ill.

Are Americans really getting more from their health care system? If so, where is it? After all, superficial evidence indicates that Americans receive fewer health care services, such as physician visits and lengths of stay in the hospital, not more, and that they pay more for them too—a classic lose-lose situation.

Fly Me to the Moon

To find the answer, let's visit a typical American hospital. It resembles few average hospitals elsewhere in the world. Our hospitals are the Cape Canaverals of the hospital world, loaded with the very latest in medical technology. Not surprisingly, they are vastly more expensive than others. The 1987 annual total expense per American hospital bed, $183,000, was more than three times as high as the expense in Germany, and four times higher than that of Canada.

Where does all this money go? A considerable amount is spent on outfitting American hospitals with the very latest in medical technology. Our ownership of medical devices dwarfs that of most other countries. For example, we had eleven multimillion-dollar MRIs per million people, while the U.K. and Canada owned only 1 machine per million, and West Germany only 3. Granted, MRIs are wonderful instruments that can provide crisp, clear pictures of our innards without surgery or pernicious X rays—but do we need so many of them? Similarly, in 1990 we owned 27 per million population of the wonderful but expensive CT scanners that enable doctors to see our innermost soft-body tissues without performing surgery, but West Germany had only 12, Canada 7, and the U.K. 4.

American doctors perform more high-technology, high-cost medical and surgical procedures too. While our cardiac surgeons completed 1,000 coronary bypass procedures per million people in 1991, their U.K. and French counterparts performed only about 400 and those in West Germany only 500. And while American cardiologists conducted nearly 1,200 procedures per million people to unclog coronary arteries, those in West Germany did fewer than half that number; those in Canada, about a third; and those in the U.K., about a seventh. We do more of other surgical procedures, too, than the Europeans. In 1980 proportionately more Americans than Europeans had a hysterectomy or hernia repair.

All Dressed Up and Nowhere to Go?

Clearly, the American health care system costs more because it has much more technology than other systems, and we use it more too. The question is whether the usage is appropriate. Do we use the technology because we need it or because it is there? The answer is important—

critics of our system assert that we are awash in wasteful technology that we use to excess.

If these critics are correct, our European and Canadian neighbors present a model of how to ration technology and keep down health care costs. "Just say no" is their motto: no to massive investments in medical research; no to purchases of medical technology; and no to seriously ill users who might need that technology—especially if they are elderly. In the U.K., for example, people over 60 are not eligible for heart transplants through the government operated health care system, although they pay the taxes that support this health care system. These desperately ill people must either pay for an expensive heart transplant out of their own pockets or die.

But, if our medical technology meets our needs and the critics of waste are wrong, then the rationing models elsewhere may not be appropriate for us after all. Indeed, the comparisons of technology use in the United States and in other developed countries discussed below suggest that the United States uses technology appropriately.

Many studies, to be sure, have demonstrated that the availability of medical resources is associated with their use, implying that the supply of medical resources creates its own unnecessary demand. But a careful examination of these studies shows that their authors are very cautious about specifying the appropriate use of medical technology. One researcher who studied the records of nearly ten thousand New York State patients who came to a hospital with a heart attack found that those treated in hospitals that were equipped with the technology that is needed to perform procedures like angioplasty or bypass surgery were much more likely to receive them than patients in hospitals that lacked such technology. Do these findings imply that the patients in areas of high availability of technology receive *unnecessary* services? No. As the researcher carefully notes, "It is worth emphasizing ... that there is no way of specifying what a clinically justifiable, or 'right' rate of service use might be in this population. . . . It is impossible to know (absent comprehensive data on costs and benefits) whether use rates in some groups are 'better' than those in others."

The rate of cardiac procedures is approximately three times higher in the United States than in Canada. One may interpret this difference in one of two ways: either we provide excessive health care or the

Canadians provide an insufficient amount. Which is it? A 1994 *Journal of the American Medical Association* found low rates of inappropriate use of cardiac procedures in both Canada and New York State. Because we performed more procedures and few were judged inappropriate, a logical conclusion from these findings is that the Canadians performed too few cardiac procedures. Who was left out in Canada? While the study did not identify them, it did note that people over 75 and women received proportionately fewer cardiac procedures in Canada than in the United States. Presumably because of the shortages in technology availability, Canadians also waited longer for health care; while 70 percent of the U.S. patients with left main coronary artery disease were operated on within 7 days, 70 percent of Canadians waited for 31 to 60 days. These delays not only lengthened the patients' period of pain and anxiety but caused a threefold increase in the risk of death or of a nonfatal heart attack.

Many technologies confer benefits that enhance the quality of life. A comparison between Americans and Canadians who underwent invasive cardiac procedures after a heart attack concluded that the Canadians, who had fewer procedures, had more cardiac symptoms and worse functional status a year after the heart attack. The study evaluated the benefits of the larger number of cardiac procedures performed on Americans than Canadians who had a heart attack. After one year, it concluded, the Americans enjoyed a significantly higher quality of life than did the Canadians. The median American returned to work twenty-three days sooner than the median Canadian, and while only 37 percent of Americans reported changes in work status due to health, 57 percent of the Canadians did so. The Canadians also reported significantly more chest pain and shortness of breath than the Americans.

These differences in quality of life were not attributable solely to the greater rate of cardiac procedures. The health status of Americans who did not undergo cardiac procedures also improved more than the Canadians, perhaps because they were more likely to be treated by a specialist. After all, in 1992 Canada had only half the number of cardiologists to serve each person as the United States.

Conversely, problems caused by technology shortages outside the United States abound. The Canadian health care system, for example, delayed the introduction of an important drug to combat the debilitating anemia that frequently accompanies dialysis for a year after it was approved in the United States.

I do not mean to pick on Canada. That country's health care system is filled with fine physicians and hospitals, but it *is* short of technology. Unfortunately, Canada is hardly the only place that delays or denies medical treatment for its citizens. A *New York Times* story noted that the United Kingdom's health care system seriously under-treats its cancer victims. Despite lower rates of tobacco consumption, the death rate for lung cancer among men was 10 percent higher there than in the United States and more than twice as high for men and women with stomach cancer, in the period 1987–1990. These differences could well be linked to significant differences in access to specialist physicians in the two countries. While the United States has 6,000 cancer specialists, the United Kingdom has only 300 to serve one-fourth as many people. Only 40 percent of the United Kingdom's cancer patients get to see specialists.

But if technology confers so many benefits, why are the average life spans in the United States only marginally longer than those in the United Kingdom and Germany, and why are they lower than Canada's? Notions of American life spans are likely affected by our relatively high rate of infant mortality. Although we spend enormous sums to prolong the lives of sick babies—their care accounts for 13 percent of hospital days even in the most stringently managed hospital, and a 1993 average stay in a neonatal unit could cost as much as $54,000—we also have much higher rates of teenage pregnancies, and resulting low-birthweight, higher-risk babies, than other countries. Our rates of teen-age pregnancies are approximately double those of the United Kingdom and Canada, and our percentage of low-birthweight babies is 12 percent higher than the United Kingdom's and 34 percent higher than Germany's and Canada's. Thus, the high infant mortality rates that impact our average life span are heavily influenced by our socio-demographic characteristics. Our average life spans might be even lower, were it not for our massive spending on technology to prolong the lives of these at-risk infants.

The positive aspect of our technology's effect on longevity becomes apparent for people who have reached 80. At that age American men can look forward to at least 15 percent more years of life than can

Germans and British. The differential odds of long life increase even for Americans over 90: A white 90-year-old American woman has a 40 percent chance of living to 95, for example, while a white Swedish woman of 90 has a 31 percent chance of reaching that age. A careful analysis of the reasons for these differences concluded that other countries are "controlling or restricting access" to technology to older people, who "would be most vulnerable" to these restrictions. While some may question whether this use of technology is appropriate, the point is that technology helps Americans to achieve longer average life spans than is commonly appreciated.

All in all, these studies offer clear support for the conclusion that our system, with its readily available medical technology and specialists, enables old, young, and in-between Americans to enjoy a better quality of life.

WHY AMERICANS RATE HOSPITAL CHARGES AS THE WORST VALUE FOR THE MONEY

If American hospitals provide an appropriate level of technology that improves the quality of life, then why are Americans so sour about the value for the money they receive? After all, they clearly appreciate medical technology. So what is the problem?

Simply put, Americans think hospitals spend too much money—much too much. Many American hospitals are too big—they have too many beds, too much technology, too many expenses—and the public knows it. As a result, hospital users in effect get hit with a double whammy: They pay both for the use of the hospital and for the hospital's excessive capacity.

The American hospital system, with 1995 occupancy of only 59.7 percent, is like a lavishly outfitted jumbo jet that flies only two-thirds full on its average trip. Although some extra capacity is needed for emergencies, the evidence of unnecessary excess capacity is substantial. One careful analysis in 1993 found that between 6 and 50 percent of the hospital beds in twenty major urban areas served no purpose. (And the number of unneeded beds is likely to increase, as clever scientists and engineers devise new drugs that keep people healthy and new MIS procedures and equipment that reduce or eliminate the need for hospitalization.) There is also some evidence of operational inefficiencies; another study claimed that eliminating the inefficiencies in hospital expenses, such as the resources expended by administrative and communication functions, could have saved $60 billion annually. A sophisticated analysis of 1987 data from more than 4,000 hospitals revealed an inefficiency level of 13.6 percent. Eliminating this inefficiency would have reduced 1991 hospital expenditures by $31 billion, the authors asserted.

Careful analyses by Jack Ashby of the U.S. Congress Prospective Payment Assessment Commission have demonstrated that hospital productivity declined from 1985 through 1993. In 1993, it declined by 2.3 percent, even while hospitals reduced the services they provided per admission (their intensity of care) by nearly 2 percent, primarily through reduced lengths of stay. In other words, in 1993, hospitals provided fewer services per admission and required more resources to do so. A 16 percent growth in the number of salaried physicians and a 10 percent climb in the number of administrators, perhaps because of the increase in integrated physician-hospital ventures at that time, caused labor inputs to rise by 2.4 percent. Supply and service and capital inputs grew even faster.

Other American industries experienced much better productivity statistics. Both the service and manufacturing sectors substantially exceeded the hospital sector labor productivity gains in the period 1980 through 1992.

Aggregate hospital productivity changes are not available in the period 1994 to 1995. During that time, hospital labor productivity increased at record levels, but capital costs grew at a faster rate. Again, the growth in integrated facilities may explain this rise in capital costs.

Although, like other productivity data, these data do not account for changes in the quality of care, whether for better or worse, they do suggest productivity concerns. In other words, hospitals spent too much, just as the American people thought they did.

Despite the need to reduce our hospital capacity and expenses, however, hospitals have so far hung in there to a remarkable extent. While the length of a hospital stay plummeted between 1984 and 1994, the average number of beds per hospital declined by only 2.3 percent. The number of hospital personnel actually increased, from 3.1 million in 1983 to 3.6 million in 1992. Hospital administrators account for the largest percentage of this increase in personnel, with their number almost doubling during this period. Their earnings increased rapidly too. In a year in which general inflation, as measured by the consumer price index, rose by about 2.8 percent, their compensation rose by 5.5 percent. Top hospital administrators are well compensated for their efforts: In 1993, on the average, the CEOs of multihospital systems received $400,000 in total compensation, while the CEOs of stand-alone hospitals earned $243,000. In view of these statistics, it is not surprising that the administrative expenses of a sample group of hospitals in western Pennsylvania grew from 14.6 percent of costs in 1983 to 20 percent in 1990.

In many ways these administrators earned their keep. For one thing they managed to maintain 1993 hospital profit levels at 5.4 percent, despite decreases in utilization and excessive capacity. In 1992 the U.S. hospital sector, which is primarily composed of not-for-profit institutions, nevertheless earned nearly $12 billion in profits. Meanwhile, the amount that nonprofit hospitals spent on uncompensated care declined as a percentage of total expenses. The simultaneous decline in charitable care and growth in profits caused a number of states to require nonprofit hospitals to provide a minimum amount of charity care.

As one Missouri state representative notes, "When hospital profits are this high, something's not right." In for-profit organizations profits are paid to the owners, who have risked their money by investing it in the business. But nonprofit hospitals have no owners. So where do their profits go? They go for four purposes: to charitable care, to support administrative activities, to invest in high technology, and lately, to form the integrated systems that hospitals hope will halt the erosion in their market share.

If You Build It, They Will Come

In the film *Field of Dreams*, an obsessive farmer played by Kevin Costner hears a voice in his head. It is not God speaking to his prophet. No, this is an American movie, and it is about baseball, and the voice gives Costner an all-American message: "If you build it, they will come." Costner obeys the voice, mows down his cornstalks, and builds a baseball diamond. Sure enough, "they"—the baseball greats of yester-year—show up.

That voice has also apparently spoken to the many hospital administrators, who annually pour billions of dollars into construction and the acquisition of expensive high-technology equipment. But contrary to *Field of Dreams,* "they" do not necessarily come. Indeed, some of these investments are barely utilized. For example, about 61.3 percent of the 150 heart transplant centers in the United States performed fewer than twelve of them a year, dropping below the minimum number recommended by the federal government for quality care. And 1992 hospital occupancy was only at 66 percent. So why do they "build" it?

One answer to this question arrived in my office one day in an elaborate box containing a number of outsized books, bound in lavish gold covers. The Health Care Advisory Board of the Governance Committee's agenda for the year had arrived, with an invitation to its annual meetings at the Ritz-Carlton, Four Seasons, and Grand hotels. Who is this Advisory Board? Judging from the opulent appearance of their mailing, I thought they might be high-flying software company CEOs, wheeling-dealing investment bankers, or stupendously wealthy business people. But no, the board members are the chief executives and chief operating officers of the leading, primarily nonprofit hospitals.

This mailing counsels members on how to stay alive. In one tome the Health Care Advisory Board of the Governance Committee outlines its approach to hospital cardiology. It points out that cardiology is a vast business for the nation's hospitals—their biggest business, in fact, accounting for almost 25 percent of hospital expenditures. The Advisory Board portrays cardiology as the "last growth market for inpatient services," which is "central to prosperity." It reassures worried readers that this gold mine has not been tapped out. "Reasons to Believe There Is Still Room at the Top in Many Local Markets," it announces in mixed-cap prose. In another article, the Advisory Board hones in on a particular favorite—chest pain emergency departments. "A tremendous way to generate huge incremental profits," it notes, particularly for hospitals that offer other, related technology-intensive services.

So how should hospitals venture into this rich last frontier? The Advisory Board has many ideas: in fact, 383 of them, including "consumer marketing" (31 ideas), and "packaging for payors" (29 ideas). Its overwhelming advice, however, is for the hospital to recruit physicians who will, in turn, refer their patients to it. Not just any physicians—no, only those physicians with a big patient pool. Good doctors will not only build a hospital's volume but can help it avoid price competition. As the Advisory Board approvingly notes, it is "Practically Impossible for Payors to Bypass World-Class Institutions with Physician, Patient Draw." In other words, insurance companies can't get too tough on a hospital that has a world-famous doctor affiliated with it.

How can a hospital persuade referring doctors to affiliate with it? The Advisory Board is all over that question. Having the latest technology available is a great lure, it avers, citing a survey in which 89 percent of cardiologists rate it as among their most important considerations in choosing a hospital. Readily available technology makes physicians' lives easier. They do not have to wait to use it. And physicians want to use high technology.

The Edifice Complex

Obviously, American hospitals have listened attentively to such advice. But they do not limit their capital investments to equipment purchases. To attract doctors and patients, they also expend billions of dollars on construction.

As recounted in the *Wall Street Journal,* for example, the Lutheran Hospital in Fort Wayne, Indiana, spent $91.2 million to rebuild its aging hospital. At the same time Parkview Memorial, the city's largest hospital, also planned to make some renovations. As Parkview's vice-president noted, "[We] are going to have to have some of the amenities [they] have. That's just part of the cost of doing business. Our doctors are going to have to have a parking lot as close to the building as we can make it. The carpet in the lobby is going to have to be replaced. The patients and physicians demand it." Although one-third of Parkview's beds were generally empty, it recently opened a $9 million maternity wing. Meanwhile, St. Joseph, the city's third largest hospital, with an occupancy rate of 42 percent, was not asleep at the wheel. It opened a medical office building in a high growth area a few miles from its downtown campus. Parkview's managers are thinking of similar sites too, so that they might "bond" better with their physicians.

What If They Do Not Come?

How is it that hospitals can seemingly squander billions of dollars on high-technology equipment and new construction, much of which will not be used? After all, in a normal market firms that invest their money foolishly in unneeded capital are soon forced out of business, because their costs are higher than their competitors' and customers usually flock to the lower-cost provider, absent quality differences among them. Hospitals, however, appear to violate these laws of economic survival; despite declining occupancy and mammoth investments in underutilized and unneeded technology and buildings, they continue to flourish, earning record profits.

How do they do it? Indirect payers help a lot. Unlike most other businesses, hospitals are not paid directly by their customers. In 1994 only an estimated 2.5 percent of hospital revenues came directly from patients. All the rest of their $342 billion in revenues that year came either from health insurance companies or the government. Insurance companies, in turn, received most of their monies from the patients' employers. In health care parlance, this bizarre payment arrangement is known as the third party system because a third party—neither the user nor the provider—pays for the service directly.

The single largest third-party hospital payer in the United States is Medicare, the government's health insurance for the elderly, which paid hospitals $101 billion in 1994. If Medicare administrators are even a little careless, payments can be made for vast amounts of unneeded, duplicate technology.

I do not mean to question the integrity and professionalism of Medicare officials, but the fact remains that not one person in the huge Medicare administrative structure would personally lose a cent if Medicare paid $485 rather than $300 per MRI scan (the actual range of Medicare payment rates for basic MRI scans in 1992). Of course, MRI scan prices vary for good reasons, such as the age and quality of the equipment. But while a consumer would find a price differential of $185 substantial—after all, people will go to a new supermarket just to save a few dollars on their food bill—Medicare's MRI payments of $237 million in 1990 were but a small fraction of the billions it spent on hospital payments that year. What are a couple of hundred million dollars in this vast sea of money?

The third-party payment system is the bedrock upon which rests the wasteful proliferation of technology. Hospitals, for their part, are so conscious of the importance of their payers and their role in determining their use of technology that patients who are insured may receive better care. A study of 38,000 patients who came to a hospital with chest pain or circulatory disorders found that those who were insured had 30 to 40 percent higher odds of receiving various life-enhancing cardiac procedures than did the uninsured. Those insured by Medicaid, the notoriously stingy health insurance for the poor, faced low odds of receiving the help that hospitals eagerly provided to patients with better-paying health insurance. (Ironically, this study was performed in Massachusetts, at a time when all the hospitals were ostensibly charitable, nonprofit institutions.) Despite the increased prevalence of managed care organizations, a 1994 research report found that hospitals continued to compete on the basis of service, not price, in 1988, much as in 1983.

It is surely no accident that the low perceived value that Americans receive for their health care money is inversely correlated with the third-party payment system. In 1994 estimates, hospitals, the worst value for the money, were 97.5 percent compensated by third parties. Doctors, whose services are also low-ranking, were 85 percent compensated by third parties. Conversely, pharmaceuticals and eyeglasses, which are only 36 and 41 percent compensated by third parties, achieved substantially higher value-for-the-money ratings. Clearly, the American public doesn't think highly of the shopping expertise of third-party payers.

Practice Makes Perfect

The proliferation of unneeded medical technology and hospital capacity is initiated by the hospitals' desperate struggle for survival and unwittingly supported by the third-party payer system. This unnecessary expenditure of capital inflicts two injuries on our health care system. First, it inflates our health care costs, and second, it likely diminishes the quality of health care we receive.

Considerable evidence demonstrates that the quality of a medical procedure is directly related to how frequently doctors perform it, or its volume. A study of 150 heart-transplant centers found that one month after the procedure was performed, the risk of death was 40 percent higher in low-volume centers. Alarmingly, more than half of the transplant centers were in the low-volume category. By contrast, patients in hospitals and physician groups that performed many open heart surgeries, like those of western Pennsylvania, had better chances of survival and easy recovery.

Why do high-volume centers achieve better results? A study of nine hospitals with consistently superior performance in a cardiac procedure noted in all of them the importance of teamwork. As one nursing administrator noted, "an open-heart patient is cared for by so many people from so many disciplines that building a team is critical." Many of the team members in that administrator's hospital have been working together for ten years or more.

Practice not only makes perfect, it also reduces costs. That cost reductions emerge from repetition is so well known in industry that the concept bears its own moniker, the "learning" or "experience curve." When average costs are plotted against volume, an experience curve takes the shape of a hyperbola, decreasing rapidly as volume increases. As the name implies, these cost reductions are presumed to occur as workers gain experience. Experienced workers make fewer of the missteps that increase costs.

The experience curve is one reason that management gurus preach that higher quality is associated with lower costs. The connection holds true in health care as well, as at the Shouldice Hospital. A 1992 study of hospitals that achieved consistently superior outcomes for a cardiac procedure revealed that the low-volume hospitals' 1991 charges averaged $35,000 or more for the procedure, while the charges of hospitals with volume of 500 or more were less than half that amount.

Americans perceive hospital charges to be the worst value for the money, then, because our third-party payment system permits too many hospitals—stuffed to the gills with too much technology, too many beds, and too many administrators—to exist. Medical technology per se is not the problem—indeed, technology may well provide a solution to the crisis in health care costs.

INNOVATIVE PRODUCERS OF MEDICAL TECHNOLOGY

Despite the clear appeal of medical technologies, most of them originate from fiercely competitive companies. The medical technology sector does not readily shelter fat cats—at least, not for long.

Medical Supply and Device Manufacturers

Medical supply and device manufacturers compete in tough, challenging markets, where existing products are continually threatened by competitors. As existing technologies mature and competitive technologies emerge, suppliers are forced to discount their prices. For example, in 1994 the average selling price of the catheters used in angioplasty *declined* by 2 percent, while the total size of the market grew by 19 percent. The ferocious competition among the many companies that manufacture angioplasty balloons caused some to discount their prices even more deeply.

This competitive battlefield motivates suppliers continually to refine the quality and cost-effectiveness of their technologies. Even Medtronic, a U.S. company whose excellent implantable pacemaker and defibrillator products make it a leader in these markets, is not resting on its laurels. In 1994, shortly after it introduced a new implantable defibrillator whose configuration reduces the hospital stay needed after implantation from 5 to 7 days to just 3 days, the company announced that the next generation of implantable defibrillators was in the works. It would reduce hospital stays even more.

Pharmaceutical Manufacturers

Like the medical device and supply sector, the pharmaceutical industry is not for the faint at heart.

For one thing, the process of discovering drugs requires enormous expenditures of money. Biology is a relatively young science, and the likelihood of making an important drug discovery is akin to that of striking oil or a precious metal. By the time a chemical compound is discovered to have some effect, the outflow of cash has still barely begun. The company must then spend substantial sums to demonstrate its safety and, then, its efficacy with hundreds, sometimes thousands of human subjects. Increasingly, the company must demonstrate a new drug's cost-effectiveness as well, testing it against other compounds that attack the same problem. For example, to convince dubious buyers of the cost-effectiveness of its expensive clot-busting drug, t-PA, the pharmaceutical firm Genentech felt it had to conduct horse-race drug trials against an older, cheaper compound. These trials alone involved over 70,000 participants and cost over $100 million.

Finally, the company must persuade government regulators that its manufacturing sites follow good manufacturing practices. If no such facility exists, as might be the case for drugs synthesized with new biotechnology fabrication techniques, the company must create a reasonable semblance of one to clear this hurdle.

After all this work, the company must convince the Patent and Trademark Office of the uniqueness of its work—on a new chemical compound or on a new use for an existing compound—in order to receive a patent that gives it a monopoly. After the company reveals the secret of its new approach in its patent application, its competitors work ferociously to discover a better agent, one with fewer side effects or lower costs. A few years after the first nonsedating allergy medications were introduced, for example, a competitor developed a nonsedating drug that did not produce the serious side effects sometimes observed with the others. Within a few years the competitor drug dominated this billion-dollar market. In today's market most of the competitor drugs are genuinely innovative. Industry analysts believe that pharmaceutical companies currently resist introducing "me-too" drugs that are neither demonstrably cheaper nor more effective.

All told, a pharmaceutical company must plunk down hundreds of millions of dollars to develop just one successful drug. (Although the exact amount of money required is the subject of considerable debate, it is clearly dimensioned in hundreds of millions.) And not every new drug is assured of a long life, despite its monopoly status, because competitors may improve it or an entirely new therapy may eliminate altogether the problem the drug addresses.

Like the medical supply and device industry, the pharmaceutical industry is heavily regulated. Enormous financial and criminal penalties are levied for violations of FDA regulations. The ex-CEO of a company that illegally tested and manufactured drugs for the treatment of heart disease and other problems was sentenced to five years in prison and fined $1.25 million. The firm he once led paid $10 million in fines and was stopped from manufacturing most of its prescription drugs. He was the seventh official of the company to be jailed or fined.

The pharmaceutical industry is a high-stakes game. To attract the substantial capital it needs to fund these risky ventures, a drug company must earn above-average returns on the capital invested in them. After all, people would have no reason to invest their money in such a risky enterprise if their returns were equal to those they could earn in much lower-risk ventures. Although pharmaceutical companies are frequently accused of price-gouging, the evidence that prices are excessive is ambiguous because some experts view the government's pharmaceutical price index as flawed. Some expert industry analysts have concluded that price increases actually represent only a modest portion of the industry's profit growth. For example, Dean Witter's analysts estimated that price increases accounted for less than 3% of the industry's double-digit profit growth between 1987 and 1993. They attributed most of the growth in profits to increased volume.

THE FUTURE OF MEDICAL TECHNOLOGY PRODUCTS

The medical technology sector is not a setting for timid souls. Participants face continual threats of technological obsolescence, substantial potential liabilities if their technologies fail, ferocious price competition, and a negative perception of their role in health care costs.

Huge companies can quickly rise and fall in this hostile environment. U.S. Surgical, for example, first experienced a meteoric rise because of its innovations in creating the catheters and instruments used in minimally invasive surgery. When it failed to maintain this innovative pace, it was nearly decimated. The rapidity of its fall echoed the speed of its rise: The company's market value decreased by $6 billion in only one and a half years.

Yet the pressure of this competitive arena seems to exhilarate its participants. They appear inspired by its Darwinian characteristics, confident that the better, more cost-effective mousetrap will win out. Those who succeed in developing such technologies enjoy the dizzying rewards of commercial success and the satisfying knowledge that they have improved people's lives. The Nobel Prizes for Medicine are but one reward earned by those who pioneered devices and new drugs and vaccines. But rewards do not linger, and the race is won by the swift.

The daring people attracted to the medical technology sector are already testing new techniques that could save 3.6 million hospital days each year and immeasurably improve people's lives. They include MIS techniques for removing brain tumors and aneurysms (stretched-out portions of the walls of blood vessels that are in danger of exploding); innovations to speed the recovery time of spinal fusions in back operations; and new devices for healing fractures. Brilliant doctors at Boston's Brigham and Women's Hospital, in conjunction with General Electric Medical Systems, have developed an MRI that enables surgeons to image the body while they are operating. As a result, they will be able to use MIS to perform surgeries that once required dangerous and expensive open procedures, like excising a tumor near the eye without removing portions of the skull. And a new miracle glue—a bone filler that stimulates fractures to heal more quickly than the casts traditionally used for the job—may substantially reduce the billions of dollars currently spent on fractures.

As impressive as these device innovations are, the promise of pharmaceutical innovations to reverse disease is nothing short of staggering. If current attempts to decipher the genetic code succeed, new medicines may well inhibit or correct the maldesigned genes that cause many diseases or that replicate unwelcome disease-causing visitors, such as the virus that causes AIDS. Such "gene therapy" and "genetic engineering" techniques will herald a new era for civilization, in which we will be freed of the debilitating diseases that presently cause so much pain, suffering, and premature death.

Of course, not all technological innovations reduce health care costs. Some innovations enable people who once would have died prematurely or endured lives filled with pain and infirmity to function more normally. Procedures to transplant new organs and CABGs on people who have suffered a heart attack are examples of such innovations. But even such cost-enhancing procedures may also reduce the prior costs of caring for these critically sick people and increase their ability to contribute to our economy.

Because today's hospital prices do not reflect the real cost of these technologies and we don't measure their effect on productivity, it is impossible realistically to predict their impact on costs. Their magnitude can be suggested by a study which estimated that MIS gallbladder procedures increased productivity by $1.3 billion in 1991. Nevertheless, many technological innovations clearly will reduce per-procedure costs, and since they are produced in ferociously competitive markets, their prices will continually be reduced.

Innovative technologies that further reduce costs will frequently be introduced. Such technological innovations will raise overall health care costs only if the growth in volume they inspire outweighs the reductions they create in unit costs. For medical devices, such increases are likely to occur only for surgical procedures that are so excruciating that patients presently endure pain or suffering rather than face them. The development of MIS techniques for live-or-die procedures, like removal of a ruptured appendix, will not cause such increases in volume. After all, such surgeries are the ones that people must have done no matter what, regardless of their willingness to "suffer in silence."

The problem with medical technology lies neither in the technology itself nor in the process for its regulation or patenting. The present FDA regulatory process appropriately safeguards the safety and efficacy of medical drugs, supplies, and devices, and the present patent process appropriately guarantees innovators the rights to the economic gains that their invention merits. The problem lies, rather, in the third-party payment system that permits the needless proliferation of technology for marketing purposes. And no matter how hard it tries, no third-party payer can ever match the efficacy of the direct user in rooting out high-cost providers who do not deliver good value for the money.

CHAPTER 10

How to Accomplish Resizing—
The Case of Deere and Company

The case of Deere and Company, the venerable $10 billion farm and industrial equipment manufacturer, is a good example of the profound impact of resizing. Its productivity increases enabled Deere simultaneously to accomplish the seemingly impossible: to bolster profits *and* increase wages *and* hold the line on prices. It's good for the customer, good for the employee, good for the stockholder—everybody wins, no one loses. Deere's transformation offers valuable lessons for the health care industry.

The placid exterior of Deere's headquarters building, a steel-and-glass architectural masterpiece nestled in the cornfields of Moline, Illinois, belies the revolutionary changes accomplished within. Deere began its transformation when its revenues plunged by $1.9 billion, between 1981 and 1986, and when its 1981 profits of $251 million reversed into 1986 losses of virtually the same amount. Although these financial reversals spurred the company into action, its transformation was no easy feat. Obstacles to change abounded. The company was large; it was steeped in a century-old, difficult-to-change culture; it was heavily unionized by the aggressive United Auto Workers; it was beset by Japanese and domestic competition; and it was devoted to the unstable and cyclical farm and construction markets. Redirecting the huge firm was like reversing an avalanche, while surrounded by snipers.

Yet in 1994 Deere's success in transforming itself was widely lauded. Although many of the companies praised in today's pop management treatises become tomorrow's dogs, in Deere's case hard data supported the applause. In the period between fiscal years 1980 and 1994, the company achieved a stunning 57 percent increase in tonnage produced per employee in North America, and from 1983 to 1994 its total manufacturing costs per ton fell by 19 percent, in constant dollars. During the 1980 to 1994 period, the total labor content of one tractor model declined by 32 percent. Deere ranked seventh in productivity gains among the nonbanking institutions included in the S&P index, with annual gains over a five-year period of 12 percent.

These dramatic gains in productivity generated substantial increases in profits. For example, Deere's Waterloo, Iowa, factory reversed a loss of $20,000 per employee in 1987 to a profit of $15,000 in 1994. Productivity drove these profit increases—not hikes in prices or reductions in wages. Throughout the period from 1983 to 1994, Deere's prices grew at slower rates than the CPI, and from 1983 to 1994 its wages grew 36 percent faster than its price increases. Indeed, Deere is such a good employer that, in both 1984 and 1994, the company was selected for inclusion in the book *The 100 Best Companies to Work for in America*.

How was this remarkable record achieved?

SMALL IS BEAUTIFUL, AND FOCUS IS FABULOUS

First, Deere rejected the two truisms that are commonly viewed as productivity-increasing solutions in the health care sector: "bigger is better" and vertical integration. To the contrary, like the 1960s gurus, Deere discovered that small is beautiful and focus is fabulous.

Instead of integrating vertically in order to produce internally products that were once supplied by outside vendors, Deere decided to do the reverse: It outsourced many of the components it once produced in-house. Then it burnished the smaller, remaining units until they gleamed. Workers once employed on sprawling assembly lines have been reorganized into focused teams—and armed with new, powerful, programmable equipment. They are kept informed by an electronic highway that runs through the company. They are nourished by training in technical and interpersonal skills. They are liberated by decentralization of power and responsibility. The changes have been guided by an integrated systems perspective: The impact of each separate change on all the other parts of the system has been thoroughly evaluated.

Why did Deere reject the "big is beautiful" solution for its productivity enhancement? Because its management reasoned that this approach simply could not work in the company. Merging Deere's many factories into a few larger ones to achieve economies of scale risked a loss of focus on employees and products. The managers of these giant factories would not know either their employees or their products very well. Costs would likely suffer, as would quality. In Deere's judgment the loss of focus substantially outweighed the benefits of "big is beautiful." After all, the benefits they would achieve by merging factories would be small, Deere's management calculated, amounting to 1 percent of costs at best.

Rejecting "big is beautiful" has enabled Deere to keep faith with the small towns in which many of its factories are located. That objective is an important one to this old-line company. Its top executives, who live in these small towns themselves, know that in many of them shutting down the factory would be like shutting down the town.

THE INTEGRATED SYSTEMS PERSPECTIVE

Although most of Deere's existing factories remained in place, they were profoundly reshaped. It implemented the focused factory concept, and to do so, like Shouldice and McDonald's, it invested heavily in technology, information, and people.

Formation of Teams

First, Deere's factories were reorganized. The company eliminated the traditional functional structure, in which workers were organized by the demands of the component manufacturing process, such as sheet metal working, machining, and welding. In this old system the component parts were manufactured, then painted, then combined into subassemblies and finally into the finished product. Vast production lines, in which each person repetitiously worked on only one function, supported this organizational structure.

Deere's new factories, by contrast, were organized into hundreds of small manufacturing "cells," each focused on one clear output. Each cell contained most of the functions it needed to produce a part. For example, the cell in Deere's Harvester Works which makes flat parts from sheet metal, assembles into a team, in one location, many separate individuals who were once scattered over the cavernous 261-acre factory.

This cell is loaded with sophisticated equipment. A laser punch-press automatically carves cut-outs into sheets of metal, which an auto-mated shear then snips free of their sheet metal host. The laser not only increases quality but also decreases costs because it can be programmed to cut many different sizes and types of parts from one sheet, thus eliminating the expense of new setups for every new part. The many different cut-out parts are then combined into a kit, which is easily assembled into the final product. The cell unit of organization virtually eliminates the substantial time once required for preparing a production line to cut each new type of part; it has obviated the need for many separate tools; it has simplified assembly; and it has reduced the number of machines requiring maintenance by 80 percent.

Cells that are focused on producing parts, rather than on the manufacturing process, have also virtually eliminated production lines. For example, manufacturing the transmission used in a fertilizer machine once required it to travel a mile through 22 stops on the production line. Now it travels only 610 feet. The conversion to cell units not only saved 77 miles per year for every transmission produced, it melded workers, once separated by miles of assembly lines, into an integrated team. Team members no longer merely repeat the same function over and over again, without ever seeing the end product. Instead, they apply their functional skills whenever they are needed. For example, the welders in the rear axle cell complete all the welds needed to produce the axle, instead of welding the same thing over and over again, never catching a glimpse of the completed object.

Clearly, the team members in a cell take great responsibility and pride in the newly visible products of their labor. Team members who once labored only in one narrow function now think of themselves as running a business rather than as a cog in a machine. Notes the manager of the Harvester operations, "At one time . . . everything was depart-mentalized by process. If you asked an employee what he did, he'd say, 'I run a drill' or 'I run a punch press.' Now an employee will tell you, 'I build markers' or 'I build frames." Successful teams have not only reduced costs and increased quality but developed new products. One team was heavily involved in developing a winch whose new design has enabled Deere to become the primary supplier of this component to one of its competitors.

Outsourcing

Deere's management has also rejected vertical integration as a way to enhance productivity. Instead, it has subjected each of its operations to a rigorous analysis to determine whether its products would be more efficiently produced internally or by external vendors. These so-called "make or buy" analyses led to considerable outsourcing of products traditionally manufactured by Deere—such as combine cabs and self-propelled sprayers. The sharp focus and large volume of these external suppliers have resulted in lower costs.

Outsourcing has been a distinct change in policy for the company. At one time Deere, like most other old-time manufacturers, was substantially vertically integrated; but many of the products it produced in-house were required in such small volumes that their overall cost was considerably higher than the cost of obtaining them from larger-volume, external producers. The quality of some low-volume, in-house production had sometimes suffered too.

Outsourcing did not imply, however, that all component products would inevitably be bought rather than made. To Deere, outsourcing was an analytic technique—an approach for determining which items would be obtained from outside—not a *fait accompli*. A rigorous analysis of its outsourcing convinced Deere, to its surprise, that it possessed a competitive advantage in producing its own powertrain components, despite the plethora of outside manufacturers. Begun in 1989, the Deere Power Systems Group had grown to nearly $800 million in sales by 1995, supplying engines and powertrain components not only to Deere but to five hundred different external customers.

Investments in Technology

Deere adopted several other productivity-enhancing techniques as well. For one, it invested heavily in technology: In 1993 alone it spent more than a million dollars a working day on research and development and $263 million in capital to increase productivity. One such purchase was a laser that cut the tubing used in axles to much finer tolerances than the human eye could achieve. As a result, the precisely sculpted pieces of tubing can now be welded together with tighter, stronger bonds.

Deere was also an early adopter of flexible manufacturing systems, which increase flexibility through standardization of parts design. For example, at one time the company's industrial and agricultural divisions used different cylinders. The engineers in each division imagined that their respective cylinders were so unique that no common design was feasible. The adoption of a flexible manufacturing system led to a series of cylinders that could be used both in medium-duty construction equipment and in heavy-duty agricultural machines. This standard cylinder family greatly simplified the design of new cylinder components.

Investments in Information

Deere also invested heavily in information. Its flexible manufacturing system was supported by extensive computer databases that catalogued the many parts the company used in manufacturing with a thirty-five-digit code. This code is now as important to the company as the Dewey decimal system is to a library. It enabled Deere to achieve the much-discussed but rarely accomplished integration of computer-aided design (CAD) with computer-aided manufacturing (CAM). With the aid of this code, design engineers who were looking for a new part could easily search the databases for an existing one that met their specifications, or they could design a new part and designate it with the code. The manufacturing engineers could more easily manufacture such designs because they were working either with well-known existing parts or with clearly described new ones.

The information highway running through the factory made CAD-CAM a reality rather than a fad. The results were quite dramatic: Parts inventories shrank, the manufacturing process was simplified, and the storage space required was reduced—all changes that profoundly reduced costs. The parts reserved for cylinders, for example, decreased by 80 percent, and all nonstandard parts were eliminated.

Investments in Human Beings

Deere's integrated systems perspective ensured that its investments in its employees were not neglected either. After all, the other resizing activities affected their work greatly. The new technology required

Deere's workers to assume new technical skills, such as programming advanced equipment, and it required new social skills of them as well, in their new roles as members of a product-focused team. The welders who once interacted primarily with other welders were now required to interact with people who had different functional skills, and to manage sophisticated robotic equipment. To teach the employees these new skills, Deere offered many courses, some of which stressed the acquisition of new interpersonal attributes even more than technical ones; for example, the course on continuous quality improvement devoted twenty-four hours to the topic of personal skills and only nine to statistical process control. This training yielded almost immediate benefits. In one case a group of four wage-earning and three salaried people who had taken a course together jointly reduced the defect rate of welds on a major component by 90 percent.

A considerable shift in the locus of power accompanied these changes. The employees who were armed with these skills were granted considerable latitude to shape their own affairs, and their roles were sharply redefined. Thus, a one-time hourly assembly-line employee now spends the bulk of his time instructing far-flung Deere customers on maintenance of their equipment. The results have been profound—so effectively did one newly empowered team reshape the production process for planters that their warranty costs were cut by half, inventory levels by 64 percent, and production cycle time by 75 percent.

My visit to the rear axle team in Deere's Moline, Illinois, factory illustrated the impact of all these changes. Although sparks were still flying from the old-fashioned welders, new robotic equipment dotted the work area too. The team leader, proudly wearing a cap emblazoned "Deere & Company: Rear Axle Company," explained to me that his team members worked as if they were a company. They produced on a schedule developed by their "clients," he said, and they worked out a complementary schedule with their "suppliers." Their "clients" are the other teams that use the rear axle as a component, while the "suppliers" include both internal Deere teams and external suppliers. The team is well informed—a large chart tracks their adherence to their schedule and to quality goals. The progress mapped on the chart is discussed during regular team meetings, which are held around a conference table located next to their work space. Deere's suppliers appreciate these changes as much as the customers do. William Evans of the Evans Manufacturing Company, a supplier of parts for the rear axle, noted that the team enabled him to cut his own inventories by 20 percent. "It has worked out great," he says.

THE LESSONS FROM DEERE'S TRANSFORMATION

Among the lessons to be learned from Deere's experiences, two are noteworthy because they fly in the face of the thinking of many health care organizations: big is not always beautiful and vertical integration is not always the answer. Rather than use these approaches, the company chose to downsize and to focus sharply on those things it could do well. Using an integrated systems perspective, it created small teams to accomplish those things; to leverage the teams with technology, information, and education; and to give employees new degrees of power and responsibility.

Deere's transformation has not only increased its productivity, it has enabled the company to maintain its soul. The small-is-beautiful focused factory approach has showed the small towns that count on Deere as an employer that they have put their trust in the right place.

Deere and Company's experiences have been replicated elsewhere. The steel industry, for example, has also discovered the power of the "small is beautiful" philosophy; minimills grew from 2 percent market share in 1960 to a nearly one-third share by 1993. The focused factory concept so dominates the personal computer industry that virtually all computers are built by outside contract electronic manufacturers. These outside manufacturers themselves are focused factories. Their focus is on the complicated job of producing the "motherboard" at the heart of the computer. But as the Deere experience also demonstrates, the focused factory concept is not the whole answer. It must be supplemented with an integrated systems perspective to improve productivity. Thus, the steel minimills that use integrated systems and invest in technology, information, and their employees achieve higher productivity than others.

When applied to the health care sector, the lessons from Deere's transformation imply a restructuring of the system into a series of focused factories. These organizational units, aimed at achieving an outcome rather than a process, are staffed with well-informed, well-trained teams of multidisciplinary, empowered personnel, who are leveraged with technology and held accountable for their results. They are a far cry indeed from today's everything-for-everybody providers and from the upsizing and downsizing remedies that are commonly prescribed for the health care system.

As more sectors of the health care system follow the Deere model of transformation, our health care costs will be controlled, our productivity as an economy will grow substantially, and the public's satisfaction with their health care system and health status will increase. But two barriers stand in the way of this transformation. One, some of the existing industry participants that will lose ground in the transformation will staunchly resist it. And two, the third-party payment system, which focuses on upsizing and downsizing as solutions, may well slow down the rapidity of the transformation. To enhance the speed of resizing, we need a governance system that enhances competition and rewards the innovators who truly increase productivity. Part 4 discusses how to make that governance system happen.

How to Make It Happen

CHAPTER II

A Consumer-Controlled Health Insurance System

In the prior parts of this book, I have described how the innovations that enhance convenience and mastery and provide focused factories and new technologies simultaneously decrease the costs of health care, improve our health, and increase the productivity of the U.S. economy.

Who can most readily accelerate the pace of these innovations? The American consumer. More than anybody else, the consumer values convenience, mastery, focused health care services, and new technology. American consumers are in the best position to assess the long-run effect of these innovations on their health status and to appreciate the impact of better health on their productivity. For example, the consumer is the one who can best weigh the costs of convenience innovations—such as vaccinations or screening devices at the work site—against their benefits, such as improved health status and fewer sick days.

On the other hand, other buyers, such as insurance companies or governments for example, will likely view these innovations as yet another benefit that may cause costs to increase, ignoring their impact on long-term national productivity. After all, the focus of other buyers is above all to lower their health care costs. They are not nearly as concerned about the relationship among health care costs, health status, and productivity as is the consumer of services. Nor are they as likely as to take a long-run view of the impact of innovations that help consumers manage their chronic diseases—focused factories or new methods of delivering support and information—or cope with serious problems, such as new surgical or pharmaceutical innovations that reduce the patient's recovery time. While buyers of health care other than consumers may well hope that people with a chronic disease or the need for a surgical procedure will have their health care services paid for by somebody else, consumers have a large stake in maintaining their health for the rest of their lives.

Let's look specifically at the other buyers of health care, such as managed care organizations or government-funded health care systems, and examine their receptivity to these innovations. As we saw in Chapter 6, when it comes to managed care, sick people complained about inconvenience and inability to obtain the care they thought they needed much more than the enrollees in traditional insurance policies. Surveys reveal similar complaints by citizens of other countries in which the government pays for all health care. For example, sick people in Canada were significantly more likely than Americans to complain of inadequate choice of specialist physicians and Germans complained of the inability to get a timely appointment with one and of inadequate choice and the poor condition of their hospitals as well.

More objective data support these complaints, such as the presence of waiting lists for health care. The existence of waiting lists for health care services is acknowledged in some government-controlled systems. Indeed, the private British health insurance company called BUPA, which had 2.7 million people covered in 1992, at that time based its appeal on its advertised promise to provide prompt care for those whom the government National Health Service couldn't see in six weeks. Those enrolled in BUPA paid twice for their health insurance: once with taxes for the government's system, and then again with payments to BUPA. Other data indicate that some are completely denied access to care. Notes the *Economist,* "In many regions, intensive-care units quietly restrict the admission of those over 75, alcoholics are not given liver transplants, and diabetic patients are not given renal [kidney] dialysis." These decisions are often equivalent to a death notice.

Plenty of evidence for waiting lists exists in Canada, another government funded system. For various forms of cancer, for example, Canadian radiation oncologists recommend that the waiting time between diagnosis and treatment should not exceed two weeks. But a study reveals that most waiting times for cancer therapy are substantially longer. For breast cancer the median waiting time between diagnosis and the postoperative radio therapy was 61.4 days. The physician author of this study says that if he were put on the waiting list for larynx cancer treatment—median waiting time more than forty days—he would "panic like hell. And then I'd go to Buffalo." Another physician notes that two- to three-month waits for a referral appointment are common. In general, according to specialists, in 81 percent of cases surgery waiting times are longer than is reasonable, and 45 percent of all patients are waiting in pain. More than half the specialists attribute the waits to shortages in capacity.

Delays like these not only require people to live with pain and debilitation, but also can worsen outcomes. Canadians who have had a heart attack do not recover as well as Americans. They are less active and report more angina; fewer state that their general health is the same as or better than it was before their heart attack. Research indicates that the lower rate and longer wait for coronary procedures in Canada may have caused these results—38 percent of U.S. patients but only 18 percent of the Canadians received an angioplasty procedure a year after their attack.

Lengthy Canadian waiting times are likely shortened somewhat because the American health care system provides Canada with a bench of health care resources. Most Canadians live within a moderate drive to a northern U.S. city, which can readily provide them with care that would otherwise be delayed. In 1991 to 1993, for example, 10 percent of those needing cancer therapy in British Columbia were served in the United States. In 1993, the Province of Ontario contracted with nearby American hospitals to provide MRIs and brain injury care; and in one Minnesota hospital's chemical dependency unit, Canadians accounted for 75 percent of the patients. In a sense, Canadians can afford to ration health care because they have the well-stocked American system nearby, as a safety valve against shortages.

Specialist care is denied in Canada, too. Although a positive appraisal of the Canadian health care system in the influential *New*

England Journal of Medicine inferred from indirect data that Canada provided more physician services and yet achieved lower costs than the United States, a careful direct observation of the level of physician services in the *Journal of the American Medical Association* found that elderly Canadians receive 25 percent fewer surgical procedures than elderly Americans. On the other hand, the elderly Canadians received more visits and consultations from physicians than the Americans. The Canadian health care system clearly emphasized inexpensive physician consultations over expensive surgical care.

Government-funded health care systems don't score well on preventive health care measures either. Significantly larger percentages of Germans and Canadians than Americans did not have blood pressure checks, breast examinations, Pap smears, and mammograms in the past year. Nor, surprisingly, did managed care organizations fare particularly well in some aspects of preventive care. For example, the smoking cessation experts cited in the *American Medical News* were "skeptical about managed care's willingness to embrace smoking-cessation services, since the long-term benefits, such as reduction in cancer rates, may accrue to competing plans as enrollment shifts." And while a Mayo Clinic expert concluded that "If there's one thing you can do to prevent illnesses in most individuals, it's to get the person to stop smoking, which is far and away the most preventable cause of death and disability in the country," he estimated that "at best" only 30 to 40 percent of managed care plans cover smoking cessation programs.

Delays in access to care, denial of high-technology specialist care, and lack of preventive care permit governments and managed care organizations to reduce their health care costs. But the "savings" are illusory—people pay for these savings by spending their "free" time in waiting for health care and we all ultimately pay for them with greater number of sick days and lower work productivity. The so-called savings in the health care budgets pop up as increases elsewhere in the economy.

Conversely, people who buy health care services for themselves appropriately value the impact of specialist care, convenience, and health promotion on their free time and productivity. They don't play accounting shell games with themselves. They know that they will pay for restrictions on needed high-technology health care services with limits to their ability to function and for lack of access to convenient, supportive health care with reductions in their free time and health status.

THE PAYER-CONTROLLED HEALTH CARE SYSTEM

Just what would a consumer be in the context of health care? Real consumers are people who weigh the price of a product against its quality. If the quality isn't good enough for the money, they don't buy it. Producers quickly get the message. They then madly innovate to provide consumers with the quality they want at the price they are willing to pay for it. The winners do well; the losers go out of business. In a real market cost control does not come about because producers limit goods or services; it comes about because producers innovate—they develop new ways to give consumers what they want. Although advocates of government-controlled health care systems rail against competition, it is key to the success of virtually every sector of our economy.

Let's take a look at this dynamic in the eyewear sector. There consumers wanted contact lenses that were easy to wear, easy to use, disposable, and inexpensive. Manufacturers continually innovated so that consumers got what they wanted. At the moment when Johnson and Johnson introduced disposable contact lenses that cost $2.50 a pair, most others still cost ten times as much. As a reward, J and J won a multihundred-million-dollar market. Consumers also wanted eyeglasses that were fashionable, easy to obtain, available in a large variety, and inexpensive. They got them. Mind you, the market cannot work miracles—you cannot buy genuine Armani frames for $49.99. But you can get a reasonable facsimile of them for that price. Why do consumers control the eyewear sector? Because they pay for most of it directly, not through an insurer.

The most dramatic modern-day example of consumer control at work is the automobile industry. Let's face it—most American cars of the 1970s were real clunkers. They were too big, too ugly, too low in quality, too difficult to handle, too unsafe, and too expensive. Do you know why? For a long time the big three manufacturers had a comfortable life, with no foreign competition. They did not pay much attention to the consumers. Nor need they have, since the consumers had few real choices. It was Detroit, mass transit, pedal power, or shoe leather. But once the German and Japanese manufacturers rose out of the ashes of World War II—whoa, did those Detroit guys ever come back to life! After the Japanese increased the number of cars they sold in the U.S. market nearly tenfold between 1969 and 1991, Detroit was all over American consumers, trying to produce the cars they wanted.

Why has this consumer-control dynamic worked in eyewear and cars but not in health care? The answer is simple: There is no consumer in most of the health care system. Instead, a third party, a government or an insurance company, pays for the services. As a result, the users do not know the costs of the services they use, and the payers do not know how the users feel about them. Little wonder that the costs of the system are a mess!

Secrets of the Tax Code

How did the health care system get into this mess? Two obscure, seemingly innocuous income tax code provisions have caused it. Eliminating them would eliminate the mess.

1. Corporations that purchase health insurance can deduct the full expense from their revenues when paying their income taxes. But individuals who buy health insurance for themselves cannot claim a full deduction on their tax returns.

2. Employees who receive health insurance benefits from their employer do not pay income taxes on the dollar value of the insurance.

These provisions cause the high costs of the American health care system because they keep consumers out of the market. They motivate employees to prefer receiving health insurance to receiving wages, and to prefer that the employer purchase their health insurance instead of purchasing it for themselves.

Imagine that your home was paid for by housing insurance that your employer purchased. You didn't pay for the insurance and you didn't pay for the house it insures yourself, so you do not know how much it cost. For all you know, your employer has paid $100,000 for a house for which you would not have paid more than $80,000. As your family grows, you ask your employer for more and more housing insurance. Why shouldn't you? It appears to be free, since you don't pay for it, and it is even better than a salary increase because you don't pay taxes on your additional housing insurance benefits. After a while, you lose all sense of what housing should cost. And your employers probably pay a lot more than you would have paid, because they have no idea of what you would consider a fair price—they pay more or less what the sellers demand.

This is the pernicious dynamic that is at work in the health care system. Let's say you need extensive dental work. If you buy your own dental insurance, you pay for it with income on which you are taxed. For example, if your employer gives you $5,000 in salary, you will not have enough money to buy a $5,000 health insurance policy with it because you will have to pay taxes on it, and you generally cannot deduct the $5,000 purchase from your tax payments. But if your employer gives you a dental insurance policy instead of a wage increase, no tax payments will be required.

These two tax provisions profoundly distort the normal purchasing process by removing the users from purchase decisions and by skewing their perceptions of the real costs. In 1992 the average American household whose head was under 54 years of age, spent more on entertainment or apparel than on health care, and in 1994 Americans paid for only 2.5 percent of their hospital bills.

When consumers do not know the costs of the things they buy, prices are likely to increase. They may even buy things they do not really want or need because those things appear to be free. Accordingly, hospitals may raise their fees to levels that consumers would not be willing to pay out of their own pockets, while the third party, who actually pays the hospital bills, has no idea whether the user considers the prices too high, too low, or just right. Or consumers may insist on health insurance coverage for items they do not really want or intend to use, simply because they do not pay for the extra coverage.

For this reason, increases in health care costs are inversely correlated with the percentage of out-of-pocket payments. Between 1982–84 and 1994 the costs of hospitals—which are 97.5 percent insured—inflated by 245.6 percent and those of physicians—85 percent insured—by 199.8 percent. But the costs of eye care—41 percent insured—rose only 133 percent. In contrast, during that same period the CPI for all nonmedical care services inflated by 163.1 percent.

Americans, for their part, want more control over their health care benefits. A 1995 report found that a third of employers provide only one health plan to their employees. That is, the employees have no choice among plans at all. About 40 percent offered only two choices. Small wonder that more than 70 percent of the respondents in a 1994 study said that they would somewhat or strongly prefer a job that allowed them a choice of benefits over an otherwise identical one that did not provide a choice. Moreover, Americans are confident of their ability to choose the best health plan. More than 90 percent of those who had a choice felt they had made the right one. Indeed, 73 percent of employees in a 1995 study were so convinced of their ability to better control health care costs that they were willing to pay a large share of the cost if their employer gave them more flexibility in choosing benefits.

CONSUMER-CONTROLLED HEALTH INSURANCE

Many variations of a consumer-control model for health care exist, but they all fundamentally propose to move the tax subsidies in the health care system and to give the monies now spent by third party payers directly to the insured. Their philosophy is that if you and I bought our own health care, costs would plummet: We would buy only what we needed, we would shop around for good values, we would penalize needlessly expensive providers, and we would reward efficient ones. In short, we would do all the things consumers normally do to make sure that they get what they want at prices they can afford to pay. In response, providers would innovate and produce the things we wanted at prices we were willing to pay.

What would people buy if they were given greater control over their health insurance dollars? Many surveys show that people most want a health insurance policy that protects them against catastrophically expensive medical events, ones that they could not afford to pay out of their own pockets. A detailed analysis of nearly 3,000 survey respondents found that when presented with fair market prices, the respondents chose health insurance policies with greater coverage for catastrophic illnesses, which also contained incentives to reduce utilization of other, less expensive medical care. Indeed, Americans' concern about the costs of such events is so great that an increasing number buy insurance for long-term care expenses which are not covered in the typical insurance policy, and pay for it out of their own pockets. By 1992, nearly three million such policies had been sold. The average 1995 premium of $1,505 required the average buyers to spend 6% of their annual income on the purchase. The pent-up demand for this form of insurance is so high that in just the first few months that it was offered, 50,000 Californians bought an innovative policy that lowered the premium by up to 30%, through incentives for users to economize on care.

Substantial evidence indicates that catastrophic health insurance policies—that is, policies that pay for very expensive medical care but which carry a large deductible that enrollees must pay out of their own pockets before insurance coverage begins—reduce health care expenditures. Even way back in 1974, the RAND insurance experiment, which enrolled nearly 6,000 people for a three to five year period, demonstrated that a catastrophic plan reduces expenditures by 31 percent relative to a plan that requires no out of pocket expenditures. For most participants, costs went down while their health status remained the same.

TRANSFERS FROM THIRD PARTIES TO CONSUMERS

Transferring purchasing power from the employer to the employee is not as simple a task as it may appear. Here are a few of the practical questions that might well arise if funds were given over to employees:

- How much money should be transferred? Employers' payments for health insurance may average the rates for their youngest, healthiest employee, their oldest, sickest one, and everybody in between. Should employees receive the amount that reflects their health characteristics? Or should they receive the average amount paid by their employer for all employees? Or should they receive some other amount?

- Should the transfer come in the form of a medical savings account, a tax credit, or some other tax-advantaged instrument?

- Should the employees be required to buy health insurance with the funds they receive? Or should they be permitted to use the funds for any purpose they wish?

- If they are required to buy health insurance, should it cover a standard benefit package and/or have a standard deductible (the amount the insured person must pay before the insurance payments kick in) and co-insurance features for a one-size-fits-all health insurance policy?

Answering these questions will involve political decisions, ones not easily arrived at. Regardless of how they are resolved, however, the impact of the transfer itself would substantially overwhelm these details. Deciding to transfer funds from employer to employee is like deciding to paint a house red—while resolving these smaller issues is like selecting the precise shade of red. The precise shade will make a visual statement, but its impact will be overwhelmed by the fact that the color is red.

The Amount of the Transfer

If all employees received a sum that equaled the average amount their employer paid for health insurance in the past, the sickest among them would probably not be able to obtain a health insurance policy for that sum, while the healthiest one would make out like a bandit. A 1996 analysis of national data revealed that, when the tax subsidy that comes from tax deductibility is included, people with private health insurance received $1,059 more in benefits than their payments if they were in fair or poor health, while those in excellent or good health lost $437. Thus, if an employers' average premium of $6,000 were transferred to employees, the family with an adult diabetic would not be able to obtain a health insurance policy because their health care costs substantially exceed this sum, while the 21-year-old junior executive would be able to buy a policy for less than $1,000.

Clearly, transferring equal amounts of money to all is not equitable. It can be corrected in either of two ways:

1. Health insurers must be required to charge everybody who lives in a certain area the same rate, regardless of their health status. This pricing mechanism is called *community rating*.

2. Health insurers are permitted to charge rates that reflect the health status of the insured. This pricing mechanism is called *experience rating*.

Although community rating superficially appears more equitable, as a practical matter it causes insurers to try to avoid sick people and to recruit well ones. Government can certainly require that insurers not discriminate against the sick, but insurers can still do it in many subtle ways. For example, insurance that covers only highly restrictive systems that offer limited choices of providers for care of chronic diseases will discourage many sick potential enrollees. Experience rating, in contrast, avoids this problem—after all, if insurers can quote a price that fairly covers the expenses of treating the sick, they have no reason to avoid insuring them. But it creates another problem: How much money should the company transfer to each employee?

The problem is not unsolvable. For example, a group of researchers devised a model that accurately predicts the expenditures of enrollees in various types of health insurance plans using characteristics that are commonly available in employee personnel files as the basis for these predictions. Thus, it is possible to adjust transfers for the risk status of the enrollee with readily available data. But this model predicted well only for enrollee groups of 1,000 or more people. Further research is needed to refine it for smaller groups. A number of purchasers of health insurance for their employees are developing various techniques for measuring the effect of health status on costs. With time, even better measures are likely to emerge.

In the choice between community- and experience-rated transfers, my personal preference is for a transfer amount that is based on the employee's health characteristics. To determine the amounts of such transfers, a company can hire an independent actuarial firm or consult standard actuarial tables. Although a transfer amount based on actuarial calculations will not be perfectly accurate, it will be considerably more accurate than a transfer of an *average* amount that reflects only the health status of the mythical "average" employee.

Experience-rated transfers of funds to buy health insurance would have other benefits too. They document the high costs of care for those with reversible destructive habits, such as smokers, and they provide incentives for insurers to reduce their costs. For example, an insurer who receives $12,000 in premiums from a smoker has a substantial incentive to innovate new methods for helping smokers kick the habit, given that their expenses could exceed $12,000 if the smoker got sick.

The Tax Status of the Transfer

Two methods have been proposed for transferring these funds to employees in a tax-neutral way.

> 1. Employees receive the money and deposit it in a medical savings account (MSA). They use some fraction of the money to purchase a health insurance policy and save the rest to pay for other health care expenses. In one version, no taxes were to be paid on any of the funds deposited in the medical savings account.

> 2. Employees receive a credit against their income tax payments in the amount of the transfer.

The financial impact of the second method would be the same for everybody. If they are equally healthy, John Rockefeller and John Doe will both receive the same tax credit, regardless of their tax status. The medical savings account method, on the other hand, would be worth more to John Rockefeller than to John Doe. If Mr. Rockefeller is in a 50 percent tax bracket, then every dollar transferred into his MSA has an equivalent pretax value of $2, while, if Mr. Doe is in a 25 percent tax bracket, then every dollar transferred into his MSA has a pretax value of $1.33. Thus, a dollar transferred into an MSA has greater value for those in higher tax brackets than for those in lower ones.

Economists like Mark Pauly of the University of Pennsylvania and the Heritage Foundation staff in Washington, D.C., have argued eloquently for the equity of the tax credit approach. On the other hand, public policy analysts—such as John Goodman and Gerald Musgrave of the National Center for Policy Analysis and Jesse Hixson of the American Medical Association, who first conceived of the idea—argue persuasively that medical savings accounts permit a closer connection between consumers and their expenditures.

Both sides have advanced strong arguments. The issue will ultimately be decided in a political context that trades off the equity of the tax-credit approach against the immediacy of the medical savings account.

Requirement to Purchase Health Insurance

The costs of some health procedures are beyond the means of even the most affluent people—for example, transplant procedures cost hundreds of thousands of dollars. Most of us need health insurance primarily to protect ourselves against these astronomically high expenses. But making the purchase of health insurance voluntary would likely eliminate the availability of moderately priced health insurance policies. The reason is that if everyone is not required to purchase health insurance, sick people will be the primary purchasers. Many well people will take the money newly-transferred to them and run. But, if only sick people sign up for health insurance, the premiums will grow sky-high, to a level virtually identical with the actual costs of treatment. A government mandate that requires the purchase of health insurance is essential to the existence of affordable health insurance policies.

Characteristics of the Required Policy

Should Americans be required to buy a specific kind of insurance policy? If they are not, well people may opt for a policy that gives them only the barest protection. Many young people may choose a policy that covers them only in the unlikely event that they are accidentally injured or contract an infectious disease such as hepatitis. If they can purchase a bare-bones policy, then other people will not be able to find affordable health insurance for expensive health care problems like heart disease. Therefore, people should be required to buy a specific kind of policy. But what kind?

CATASTROPHIC HEALTH INSURANCE POLICY. The purpose of insurance is to protect people from financial ruin. The minimum health care policy that people should be required to buy, then, should pay for all expenses that exceed what they can reasonably afford to pay out of their pockets. For example, people who earn $50,000 a year probably could afford to pay about $500 out of pocket for health care, while those who earn $200,000 realistically could pay a much higher amount. The minimum required health insurance policy should be one that protects people against health care expenses that they otherwise cannot afford to pay.

This kind of insurance policy is called a *catastrophic* policy. It is precisely the kind of policy most Americans want. In a 1996 survey 82 percent of the respondents, the highest number, wanted catastrophic health coverage, and 76 percent, the second highest, wanted coverage for long-term care and disability.

How would the universal purchase of a catastrophic policy be enforced? The IRS would require taxpayers to demonstrate that they have purchased a health insurance policy that covers all the health care expenses that they could not afford to pay personally. They would be required to provide evidence in the current year that they have purchased a policy that will be in effect a year from now. Those who could not provide such evidence would be fined and required to pay the IRS to purchase such a policy. The IRS has already implemented this kind of review mechanism for taxpayers who place their monies in tax-exempt vehicles for child-care or medical expenses. Those who cannot provide evidence that they have used the monies in the intended way forfeit the funds they have deposited.

How can the IRS evaluate the adequacy of the coverage in an individual's health insurance policy? Congress must first decide how much taxpayers in each income bracket must pay out of pocket before insurance kicks in. (Tying health insurance payments to income would not be novel: In 1993 industry consultants estimated that 10 to 15 percent of employers coupled health insurance payments to employees' earnings.) The IRS could then simply check whether the taxpayer's income matched the coverage provided by their health insurance policy. The key figure in the policy would be the insured's *out-of-pocket maximum*—the maximum amount of money the insured would pay before the health insurance kicked in. The IRS could ensure that this maximum is equal to the level of coverage required for a person in that income bracket. For example, if Congress decides that someone with an income of $80,000 must buy a health insurance policy that covers all expenses above $2,000, the IRS could check that a person with that income has purchased a policy with a $2,000 out-of-pocket maximum.

What kind of health care expenses should the mandatory catastrophic policy cover? Should it pay for nursing home care for long-term illnesses and rehabilitation? Should it include acupuncture, massage therapy, or cardiovascular fitness? Should it embrace expensive, experimental procedures of indeterminate efficacy? To date, the health care expenses covered by insurance policies are usually limited to those provided by practitioners of traditional medicine in hospitals, homes, and the physicians' offices. Many expensive health care expenses are not covered: Stays in nursing homes are primarily paid for by individuals or by Medicaid, not by traditional health insurance; many victims of deadly diseases struggle to pay for new treatments whose costs are not covered by their health insurance policies; and alternative medicine and wellness activities are paid primarily by the individual. But if the purpose of an insurance policy is to protect individuals against health care expenses that they cannot afford to pay for themselves, then clearly the mandatory policy should cover costly long-term care expenses and even preventive health care, for those who cannot afford to pay for them directly.

Should the mandatory insurance policy pay for expensive, experimental treatments for serious illnesses? At present, when managed care organizations and other health insurers deny payment for these procedures, on the grounds that their efficacy is unknown, they are roundly castigated in the media, and they sometimes lose court cases. If insurers are held responsible for making experimental treatments available to all enrollees, then the mandatory policy may as well include coverage for them. But the cost of offering such coverage might well explode, given the inflation caused by any health insurance coverage that removes the consumer from direct oversight of the payments. If the costs became unconscionable, the consumer-controlled health care market would ultimately resist paying for them, and insurers could offer policies whose costs adjust appropriately for the inclusion or absence of such coverage.

Some health care providers worry that insurance policies that have large out-of-pocket maximums create substantial financial risks for them. They fear that patients simply won't pay their bills. But to solve this problem, credit card vendors are ready to step into the breach. Already bank credit cards, such as those issued by MultiOne

Financial Services of Chesapeake, Virginia, permit customers to pay off their out-of-pocket hospital charges over a ninety-day period or even longer. Notes the vice-president of MultiOne, "The market is incomprehensibly huge." Visa too has entered the market, with an estimated $6.8 billion in 1995 health care charges. Higher-income individuals who opt for high out-of-pocket policies will be able to obtain commensurately large lines of credit. Like hotels and automobile rental firms, health care providers will be able to secure payment simply by charging the customer's credit card.

STANDARD BENEFIT PACKAGE POLICY. Rather than coverage that corresponds to income, some people might prefer a health insurance policy that specifies a minimum benefit package or one that provides the same level of health insurance coverage to everybody. But either of these alternatives would seriously undermine the efficacy of a consumer-controlled health insurance system. The consumer-controlled approach essentially relies on the fact that the public can control health care costs better than a government or managed care organization because the public will shop for health care more carefully and effectively than any surrogate acting on their behalf. Limits that are placed on Americans' ability to shop for health care will seriously compromise their ability to make the health care system more efficient. Requiring a standard benefit package or a one-size-fits-all policy would impose limits galore.

Requiring a standard benefit package would cause two distortions. First, most people would opt to receive their health care services in the sites that are included in the standard benefit package rather than in the most cost-effective setting. For example, removal of impacted wisdom teeth was once insured only if the procedure was performed in a hospital. Although the surgery was performed more cheaply and conveniently in the office of an oral surgeon, some people chose the hospital site because the procedure there was insured—and thus apparently "free"—while the office-based procedure required full payment by the patient.

Are insurers likely to continue to make this kind of mistake in specifying standard benefit packages? Certainly they have smartened up over time, as information about the cost-effectiveness of different procedures is increasingly available. But even today requiring a standard benefit package is likely to distort the market because its contents would inevitably be heavily politically influenced. For example, proponents of mental health therapy lobbied ferociously to ensure that it would be included among the benefits in the 1996 health care reform legislation. Four Senators shared tragic stories about friends or relatives who suffered from mental illness and inadequate insurance coverage. On the other hand, business representatives argued strongly that generous coverage of mental health care would derail cost-control efforts. "There has always been a feeling that mental health benefits are harder to define and softer in their definitions than a discrete physical condition and therefore more prone to excessive litigation and potential abuse," noted one. The battle became very contentious. The intrinsically political nature of standard benefit packages is underscored by the incessant harping on their importance by various health care sector representatives in prior health care reform debates.

Absent a standardized benefit package, however, consumers can make up their own minds about which provider best meets their needs. Consumers will base their decisions on the provider's cost, quality, convenience, perhaps follow-up, and level of interest in the patient, and not on the provider's political clout. When users can freely select the sites in which services are provided, the health care system will become more cost-effective.

Are consumers smart enough to make such decisions themselves, or do they need a standard benefit package to limit the possibility of error? If they have access to the cost-effectiveness analyses that insurers use to create benefit packages, they can be at least as well-informed as the insurers.

Some argue that standard benefit packages enable users readily to compare different health insurance packages. But the same consumers who successfully manage to compare cars and computers that come with a variety of different options, are also likely to successfully evaluate health insurance that comes with a variety of different options. Potential car buyers can find exhaustive information about the pros and cons of different automobile options in magazines like *Consumer Reports.* Just so, potential purchasers of health insurance would likely find a wide array of information sources about the value of different

benefit options. Finally, the prevalence of focused factories that provided a clear, complete array of services for certain diseases and
surgical procedures would considerably ease the process of comparison shopping.

In any other industry the notion of limiting consumer purchases
to a standard array of goods would be ludicrous. Can you imagine the
government's limiting you to a standard choice of food, or housing,
or car? American consumers will simply not accept such limitations:
They intuitively grasp that any "standard" package would benefit
producers more than themselves. Indeed, a 1994 survey revealed that
nearly two-thirds of Americans said they would be less likely to vote
for a member of Congress who had voted for government control of
benefits selection.

ONE-SIZE-FITS-ALL POLICY. Another alternative to the mandatory catastrophic policy is the one-size-fits-all policy: a health insurance policy with, say, a $250 out-of-pocket maximum for all users.
This option would be simpler to administer than the catastrophic
insurance policy; it requires the IRS merely to check whether the
taxpayer purchased a $250 out-of-pocket maximum policy rather than
to match each individual policy's out-of-pocket maximum to the
person's income level. (Of course, in these days of computerized
record-keeping, matching one item on a form with another is hardly a
mammoth undertaking; nevertheless, the one-size-fits-all policy
would undoubtedly simplify administration.)

But this simplification would come at a substantial cost: It would
undermine the consumer-control model in its fundamentals. Consumers can be expected to affect health care costs only when they pay
for them out of their own pockets. Their level of interest in shopping
wisely for the uninsured portion of their health care expenses is clearly
related to the magnitude of this uninsured portion. For example, those
who earn $70,000 a year will likely take great interest in finding the best
buys if the out-of-pocket maximum on their policies is $2,500; but if
that maximum slips down to $250 or so, they are not likely to be as
interested in managing what seems to them so small a sum.

A one-size-fits-all health insurance policy would inevitably push
the out-of-pocket maximum down to a level that all employed people,

no matter how rich or poor, could afford to pay. At this low level a large number of consumers would likely lose interest in shopping for the best value. By reducing the number of shoppers, the one-size-fits-all health insurance policy seriously undermines the consumer-control approach.

ARGUMENTS AGAINST CONSUMER-CONTROLLED HEALTH INSURANCE

Some may contend that consumer purchase of health insurance is infeasible because consumers cannot create markets large enough for risks to be effectively spread. Instead, insurance must be purchased by large buyers, such as giant corporations or the government, that can create a large enough group.

But if a consumer-based risk pool is prohibitively small in health insurance, then how do the consumer-based markets for homeowners and automobile insurance function? In fact, large risk pools are created when many people buy insurance policies. An insurance company can create a large pool in many ways, drawing from a large number of individual buyers, from a few buyers who represent many individual employees, or from some combination of the two. For example, a risk pool of one million people can be created either from a million individual buyers or from ten large buyers each representing a hundred thousand employees.

Others may argue that a consumer-controlled model would enlarge the administrative costs of the health care system because it would increase the bewildering welter of coding forms and billing arrangements that exists today and the costs of automation.

True, standardization would save money. One expert estimated that as much as 7 percent of medical expenditures could be saved if the industry switched from a manual system to a nationwide electronic interchange system and standardization would save even more. But standardization can be achieved in a consumer-controlled market. After all, the grocery industry managed to standardize its bar codes without any government oversight. In the early 1970s it adopted the uniform product codes that are now visible on virtually every manufactured item sold in a supermarket. The standardization greatly reduced customer waiting time in checkout lines and the expense of marking prices in stores. In the health care sector a standardization process, led by the industry itself, would yield similar results.

How large are the administrative costs of a consumer-control system? Examining the billing expenses of other industries that deal with multiple customers may shed light on this question. The retailing industry, for example, deals with tens of millions of customers. In 1994 all department stores spent 1.26 percent of net sales on collections and another 1.54 percent on accounting and information, for a total of less than 3 percent.

Although selling insurance to individuals may cost more than selling to large groups, the economies that would result from individuals' control over their health care would overwhelm the increased selling costs. Further, catastrophic insurance policies substantially lower administrative insurance expenses because they eliminate insurance payments for frequent, low-cost health care, such as routine doctors' visits.

ARE AMERICANS SMART ENOUGH TO BUY THEIR OWN HEALTH CARE?

Some contend that Americans cannot be trusted to buy their own health care wisely. For example, Lawrence Lewin, the head of a Beltway consulting firm, said "The approach of trying to give people the purchasing power to operate in the current insurance market assumes too much about individual purchasing abilities." Eli Ginzberg, an economist who is a long-time advocate of a government-controlled health care system, agrees. In a 1995 editorial entitled "A Cautionary Note On Market Reforms in Health Care," he cites a thirty-two year old paper by a noted economist in support of his opinion that "Consumers are not well qualified to decide on the health care they need."

A vast body of research literature appears to support their opinions. On the basis of answers to hypothetical questions, the literature concludes that most people have various irrational biases; they prefer the status quo even when change is beneficial; they are heavily influenced by the context in which a question is asked, answering the same questions in different ways if the context framing the question alters; and they prefer an error that is based on no action to one that is based on conscious action.

Although the research is well done, one can question the relevance of conclusions derived from answers to one-time questioning mostly of students to purchase decisions involving substantial sums of money that are made every year. To take but one example, if the status quo bias were indeed prevalent, then consumers would not change their buying habits. But, as discussed in Chapter 2, a retailing revolution occurred in response to consumer preferences. Three pieces of research examine the insurance decision-making process of real consumers. Although all three conclude that consumer behavior illustrates various biases, their research does not necessarily support this opinion, as discussed in detail in the end note to this chapter.

Last, the literature on cognitive biases in decision-making does not generally address the issue of whether some people are freer of biases than others. So even if we agree that consumers are as irrational as some of these studies contend, and, therefore, should not be trusted to purchase their own health care, who, then, should we trust? The record of the insurers and governments who have paid for health care purchases to date is hardly stellar. Even technocratic experts make irrational decisions. For example, one review of distortions in insurance markets notes that "surveys of actuaries and underwriters indicate that the insurers price policies for ambiguous events, such as earthquakes ... higher than would be suggested by ... models. These pricing decisions could be due primarily to biases similar to those exhibited by consumers ..."

The Efficacy of Consumer-Controlled Health Care Plans

The Federal Employees Health Benefits Program (FEHBP) offers far clearer, more direct, and more persuasive evidence of the ability of consumers to control costs when they are offered a large number of health insurance options, sufficient information to evaluate them, and a financial incentive to pick the most cost-effective ones. The FEHBP enables the 2.7 million federal employees and retirees to choose from among four hundred health insurance plans. (Four to twenty plans are offered in each federal region.) The government pays up to a certain maximum dollar amount for each plan and up to 75 percent of the cost of a plan. Thus, an employee who chooses an expensive plan must pay more for it. Finally, the employees are advised by the government and a number of consumer organizations on how to evaluate the quality and price ratings of the plans.

The results? The FEHBP's premiums have risen at rates 40 percent *lower* than those of medium and large employers. In 1995 its premiums actually declined by 4 percent. Meanwhile, it has expanded its coverage. (Although the power of consumer-controlled plans has also been demonstrated at *Forbes* and at the Golden Rule Insurance Company, they are on a smaller scale and have been operating for a shorter period of time.)

In one survey supposedly ignorant Americans gave the highly accurate average assessment of $5,157 as the value of their employer-provided health benefits. To contend that Americans are ill-informed about health care is to ignore the tidal wave of information that fills the daily media precisely because of their vast interest in the subject. Even back in the 1970s, the RAND insurance experiment showed that when Americans controlled their health care expenses, they reduced costs without inflicting damage to their health status (except for poor adults whose blood pressure rose and vision deteriorated with RAND's high deductible plans).

At present, nevertheless, the American public clearly lacks the information it needs to choose among providers and insurers. Over two-thirds of the respondents in a 1995 study said they needed "a lot more information" to make good decisions about their choice of doctors and health plans. A consumer-controlled health care market would cause an explosion of such information: Surveys of health care practitioners, like the Zagat restaurant surveys; *Consumer Reports* evaluations of procedures, insurers, and technology; and local equivalents of *Boston* magazine's annual "Best Doctors in Boston" feature would mushroom.

Beauty Is in the Eye of the Beholder

Of course, not all Americans would make perfectly wonderful choices if they were permitted to buy their own health care. First, notions of what is "wonderful" depend on the individual. My own family members, who buy only American cars, might be judged imprudent by those who prefer Japanese, German, or Swedish automobiles. The dentist I favor for his remarkable skill and devotion is not as busy as the younger dentist just around the corner. Although people will always make judgments about each other's choices—"Can you believe he drives a Chevy?" or "She goes to that old quack!"—such choices are not conclusively right or wrong; they are merely legitimate differences of opinion.

But some people clearly are incapable of making intelligent choices. Those who cannot digest consumer information about cars, computers, and investment options are likely to be equally incapable of digesting consumer information about their health care options. Fortunately, the market mechanism protects these people to a substantial extent. The market responds to the desires of opinion leaders, who in turn ultimately influence the majority of people. As long as the opinion leaders make intelligent choices, lemons and scams are minimized. The large markets for consumer goods provide evidence that this protection works. For example, although the personal computer is a very complicated consumer item, few lemon models or scams exist. Clearly not every person who buys a computer is capable of evaluating it, but enough people who can assess the quality of a computer exist to eliminate the duds. The mutual fund industry also owes its success to this same dynamic.

Just the Facts

That said, in my opinion the government will have to ensure the validity of consumer information on health care, just as it presently ensures the validity of the financial information provided by companies that raise money from others. The Securities and Exchange Commission requires the publication of certain information from the corporations under its jurisdiction and audits its accuracy. Similar laws should require the disclosure, analysis, and dissemination of both financial and nonfinancial data from health insurers and health care providers. In addition, the government should ensure that all providers are financially viable and unlikely to slip into bankruptcy.

Some advocates of minimal government may argue that such regulation is unnecessary because the market will identify fraudulent or financially hazardous providers and insurers; for example, health insurer A will advertise that its rival B is using false data or is on the brink of bankruptcy, in an attempt to gain customers for itself. Maybe so, but in this arena the consequences of fraudulent information are so grave that I would opt for governmental requirements rather than rely on the market mechanism. Indeed, the SEC was established in part because the market failed to provide investors with the information they needed; before passage of SEC legislation, some publicly traded firms did not publish annual reports or hold meetings with their stockholders. Thus, the history of corporate information disclosure strongly argues for a government role in the disclosure, analysis, and dissemination of health care information.

The SEC, however, has delegated some of its powers to specify and audit information disclosure to the independent accounting profession. The Financial Accounting Standards Board (FASB), composed of accountants, businesspeople, members of the public, and academics, promulgates standards of accounting disclosure for various economic events. Certified public accountants then use these standards to audit the financial statements and other information that corporations are required to disclose and disseminate and to render an opinion about whether they comply with these standards.

THE ROLE OF GOVERNMENT

All in all, a consumer-controlled health care system would transfer to consumers, in a tax-neutral way, the monies now spent on their behalf for the purchase of health insurance. Consumers would be required to buy a health insurance policy that protects them against health care expenses that they could not afford to pay out of their own pockets. The government's role would be, first, to ensure that the transfer took place and second, to ensure that consumers purchased the required minimum-coverage health insurance policy. The government, through a private professional group, would also vet the information that consumers use to appraise their health care purchases, just as the SEC vets the financial information disseminated by corporations through certified public accountants and the FASB. It would also audit the financial integrity of the insurers. Finally, the government would prosecute consumers who misstated their health status and fraudulently obtained a greater transfer of funds or purchased less health insurance than their health status warranted; it would also prosecute insurers who discriminated against the sick.

To some readers, these governmental functions may seem numerous indeed. How can so many government functions possibly accord with a consumer-controlled marketplace? After all, doesn't control by consumers explicitly mean a much-reduced role for the government?

To answer this question, let us examine the decentralized firms in the corporate world that are intellectual cousins to consumer-controlled health care providers and insurers. These firms fervently believe in giving power to the people.

Johnson and Johnson

By any measure, Johnson and Johnson is an extraordinary organization. This decentralized firm offers ubiquitous, well-regarded products, ranging from Band-Aids to Tylenol. It is renowned for its ethical behavior, as exemplified by its immediate disclosure of evidence of tampering with its best-selling Tylenol medication; and it earns spectacular financial returns. Moreover, J and J's superlative management is rarely caught by surprise. They achieve what they promise. Wall Street analysts generally give great credence to J and J's predictions of its future, and they reward it with favorable coverage.

Most observers of J and J trace its success to its decentralization. In 1996 the firm consisted of 167 operating companies. The decentralization was largely spurred by General Robert Wood Johnson, who noted that "the value of splitting up huge centralized, concentrated operations is principally the restoration of human values which are submerged . . . when . . . all . . . operations [are put] under one roof." The philosophy is carried on by the present CEO, Ralph Larsen, who says, "The quickest way to destroy morale is to issue edicts from [headquarters]. We do best when we take the time to describe the problem and let them come up with a solution."

How does J and J achieve its remarkable results? One might think that a "hands-off" top management carelessly approves the yearly budgets presented by managers of its separate companies and then every so often audits the budgeted versus actual results, somewhat like an indulgent, negligent, but loving parent. Nothing could be further from the truth. Instead, the managers of J and J's decentralized units are subjected to continual, probing interrogation by many levels of managers. A J and J company called Codman and Shurtleff, for example, holds year-round reviews of its budgets and results that involve *all* layers of J and J management.

When I discuss Codman and Shurtleff with my students at the Harvard Business School—we use it as a case study—some are initially shocked: "Is this how decentralization works? If so, when do the managers of the decentralized units have time to do their jobs? They seem to spend all their time in responding to their superiors." Some students' implicit beliefs that decentralized management is equivalent to "hands-off" management is turned on its head. But most of them eventually come to feel that J and J's method of managing decentralization achieves the best of all possible worlds: It simultaneously empowers decentralized managers so that they are free to achieve excellent results in their own local businesses—while maintaining control of the whole. J and J's top management team achieves what all managers dream of doing—they deliver on their promises, year after year, by simultaneously empowering their managers and holding their feet to the fire.

Alfred Sloan, the architect of General Motors, articulated these two opposing principles for decentralization of GM in 1920 (as noted by the late Richard F. Vancil in his seminal work, *Decentralization*):

1. The responsibility attached to the chief executive of each operation shall in no way be limited.

2. Certain central organizational functions are absolutely essential to the logical development and proper control of the corporation's activities.

Forty years later, in his autobiographical *My Years with General Motors,* Sloan conceded the contradictions in these two principles, but he noted:

Interaction, however, is the thing, and . . . I still stand for [those] fundamentals. Its basic principles are in touch with the central problem of management as I have known it to this day.

The role of government in a consumer-controlled health care system resembles the role of top management in a decentralized firm like

J and J. Government would determine the minimal amount of money that individuals must spend; it would ensure that individuals received those funds from those who previously purchased health care services for them; it would audit individuals who use the money to buy health care; it would assure the quality and availability of information about health care providers; and it would prosecute consumer and provider fraud.

Although this role may appear overwhelming, the key to the consumer-control approach is that individuals would make the decisions about the health care they purchase, not government bureaucrats or managed care technocrats.

IMPACT ON ACADEMIC MEDICAL CENTERS

The consumer-controlled health care system would bear little resemblance to the present one. Its focused factories would deliver integrated health care for chronic diseases and frequently performed procedures, replacing the present jumble of multipurpose providers. Costs would be controlled by powerful medical technologies that provide earlier diagnoses, better prevention, and more effective and efficient cures; by newly convenient sources of health promotion and information that will increase Americans' abilities to care for themselves; and by focused factories.

So far, so good. But this system might also claim an important victim—our great academic medical centers that train students, conduct research, and provide the most advanced, complex procedures. Medical apprenticeships would certainly change in the new system. Many residents would learn more of their craft in the focused factories in which they would ultimately practice, rather than in academic medical centers.

Some administrators of research hospitals may also fear that a price-competitive health care system would result in a loss of revenues used for support of research. Research grants do not fully cover a hospital's costs of carrying out research, they claim, so research must be subsidized by patient-care revenues. A consumer-controlled health care system would no longer permit academic medical centers to inflate their patient care charges with subsidies for research. Implicitly, these executives worry that Americans would not pay the full costs of research directly.

But their concern is likely misplaced. Americans so greatly admire medical technology that delays in the development of new drugs and devices were their number-one concern about health care reform. Both the general public and business sector demonstrate their high regard for medical research not only with words but with lots of money. Between 1978 and 1988 medical research expenses tripled to around $19 billion. Because of the financial promise of new medical discoveries, private funding of research has increased at rates that surpass even those of health care costs. In 1994 public sector expenditures were at $14 billion. The U.S. government devotes a much larger share of its funding for academic and related research to biological, medical, and agricultural science than do the governments of European countries and Japan. And these expenditures on research have increased far more than those of other countries.

The new system may force research hospitals to recognize that the costs of their research are much higher than they had previously calculated. Would the American public and American industry recoil from funding research if they knew that its real cost was, say $60 billion? I do not know. Congressional committees reviewing the national budget would undoubtedly try to assess whether the results of the research efforts were worth $60 billion. If they were, the research would continue; if not, it would be scaled back. In either case, research would be evaluated in light of accurate assessments of its true costs, which are currently unavailable.

THE EFFECTS OF A CONSUMER-CONTROLLED HEALTH CARE SYSTEM

In a consumer-controlled system an average family may receive around $6,000—the payment their employers once spent for their health insurance. They could use this money to duplicate the health insurance package they currently receive with its $400 deductible and $2,000 out-of-pocket maximum. Alternatively, they could buy another lower-cost health insurance plan. A $1,000/deductible, $2,000 out-of-pocket maximum plan could save this family about $400, while a $2,000/deductible, $3,000 out-of-pocket maximum plan could save them about $1,200.

Suppose this family earns more than $100,000 a year and can afford a $2,000 deductible and $3,000 out-of-pocket maximum policy, and thus save "their" $1,200. How will they choose such a policy? Their employer, an independent insurance broker, or an Internet- or mail-based insurance broker can provide them with a number of options. All of the options will offer insurance coverage for health expenses that cost more than $2,000. Some insurers will offer a package of focused factories; others a standard medical benefits package (specifying so many days in a hospital, so many physician visits, and so on); still others various managed care options; and providers may offer their own integrated health care delivery system as a source of care.

The prices for all of these options will vary considerably. The family will evaluate the costs, quality, and variety and select the insurer that provides the combination of features that best fulfills their needs. A family that is new to the area might select a managed care or integrated health care delivery system, while one that has members with chronic diseases might favor an insurance policy that covers the services of a focused factory whose quality they admire.

Insurance companies will continually seek out new, cost-effective ways to provide health care services. Such innovations will enable them to win new customers. Providers will also create new ways to meet the needs of family members who must now pay for the first $2,000 of their health care expenses. For example, mammography units will advertise in order to win Mom's patronage. In the past, when her health insurance paid for her mammogram, she had no idea what it cost. But now that she must pay for it out of her own pocket, she turns into a super–health care shopper. She is concerned not only with the price of the mammogram but with the quality of the machine, the accuracy of the interpretation, and the convenience, expertise, and courtesy of the staff.

Some worry that high-deductible health insurance policies would cause Americans to forgo important health-promotion measures. But because health status is significantly associated with factors other than health insurance, such as education and convenience (see Chapters 2 and 3), the absence of low-deductible health insurance is likely not to be so pivotal. In cancer screening, for example, Canadian national rates were as low as U.S. rates for poor women, despite the longstanding presence of universal insurance in Canada. Indeed, the American women had higher rates of health mastery than their Canadian counterparts, as manifested by exercise, weight control, smoking, and seatbelt use. In both countries, education was highly correlated with rates of cancer screening. The study's authors speculate that the large number of ambulatory radiology centers for mammography in the United States increases convenience and use, while the smaller number of hospital-based radiology centers in Canada reduces it.

Because the deductible is set at the amount that people can afford to pay out of their own pocket, they will not be financially constrained in their health-promotion spending. Further, lack of convenience, not lack of money, is a major barrier to the use of many health-promoting activities. A consumer-controlled health care system would motivate providers to innovate new, convenient ways to deliver health-promoting services, especially at work sites or schools, or at malls, during nonworking hours. And chronic disease–focused factories that want to establish a long-term relationship with their customers would provide health-promoting activities now that would reduce future therapeutic expenditures. Last, because the premiums will be risk-adjusted, insurers will have an incentive to provide preventive health care measures that will reduce the actual expenses of their enrollees.

Thus, a consumer-controlled health care system may well *increase* the level of health-promoting activities rather than decrease it. Nevertheless, if subsequent analysis reveals a reduction, or an insufficient level, of health-promoting activities, Congress could act to qualify them for tax credits or deductions, thus substantially reducing their cost to the user, or it could create other programs to support these important activities.

INNOVATION IN A CONSUMER CONTROLLED, GOVERNMENT CONTROLLED, AND MANAGED CARE CONTROLLED SYSTEM

Innovation is key to the transformation of the American health care system. If we don't put obstacles in their way, entrepreneurs will create the focused factories, technology, and customer-responsive health care organizations that will revolutionize the industry.

How would the different governance models encourage the entrepreneurs that make innovation happen?

Innovation in a System Controlled by the Government

In a government controlled system the government would specify the amount it would pay doctors and other health care providers. Providers who spent more than the specified sum or who provided benefits other than those specified would be out of luck. In this way a government system would put a very effective lid on health care costs.

But government is not entrepreneur-friendly. For one thing, the health care system would be implemented through government payments to existing providers—a certain percentage of the total health care budget to hospitals, a certain percentage to physicians, and so on. Providers would lack incentives to lower their costs, since the primary reward for lowering their costs would be a reduced allocation from the government in the next period. As a result, entrepreneurs with new ideas would have to convince the government to sponsor them, because existing providers would lack the incentive to do so. Perhaps for this reason there are more than 1,500 free-standing ambulatory surgery centers in the U.S. and only a few in all of Canada.

Many entrepreneurs are left cold by the prospect of entering a market with only one customer, especially when that customer is the government. Although the market would be enormously large—the entire United States—it would also be enormously risky. Entrepreneurs who failed to sell an idea to the government—their only possible customer—could not go elsewhere. Furthermore, because the customer is a government, the process of innovation could easily become politicized, and the government might easily refuse to pay on a timely basis.

Finally, providers who are paid a flat reimbursement for a particular procedure would spend considerable energy defining the patient's characteristics in a manner that provided the most profitable payment. Such efforts to "game the system" sap energies that could better be devoted to innovation.

The bottom line is that countries with government funded systems do not provide hospitable environments conducive to innovations. Indeed, an innovation like the surgical sutures initially developed in Hungary, and a noninvasive diagnostic technique invented in the United

Kingdom, languished in their home countries until they were commercialized by U.S. firms in the innovation-friendly American system.

Nonetheless, a government funded system, in theory, should ease the path of entrepreneurs whose ventures would reverse destructive health habits. At present, it is in no one's interest to support such efforts. An insurance company's program to encourage people to quit smoking, for example, would bring it many costs but few immediate benefits. After all, it would not benefit from the lower health care costs eventually incurred by those who stopped smoking but subsequently switched to a different insurance company.

A government system could change all that. With only one insurer, no one could switch insurance companies. Thus, the one insurer—the government—would have an incentive to encourage people to modify life-threatening behavior. But, let's face it: Governments are more noted for their willingness to borrow from the future than to invest in it. The data about the relatively lower levels of some health-promoting activities in Canada and Germany than in the U.S. discussed above provide additional support for this assertion.

Innovation and Managed Care
How entrepreneur-friendly are managed care organizations likely to be?

Not very.

Entrepreneurial ventures usually start small and grow larger if they are successful. But the needs of large managed care organizations cannot be met by small ventures. (Not surprisingly, very large companies are not usually noted for their innovations.) Furthermore, the small number of potential buyers would considerably increase an entrepreneur's risk of failure.

Because managed care organizations are thought to favor vertically integrated health care providers, the primary incentive for innovation would originate from them. In theory, these providers should be responsive to innovative, lower-cost ways of providing health care services because they receive a flat price for providing all of their clients' health care needs. If they are innovative in controlling their costs, they can cut their prices, increase their enrollment, and enlarge their profits.

But a review of the behavior of large, vertically integrated firms in other industries suggests that they try to avoid price competition and compete on other bases, such as marketing and product differentiation. For example, American cigarette companies have historically avoided price competition, preferring to compete by offering brands with different images, shapes, and flavors. Vertically integrated health care providers might well compete in the same way. After all, price competition courts potential ruin as successive waves of price-cutting cut into profits.

Still, concern that very large providers would have destructive effects on innovation may be misplaced because little evidence suggests that vertical integration of health care services is either desirable or managerially feasible. To the contrary, considerable evidence suggests that it is not. For instance, Kaiser Permanente, the best model of a vertically integrated health care organization, covers only 7 million people, not 250 million, and its attempts to replicate itself outside its home ground of California have not met with roaring success. Its market success in California may be attributable to unique, nonreplicable circumstances—to its long history and the unusual group of providers and clients in that state—rather than to vertical integration.

As discussed in Chapter 7, managerial problems blocked Humana's attempts to integrate its hospitals with a managed care insurance product. Its hospital managers grew dispirited when the hospitals became a mere link in a vertically integrated chain instead of the star jewel of the company. Meanwhile, Humana's top management's energies were diverted away from its faltering hospitals and toward its new health insurance divisions. Prophetically, Humana ultimately cleaved itself into two independent companies, one a hospital chain and the other a health insurance company, abandoning its vertical integration strategy.

If vertical integration were a sure-fire, cost-reducing strategy, then most American businesses would already be vertically integrated. But they are not. Instead, many of the firms that attempted vertical integration in the past backed off when they discovered that their knowledge of a *market* did not necessarily translate into effective knowledge of the separate *businesses* in the market. Time, for example, sold its paper-producing facility when it discovered that the skills needed to produce the paper on which magazines are printed are different from those required to run a magazine empire.

Hence the vertically integrated organizations that are central to managed care are themselves unlikely to succeed. But, if they did, they might well squelch the entrepreneurial fervor that is currently transforming the health care system.

Encouraging Technological Innovation

Even in our current health care system, innovations in medical technology are not easy to implement. They are very expensive to develop, and they must clear massive regulatory hurdles before they can be brought to market.

The saga of Genentech illustrates the risks that technology entrepreneurs now face. Genentech developed what leading cardiologists believed to be a magic bullet to dissolve blood clots. It was widely expected to be the biotechnology equivalent of a world champion—a billion-dollar-a-year drug. But it encountered one unexpected defeat after another. First, the Food and Drug Administration surprisingly requested additional data before it would permit the drug to be marketed. Then Medicare granted only limited reimbursement for the drug. Then foreign research findings appeared to demonstrate that a lower-cost drug was equally effective. Finally, cardiologists came to doubt the Genentech drug's efficacy. After hundreds of millions of dollars of investment, the drug's sales revenues in 1992 were a fifth of what the company had initially expected.

The pharmaceutical industry estimates that when all costs are included, the cost of bringing a new drug to market averages $250 million. Although this figure is widely disputed, it is generally thought to be of the right order of magnitude; that is, bringing a new drug to market requires at least $100 million. Years after bringing its clot solvent to market, Genentech spent yet another $55 million on clinical trials that it hoped would demonstrate the drug's cost-effectiveness.

Such substantial financial risks are somewhat tempered by the fact that once a drug clears FDA hurdles, the costs are likely to be reimbursed by at least some of the many payers of health care. But a government or managed care system would increase the risk of nonreimbursement, since medical technology companies would have only one or a few potential customers. This business equivalent of putting all the eggs in one basket would surely reduce the availability of the huge capital sums required for medical technology innovation.

Willem Kolff of the University of Utah is a brilliant Dutch physician who not only invented the first artificial organ—the kidney dialysis machine—but pioneered the first artificial heart. His story epitomizes the impact of stultifying environments on innovators. Kolff was advised by his Dutch peers to emigrate to the United States. "Only the U.S. medical system can accept someone as wild as you," they said.

THE UNINSURED

The large number of people without health insurance represent one of the worst failing of the American health care system. A 1993 survey found that 53 million adults 18 to 64 years old were uninsured for some period in the prior two years. Lack of health insurance prevented one third of the uninsured from receiving needed care and nearly three-fourths delayed seeking health care services for financial reasons. A 1996 report found that the uninsured had significantly lower rates of preventative health care services, such as a blood pressure check, than the insured.

The majority of the uninsured said that the high cost of health insurance coverage was a key factor in their uninsured status. The defeat of the Clintons' health reform proposals, which would have provided insurance coverage for all Americans, demonstrated that Americans are not prepared to pay the extra taxes needed to achieve universal health insurance. A substantial portion could afford to buy health insurance, with some support, if a lower-cost version were widely available. Eight percent of them earned more than $50,000 per year; eight percent earned between $35,001 and $50,000; and thirteen percent earned more than $25,000 but less than $35,000. A consumer-controlled health insurance system could help the uninsured in two ways. First, a widespread market for catastrophic health insurance will lower the price of an insurance policy substantially, and will make this form of insurance more widely available. A 1996 study showed that "if everyone switched to . . . high deductibles . . . health care costs would decline by between 6% and 13%." Purchases of health insurance are sensitive to its price. A 1994 study estimated that a one percent cost increase reduces the probability that a self-employed person would be insured by 1.8 percent. Second, the newly available tax deduction will enable even unemployed individuals to receive a tax subsidy for the purchase of health insurance, thus widening the market for insurance, lowering its costs, and increasing its availability.

A consumer-controlled health care system will directly help the poor uninsured who cannot afford to pay for health insurance out of their own pockets. At the present time, Medicaid, our nation's health insurance program for the poor, pays for almost 52 percent of nursing home expenses. A substantial percentage of those covered by Medicaid in nursing homes were indigent primarily because they lacked insurance for long-term care. A catastrophic health insurance system will greatly expand the market for long-term care insurance. It will thus free up Medicaid money for the poor because the middle-class people who now claim a large fraction of Medicaid's budget for their long-term care needs will, in the future, be covered by their own long-term care insurance policies. In addition, because the consumer-controlled health care system encourages the innovations that will increase the efficiency of the system, the provision of adequate health insurance for the uninsured will not be as costly in the future.

Providing health insurance for the uninsured is not enough, however. Many studies document that those covered by Medicaid demonstrate worse health status, in many dimensions, than the uninsured. Education to create good health and support to eliminate health destroying habits are the keys to public health. We must ensure that our elementary and secondary educational system helps students to manage their health and that supportive, convenient health promoting innovations are available to the poor as readily as to other segments of our society.

Although 1996 legislative reforms in health insurance may succeed in eliminating the cruel barrier that many sick people now encounter when they attempt to obtain health insurance, we must strive to improve the availability of health insurance and of helpful innovations even further. A consumer-controlled health care system will help us to accomplish these goals, even in the absence of new tax revenues to help pay for the health insurance needs of the poor uninsured.

CONSUMER CONTROL: A BETTER ALTERNATIVE

Managed care or a government-controlled system might well squelch the innovations that are currently transforming the American health care system.

Innovation flourishes best in a market system, in which buyers and sellers can interact freely. Even for complex products like personal computers and automobiles, the market works extraordinarily well. Indeed, both types of products have become better, available in far greater variety, and less expensive as a proportion of income because of the free market. It is difficult to imagine that these results would have been obtained if the federal government had been limiting who could buy and sell these products, designing their characteristics, and as it would in a government system, even specifying the budgets of the manufacturers.

Many of the health care cost problems result from the fact that health care expenditures are paid for by somebody other than the user, usually an insurance company or a government organization. Indeed, 97.5 percent of hospital expenses are paid by someone other than the patient. Payment by third parties has led to an absence of consumer vigilance, which in turn has allowed costs to explode. In a personal anecdote, when I called a hospital to correct a mistake on my bill, I was told, "Why are you bothering to do this? You're not paying for it."

Consumer-control would restore consumer cost vigilance. When the funds now spent on insurance by employers—averaging about $4,900 to $6,600 per family—are returned to consumers in a way that reflects their individual characteristics, they would then be required to purchase a health insurance policy on their own, subject to IRS enforcement. At a minimum, individuals would be required to purchase policies that protected them against catastrophic health care expenses. For example, they might be required to purchase a policy that would pay for all health care services that cost more than 5 percent of their annual income. They could also choose, of course, to replicate the more generous coverage they presently have.

In this system people would newly consider the costs of the health care products and services they use. A consumer-controlled system would allow Americans to decide how to spend their money. They could freely select the health insurance policy that best meets their needs. Some would choose to continue their present coverage; others might prefer a catastrophic policy that costs far less than their present insurance—up to thousands of dollars less—and then spend the difference on other needs or save it. If they opted for a high out-of-pocket expense policy, they would shop carefully for the health services for which they themselves paid.

Because consumer-controlled health care would be market-driven, it would support entrepreneurial ventures. Health insurers would have an incentive to design cost-effective policies that would appeal to people spending their "own" money. Furthermore, because the consumer-control model defines insurance coverage in dollar terms rather than benefit packages, providers would not have to lobby insurers for coverage of their services. New entrepreneurial health care services would be automatically covered by insurance policies.

This new health care system is now being created by the people—by entrepreneurial people—for the people—for efficiency-, convenience-, mastery-, and medical technology–loving people. The government can ensure that this system will not perish from the earth, by protecting us against undercapitalized insurers, false information, price-fixing, restraint of trade, ineffective or harmful technology, and discrimination against the sick and the poor.

But would you want the government to do your health care shopping for you? How about a managed care organization? Would you entrust somebody else, a government or an agent, to buy your food or your housing for you? Of course not. So why should we entrust others to buy our health care for us? The key to this entrepreneurial revolution is consumer control of the health care system.

CHAPTER 12

How to Make it Happen:
New Rules, New Tools

The new market-driven health care system is changing all the rules of the game. What follows are the new tools that will help you—providers, payers, and users—get the most out of it.

TOOLS FOR PROVIDERS OF HEALTH CARE SERVICES

The health care providers who flourish in this new market-driven system will give customers the mastery and convenience and the focused, cost-effective services they want.

It's easy enough to say, but how will they get it done? By following these rules of successful service entrepreneurs.

Pay Attention to the Customer

Listen to what your customers want with open ears and an open mind, without defense or pretense. Don't call them patients. Don't fight their assertiveness. Don't give them hype. Give them the real convenience they want—the kind they can measure with newly found "free" time. Value your customers' time as if it were your own. Provide them with the pragmatic information they need to overcome destructive habits and to manage their health status: vague, vacuous, self-serving, "soft-sell" information is not welcomed by well-informed customers. Help them to help themselves. Use their assertiveness and energy as levers for improving their health. Remember, the more they do themselves, the better their health will be, and the lower your costs.

Don't just listen to your customers. For eye-opening advice, listen to the customers you don't have too—the ones who prefer your competitor.

Focus, Focus, Focus

Throw out the general purpose, everything-for-everybody model. All too often it provides "nothing for nobody." Focus on your strengths—they might be insurance, or a certain kind of technology, or distribution, or information, or integrated care for a chronic disease, a high-volume surgical procedure, for diagnostic health care, or general health care—and design the integrated operating system that will lower the costs and optimize the quality of your focused factory.

Learn from the Rockettes

Take a leaf (a french fry?) out of McDonald's seven-hundred-plus-page operations manual or the success stories presented by Deere and Company and the Shouldice Hospital. Make sure that all the elements of your operating system are integrated and that you recruit the right kind of employees, train them well, measure their performance, leverage them with technology, reward them generously, and enliven the system with information. Your operating system should resemble a well-choreographed dance, whose disparate elements have been integrated into a harmonious whole.

Resist the Edifice Complex

Here is a Herzlinger Investment Rule: Short the stock of a company whose CEO is building a lavish new headquarters building.

Bricks and mortar are distractions. You are not in the real estate business. You are not an architect. You are not an interior decorator. The process of becoming one will chew up a lot of time that would be better spent on other managerial activities.

Bricks and mortar are albatrosses—fixed costs that dangle from your neck, dragging you and the enterprise down.

Fixed costs don't come just in the form of buildings. They come as other acquired assets too. Think hard before you acquire any other organization. Remember—many assets are really liabilities—money pits that consume your time and capital.

Lower Your Costs, Don't Raise Your Prices

Successful enterprises become more productive over time. They succeed by getting more output out of every unit of input—not by raising their prices.

Enterprises that raise prices open a big window of opportunity for their competitors, who can win their customers simply by underpricing them. Enterprises that lower their costs create sustainable competitive advantage.

Anybody can raise prices; lowering costs requires real talent.

Use Technology Wisely

Technology can be your friend or your foe.

If you use it primarily as a marketing tool, technology will be your foe. It will merely increase your costs. (See "Resist the Edifice Complex," above.)

But if you use it to enhance the productivity of the health care process, it will be your friend. The new market-driven health care system will reward cost-effective providers.

Don't Let the Dogma Grind You Down

Medicine is a young science, in which no one has a lock on the truth.

Nobody has unraveled all of Mother Nature's mysteries, yet medicine is surprisingly prone to orthodoxy. Make sure you obtain advice from the widest possible range of sources about what works and what doesn't. One pharmaceutical company, for example, evaluates various biotechnology licensing options with a unit that is completely separate from its large, brilliant research department. The company fears that its own scientists will deprecate anything that was "not invented here."

Be Ethical

Don't seek competitive advantage in unethical ways—by discriminating against sick or poor people or by denying people the health care services they need.

Such tactics are not only unethical, they are downright stupid. As some managed care providers who denied people services discovered to their horror, you can't fool all of the people all of the time. At least, not in a market-driven democracy. Sooner or later our aggressive media and activist consumers will put an unethical provider on the equivalent of the front cover of *Time* magazine and on the losing end of a multimillion-dollar lawsuit.

Breadth Beats Depth

Don't fall for the lure of vertical integration. It sounds good, no question about it—a seamless system that provides all the health care your customers need. But do you remember all the problems you have experienced in running just your corner of the health services world? Do you really think you can solve all those problems *and* all the new ones that a vertically integrated system will bring?

Breadth beats depth—a horizontally integrated chain of focused factories will amplify your strengths in each of the separate units that compose the chain. It is a much more feasible and effective strategy than vertical integration.

Don't Get Big for Bigness's Sake

Don't think of horizontal integration as a way of blocking competitors. Think of it as a way of getting really good at what you do. If you enlarge your enterprise solely to block competition, you're in the wrong country. The American legal system and competitive markets do not believe that this form of big is beautiful. Government regulators will sink their teeth into your neck, tying you up in draining restraint-of-trade lawsuits. Meanwhile, more efficient, nimbler competitors will steal your customers.

Measure Results: Your Own and Your Competitors'

What gets measured gets done. If you promise your customers convenience, measure how much time they spend to obtain what they need. If you promise them helpful information and support, measure whether they find what you provide to be helpful—and measure the changes it has created in their behavior.

Don't kid yourself in the measurement process. Don't permit yes-men to massage the data to produce the results you want to see. Don't ignore results you don't like. And don't let success go to your head—your good results will only cause your competitors to emulate you.

Use objective outsiders to do the measuring. Use "mystery shoppers" to tell you what it feels like to be one of your customers. Don't let your people know when the measurement will be done.

Take measurements consistently. Don't bury the results in a file marked "Feedback." Use them actively in continually recreating your operations.

Above all, don't believe your own press. You are at your most vulnerable when your measurement results are at their most flattering.

RULES FOR PROVIDERS OF MEDICAL TECHNOLOGY

Focus, Focus, Focus

Zoom in on products that help a focused factory deliver care for a chronic disease, a particular procedure, or diagnostic care. Say farewell to everything-for-everybody products and back-slapping salespeople. We're talking specialists here—real specialists, in the new health care system.

Banish "Me Toos"

No more bells and whistles, rhinestones, and bows. If your new product is not clearly more cost-effective when compared to its nearest competitors, wave it a fond farewell. Be prepared to back up your claims of cost-effectiveness with hard, scientific data that also prove the safety and efficacy of your technology.

Banish "Not Invented Here"

Focused factories exist in medical technology too. The biotechnology companies that develop new drugs or new ways to discover them, the firms that provide assistance in navigating FDA requirements or in conducting clinical trials, the software jocks who can provide your sales force, and you, with new ways of looking at your customer—these are all focused factories.

Use their services. Resist the pernicious "not invented here" syndrome. Focused factories will likely serve your needs better than your internal people because they focus on only one thing, and they do it over and over and over again.

Remember—if you don't use them, your competitors will.

Don't Be Greedy

Sure, you have a patent. Sure, you're in a very risky business. Sure, your investors deserve a good return on their money—one that is commensurate with the substantial risks of the medical technology business.

But don't be greedy. Remember, some medical technologies, like drugs, are not covered by customers' health insurance, and they can be expensive. All of your customers are sick—they have no choice but to use your technology—and some are poor too.

Test out your pricing strategy with some outside consumer-focus groups. Don't let insiders tell you what you want to hear—that you deserve the highest possible price. Those guys won't be around to tell you what you don't want to hear—that the crew from *60 Minutes* is at your door.

RULES FOR PAYERS AND GOVERNMENTS

The new market-driven health care system puts you into a new role. You are no longer the direct buyer of health insurance and health services. Your employees (in the case of a business) and your voters (in the case of a government) will now fulfill that role. Your new job is to make the system work, to help your people buy smart without smothering them. Because your new role most closely resembles that of a parent, the rules you need to follow are parenting rules.

Innovate, Don't Ration

A "just say no" diet reduces health care costs by rationing—denying people access to some health care services. Instead of rationing, let consumers figure out for themselves what they need, and trust the market to create the innovative solutions that will provide it, at a price they are willing to pay.

Innovators have created such solutions for the poultry, automobile, computer, cancer care, and eyewear markets. If you give them a chance, they will do it in the rest of the health care sector too.

Transfer the Right Sum of Money

The market-driven health care system will lower your costs and increase your productivity—but customers need shopping money. Give them the money they need to obtain the health care they deserve.

Don't play games in transferring the money from you to them. Transfer all the money you would have spent; don't hold back "little" sums for yourself. If you fool around, they will find out about it and waste some of the energy they should spend on shopping in getting mad at you.

Trust Your People

Your people are smart. Some of them are smarter than you; some are much smarter. Don't bind up their intellects, energy, and creativity with restrictions that are supposed to "help" them. They can help themselves, thank you very much.

The more rules you make, the more energy they will spend in getting around them. Give them room. Let them fly.

Enforce the Rules

A market filled with liars and cheats cannot function. Follow Johnson and Johnson's lead: Install tough auditing systems to make sure that people use the money you gave them in the way it was intended—to buy health insurance and not for a down payment on a new car.

Spend a lot of money in enforcing the rules and punishing those who break them. If people don't buy health insurance or if they lie about such choices as smoking, throw the book at them. Make an example of these scofflaws, so those others who are tempted to play games will see their pain.

Audit your providers too. Don't take anybody's word for anything, no matter how prestigious their affiliation or how holy their cause. Remember the university-affiliated cancer center that killed a patient with vast overdoses of cancer drugs? Remember the hospital that cut off the one good leg? Remember the religious facility for children whose head was accused of sexually abusing them?

Remember them when providers ask you to "trust" them because they are on the side of the angels.

Watch Out for Rules That "Protect" Consumers

Rules meant to "protect" consumers may protect regulators more than consumers. Licensing laws meant to "protect" consumers from unscrupulous providers may primarily protect existing providers from new competitors. Standard benefit packages meant to "protect" consumers from the hard job of selecting the health care providers they want may instead protect existing providers from innovators.

RULES FOR USERS

Be Informed

The market-driven health care system will provide you with a lot of new choices and the money with which to buy them.

Be smart. Get the information you need to make the right choices of health insurance and providers. Don't pretend to know what you're doing if you don't. Educate yourself. At the very least, ask the smartest people you know—the ones who have been through a similar experience—for advice.

Be Honest

Don't lie about your health status in order to get more money or lower your health insurance rates.

Use the transfer money you received to buy health insurance, not for fancy duds or fancy dining.

If you cheat, sooner or later you will get caught. And you will spoil the system for the rest of us too. Remember, we're all in the same boat in this market-driven health care system. When you cheat the system, you're hurting everybody else. And you will painfully discover that it is not nice to fool your fellow Americans.

Be Assertive

Demand convenience, information, support, and low-cost, high-quality services. Demand the very best providers who have had a lot of experience. Demand information to help you make decisions. Don't settle for hype or catchy jingles. Get real, hard information. Demand courtesy, promptness, and support.

Remember: When it comes to health care, it is your body, your time, your money, and your life. You deserve the best for them. Demand it.

Be a Good Customer
Be courteous, prompt, and supportive of your providers. Be assertive—but not obnoxious. Build long-term relationships with your providers. They'll do a lot more for you, especially if you have a chronic problem, if they know that you're in there for the long haul.

Take Your Health Into Your Own Hands
The new market-driven health care system puts you in charge of your own health by giving you the money to buy the health care you need.

If you can't find the service you want at a price you're willing to pay, keep looking. A savvy competitor wants your business.

If you want to alter destructive lifestyle habits, use your health care dollars to get help.

If you want to spend the money wisely, use it for preventive health care measures, like vaccinations and mammograms.

You're in charge now, friend.

I wrote this book to provide consumers, providers, and payers with a map of the new market-driven health care system and with the rules for navigating it.

I hope that the new map will lead to your health!

NOTES

Preface

p. ix   *And while they have rejected . . .*: Timothy Egan, "Campaigning on Portents of Doom and Boom," *New York Times,* Sept. 8, 1996, sec. 4, 4.

p. x   *yet, paradoxically, Americans . . .*: Karen Donelan et al., "All Payer, Single Payer, Managed Care, No Payer: Patients' Perspectives in Three Nations," *Health Affairs,* vol. 15, no. 2 (Summer 1996), 254–66.

p. x   *and they think highly . . .*: George Gallup, Jr., *The Gallup Poll: Public Opinion 1987* (Wilmington, Del.: Scholarly Resources, 1988), 165, 166.

p. x   *I first noticed . . .*: Regina E. Herzlinger, "Case: Hyatt Hill Health Center," in Regina E. Herzlinger and Denise Nitterhouse *Financial Accounting and Managerial Control for Nonprofit Organizations* (Cincinnati, Oh.: SouthWestern Publishing, 1994), 392–95.

p. xi   *Although medicine has been practiced . . .*: Brian Inglis, *A History of Medicine* (Cleveland, Oh.: World Publishing, 1965), 161.

p. xi   *Even the anesthetics . . .*: Ibid., 148, 151.

p. xii   *This shaky scientific footing . . .*: Harold M. Schmeck, Jr., "Study of Chimps Strongly Backs Salt's Link to High Blood Pressure," *New York Times,* Oct. 3, 1995, C3; Thomas H. Maugh II, "Study Questions Benefits of Curbing Salt," *Los Angeles Times,* May 22, 1996, A20.

p. xii   *For example, when one study . . .*: John Wennberg and Alan Gittelsohn, "Variations in Medical Care Among Small Areas," *Scientific American,* vol. 246, no. 4 (Apr. 1982), 120–34.

293

p. xii   *Our once-world-champion* . . . : Lester C. Thurow, "A World-Class Economy: Getting Back into the Ring," *Technology Review,* vol. 88 (Aug. 1985), 26.

p. xii   *For example, focused steel minimills* . . . : Steven Greenhouse, "Mini-Mills: Steel's Bright Star," *New York Times,* Feb. 24, 1984, D1.

p. xiii *At the same time, that the* . . . : U.S. Bureau of the Census, *Statistical Abstract of the United States, 1995,* 115th ed. (Washington, D.C.: Government Printing Office, 1995), 416, table 653.

Introduction

p. xix   *McDonald's can turn out* . . . : *Performance at a Glance* (Oak Brook, Ill.: McDonald's Corp., 1996).

p. xix   *but at a hospital* . . . : Doug Stanley, "Amputee Recovering After Wrong Leg Taken," *Tampa Tribune,* Feb. 28, 1995, A1.

p. xix   *An HMO turned down* . . . : Erik Larson, "The Soul of an HMO," *Time,* Jan. 22, 1996, 44–52.

p. xix   *Are we doomed* . . . : Richard Saltus, "Errors Detailed in Kidney Removal," *Boston Globe,* Jun. 1, 1996, B1.

p. xx   *Some of the many good people* . . . : Charles J. Dougherty, "The Costs of Commercial Medicine," *Theoretical Medicine,* vol. 11 (1990), 275–86.

p. xx   *McDonald's may be a miracle* . . . : Paul Starr, *The Social Transformation of American Medicine* (New York: Basic Books, 1982).

p. xx   *As a retired professor of medicine* . . . : Arnold S. Relman, "Bean Counters Shouldn't Control Doctors," *Newsday,* Sept. 30, 1993, 101.

p. xx   *Are there no lessons* . . . : "America's Fantastic Factories," *Economist,* Jun. 8, 1996, 19.

p. xx   *What is at stake* . . . : Barbara Sande Dimmitt, "Follow the Money," *Business and Health,* vol. 14 (Jan. 1996), 6.

p. xx   *If all the dollars* . . . : Ibid.

p. xx   *The system annually delivers* . . . : U.S. Bureau of the Census, *Statistical Abstract of the United States, 1995,* 115th ed. (Washington, D.C.: Government Printing Office, 1995), 9, table 4.

p. xx   *provides 762 million visits* . . . : Ibid., 123, table 179.

p. xx   *and enables 539 million days* . . . : U.S. Department of Health and Human Services, *Health United States, 1994* (Washington, D.C.: Government Printing Office, 1994), 178, table 83.

p. xx   *U.S. medical technology is so good* . . . : Matthew Q. Edwards, "Medical and Dental Instruments and Supplies," *U.S. Industrial Outlook,* Jan. 1994, 44.

p. xx   *Our researchers are the Chicago Bulls* . . . : "Awards—Nobel Prizes," *The World Almanac and Book of Facts, 1996* (Mahwah, N.J.: World Almanac Books, 1996), 324.

p. xxi   *And if you're old* . . . : Gina Kolata, "After 80, Americans Live Longer than Others," *New York Times,* Nov. 2, 1995, B14.

p. xxiii *Some drugs* . . . : *The Contribution of Pharmaceutical Companies* (New York: Boston Consulting Group, 1993), 126.

p. xxiii *The news sciences incorporated* . . . : Craig Venter, letter to author, Jul. 1996.

p. xxiv *The clearest evidence* . . . : Keith Naughton, "Revolution in the Showroom," *Business Week,* Feb. 19, 1996, 70.

p. xxv   *In the 1990s the venerable Eastman Kodak* . . . : "Back in Focus," *Forbes,* Jan. 1, 1996, 114.

p. xxv   *McDonald's, the ubiquitous hamburger* . . . : Stephen Drucker, "Who Is the Best Restaurateur in America?" *New York Times Magazine,* Mar. 10, 1996, 45.

p. xxv   *If it were easy Woolworth's* . . . : Laura Bird, "Woolworth Posts $42 Million Loss for Its 2nd Period," *Wall Street Journal,* Aug. 19, 1994, B2.

p. xxv   *the medical device company* . . . : *Market Value: U.S. Surgical Corporation: 12/90–12/95* (Bloomberg's Financial Market, 1996).

p. xxvi *Although most physicians* . . . : American Board of Family Practice, *Rights and Responsibilities: Part II* (Lexington, Ky.: American Board of Family Practice, 1987), 65.

p. xxvi *the physician who wrote* . . . : John R. Egerton, "Why I Let Patients Tell Me What Treatments They Need," *Medical Economics,* vol. 67, no. 2 (Jan. 22, 1990), 123.

Chapter 1: The Consumer Revolution

p. 3   *"Did you hear about Quick Pharm"* . . . : The name Quick Pharm is apocryphal and the ailments of Susan's family members are inspired by many such conversations.

p. 6   *In 1960 only 60 percent* . . . : U.S. Bureau of the Census, *Statistical Abstract of the United States, 1994,* 114th ed. (Washington, D.C.: Government Printing Office, 1994), 396, table 616; 401, table 625.

p. 6   *While in 1960 . . .* : Census Bureau, *Statistical Abstract, 1994,* 401, tables 624, 625.

p. 6   *Some two-thirds . . .* : Ellen Graham, "Teenagers: The Lessons That 'Junky Jobs' Teach," *Wall Street Journal,* Jul. 13, 1994, B1.

p. 6   *In 1960 only 28 percent . . .* : Census Bureau, *Statistical Abstract, 1994,* 402, table 626.

p. 6   *Many of them want . . .* : Ellen Galinsky, James T. Bond, and Dana E. Friedman, *The Changing Workforce* (New York: Families and Work Institute, 1993), 65.

p. 6   *Over 6 percent of those employed . . .* : Census Bureau, *Statistical Abstract, 1994,* 405, table 633.

p. 6   *Full-time workers spent 138 hours . . .* : Girl Scouts of the USA, *Environmental Scanning Report 1994–1996* (New York: Girl Scouts of the USA, 1993), 33.

p. 6   *In 1992 the average worker . . .* : Galinsky, *Changing Workforce,* 9, 55.

p. 6   *Meanwhile, between 1970 and 1993 . . .* : Census Bureau, *Statistical Abstract, 1994,* 68, table 83.

p. 6   *The Census Bureau estimates . . .* : Sue Shellenbarger, "The Aging of America Is Making 'Elder Care' a Big Workplace Issue," *Wall Street Journal,* Feb. 16, 1994, A1.

p. 6   *The 7 percent of workers . . .* : Galinsky, *Changing Workforce,* 58, 60.

p. 6   *For example, in the United Kingdom . . .* : Philip Bassett, "When Two Jobs Are All in a Day's Work," *The Times,* June 13, 1995, p. 29.

p. 7   *Today's workers with employed spouses . . .* : Galinsky, *Changing Workforce,* 74.

p. 7   *Understandably, most of them complain . . .* : Ibid., 75.

p. 7   *A furniture retailer notes . . .* : Elaine Louie, "Retailers Provide Instant Furniture," *New York Times,* Aug. 4, 1994, C2.

p. 7   *In 1960 only 41 percent . . .* : Census Bureau, *Statistical Abstract, 1994,* 157, table 232.

p. 7   *Even 50 percent of those 75 and older . . .* : Ibid., 158, table 234.

p. 7   *Fifty-seven million people . . .* : Ibid., 193, table 300.

p. 7   *12 million people who themselves paid . . .* : U.S. Bureau of the Census, *Statistical Abstract, 1993* (Washington, D.C.: Government Printing Office, 1993), 423, table 665.

p. 7   *The students in the top 60 percent . . .* : Census Bureau, *Statistical Abstract, 1, 1994,* 174, table 264.

p. 8   *American College Testing Program . . .* : Ibid., 174, table 265.

p. 8   *The proficiency scores . . .* : Ibid., 175, table 266. Scores in nine out of twelve categories were unchanged or improved. Scores start in 1976 in science, 1977 in mathematics, 1983 in writing, and 1979 in reading.

p. 8   *In 1992, 102 million . . .* : Gretchen Morgenson, "The Fall of the Mall," *Forbes,* May 24, 1993, 106–112.

p. 8   *consumer purchases from the home . . .* : Census Bureau, *Statistical Abstract, 1994,* 786, table 1281.

p. 8   *Although the wares . . .* : Ellen Neuborne, "Nordstrom Turns to Home Shopping," *USA Today,* May 18, 1993, 1B.

p. 8   *When their merchandising skills . . .* : Suzanne Bilello, "A Growing TV Audience Goes Bargain Hunting," *Newsday,* Sept. 27, 1993, 29.

p. 8   *For those who still . . .* : U.S. Bureau of the Census, *1992 Census of Retail Trade* (Washington, D.C.: Government Printing Office, 1994), US-11–12. Total 1992 retail sales at outlets where people go to see the merchandise. One trillion dollars includes $245 billion at general merchandise stores, $395 billion at automotive dealers, $101 billion at apparel and accessory stores, $93 billion at furniture and home furnishings stores, $77 billion at drug and proprietary stores, $66 billion at miscellaneous shopping goods stores, and $29 billion at other miscellaneous shopping goods stores.

p. 9   *Stores that sell linens . . .* : Michelle C. Hollow, "Bigger Is Better: Superstores Spur Wave of Opportunities," *Discount Store News, HomeMarket Trends Supplement,* vol. 32, no. 7 (Apr. 5, 1993), S4.

p. 9   *No wonder Sears . . .* : Steven Simons, "Death of Mail Order Is Greatly Exaggerated," *DM News,* Apr. 26, 1993, 51.

p. 9   *For example, SuperSports . . .* : Debra Hazel, "Are Sporting Goods Next? Superstores Challenge Small Operators," *Chain Store Age Executive,* vol. 69, no. 6 (Jun. 1993), 27.

p. 9   *And stores like the venerable Sears . . .* : Kevin Kelly, "The Big Store May Be on a Big Roll," *Business Week,* Aug. 30, 1993, 85.

p. 9   *Telephone Doctor . . .* : Barbara Marsh, "Oh It's You, We Were Hoping You'd Call, Please Hold," *Wall Street Journal,* Jun. 9, 1994, B2.

p. 9   *The prices of the ubiquitous Wal-Mart . . .* : "The Evolution of Wal-Mart," *Harvard Business Review,* May–Jun. 1993, 82.

p. 9   *Notes an observer . . .* : Alex Beam, "Meltdown Main St.," *Boston Globe,* Oct. 27, 1993, 11.

p. 9   *No wonder sales revenues . . .* : "Attention Shoppers!" *Business Week,* Aug. 22, 1994, 8.

p. 10   *One superstore executive* . . . : Michelle C. Hollow, "Bigger Is Better," *Business Week,* Aug. 22, 1994, 8.

p. 10   *Its CEO was dismissed* . . . : Bill Vlasic and Keith Naughton, "Kmart: Who's in Charge Here?" *Business Week,* Dec. 4, 1995, 104.

p. 10   *Yet while Kmart* . . . : Barnaby J. Feder, "Message for Mom and Pop," *New York Times,* Oct. 24, 1993, sec. 3, p. 4.

p. 10   *The mall in Menlo Park* . . . : Nancy Kennedy, "Malls Add Services to Keep Customers," *New York Times,* Oct. 17, 1993, sec. 13NJ, p. 1.

p. 10   *Charles Schwab, founder* . . . : "The Schwab Revolution," *Business Week,* Dec. 19, 1994, 88–98.

p. 11   *Motley Fool, a computer service* . . . : Arthur Armstrong and John Hagel III, "The Real Value of On-Line Communities," *Harvard Business Review,* May–Jun. 1996, 134.

p. 11   *Notes Rose Wunder* . . . : "Schwab Revolution," 89, 91.

p. 11   *Beginning with Julia Child's* . . . : Simone Beck, Louisette Bertholle, and Julia Child, *Mastering the Art of French Cooking* (New York: Alfred Knopf, 1961).

p. 13   *"Ranked best in its class"* . . . : Buick Park Avenue, "Clearly the Quality Shines Through," magazine advertisement, 1994. Featured with permission of Buick Motor Division.

p. 13   *The company hired a* . . . : David Woodruff, "Bug Control at Chrysler," *Business Week,* Aug. 22, 1994, 26.

p. 13   *To the contrary* . . . : Census Bureau, *Statistical Abstract, 1994,* 469, table 715.

p. 13   *the price index* . . . : Ibid., 489–90, table 748. (Between 1985 and 1992, mean family income increased 33 percent in current dollars. The Consumer Price Index for new vehicles increased 22 percent in the same years.)

p. 13   *Inside, Lonnie Reeder* . . . : "Revolution in the Showroom," *Business Week,* Feb. 19, 1996, cover and 74.

p. 14   *As a result of Florida's* . . . : Douglas Lavin, "Volkswagen, Porsche and Jaguar Lead in Complaints of 'Lemons,' Florida Says," *Wall Street Journal,* Aug. 19, 1994, B2.

p. 14   *Woolworth's, the retailing giant* . . . : Laura Bird, "Woolworth Posts $42 Million Loss for Its 2nd Period," *Wall Street Journal,* Aug. 19, 1994, B2.

p. 14   *No single factor explains* . . . : Howard Rudnitsky, "How Sam Walton Does It," *Forbes,* Aug. 16, 1982, 42.

p. 15   *After all, he had been only* . . . : John Ingham and Lynne B. Feldman, *Contemporary American Business Leaders: A Biographical Dictionary* (Westport, Conn.: Greenwood Press, 1990), 728.

p. 15   *His most notable accomplishment* . . . : "Ted Turner," *The Complete Marquis Who's Who Biographies* (New Providence, N.J.: Reed Reference Publishing, 1995).

Chapter 2: When Patients Won't Remain Patient

p. 16   *According to a recent* . . . : Jonathan E. Fielding, William G. Cumberland, and Lynn Pettitt, "Immunization Status of Children of Employees in a Large Corporation," *Journal of the American Medical Association,* vol. 271, no. 7 (Feb. 16, 1994), 525–30.

p. 17   *In general, fewer preschool* . . . : Henry D. Mustin, Victoria L. Holt, and Frederick A. Connell, "Adequacy of Well-Child Care and Immunization in U.S. Infants Born in 1988," *Journal of the American Medical Association,* vol. 272, no. 14 (Oct. 12, 1994), 1111–15.

p. 17   *A detailed analysis* . . . : Fielding, "Immunization Status of Children of Employees."

p. 17   *Although Americans hold* . . . : American Medical Association, *Public Opinion* . . . *Health Care Issues* (Chicago, Ill.: American Medical Association, 1994), 16–17.

p. 17   *They consider physicians' office* . . . : Haya R. Rubin et al., "Patients' Ratings of Outpatient Visits in Different Practice Settings," *Journal of the American Medical Association,* vol. 270, no. 7 (Aug. 18, 1993), 837.

p. 17   *During the years* . . . : American Medical Association, *Trends in U.S. Health Care 1992* (Chicago, Ill.: Center for Health Policy Research, 1993), 120.

p. 18   *When G. Kirk Raab* . . . : Marilyn Chase, "Whose Time Is Worth More: Yours or the Doctor's?" *Wall Street Journal,* Oct. 24, 1994, B1.

p. 18   *People find inconvenience* . . . : Rubin et al., "Patients' Ratings," 838.

p. 18   *Consider the case* . . . : Susan C. Rosenfeld, "So You Want to Join an H.M.O.? Good Luck," *New York Times,* Aug. 9, 1994, A23.

p. 19   *Adds Consumer Reports* . . . : "Are HMOs the Answer?" *Consumer Reports,* Aug. 1992, 521.

p. 19   *A 1995 Journal of the American* . . . : Andrew B. Bindman et al., "Preventable Hospitalizations and Access to Health Care," *Journal of the American Medical Association,* vol. 274, no. 4 (Jul. 26, 1995), 305–311.

p. 19 *For example, the 30 million . . .* : U.S. Bureau of the Census, *Statistical Abstract of the United States, 1995* (Washington, D.C.: Government Printing Office, 1995), 141, table 215.

p. 19 *and the 591,000 women . . .* : HIAA, *Source Book of Health Insurance Data 1992* [Washington, D.C.: Health Insurance Association of America (HIAA), 1992], 54.

p. 20 *My friend with the foot . . .* : The name of the protagonist has been omitted from this true story. It has been reviewed for accuracy by Dr. Michael Robinson.

p. 21 *But she did start . . .* : Kate R. Lorig and James Fries, *The Arthritis Help Book* (Reading, Mass.: Addison-Wesley, 1990).

p. 22 *One examination of . . .* : "Disabling Foot Disorders in the Elderly," *Journal Watch*, vol. 15, no. 12 (Jun. 15, 1995), 99.

p. 23 *A nationwide survey . . .* : Elizabeth R. Zell et al., "Low Vaccination Rates of U.S. Preschool and School Age Children," *Journal of the American Medical Association*, vol. 271, no. 11 (Mar. 16, 1994), 833–39.

p. 23 *A study based on . . .* : Jessica Primoff Vistnes and Vivian Hamilton, "The Time and Monetary Costs of Outpatient Care for Children," *American Economic Association Papers and Proceedings* (May 1995), 117–21.

p. 24 *Similarly, an analysis of 803 families . . .* : Carlos A. Moreno, "Utilization of Medical Services by Single-Parent and Two-Parent Families," *Journal of Family Practice*, vol. 28, no. 2 (1989), 198.

p. 24 *Other studies found . . .* : Center for the Future of Children, *The Future of Children*, vol. 4, no. 3 (Winter 1994), 32–34.

p. 24 *More women in single . . .* : Moreno, "Utilization," 196.

p. 24 *An intensive analysis . . .* : Ann S. Bates et al., "Risk Factors for Underimmunization in Poor Urban Infants," *Journal of the American Medical Association*, vol. 272, no. 14 (Oct. 12, 1994), 1108.

p. 24 *Similarly, an analysis of the disparate . . .* : Center for the Future of Children, *Future of Children*, 33.

p. 24 *For example, lower-income Scottish . . .* : David J. Torgerson, Cam Donaldson, and David M. Reid, "Private Versus Social Opportunity Cost of Time," Health Economics Research Unit, discussion paper, University of Aberdeen, Scotland, Aug. 1993.

p. 25   *One early stage analysis . . .* : Paul E. Greenberg, Stan N. Finkelstein, and Ernst R. Berndt, "Economic Consequences of Illness in the Workplace," *Sloan Management Review* (Summer 1995), 26–28.

p. 25   *Many of these expenses . . .* : Ibid., 29.

p. 25   *The rise in absenteeism . . .* : "1995 CCH Unscheduled Absence Survey," *Human Resource Management: Ideas and Trends* 354 (May 24, 1995), 85–95.

p. 25   *Similarly, if each of the 704 million . . .* : U.S. Department of Health and Human Services, *Health United States, 1993* (Hyattsville, Md.: Public Health Service, 1994), 176.

p. 26   *As a result, Costa Rica . . .* : Barbara A. Tenenbaum, ed., "Costa Rica," *Latin American History and Culture* (New York: Charles Scribner's Sons, 1996), 287.

p. 26   *And in both Japan and Canada . . .* : Paul Sperry, "Hidden Costs of National Health," *Medical Benefits,* Apr. 30, 1994, 4–5.

p. 26   *(Although the United States . . .* : Hewitt Associates, "Summary of Country Statutory Compensation and Benefits" (Lincolnshire, Ill.: Hewitt Associates, n.d.).

p. 26   *For example, a recent article . . .* : "What Should Women Over 50 Do?" *Harvard Health Letter,* vol. 19, no. 8 (Jun. 1994), 3–4.

p. 27   *Because of their lower costs . . .* : John R. Borzilleri, *Pharmaceutical Industry—No Turning Back* (New York: Dean Witter, 1994), 15.

p. 28   *The health insurance, . . .* : Watson Wyatt Worldwide and Washington Business Group on Health, "Is Cost Everything? Getting Value for Your Health Care Dollar," *Medical Benefits,* Apr. 15, 1996, 4.

p. 28   *For example, one federal . . .* : Thomas M. Burton, "Doctor Charged with Kickbacks from Caremark," *Wall Street Journal,* Sept. 22, 1994, B7.

p. 28   *Similarly, T² Medical . . .* : George Anders, "T² Sets Accord in Fraud Case, To Pay Penalty," *Wall Street Journal,* Sept. 26, 1994, A2.

p. 29   *The Mid America Dental . . .* : Eric Morganthaler, "Worth a Trip," *Wall Street Journal,* Dec. 9, 1993, A1, A10.

p. 29   *Customers are sensitive to the costs . . .* : *EBRI Databook on Employee Benefits* [Washington, D.C.: Employee Benefit Research Institute (EBRI), 1992], 31.

p. 29   *As a result of the favorable perception . . .* : Morganthaler, "Worth a Trip."

p. 29   *I began by . . .* : "Buying Glasses," *Consumer Reports,* vol. 58, no. 8 (Aug. 1993), 495–503.

p. 30   *Although Opticians are* . . . : National Eye Institute, letter to author, Jul. 26, 1996.

p. 30   *a graduate of* . . . : Ibid.

p. 31   *Eyewear prices had inflated* . . . : Census Bureau, *Statistical Abstract, 1995,* 78, table 25.

p. 31   *while hospitals' and doctors' prices* . . . : Ibid.

p. 31   *Because the customer* . . . : "Buying Glasses," *Consumer Reports,* 496.

p. 32   *For example, the hundreds* . . . : Lenscrafters and Pearle Vision, Lenscrafters letter to author Jul. 15, 1996; Pearle Vision letter to author from Jeff Smith, Professional Affairs Department, Jul. 17, 1996.

p. 32   *The* Consumer Reports *survey* . . . : "Buying Glasses," *Consumer Reports,* 500.

p. 32   *No wonder the overall satisfaction* . . . : Ibid., 502.

p. 32   *The first hard contact lenses* . . . : Dr. Linda Bennett, letter to author, Aug. 15, 1996.

p. 32   *Johnson and Johnson, for example* . . . : Brian O'Reilly, "J&J Is on a Roll," *Fortune,* Dec. 26, 1994, 178.

p. 32   *Ultimately, mail-order houses* . . . : Joseph T. Barr, "Alternative Dispensers Dominate Discussion of 1993," *Spectrum,* Jan. 1994, 9.

p. 33   *Their incomes have inflated* . . . : American Medical Association (AMA), *Socioeconomic Monitoring System 1991, 1994* (Chicago, Ill.: AMA, 1991, 1994).

p. 33   *In 1990, 97 percent* . . . : *EBRI Databook on Employee Benefits,* 248.

p. 33   *Indeed, when I used* . . . : Dr. Stanley Pearle of Pearle Vision in Dallas; Charles M. Stroupe of the Wesley-Jesson Corporation in Chicago; and David M. Browne of Lenscrafters in Cincinnati commented on these sections.

p. 33   *In the 1970s* . . . : U.S. Senate, Committee on Small Business, Subcommittee on Monopoly and Anti-competitive Activities, *Restrictive and Anti-competitive Practices in the Eyeglass Industry* (Washington, D.C.: Government Printing Office, 1973), 11–12.

p. 34   *The extensive testimony* . . . : Ibid.

p. 35   *Senator Haskell* . . . : Ibid., 19.

p. 35   *A study conducted by* . . . : Ibid., 26.

p. 36   *Dr. Pearle explains* . . . : Dr. Stanley Pearle, letter to author, Feb. 25, 1992.

p. 36   *Its prices have been rated* . . . : "Getting Framed," *Washingtonian*, Oct. 1990, 217.

p. 36   *Additionally, notes the publisher* . . . : Susana Barciela, "Optical Chain Has Single Vision: Low Prices," *Miami Herald*, Apr. 12, 1993, "Business Monday," 7.

p. 36   *The 24 percent* . . . : Harris-Equifax, *Health Information Privacy Survey* (New York: Louis Harris and Associates, 1993), 35.

p. 37   *Health Stop's aim* . . . : Regina E. Herzlinger, "Health Stop, A," *Creating New Health Care Ventures* (Gaithersburg, Md.: Aspen Publishers, 1992), 268–70.

p. 37   *Buoyed by a massive investment* . . . : Ralph T. King, Jr., "Hambrecht, in Financial Comeback, May Go Public with Sale of 20% Stake," *Wall Street Journal*, May 17, 1996, B2.

p. 38   *The managers of hospital* . . . : "Clinics Alter Brisk Emergency-Room Style," *New York Times*, Feb. 11, 1993, B2.

p. 38   *Ironically, some centers* . . . : For example, Boston's Beth Israel Hospital now owns the former Health Stop on Massachusetts Avenue in Cambridge. Sharon W. Reich, letter to author, Sept. 16, 1996, reviewed the history of Health Stop.

p. 39   *Even a busy hospital* . . . : Institute for Health Care Improvement, *Reducing Delays and Waiting Time* (Boston, Mass.: Institute for Health Care Improvement, 1996).

p. 39   *Health Stop's management* . . . : Bama Rucker, letter to author, Jul. 15, 1996.

p. 42   *After all, over a million* . . . : Census Bureau, *Statistical Abstract, 1993*, 138, table 211.

p. 43   *Notes the* Economist . . . : "Salick's Salve," *Economist*, Jul. 23, 1994, 62.

p. 45   *They understand how to provide* . . . : David Maister, *The Psychology of Waiting Lines* (Boston, Mass.: Harvard Business School Case Services, 1984).

p. 45   *For example, within their* . . . : P. Eugene Jones and James F. Cawley, "Physician Assistants and Health System Reform," *Journal of the American Medical Association*, vol. 271, no. 16 (Apr. 27, 1994), 1266–72.

Chapter 3: Give Me Mastery or Give Me Death: The New Health Care Activist

p. 47   *I looked up the menopause treatment* . . . : *Merck Manual of Diagnosis and Therapy* (Rahway, N.J.: Merck & Co., 1992), 1793–94.

p. 48   *Do you know a good one?* . . . : The details of this conversation and the exact characteristics of the doctor are composites drawn from many such conversations. Personal correspondence with women mentioned July, 1996.

p. 48   *As one advertising* . . . : Ronald Henkhoff, "Why Every Red-Blooded Consumer Owns a Truck," *Fortune*, May 29, 1995, 9.

p. 48   *At his sixty-fifth* . . . : Sam's story is a pastiche of many such stories.

p. 48   *Between 1968 and 1976, the lives* . . . : Lee Goldman and E. Francis Cook, "The Decline in Ischemic Heart Disease Mortality Rates," *Annals of Internal Medicine*, vol. 101, no. 6 (Dec. 1984), 833.

p. 48   *During that period* . . . : Ibid., 825.

p. 48   *Between 1980 and 1990, it plunged* . . . : U.S. Department of Health and Human Services, *Health United States, 1993* (Washington, D.C.: Government Printing Office, 1994), 103.

p. 48   *By 1991, the year* . . . : Ibid., p. 47.

p. 49   *During that period* . . . : Goldman and Cook, "Decline in Ischemic Heart Disease Mortality Rates," 833.

p. 49   *in 1993, they accounted* . . . : Health Insurance Association of America, "Source Book of Health Insurance Data," *Medical Benefits*, May 15, 1994, 8.

p. 49   *In a 1987 report* . . . : The American Board of Family Practice, *Rights and Responsibilities: Part II* (Lexington, Ky.: American Board of Family Practice, May 1987), 38.

p. 49   *While a 1994 survey* . . . : This survey was performed for a corporation that prefers to remain anonymous. Authorizing letter Oct. 1996.

p. 50   *A "healthy lifestyle"* . . . : Ruth E. Patterson et al., "Health Lifestyle Patterns of U.S. Adults," *Medical Benefits*, Oct. 15, 1994, 11.

p. 50   *T. George Harris, the founder* . . . : Correspondence with the author, 1995.

p. 50   *Janine Jocinto Sharkey* . . . : Leslie Laurence, "The Proactive Patient," *Town and Country*, vol. 148, no. 5173 (Oct. 1994), 126.

p. 50   *The* Wall Street Journal . . . : Laura Johannes, "Patients Delve into Databases to Second-Guess Doctors," *Wall Street Journal,* Feb. 26, 1996, B1.

p. 51   *Some activists disregard* . . . : Wendy Bounds, "Sick of Skyrocketing Costs, Patients Defy Doctors and Shop for Cheaper Treatment," *Wall Street Journal,* Feb. 16, 1993, B1.

p. 51   *Andy Grove, the CEO* . . . : Andy Grove, "Taking On Prostate Cancer," *Fortune,* May 13, 1996, 72.

p. 51   *In the heat of her* . . . : Novalis Corporation, "American Values and Health Care Reform," *Medical Benefits,* Mar. 30, 1993, 7.

p. 52   *In the quest for good health* . . . : The per-capita consumption and the rates of change were calculated from data in U.S. Bureau of the Census, *Statistical Abstract of the United States, 1992* (Washington, D.C.: Government Printing Office, 1993), 147.

p. 52   *Americans have quaffed* . . . : Maxim Lenderman, "NBPA's Green Day at Pepsi," *Beverage World,* May 1996, 41.

p. 52   *From 1983 to 1993, the percentage* . . . : *Prevention Index, 1994* (Emmaus, Pa.: Rodale Press, 1994), 30.

p. 53   *In 1990 over 40 percent* . . . : Census Bureau, *Statistical Abstract, 1995,* 145, table 221.

p. 53   *and the number who claim to exercise* . . . : Cynthia Crossen and Ellen Graham, "Good News—and Bad—About America's Health," *Wall Street Journal,* Jun. 28, 1996, R1.

p. 53   *Busy Americans exercise* . . . : Gregory D. Curfman, "Is Exercise Beneficial or Hazardous to Your Heart?" *New England Journal of Medicine,* vol. 329, no. 23 (Dec. 2, 1993), 1730–31.

p. 53   *Surprisingly, the very word* . . . : Kenneth H. Cooper, *1993 Healthtrac Foundation Prize Recipient Lecture* (Palo Alto, Calif.: Healthtrac Foundation, 1994), 1–2.

p. 53   *Indeed,* Billboard *magazine* . . . : Nanci Hellmich, "Yoga Videos," *USA Today,* Aug. 4, 1994, 5D.

p. 53   *In 1996, 23 percent of Americans* . . . : Crossen and Graham, "Good News—and Bad—About America's Health," R1.

p. 53   *The market for* . . . : Frost and Sullivan, *U.S. Home Diagnostics and Monitoring Product Markets* (New York: Frost and Sullivan, 1994), 1.

p. 53   *The value of the vitamin* . . . : Donaldson, Lufkin, and Jenrette Securities, *General Nutrition Companies, Inc.* (New York: Donaldson, Lufkin, and Jenrette, 1993), 6.

p. 53   *The 18 million women* . . . : Milt Freudenheim, "Rearranging Drugstore Shelves," *New York Times,* Sept. 27, 1994, D1.

p. 53   *Although many addiction experts* . . . : Philip J. Hilts, "Is Nicotine Addictive? It Depends on Whose Criteria You Use," *New York Times,* Aug. 2, 1994, 3.

p. 54   *the percentage of adults smoking* . . . : U.S. Department of Health and Human Services (DHHS), *Health United States, 1994* (Washington, D.C.: Government Printing Office, 1994), 155, table 64.

p. 54   *These changes have not* . . . : Census Bureau, *Statistical Abstract, 1993,* 96, table 128.

p. 54   *A dramatic example* . . . : North America Case Line, "Groundbreaking Research Establishes Employee Role in Reducing Health Care Costs," *Medical Benefits,* Feb. 28, 1994, 3.

p. 54   *Indeed, Medicare* . . . : DHHS, *Health United States, 1994,* 219, 243.

p. 54   *The 5 percent of national health care* . . . : James D. Lubitz and Gerald F. Riley, "Trends in Medicare Payments in the Last Year of Life," *New England Journal of Medicine,* vol. 328, no. 15 (Apr. 15, 1993), 1092. Thirty percent of Medicare expenditures, which are 17 percent of total health care spending, were for the last year of life. [5% = (30%)(17%)].

p. 54   *One study estimated* . . . : Ezekiel J. Emanuel and Linda L. Emanuel, "The Economics of Dying," *New England Journal of Medicine,* vol. 330, no. 8 (Feb. 24, 1994), 543.

p. 55   *The condition of the* . . . : Thomas T. Perls, "The Oldest Old," *Scientific American,* vol. 273, no. 1 (Jan. 1995), 75.

p. 55   *Further, although health* . . . : James F. Fries, "The Compression of Morbidity: Near or Far?" *Millbank Quarterly,* vol. 67, no. 2 (1989), 208–32.

p. 56   *Fries's hypothesis* . . . : George Pickett and William F. Bridges, "Prevention, Declining Mortality Rates, and the Cost of Medicare," *American Journal of Preventive Medicine,* vol. 3, no. 2 (1987), 6, 7.

p. 56   *A 1996 Dutch study* . . . : Wilma J. Nusselder et al., "The Elimination of Selected Chronic Diseases in a Population," *American Journal of Public Health,* vol. 86, no. 2 (Feb. 1996), 191.

p. 56   *With a colleague, Fries . . .* : J. Paul Leigh and James F. Fries, "Health Habits, Health Care Use and Costs in a Sample of Retirees," *Inquiry* 29 (Spring 1992), 44–54.

p. 56   *Conversely, the prevalence . . .* : Census Bureau, *Statistical Abstract, 1995,* 141, table 215, and U.S. Department of Health and Human Services, *Vital and Health Statistics, 1993* (Washington, D.C.: Government Printing Office, December 1994), 80, table 57.

p. 56   *For example, one inexpensive . . .* : J. Paul Leigh et al., "Randomized Controlled Study of a Retiree Health Promotion Program," *Archives of Internal Medicine,* 152 (Jun. 1992), 1201–1206.

p. 56   *Similarly, a self-help program . . .* : Kate R. Lorig, Peter D. Mazonson, and Halsted R. Holman, "Evidence Suggesting that Health Education for Self-management in Chronic Arthritis Has Sustained Health Benefits While Reducing Health Care Cost," *Arthritis and Rheumatism,* 36 (April 1993), 439–46.

p. 56   *To assess the importance . . .* : Census Bureau, *Statistical Abstract, 1995,* 141, table 215, and 15, table 14.

p. 57   *Despite these activist successes . . .* : DHHS, *Health United States, 1993,* 101.

p. 57   *The poor rate . . .* : Ibid., 101, 62.

p. 57   *and men fare less well than women . . .* : Ibid.

p. 57   *For example, the incidence . . .* : DHHS, *Health United States, 1992,* 109, 97.

p. 57   *Over a quarter of the population . . .* : DHHS, *Health United States, 1993,* 103.

p. 57   *despite new food fads . . .* : *Prevention Index, 1994,* 30.

p. 57   *Excessive consumption of alcohol . . .* : J. Michael McGinnis and William H. Foege, "Actual Causes of Death in the United States," *Journal of the American Medical Association,* vol. 270, no. 18 (Nov. 10, 1993), 2207–12.

p. 57   *In total these lifestyle . . .* : Ibid.

p. 57   *For example, smokers . . .* : Kevin Fiscella and Peter Franks, "Cost-Effectiveness of the Transdermal Nicotine Patch as an Adjunct to Physicians' Smoking Cessation Counseling," *Journal of the American Medical Association,* vol. 275, no. 16 (Apr. 24, 1996), 1249.

p. 57   *Tobacco, for example . . .* : McGinnis and Foege, "Actual Causes of Death in the United States," 2207–12.

p. 58   *In a 1989 study* . . . : Jeffrey S. Harris, "What Employers Can Do About Medical Care Costs," in *Care and Cost,* ed. Kenneth McLennan and Jack A. Meyer (Boulder, Colo.: Westview Press, 1989), 180–81.

p. 58   *The Health Insurance Association* . . . : Health Insurance Association of America, "Source Book of Health Insurance Data," *Medical Benefits,* May 15, 1994, 8.

p. 58   *Notes one physician* . . . : Paula Moyer, "Twin Cities Plans Collaborate on Asthma Management," *Managed Healthcare,* May 1996, 75.

p. 58   *Adds a pharmacist* . . . : Liz Meszaros, "Breathing Lessons," *Managed Healthcare,* May 1966, S27.

p. 58   *Similarly, many experts feel* . . . : Michael J. Major, "DSM and Diabetes," *Managed Healthcare,* Sept. 1995, 40.

p. 59   *One study found, no doubt* . . . : "Crossing the Divide from Vaccine Technology to Vaccine Delivery," *Journal of the American Medical Association,* vol. 272, no. 14 (Oct. 12, 1994), 1138.

p. 59   *Other studies showed* . . . : Major, "DSM and Diabetes," 40.

p. 59   *did not provide their patients* . . . : Meszaros, "Breathing Lessons," S30.

p. 59   *and did not even ask* . . . : "Patients Want to Be Asked About Functional Status," *Journal Watch,* vol. 15, no. 6 (Mar. 15, 1995), 52.

p. 59   *Americans can obtain* . . . : Ulrich's *International Periodicals Directory 1996* (New Providence, N.J.: R. R. Bowker, 1996), 5198.

p. 59   *Even brief periods of physician advice* . . . : Richard D. Hurt et al., "Nicotine Patch Therapy for Smoking Cessation Combined With Physician Advice and Nurse Follow-Up," *Journal of the American Medical Association,* vol. 271, no. 8 (Feb. 23, 1994), 595.

p. 59   *A twenty-four-hour telephone health service* . . . : Geoffrey Leavenworth, "Informed Employees Make Better Health Consumers," *Preventive Medicine, supp. A: Business and Health,* vol. 13, no. 13 (1995), 7–8.

p. 59   *Computer-generated calls* . . . : "Computer-generated Phone Calls Increase Clinic Visits," *Journal Watch,* vol. 15, no. 17 (Sept. 1, 1995), 139.

p. 60   *As one spokesperson notes* . . . : Stephen L. Davidow, "Compliance with Asthma Treatment Guidelines Improves Symptoms," *Update: Health Outcomes Institute,* vol. 2, iss. 3 (Fall 1995), 4.

p. 60   *Finally, a six-year follow-up* . . . : Gilbert J. Botvin et al., "Long-term Follow-up Results of a Randomized Drug Abuse Prevention Trial in a White Middle-class Population," *Journal of the American Medical Association,* vol. 273, no. 14 (Apr. 12, 1995), 1106.

p. 60   *Kate Lorig of Stanford University* . . . : Lorig, Mazonson, and Holman, "Evidence Suggesting that Health Education."

p. 60   *All participants receive* . . . : Kate R. Lorig and James F. Fries, *The Arthritis Help Book* (Reading, Mass.: Addison-Wesley, 1990).

p. 60   *In scholarly parlance* . . . : Patrick McGowan and Lawrence W. Green, "Arthritis Self-management in Native Populations of British Columbia," *Canadian Journal on Aging*, vol. 14, supp. 1 (1995), 205.

p. 61   *The results have been* . . . : Ibid.

p. 61   *The relationship between* . . . : In their article, "Schooling and Health," Phillip Farrell and Victor R. Fuchs demonstrated that a personality trait associated with education, and not education per se, caused educated people to abstain from smoking. But the relevance of their study, based on 1979 data, today is questionable. Further, the study treats all education as equivalent; but Lorig's work clearly shows that education that empowers individuals is unusually effective. Phillip Farrell and Victor R. Fuchs, "Schooling and Health," *Journal of Health Economics* (1982), 217–30.

p. 61   *For example, women in Thailand* . . . : World Bank, *World Development Report, 1993* (New York: Oxford University Press, 1993), 43.

p. 61   *Last, as Leonard Sagan* . . . : Leonard Sagan, *The Health of Nations* (New York: Basic Books, 1987), 180.

p. 61   *Between 1960 and 1986* . . . : Statistical Bulletin, "The Widening Gap between Socioeconomic Status and Mortality," *Medical Benefits*, May 30, 1994, 8.

p. 61   *Only 17 to 27 percent* . . . : Sagan, *Health of Nations*, 177.

p. 62   *Income undoubtedly* . . . : Peter Franks et al., "Health Insurance and Subjective Health Status: Data from the 1987 National Medical Expenditure Survey," *American Journal of Public Health*, vol. 83, no. 9 (Sept. 1993), 1297.

p. 62   *Similarly, although race* . . . : "Prevalence of Selected Risk Factors for Chronic Disease by Education Level in Racial/Ethnic Populations— United States, 1991–1992," *Journal of the American Medical Association*, vol. 273, no. 2 (Jan. 11, 1995), 100.

p. 62   *Better educated* . . . : *Prevention Index, 1994.*

p. 62   *The effect of education* . . . : World Bank, *World Development Report, 1993*, 44.

p. 62   *In Porto Alegre . . .* : Ibid.

p. 62   *In the United States . . .* : DHHS, *Health United States, 1993* (Washington, D.C.: Government Printing Office, 1993), 156, table 65.

p. 62   *In the United States . . .* : Morbidity and Mortality Weekly Report, "Cigarette Smoking Among Women of Reproductive Age—United States, 1987 to 1992," *Medical Benefits*, Nov. 30, 1994, 2.

p. 62   *Similarly, while 44 percent . . .* : *Prevention Index, 1994*, 11.

p. 63   *A similar pattern prevails . . .* : World Bank, *World Development Report, 1993*, 44.

p. 63   *Because education and the prevalence . . .* : Census Bureau, *Statistical Abstract, 1995*, 119, table 171.

p. 63   *The clearest evidence . . .* : Douglas Black et al., *The Black Report, Inequalities in Health* (New York: Penguin Books, 1990), 271.

p. 63   *Differences in the availability . . .* : Ibid., 272.

p. 63   *Although the differences . . .* : Ibid., 44, 123.

p. 63   *All these causes . . .* : Lester Breslow and J. E. Enstrom, "Persistence of Health Habits and Their Relationship to Mortality," *Preventative Medicine*, Sept. 4, 1980, 469–83.

p. 63   *Similar patterns prevailed . . .* : *Black Report*, 91.

p. 63   *Similarly, the Finnish . . .* : Ibid., 90.

p. 64   *The lowest social groups . . .* : Ibid., 277.

p. 64   *All in all . . .* : Ibid., 281.

p. 64   *Health club membership . . .* : "Health Clubs," *Consumer Reports*, vol. 61, no. 1 (Jan. 1996), 27.

p. 64   *All in all, sales of athletic clothing . . .* : Debra Hazel, "Are Sporting Goods Next?" *Chain Store Age Executive* (June 1993), 27.

p. 65   *As co-author of the best-selling . . .* : James F. Fries and Donald M. Vickery, *Take Care of Yourself: A Consumer's Guide to Medical Care* (Reading, Mass.: Addison-Wesley, 1989).

p. 65   *And as a medical researcher . . .* : James F. Fries, Lawrence W. Green, and Sol Levine, "Health Promotion and the Compression of Morbidity," *Lancet*, no. 8631 (Mar. 1989), 481–83.

p. 65   *In a test . . .* : Leigh and Fries, "Health Habits, Health Care Use."

p. 65   *Similarly, the Aetna insurance . . .* : Bruce Shutan, "Self Care: A Resource Untapped," *Medical Benefits*, April 30, 1994, 12.

p. 65   *Consider a common problem . . .* : "Hemorrhoids," *Nutrition Health Review,* Spring 1992, 12. Received from Mark Haverland, Jan. 12, 1994.

p. 66   *For example, Access Health . . .* : *Access Health: The 1995 Annual Report* (Rancho Cordova, Calif.: Access Health, 1996), 1, 14, 20.

p. 66   *What fueled this . . .* : Ibid.

p. 66   *Notes a* Fortune *magazine . . .* : Shawn Tully, "Access Health Marketing. Remedy: Educate the Patient," *Fortune,* Feb. 7, 1994, 134.

p. 67   *When compared with . . .* : Michael C. Fiore et al., "The Effectiveness of the Nicotine Patch for Smoking Cessation," *Journal of the American Medical Association,* vol. 271, no. 24 (Jun. 22, 1994), 1940–47.

p. 67   *One analyst notes . . .* : Ronald Nordmann and Cathy Wargo, *Cygnus Therapeutic Systems* (New York: PaineWebber, 1994).

p. 67   *Becker and his colleague . . .* : Gary S. Becker and Michael Grossman, "The Senate's Health Care Follies," *Wall Street Journal,* Aug. 9, 1994, A12.

p. 68   *Nevertheless, an editorial . . .* : David Satchere and Michael Eeriksen, "The Paradox of Tobacco Control," *Journal of the American Medical Association,* vol. 271, no. 8 (Feb. 23, 1994), 627.

p. 68   *In 1993, the medical costs . . .* : Phillip J. Hilts, "Sharp Rise Seen in Smokers' Health Care Costs," *New York Times,* Jul. 8, 1994, A12.

p. 68   *Once they become sick . . .* : Regina E. Herzlinger, "Center for Nutritional Research," *Creating New Health Care Ventures* (Gaithersburg, Md.: Aspen, 1992), 208.

p. 69   *In a 1995 survey . . .* : American Sports Data, *American Attitudes Towards Healthy Lifestyle Incentives* (Boston, Mass.: International Health Racquet and Sportsclub Association, 1995), 10.

p. 69   *That unhealthy lifestyle . . .* : Stephen D. Brink, "Health Risks and Their Impact on Medical Costs," *Medical Benefits,* Apr. 15, 1995, 1.

p. 69   *Another analysis confirmed . . .* : "Preventive Medicine," *Business and Health,* supp. A, vol. 13, no. 3 (1995), 5.

p. 69   *In 1990, Americans . . .* : David M. Eisenberg et al., "Unconventional Medicine in the United States," *New England Journal of Medicine,* vol. 328, no. 4 (Jan. 28, 1993), 246–52.

p. 70   *In France, for example . . .* : Marlise Simons, "So It's Not What Doctor Ordered: Herbs Are In," *New York Times,* Apr. 11, 1994, A4.

p. 70   *Although visits to . . .* : Eisenberg, "Unconventional Medicine," 252.

p. 71   *The late Lewis Thomas* . . . : Lewis Thomas, *The Youngest Science* (New York: Viking Press, 1983).

p. 71   *You think that* . . . : "Debugging the System," *Harvard Health Letter,* vol. 19, no. 8 (Jun. 1994), 1–2.

p. 72   *In fact, breast implants* . . . : William Cronnie, "Study: Leaky Breast Implants May Reduce Cancer Risk," *Harvard University Gazette,* Aug. 12, 1994, 1.

p. 72   *A study of 20,000 patients* . . . : Sheldon Greenfield et al., "Variations in Resource Utilization Among Medical Specialties and Systems of Care," *Journal of the American Medical Association,* vol. 267, no. 12 (Mar. 25, 1992), 1624–30.

p. 72   *French medicine relies* . . . : Lynn Payer, "Borderline Cases," *Sciences,* vol. 30, no. 4 (Jul. 1, 1990), 38.

p. 72   *Although Galen is honored* . . . : "Galen," *New Encyclopaedia Britannica,* vol. 5 (Chicago: Encyclopaedia Britannica, 1994), 82.

p. 73   *As a result, creators of legitimate* . . . : Sherwin B. Nuland, "Medical Fads: Bran, Midwives and Leeches," *New York Times,* Jun. 25, 1995, sec. 4, p. 16.

p. 73   *As Brian Inglis* . . . : Brian Inglis, *The History of Medicine* (Cleveland: World Publishing, 1965), 148–49.

p. 73   *As Inglis recounts* . . . : Ibid., 150.

p. 73   *The obstetrician, Ignaz* . . . : Ibid., 152–54.

p. 73   *When an Australian researcher* . . . : *Harvard Health Letter,* vol. 19, no. 8 (Jun. 1994), 1.

p. 73   *Stung by the lack of support* . . . : Barry J. Marshall, "Helicobacter Pylori: The Etiologic Agent for Peptic Ulcer," *Journal of the American Medical Association,* vol. 274, no. 13 (Oct. 4, 1995), 1064.

p. 74   *Notes an editorial* . . . : Robert L. Kane and Judith Garrard, "Changing Physician Prescribing Practices," *Journal of the American Medical Association,* vol. 271, no. 5 (Feb. 2, 1994), 393–94.

p. 74   *One physician said* . . . : "NIH Consensus Panel Urges Antimicrobials for Ulcer Patients," *Journal of the American Medical Association,* vol. 271, no. 11 (Mar. 16, 1994), 808.

p. 74   *To test whether* . . . : L. McTier Anderson, "Marketing Science: Where's the Beef?" *Business Horizons,* Jan.–Feb. 1994, 10.

p. 74   *In 1965, when Congress* . . . : "Incalculably Inaccurate," *Economist,* Aug. 20, 1994, 22.

p. 75   *For example, although the connection* . . . : World Bank, *World Development Report, 1993,* 12, 132, 205.

p. 75   *As some epidemiologists* . . . : Sarah Tilton Fries, letter to author, Jul. 16, 1996.

p. 75   *For example, despite the massive* . . . : L. McTier Anderson, "Marketing Science: Where's the Beef?" 14.

p. 76   *For example, the efficacy* . . . : Jerry Avorn et al., "Reduction of Bacteriuria and Pyuria After Ingestion of Cranberry Juice," *Journal of the American Medical Association,* vol. 271, no. 10 (Mar. 9, 1994), 751–54.

p. 76   *Notes from Ventre* . . . : Regina E. Herzlinger, "North Shore Birth Center," *Creating New Health Care Ventures* (Gaithersburg, Md.: Aspen, 1992), 361; case study reviewed and cleared by Beverly Hospital.

p. 77   *Nurse-midwives* . . . : "Non-Physician Providers, The State of Health Care in America," *Business and Health* (Montvale, N.J.: Business and Health, 1994), 50.

p. 77   *The history of birth* . . . : Herzlinger, "North Shore Birth Center."

p. 77   *While the death rate* . . . : DHHS, *Health United States, 1994,* 128, table 45.

p. 77   *Cesarean section* . . . : Geoffrey Cowley, "What High Tech Can't Accomplish," *Newsweek,* Oct. 4, 1993, 60.

p. 77   *up from one of every twenty* . . . : Health Letter, "Unnecessary Cesarean Sections," *Medical Benefits,* Jul. 30, 1994, 5.

p. 77   *Although the "right" number* . . . : Ibid.

p. 77   *Noted the president* . . . : Herzlinger, "North Shore Birth Center," 362.

p. 77   *Observes Dorothy Kuell* . . . : Ibid., 360.

p. 78   *Small wonder* . . . : Ibid., 361.

p. 78   *Women who use* . . . : Fran Ventre, letter to author, Aug. 26, 1996.

p. 78   *Noted the budget director* . . . : Herzlinger, "North Shore Birth Center," 365.

p. 79   *Despite its good* . . . : Miriam Zoll, "Birth Center Conflicts Cited for Resignation," *Beverly Times,* Dec. 13, 1984.

p. 79   *A good example* . . . : Whole Foods Market, *Team Member General Information Guidebook* (Austin, Tex.: Whole Foods Market, 1993), 25.

p. 80   *Notes the guidebook* . . . : Ibid., 24.

p. 81   *By August of 1996* . . . : "NASDAQ National Market," *New York Times,* Aug. 20, 1996, D18.

p. 82   *Because of health activists* . . . : Robertson, Stephens and Company, "Vestro Foods Inc.," *Portfolio Notes* (Jun. 23, 1994), 40.

Chapter 4: The Health Care System That Provides Convenience and Mastery

p. 88   *Typically, the process* . . . : P. W. Turnbull and A. Meenaghan, "Diffusion of Innovation and Opinion Leadership," *European Journal of Marketing,* vol. 14, no. 1 (1980), 3–33.

p. 89   *Indeed Boston's Institute* . . . : Institute for Health Care Improvement, *Conference proceedings: National Congress on Reducing Delays and Waiting Times in Health Care,* July 23–24, 1996 (Boston: Institute for Health Care Improvement, 1996).

p. 89   *My former assistant* . . . : Stacy Shore, letter to author, Jul. 1996.

p. 91   *As a special April* . . . : Joseph Burns, "Measuring Health Care Quality," *Medical Benefits,* Apr. 1996.

p. 91   *So why do those who purchased* . . . : U.S. Department of Health and Human Services, *Health United States, 1994* (Washington, D.C.: Government Printing Office, 1994), 225.

p. 92   *In 1965, for example* . . . : Ibid.

p. 92   *In the period 1984 to 1991* . . . : *EBRI Databook on Employee Benefits* (Washington, D.C.: Employee Benefits Research Institute, 1992), 260.

p. 92   *By 1990 medically* . . . : Ibid., 31.

p. 92   *Even after years* . . . : The Conference Board, "Transforming the Benefit Function," *Medical Benefits,* Jan. 15, 1996, 7.

p. 93   *In 1992 per capita out-of-pocket* . . . : John R. Borzilleri, *Pharmaceutical Industry—No Turning Back* (New York: Dean Witter, 1994), 16, table 10.

p. 93   *In 1993 most Americans* . . . : U.S. Bureau of the Census, *Statistical Abstract of the United States, 1993* (Washington, D.C.: Government Printing Office, 1993), 454–55.

p. 93   *Spurred by the magnitude* . . . : Norma Harris, "How Hospitals Measure Up," *Business and Health,* Aug. 1994, 20–24.

p. 93   *Some health insurance plans* . . . : George Anders, "Three HMOs Evaluate Themselves," *Wall Street Journal,* Nov. 16, 1993, B1.

p. 93   *In various states* . . . : *Update* (Bloomington, Minn.: Health Outcomes Institute, Summer 1994), 4.

p. 93   *Industry standard-setting*...: "JCAHO Unveils Simplified Rating System," *Modern Healthcare,* Aug. 1, 1994, 6.

p. 93   *And the National Committee*...: National Committee for Quality Assurance, "HEDIS Pilot Report Card Project," *Medical Benefits,* Feb. 28, 1994, 6.

p. 93   *The independent Health Outcomes*...: *Update, The Newsletter of the Health Outcomes Institute,* 4 (Summer 1994), 4.

p. 94   *Currently estimated at $10 to $15 billion*...: John Morrissey, "Information Systems; Data Sector Has Wall Street's Attention," *Modern Healthcare,* Feb. 5, 1996, 30.

p. 94   *The Westborough*...: John Kordash, letter to author, Jul. 1996.

p. 94   *Notes an unusually tart review*...: Thomas M. Gill and Alvan R. Feinstein, "A Critical Appraisal of the Quality of Quality-of-Life Measurements," *Journal of the American Medical Association,* vol. 272, no. 8 (Aug. 24–31, 1994), 619.

p. 95   *National magazines*...: "The Honor Roll," *U.S. News and World Report,* Jul. 24, 1995, 51.

p. 95   *For example, GTE*...: Paul Magnusson and Keith H. Hammonds, "Health Care: The Quest for Quality," *Business Week,* Apr. 8, 1996, 104.

p. 95   *The demand for*...: Jeremy Brody, letter to author, Jul. 15, 1996.

p. 95   *A consumer watchdog*...: "Consumer Group Slams JCAHO Regulator Record," *Modern Healthcare,* Jul. 15, 1996, 6.

p. 95   *The system for rating*...: Christine Woolsey, "Buyers Go It Alone on Quality," *Business Insurance,* May 22, 1995, 1.

p. 95   *In the August 1996 issue*...: "Latest *Consumer Reports* Rates Managed Care Plans," *American Medical News,* Aug. 12, 1996, 4.

p. 95   *The magazine was so dissatisfied*...: "How Good Is Your Health Plan?" *Consumer Reports,* vol. 61, no. 8 (Aug. 1996), 34, 35.

p. 96   *Choosing a doctor*...: "Governor William F. Weld Signs Physician Profile Bill," press release, Commonwealth of Massachusetts Executive Department, Aug. 9, 1996.

p. 96   *Notes the CEO*...: "Health Care: The Quest for Quality," *Business Week,* Apr. 8, 1996, 104–106.

Chapter 5: Options for the Productivity Revolution

p. 99   *The doctors gave me . . .* : Helen Dewar, "Biden, Home on the Hill," *Washington Post,* Sept. 8, 1988, C1; Senator Joseph Biden, conversation with author, reviewed by Matt Baumgart of Senator Biden's office, Summer 1996.

p. 100   *But like the senator . . .* : Health Research Institute, "Health System Reform: Employers', Unions' and Citizens' Views, and a Comparative Analysis," *Medical Benefits,* Sept. 15, 1993, 8.

p. 100   *And like him too . . .* : Health Insurance Association of America, "National Attitudes Toward Health Care Financing Reform," *Medical Benefits,* Feb. 29, 1992, 12.

p. 101   *In one large-scale survey . . .* : Louis Harris and Associates, *Comparing Health Systems: An International Survey of Consumer Satisfaction* (Boston: Harvard Community Health Plan, 1990).

p. 101   *For example, fewer Canadians . . .* : Ibid, 9.

p. 101   *A 1996 report . . .* : Karen Donelan et al., "All Payer, Single Payer, Managed Care, No Payer: Patients' Perspectives in Three Nations," *Health Affairs,* vol. 15, no. 2 (Summer 1996), 254–65.

p. 101   *Americans also support . . .* : Harvard Community Health Plan (HCHP), *An International Comparison of Health-Care Systems: Harvard Community Health Plan Annual Report, 1990* (Brookline, Mass.: HCHP, 1991), 11–21.

p. 101   *In 1994, pharmaceutical firms . . .* : *The PhRMA Industry Profile* [Washington, D.C.: Pharmaceutical and Research Manufacturers of America (PhRMA), 1996], table 12.

p. 101   *generating a trade surplus . . .* : Jonathan C. Menes, "Highlights of Outlook '94," *U.S. Industrial Outlook* (Washington, D.C.: U.S. Dept. of Commerce), Jan. 1994, 17. Surplus is for 1993.

p. 101   *The medical device industry . . .* : "U.S. Exports of Medical Devices Advance 10% in 1994," *Medical Device and Diagnostic Industry,* vol. 17, iss. 5 (May 1995), 14.

p. 101   *In a pleasant reversal . . .* : Ibid.

p. 102   *For example, Caremark International . . .* : Mari Edlin, "Going After the Global Marketplace," *Managed Healthcare,* vol. 5, no. 8 (Aug. 1995), 33.

p. 102   *For example, in 1989 . . .* : National Science Board (NSB), *Science and Engineering Indicators—1991* (Washington, D.C.: Government Printing Office, 1991), 344.

p. 102   *In that year American . . .* : Ibid., 342.

p. 102   *Between 1985 and 1990 . . .* : "Awards—Nobel Prizes," *The World Almanac and Book of Facts, 1996* (Mahwah, N.J.: World Almanac Books, 1996), 324; Between 1985 and 1990, nine Americans, one Japanese, one Briton, and one Italian-American won the Nobel Prize in Medicine and Physiology.

p. 102   *The average U.S. drug . . .* : NSB, *Science and Engineering Indicators—1991*, 442.

p. 102   *In a 1993* Business Week . . . : Peter Coy, "The Global Patent Race Picks Up Speed," *Business Week,* Aug. 9, 1993, 57–62.

p. 102   *Respondents to a 1991 survey . . .* : NSB, *Science and Engineering Indicators—1991*, 449.

p. 102   *Indeed, in 1990, 72 percent . . .* : Ibid., 463.

p. 102   *While 68 percent of Americans . . .* : Ibid., 466.

p. 103   *Survey respondents overwhelmingly . . .* : Public Agenda Foundation, *Faulty Diagnosis* (New York: Public Agenda Foundation, 1992), 4.

p. 103   *In contrast, the citizens of Canada . . .* : Harvard Community Health Plan, *An International Comparison,* 10–11.

p. 103   *In 1992 total per-capita . . .* : National Center for Health Statistics (NCHS), *Health United States, 1994* (Hyattsville, Md.: Public Health Service, 1995), 220.

p. 103   *The United States spent substantially . . .* : Ibid.

p. 103   *Since 1982 health care . . .* : U.S. Bureau of the Census, *Statistical Abstract of the United States, 1995,* 115th ed. (Washington, D.C.: Government Printing Office, 1995), 493–94, table 762.

p. 103   *In 1989 American corporations' profit . . .* : Katherine Levit and Cathy Cowan, "The Burden of Health Care Costs: Business, Households, and Governments," *Health Care Financing Review,* 12 (Jan. 1990), 131.

p. 103   *Medicare and Medicaid payments . . .* : NCHS, *Health United States, 1994,* 244, 247. Between 1991 and 1992, Medicare payments per person served increased by 8.1 percent, and Medicaid payments per recipient increased by 7.8 percent.

p. 103   *outstripping increases . . .* : Census Bureau, *Statistical Abstract, 1995,* 299, 492. Between 1991 and 1992, total per-capita tax revenues increased by 5.3 percent.

p. 104   *While the wages and salaries . . .* : NCHS, *Health United States, 1994,* 227.

p. 104   *The percentage of health care costs . . .* : Ibid., 229.

p. 104   *but some expensive items . . .* : Ibid., 230.

p. 104   *The elderly and chronically ill . . .* : U.S. Bureau of Labor Statistics, *Consumer Expenditures in 1993,* report 885 (Washington, D.C.: U.S. Department of Labor, 1994), 8.

p. 104   *And the 35.3 percent . . .* : NCHS, *Health United States, 1994,* 240.

p. 104   *Small wonder that the uninsured . . .* : Louis Harris and Associates, *Comparing Health Systems: An International Survey of Consumer Satisfaction* (Boston: Harvard Community Health Plan, 1990), 21, 22, 24.

p. 104   *The factors within the industry . . .* : Sally T. Burner and Daniel R. Waldo, "National Health Expenditure Projections, 1994–2005," *Health Care Financing Review,* vol. 16, no. 4 (Jun. 22, 1995), 221.

p. 104   *No wonder that in a 1996 report . . .* : Watson Wyatt Insider, "What's Going On?" *Medical Benefits,* vol. 13, no. 9 (May 15, 1996), 7–8.

p. 105   *The many types of managed care . . .* : "HMO-PPO Digest, 1995," *Medical Benefits,* Mar. 15, 1996, 1.

p. 105   *In 1995 the number . . .* : "Study Documents Brisk Merger-Acquisition Pace," *Modern Healthcare,* Feb. 26, 1996, 3.

p. 106   *The number of integrated . . .* : SMG Market Letter, "IHN Market Continues Steady Growth and Evolution," *Medical Benefits,* vol. 13, no. 10 (May 30, 1996), 6.

p. 106   *The importance of organizational . . .* : Howard Gleckman et al., "The Technology Payoff," *Business Week,* Jun. 14, 1993, 57.

p. 107   *They may worry that neither diet . . .* : Health Research Institute, "Health System Reform: Employers', Unions', and Citizens' Views, and a Comparative Analysis," *Medical Benefits,* Sept. 15, 1993, 8.

Chapter 6: Downsizing: The "Just Say No" Diet

p. 108   *In "Slashed and Burned," . . .* : Alex Markels and Matt Murray, "Slashed and Burned," *Wall Street Journal,* May 14, 1996, 1.

p. 108   *Although American firms shrank . . .* : Andrew J. Filardo, "Has the Productivity Trend Steepened in the 1990s?" *Federal Reserve Bank of Kansas City, Economic Review* (Fourth Quarter 1995), 41–59.

p. 109   *Early-stage HMOs . . .* : Mark S. Foster, *Henry J. Kaiser: Builder in the Modern American West* (Austin: University of Texas Press, 1989), 214; Dr. L. Zendle, letter to author, Oct. 22, 1996.

p. 109　*They typically contracted . . .* : Harold Luft, *Health Maintenance Organizations* (New York: Wiley-Interscience, 1981), 14.

p. 109　*Not surprisingly, most of . . .* : "How Good is Your Health Plan?" *Consumer Reports*, Aug. 1996, 35; "America's Best HMOs," *Newsweek*, Jun. 24, 1996, 61.

p. 109　*An influential . . .* : Willard G. Manning et al., "A Controlled Trial of the Effect of a Prepaid Group Practice on Use of Services," *New England Journal of Medicine*, vol. 310, no. 23 (Jun. 7, 1984), 1505.

p. 109　*Simultaneous research findings . . .* : John Wennberg and Alan Gittelsohn, "Variations in Medical Care Among Small Areas," *Scientific American*, vol. 246, no. 4 (Apr. 1982), 120–34.

p. 109　*For example, one essay . . .* : Theodore R. Marmor, Morris L. Barer, and Robert G. Evans, eds., "The Determinants of a Population's Health," *Why Are Some People Healthy and Others Not?* (New York: Aldine de Guyten, 1994), 218, 221.

p. 110　*Nevertheless, the combination . . .* : U.S. Department of Health and Human Services, *Health United States, 1994* (Washington, D.C.: Government Printing Office, 1994), 242, table 137.

p. 110　*New types of HMOs . . .* : Ibid.

p. 110　*In twenty metropolitan areas . . .* : Lawrence O. Gostin, "Law and Medicine," *Journal of the American Medical Association*, vol. 275, no. 23 (Jun. 19, 1996), 1818.

p. 111　*Alain Enthoven, a distinguished . . .* : "Alain Enthoven," *Marquis Who's Who in America* (Providence, N.J.: Reed Reference Publishing, 1995); Alain C. Enthoven and Richard Kronick, "Universal Health Insurance Through Incentives Reform," *Journal of the American Medical Association*, vol. 265, no. 19 (May 15, 1991), 2532–36.

p. 111　*Modern-day systems . . .* : Robert Lilienfeld, *The Rise of Systems Theory* (New York: John Wiley & Sons, 1989), 103–104.

p. 111　*So successful were . . .* : David Halberstam, *The Best and the Brightest* (Greenwich, Conn.: Fawcett Publications, 1973), 278.

p. 111　*As recounted by . . .* : Ibid., 304.

p. 112　*As one observer . . .* : Clark Murdock, "McNamara, Systems Analysis, and the Systems Analysis' Office," *Sociological Review*, vol. 22, no. 1 (Feb. 1974), 93.

p. 112　*New York City's Mayor . . .* : Lilienfeld, *Rise of Systems Theory*, 122.

p. 112   *As McNamara's assistant* . . . : Charles J. Hitch and Roland N. McKean, *The Economics of Defense in the Nuclear Age* (New York: Athenaeum, 1966), v.

p. 112   *The* New York Times *notes* . . . : John Hubner, "The Abandoned Father of Health-Care Reform," *New York Times*, Jul. 18, 1993, sec. 6, 24.

p. 112   *A consultant to Kaiser* . . . : Adam Peck, "Easier to Explain Than Execute," *Managed Healthcare*, Aug. 1993, 10.

p. 112   *He particularly admires* . . . : Ibid., 36.

p. 113   *With 6.9 million* . . . : Dr. David Lawrence, letter to author, July 1996; Louise Kertesz, "Kaiser Retools to Fight for Lost Ground," *Modern Healthcare*, Jul. 17, 1995, 34.

p. 113   *Enrollees can obtain* . . . : *Kaiser Permanente. 1992 Annual Report* (Oakland, Calif.: Kaiser Permanente, 1993), 3–4.

p. 113   *Its customers* . . . : Foster, *Henry J. Kaiser,* 214.

p. 114   *One study showed* . . . : "The Hay Report," *Medical Benefits*, Mar. 15, 1996, 10. Managed care organizations may also reduce out-of-pocket enrollee expenses.

p. 114   *A front-page headline* . . . : Jerry Geisel, "Health Plan Costs Remaining Stable," *Business Insurance*, Jan. 29, 1996, 1.

p. 114   *In a thoughtful analysis* . . . : Jack Zwanziger and Glenn A. Melnick, "Effects of Competition on the Hospital Industry: Evidence from California," *Competitive Approaches to Health Care Reform*, edited by R. Arnold, R. Rich, and W. D. White (Washington, D.C.: Urban Institute Press, 1993), 111–38.

p. 115   *A 1996 report by* . . . : Graef S. Crystal, "Managed Care CEOs: 'It's Great to be the King,' " *Medical Benefits*, Mar. 15, 1996, 5.

p. 115   *The marketing and administrative* . . . : David J. Lothson, *HMO Industry* (New York: PaineWebber, 1996), 28.

p. 115   *Nonprofit managed care* . . . : McKinsey & Co., *1995 Health Care Annual* (New York: McKinsey & Co., 1995), 272–73, 270.

p. 115   *comparable to that of* . . . : U.S. Department of Commerce, *Statistical Abstract 1993* (Washington, D.C.: Governing Printing Office, 1993), 553, table 890.

p. 115   *United Healthcare* . . . : George Anders, "HMOs Pile Up Billions in Cash," *Wall Street Journal*, Dec. 21, 1994, A1.

p. 116   *Their average 1994* . . . : McKinsey & Co., *1995 Health Care Annual,* 259, 273.

p. 116   *And while HMOs earned . . .* : Ibid., 252, 270.

p. 116   *A 1995 Congressional Budget . . .* : Congressional Budget Office (CBO), *The Effects of Managed Care and Managed Competition* (Washington, D.C.: CBO, 1995), 2.

p. 116   *HMO members generally . . .* : Robert H. Miller and Harold S. Luft, "Managed Care Plan Performance Since 1980," *Journal of the American Medical Association,* vol. 271, no. 19 (May 18, 1994).

p. 116   *For example, one study . . .* : John Rapoport et al., "Resource Utilization Among Intensive Care Patients: Managed Care vs. Traditional Insurance," *Medical Benefits,* Dec. 30, 1992, 4.

p. 116   *Finally, managed care . . .* : Spencer Foreman, "Managing the Physician Workforce," *Health Affairs,* vol. 15, no. 2 (Summer 1996), 243–49.

p. 116   *A University of Michigan . . .* : John E. Billi et al., "Potential Effects of Managed Care on Specialty Practice at a University Medical Center," *New England Journal of Medicine,* vol. 333, no. 15 (Oct. 12, 1995), 982.

p. 117   *Numerous front-page stories . . .* : See, for example, Michael A. Hiltzik, "Drawing the Line: An HMO Dilemma," *Los Angeles Times,* Jan. 17, 1996, A1.

p. 117   *A 1996 cover story . . .* : Erik Larson, "The Soul of an HMO," *Time,* Jan. 22, 1996, 44–52.

p. 117   *Notes a spokesman . . .* : Michael Meyer and Andrew Murr, "Not My Health Care," *Newsweek,* Jan. 10, 1994, 38.

p. 118   *A former medical . . .* : "The Cancer Wars at HMOs," *U.S. News and World Report,* Feb. 5, 1996, 70.

p. 118   *A 1994 survey . . .* : "Group Health Exclusions for Experimental Procedures," *Medical Benefits,* Sept. 15, 1994, 4–5.

p. 118   *Insurers like Blue Shield . . .* : Dr. Richard Cornell, letter to author, Jul. 1, 1996.

p. 118   *For example, Forbes . . .* : Gloria Lau, "The Heart Hassle," *Forbes,* Jun. 3, 1996, 161; also Medtronic representative, letter to author, July 1996.

p. 118   *A panel convened . . .* : Gina Kolata, "Cancer Care at HMOs: Do Limits Hurt?" *New York Times,* Oct. 26, 1994, C11.

p. 118   *A study of the results . . .* : Anna Lee-Feldstein, Hoda Anton-Culver, and Paul J. Feldstein, "Treatment Differences and Other Prognostic Factors Related to Breast Cancer Survival," *Journal of the American Medical Association,* vol. 271, no. 15 (Apr. 20, 1994), 1167.

p. 119   *A Duke University* . . . : Ron Winslow, "Study Compares Role of Doctors in Cardiac Cases," *Wall Street Journal,* Nov. 15, 1995, B6.

p. 119   *On the other hand* . . . : Sheldon Greenfeld et al., "Outcomes of Patients
with Hypertension and Non-insulin-dependent Diabetes Mellitus
Treated by Different Systems and Specialties," *Journal of the American
Medical Association,* vol. 274, no. 18 (Nov. 8, 1995), 1436–44.

p. 119   *The study's co-author* . . . : RAND Corporation, "Outcomes for Adult
Patients with Depression Under Prepaid or Fee-for-Service Financing,"
Medical Benefits, Aug. 15, 1993, 10.

p. 119   *One analysis of 10,000* . . . : Dolores G. Clement et al., "Access and Outcomes of Elderly Patients Enrolled in Managed Care," *Journal of the
American Medical Association,* vol. 271, no. 19 (May 18, 1994), 1487–92.

p. 119   *Many prior studies* . . . : John M. Eisenberg, "Economics," *Journal of the
American Medical Association,* vol. 273, no. 21 (Jun. 7, 1995), 1671.

p. 119   *Virtually all reviewers* . . . : Miller and Luft, "Managed Care Plan Performance," 1516.

p. 119   *Thus, for example, elderly* . . . : Kolata, "Cancer Care at HMOs."

p. 119   *A 1995 California report* . . . : Louise Kertesz, "California Report Card
Finds HMOs Just Average," *Modern Healthcare,* Jul. 1, 1996, 2.

p. 119   *But a recent medical* . . . : Dana Gelb Safran, Alvin R. Tarlov, and
William H. Rogers, "Primary Care Performance in Fee-for-Service and
Prepaid Health Care Systems," *Journal of the American Medical Associa-
tion,* vol. 271, no. 20 (May 25, 1994), 1583.

p. 120   *Undoubtedly, the public* . . . : Robert Wood Johnson Foundation et al.,
"Sick People in Managed Care Have Difficulty Getting Services and
Treatment," *Medical Benefits,* Aug. 30, 1995, 6–7.

p. 120   *A 1996 report also* . . . : Karen Donelan et al., "All Payer, Single Payer,
Managed Care, No Payer: Patients' Perspectives in Three Nations,"
Health Affairs, vol. 15, no. 2 (1996), 254–66.

p. 120   *Even the industry's* . . . : Louise Kertesz, "HMOs Plan Campaign to
Fight Bad Image," *Modern Healthcare,* Jan. 1, 1996, 3.

p. 120   *As for doctors, Dr. Warren* . . . : "Letters," *New York Times,* Feb. 26, 1995,
D24.

p. 120   *Two studies support* . . . : CBO, *Effects of Managed Care,* 19; Amy K.
Taylor, Karen M. Beauregard, and Jessica P. Vistnes, "Who Belongs to
HMOs: A Comparison of Fee-for-Service vs. HMO Enrollees," *Medical
Care Research and Review,* vol. 52, no. 3 (Sept. 1995), 389–408.

p. 120 *To be sure, the latter . . .* : Teresa Fama, Peter D. Fox, and Leigh Ann White, "Do HMOs Care for the Chronically Ill?" *Health Affairs,* vol. 14, no. 1 (Spring 1995), 234–43.

p. 121 *In both studies . . .* : Harold S. Luft and Robert H. Miller, "Patient Selection in a Competitive Health Care System," *Health Affairs,* vol. 7, no. 3 (Summer 1988), 97–119; Miller and Luft, "Managed Care Plan Performance," 1518.

p. 121 *Similarly, a detailed . . .* : Fred J. Hellinger, "Selection Bias in HMOs and PPOs," *Inquiry,* vol. 32 (Summer 1995), 134–242.

p. 121 *The General Accounting Office . . .* : General Accounting Office (GAO), *Medicare: Changes to HMO Rates Setting Are Needed to Reduce Program Costs;* and GAO, *Medicare Managed Care: Growing Enrollment Adds Urgency to Fixing HMO Payment Problem* (Washington, D.C.: GAO, Sept. 1994 and Nov. 1995).

p. 121 *A financial analyst noted . . .* : David J. Lothson, *Industry 1996 Outlook: Red Flags* (New York: PaineWebber, 1996), 11.

p. 121 *One three-area study . . .* : Mark A. Kaiser, "Managed Care and Cost Control," *Medical Benefits,* Feb. 28, 1994, 7.

p. 121 *More systematic evidence . . .* : James C. Robinson, "HMO Market Penetration and Hospital Cost Inflation in California," *Journal of the American Medical Association,* vol. 266, no. 19 (Nov. 20, 1991), 2719–23.

p. 121 *These results have been . . .* : Zwanziger and Melnick, "Effects of Competition on the Hospital Industry: Evidence from California," 123.

p. 121 *Managed care may . . .* : Joel H. Goldberg, "Doctors Struggle to Keep Their Earnings Up," *Medical Economics,* Sept. 11, 1995, 184–202.

p. 122 *In November 1994 . . .* : "Managed Care Savings, Quality Less Than Expected," *BBI Newsletter,* vol. 17, no. 11 (Nov. 1994), 193–94.

p. 122 *That this legislation . . .* : Group Health Association of America, "The Cost Impact of 'Any Willing Provider' Legislation," *Medical Benefits,* Jul. 30, 1994, 4; Karen McAllister, "A Few Dark Tales," *Arkansas Democrat Gazette,* Mar. 31, 1996, A1.

p. 122 *But providers are not . . .* : "Managed Care Savings," *BBI Newsletter,* 193.

p. 122 *Survey after survey . . .* : See, for example, Karen Davis et al., "Choice Matters: Enrollees' Views of their Health Plans," *Health Affairs,* vol. 14, no. 2 (Summer 1995), 99–112.

p. 122   *A large medical outcomes . . .* : Haya R. Rubin et al., "Patients' Ratings of Outpatient Visits in Different Practice Settings," *Journal of the American Medical Association,* vol. 270, no. 7 (Aug. 18, 1993), 835.

p. 122   Newsweek*'s 1996 HMO . . .* : "America's Best HMOs," *Newsweek,* Jun. 24, 1996, 61.

p. 122   *The study also found . . .* : Haya Rubin et al., "Patients' Ratings of Outpatient Visits in Different Practice Settings," 835, 840.

p. 122   *In June 1994 . . .* : *Marion Merrell Dow Managed Care Digest/Update Edition/1994* (Kansas City, Mo.: Marion Merrell Dow, 1994), 9.

p. 122   *In 1995, for example . . .* : Watson Wyatt Insider, "FHP Scraps Staff Models, Keeps IPAs," *Medical Benefits,* Jul. 30, 1995, 5.

p. 123   *A systematic analysis . . .* : Douglas R. Wholey and Jon B. Christianson, "Product Differentiation Among Health Maintenance Organizations: Causes and Consequences of Offering Open-Ended Products," *Inquiry,* vol. 31 (Spring 1994), 36.

p. 123   *The Congressional Budget . . .* : CBO, *Effects of Managed Care,* 3.

p. 123   *The once-mighty Kaiser . . .* : *Marion Merrell Dow Managed Care Digest, HMO Edition,* 1994 (Kansas City, Mo.: Marion Merrell Dow, 1994), 8, 10.

p. 123   *It is not always . . .* : Louise Kertesz, "Kaiser Retools to Fight for Lost Ground," *Modern Healthcare,* Jul. 17, 1995, 34.

p. 123   *and it has faltered . . .* : *Perspectives: Kaiser Permanente* (Oakland, Calif.: Kaiser Permanente, Feb. 1996), 4.

p. 123   *Kaiser "members' . . .* : U.S. House of Representatives Subcommittee on Oversight and Investigations, *Hearings on Kaiser Permanente Health Plan: Organization and Financial Practices,* May 27, 1993.

p. 123   *When the company . . .* : Louise Kertesz, "Kaiser Physicians Unhappy with Changes, Memo Shows," *Modern Healthcare,* Feb. 19, 1996, 12.

p. 124   *The President of . . .* : House, John D. Dingell, opening statement of the Subcommittee on Oversight and Investigations, May 27, 1993.

p. 124   *In one of Kaiser's markets . . .* : William P. Barrett, "Dr. Hustle," *Forbes,* Dec. 21, 1992, 110–13.

p. 124   *Even as overall membership . . .* : *Marion Merrell Dow Managed Care Digest, HMO Edition, 1994,* 8, 10.

p. 124   *FHP, the California based . . .* : Mary Chris Jaklevic, "FHP Drops Staff-model Operations," *Modern Healthcare,* Jul. 3, 1995, 9, 11.

p. 124   *FHP also notes . . .* : Ibid.

p. 125   *Its North Carolina region* . . . : *Perspectives: Kaiser Permanente* (Oakland, Calif.: Kaiser Permanente, Mar. 1996), 3.

p. 125   *So tumultuous is the environment* . . . : Michael L. Millenson, "HMO Goliath Ready for Reform," *Chicago Tribune,* May 7, 1994, 2.

p. 126   *Martin Feldstein, the economist* . . . : Martin Feldstein, "The Economics of Health and Health Care: What Have We Learned? What Have I Learned?" *AEA Papers and Proceedings: The Economics of Health and Health Care,* May 1995, 30.

p. 126   *Warns Dr. Sherwin Nuland* . . . : Sherwin B. Nuland, "Medical Fads: Bran, Midwives and Leeches," *New York Times,* Jun. 25, 1995, sec. 4, 16.

p. 126   *In "The Philosophical Basis* . . . : David F. Horrobin, "The Philosophical Basis of Peer Review and the Suppression of Innovation," *Journal of the American Medical Association,* vol. 263, no. 10 (Mar. 10, 1990), 1441.

p. 127   *In early 1996, other* . . . : American Association of Health Plans, "State Managed Care Legislative Activity," *Medical Benefits,* Apr. 30, 1996, 4.

p. 127   *As PaineWebber's* . . . : David J. Lothson, *HMO Industry* (New York: PaineWebber, 1996), 1.

Chapter 7: Upsizing—The "Big Is Beautiful" Diet

p. 128   *By 1921 Ford paid* . . . : Alfred D. Chandler, Jr., *Scale and Scope: The Dynamics of Industrial Capitalism* (Cambridge, Mass.: Harvard University Press, 1990), 205.

p. 129   *Did not Alfred Sloan* . . . : Alfred D. Chandler, Jr., *Strategy and Structure: Chapters in the History of the Industrial Enterprise* (Cambridge, Mass.: Massachusetts Institute of Technology, 1962), 130.

p. 129   *And because GM* . . . : "Taking GM Apart," *Economist,* Dec. 25, 1993, 91.

p. 129   *GM got big* . . . : Chandler, *Strategy and Structure,* 130.

p. 129   *In 1994, for example, 650* . . . : Sandy Lutz, "Let's Make a Deal," *Modern Healthcare,* Dec. 19–26, 1994, 47–52.

p. 129   *Managed care organizations* . . . : Timothy N. Troy, "Managed Care's Merger Mania," *Managed Healthcare,* Nov. 1995, 32.

p. 129   *For example, Glaxo Holdings* . . . : Joseph Weber, "Robust and Ready to Brawl," *Business Week,* Jan. 8, 1996, 98.

p. 129   *And three pharmaceutical* . . . : Joseph Weber, "Not the Best Prescription for Growth," *Business Week,* Oct. 30, 1995, 124.

p. 130   *From its inception in 1987* . . . : Zachary Schiller et al., "Balance Sheets that Get Well Soon," *Business Week,* Sept. 4, 1995, 80.

p. 130   *For example, it boasts* . . . : Glenn Reicin et al., *Columbia/HCA* (New York: Morgan Stanley, 1994), 1.

p. 130   *"We're now a* . . . : "Large Wave: Big Is Back in Style As Corporate America Deals, Buys and Merges," *Wall Street Journal,* Aug. 4, 1994, A1, A6.

p. 130   *Columbia's strategy* . . . : Joseph Chiarelli, *Columbia/HCA* (New York: J.P. Morgan Securities Inc., Nov. 28, 1995), 3.

p. 131   *In El Paso, Texas* . . . : Schiller et al., "Balance Sheets," 81, 84.

p. 131   *In the opinion* . . . : Chiarelli, *Columbia/HCA,* 3.

p. 131   *The merger of two* . . . : Helen T. O'Donnell and Ken Weakley, *The Prognosis: Hospital Management/Health Care Services* (New York, N.Y.: PaineWebber, 1995), 5.

p. 131   *Horizontally integrated* . . . : Lori M. Price and Kathleen Baxley, *Health Care Services: Medical Care America* (New York, N.Y.: Oppenheimer & Co., Inc., Mar. 24, 1994), 2, 4.

p. 131   *No wonder that Medical* . . . : Ibid.

p. 131   *A 1995 comparison* . . . : David Dranove and Mark Shanley, "Cost Reductions or Reputation Enhancement as Motives for Mergers: The Logic of Multihospital Systems," *Strategic Management Journal,* vol. 16 (1995), 72.

p. 131   *A 1996 analysis* . . . : Jeffrey A. Alexander, Michael T. Halpern, and Shoou-Yih D. Lee, "The Short-term Effects of Mergers on Hospital Operations," *Health Services Research,* vol. 30, no. 6 (Feb. 1996), 828–47.

p. 131   *A 1995 analysis* . . . : Gloria Bazzoli and Steven Andes, "Consequences of Hospital Financial Distress," *Hospital and Health Services Administration,* vol. 40, no. 4 (Winter 1995), 481.

p. 132   *As for HMOs* . . . : Roger Feldman, Douglas Wholey, and Jon Christianson, "Effects of Mergers on Health Maintenance Organization Premiums," *Health Care Financing Review,* vol. 17, no. 3 (Spring 1996), 171.

p. 132   *In Minneapolis* . . . : Adam Peck, "Reform Debaters Eye Minnesota," *Managed Healthcare,* Jan. 1994, 32.

p. 132   *By 1994 one* . . . : Richard Wolf, "Minnesota Health Plan Touted as a Model," *USA Today,* Jan. 17, 1994, 8A.

p. 132   *By 1994 the city's* . . . : Paul B. Ginsberg and Nancy J. Fasciano, eds., *The Community Snapshots Project* (Princeton, N.J.: Robert Wood Johnson Foundation, 1996), 1.

p. 132   *two of them were so large* . . . : Susan H. McBride, "A Tale of Twin Cities," *Managed Healthcare,* Aug. 1995, 37.

p. 132   *The rest of the provider* . . . : Ibid., 43.

p. 132   *compared with 31 percent* . . . : Penny L. Havelick, *Medical Groups in the U.S.* (Chicago: American Medical Association, 1996), 7, 143; Martin L. Gonzalez, ed., *Socioeconomic Characteristics of Medical Practice 1996* (Chicago: AMA, 1996), 6.

p. 133   *By 1996, 10 percent* . . . : Mary Chris Jaklevic, "Buying Doc Practices Often Leads to Red Ink," *Modern Healthcare,* Jun. 3, 1996, 39.

p. 133   *A 1994 survey found* . . . : Ernst & Young, *Physician Hospital Organizations: Profile 1995* (Washington, D.C.: Ernst & Young LLP, 1995), 1.

p. 133   *But hospitals were* . . . : Kelly Shriver, "Study: Most Hospitals Will Try Integration Despite Obstacles," *Modern Healthcare,* Dec. 12, 1994, 4.

p. 133   *Three of these giant* . . . : Weber, "Robust and Ready to Brawl," 98.

p. 133   *The horizontally integrated* . . . : Lori Price and Kathleen Baxley, *Health Care Services: Columbia/HCA Healthcare Corporation* (New York: Oppenheimer and Co., Inc., Oct. 21, 1994), 9.

p. 133   *In 1996 Michigan's* . . . : Henry Ford Health System, *Henry Ford Health System Fact Sheet* (Detroit: Henry Ford Health System, 1996), 1.

p. 133   *Physicians are increasingly* . . . : Mary Chris Jaklevic, "Staying Single," *Modern Healthcare,* Oct. 3, 1994, 71–80.

p. 134   *If vertical integration* . . . : "American Business," *Economist,* Sept. 16, 1995, 6.

p. 134   *And why is General* . . . : "Taking GM Apart," *Economist,* Dec. 25, 1993, 91.

p. 134   *General Motors, like* . . . : Susan Helper, "Strategy and Irreversibility in Supplier Relations," *Business History Review,* vol. 65, no. 4 (Dec. 22, 1991), 782–83.

p. 134   *A Business Week article* . . . : John A. Byrne, "The Horizontal Corporation," *Business Week,* Dec. 20, 1993, 76–81.

p. 134   *A 1994 survey* . . . : "The Celling Out of America," *Economist,* Dec. 17, 1994, 63–64.

p. 134   *Opel, the German car manufacturer* . . . : Karen Lowry Miller and Kathleen Kerwin, "GM's German Lessons," *Business Week,* Dec. 20, 1993, 67.

p. 135   *For one thing* . . . : Minnesota COACT, *Strangled Competition* (St. Paul, Minn.: Minnesota COACT, 1995), xi.

p. 135   *One report revealed* . . . : "The Impact of Managed Care on U.S. Markets," *Medical Benefits,* Feb. 29, 1996, 4.

p. 135   *The three giants share* . . . : Eric Weissenstein, "Cut Out the Middleman," *Modern Healthcare,* Jul. 3, 1995, 28–29.

p. 135   *This cost-reducing* . . . : Ron Winslow, "Employer Group Rethinks Commitment to Big HMOs," *Wall Street Journal,* Jul. 21, 1995, B1, B4.

p. 135   *Most Economics textbooks* . . . : See, for example, Edwin Mansfield, *Applied Microeconomics* (New York: Norton, 1994), 445.

p. 135   *Their role in promoting* . . . : Joyce Lapointe, letter to author, Aug. 8, 1994.

p. 136   *In contrast* . . . : Mansfield, *Applied Microeconomics,* 445.

p. 136   *Large firms that own* . . . : Ibid.

p. 136   *For example, both General* . . . : William J. Cook and Warren Cohen, "Hitting the Brakes Hard," *U.S. News and World Report,* vol. 113, no. 18 (Nov. 9, 1992), 78.

p. 136   *and IBM* . . . : Andrew J. Kessler, "Is There Any Hope for IBAppleola?" *Forbes,* Dec. 19, 1994, 319.

p. 136   *A Minnesota consumer* . . . : Minnesota COACT, *Strangled Competition,* xiii.

p. 136   *As evidence* . . . : Ibid.

p. 136   *By contracting with* . . . : Buyers' Health Care Action Group, *BHCAG Enhanced Competitive Model* (Bloomington, Minn.: BHCAG, 1995), 2.

p. 137   *For their part* . . . : Ginsberg and Fasciano, *Community Snapshots Project,* 2.

p. 137   *A 1995 survey showed* . . . : Jaklevic, "Buying Doc Practices," 39.

p. 137   *A 1996 Modern Healthcare* . . . : Louise Kertesz, "Systems Begin Pruning HMOs from Holdings," *Modern Healthcare,* Jun. 17, 1996, 77.

p. 137   *Notes an executive* . . . : Jaklevic, "Buying Doc Practices," 42.

p. 137   *Similarly, a consultant* . . . : Kertesz, "Systems Begin Pruning HMOs," 82.

p. 137   *A study of twelve*...: Robin R. Gillies et al., "Conceptualizing and Measuring Integration," *Hospitals and Health Services Administration,* vol. 38, no. 4 (Winter 1993), 484.

p. 138   *Two observant writers*...: Douglas A. Conrad and William L. Dowling, "Vertical Integration in Health Services: Theory and Managerial Implications," *Health Care Management Review,* vol. 15, no. 4 (Fall 1990), 21.

p. 138   *In a 1993 survey, fewer*...: Heidrick & Struggles, *Leading Change* (Chicago: Heidrick & Struggles, 1993), 7.

p. 138   *The pharmaceutical companies*...: Weber, "Robust and Ready to Brawl," 98.

p. 138   *For some, the market*...: Joseph Weber, "Not the Best Prescription for Growth," *Business Week,* Oct. 30, 1995, 124.

p. 138   *In 1996 a* Wall...: E. S. Browning and Thomas M. Burton, "Lilly's PCS Receives Rx: A Write-Down," *Wall Street Journal,* Jul. 30, 1996, C1.

p. 138   *Morgan Stanley's*...: Paul A. Brooke, *Merck (MRK): Second Quarter Bumps Estimates* (New York: Morgan Stanley, 1996), 1–2.

p. 138   *After all, most*...: Oliver E. Williamson, "The Vertical Integration of Production," *American Economic Association Papers and Proceedings: Response to Market Imperfection,* vol. 61 (May 1971), 122.

p. 139   *Third, the acquirer*...: Henry W. Chesbrough and David J. Teece, "When Is Virtual Virtuous?" *Harvard Business Review,* Jan.–Feb. 1996, 65–73.

p. 139   *Last, the "transaction*...: See, for example, Benjamin Klein, Robert G. Crawford, and Armen A. Alchian, "Vertical Integration, Appropriable Rents, and the Competitive Contracting Process," *Journal of Law and Economics,* vol. 21 (Oct. 1978), pp. 297–326; Oliver E. Williamson, "The Economics of Organization," *American Journal of Sociology,* vol. 87, no. 3 (1981), 548–77.

p. 139   *As the Pulitzer Prize*...: Alfred Chandler and H. Daems, eds., *Managerial Hierarchies* (Cambridge, Mass.: Harvard University Press, 1980), as cited by Srinivasan Balakrishnan and Birger Wernerfelt, *Strategic Management Journal,* vol. 7 (1986), 350.

p. 139   *Yet, the automobile*...: Scott E. Masten, James W. Meehan, and Edward A. Snyder, "Vertical Integration in the U.S. Auto Industry," *Journal of Economic Behavior and Organization,* vol. 12 (1989), 265–73; Kirk Monteverde and David J. Teece, "Supplier Switching Costs and Vertical Integration in the Automobile Industry," *Bell Journal of Economics,* vol. 13, no. 1 (Spring 1982), 206–13.

p. 139   *Instead the industry chose* . . . : Richard N. Langlois and Paul L. Rob-
          ertson, "Explaining Vertical Integration: Lessons from the American
          Automobile Industry," *Journal of Economic History,* vol. 49, no. 2 (Jun.
          1989), 374.

p. 139   *The industry was* . . . : Michael H. Riordan, "Ownership Without Con-
          trol," *Journal of the Japanese and International Economies,* vol. 5, no. 2
          (Jun. 1994), 101–19; Sanford J. Grossman and Oliver D. Hart, "The
          Costs and Benefits of Ownership," *Journal of Political Economy,* vol. 94,
          no. 4 (1986), 651–719.

p. 140   *A 1994 report of* . . . : Kelly J. Devers et al., "Implementing Organized
          Delivery Systems: An Integration Scorecard," *Health Care Management
          Review,* vol. 19, no. 3 (Summer 1994), 10.

p. 140   *They include the* . . . : Lawrence R. Burns and Darrell P. Thorpe,
          "Trends and Models and Physician-Hospital Organization," *Health
          Care Management Review,* vol. 18, no. 4 (Fall 1993), 7–20.

p. 140   *The entrepreneurial* . . . : Zachary Schiller, "Humana Wheels Itself to
          Surgery," *Business Week,* Jan. 25, 1993, 58–59.

p. 141   *Even in the 1960s* . . . : David Jones, letter to author, Jul. 1996. I am
          grateful for his review of this section.

p. 141   *The system was* . . . : As reviewed by David Jones.

p. 141   *At one point* . . . : Regina E. Herzlinger, *Creating New Health Care
          Ventures* (Gaithersburg, Md.: Aspen, 1992), 325.

p. 141   *Jones operated* . . . : Datastream (a financial electronic database).

p. 141   *On a one-to-ten* . . . : Herzlinger, *Creating New Health Care Ventures,*
          315.

p. 141   *Meanwhile, hospital* . . . : Judith Nemes, "For-profit Hospitals Waving
          Goodbye to Era of High Prices," *Modern Healthcare,* Mar. 22, 1993, 33.

p. 142   *The cost of* . . . : Gary M. Fournier and Jean M. Mitchell, "Hospital
          Costs and Competition for Services," *Review of Economics and Statis-
          tics,* vol. 74, no. 4 (Nov. 1992), 633.

p. 145   *Ironically, the vertically* . . . : Herzlinger, *Creating New Health Care
          Ventures,* 312.

p. 145   *The physicians' indifference* . . . : Ibid.

p. 146   *Ownership may even* . . . : "Survey: Doc Practice Buys Don't Boost Pay,"
          Modern Healthcare, Feb. 19, 1996, 34.

p. 146   *Popular business writers* . . . : See, for example, Kathryn Rudie Harrigan, "Matching Vertical Integration Strategies to Competitive Conditions," *Strategic Management Journal*, vol. 7 (1986), 535–55.

p. 147   *Managing any one . . .* : Gregory N. Herrle and William M. Pollock, "Multispeciality Medical Groups: Adapting to Capitation," *Journal of Health Care Finance*, vol. 21, no. 3 (Spring 1995), 37–43.

p. 147   *Vertical integration has beneficial . . .* : Marvin B. Lieberman, "Determinants of Vertical Integration: An Empirical Test," *Journal of Industrial Economics*, vol. 39, no. 5 (Sept. 1991), 451–66; Forest Reinhardt, *Vertical Integration in Forest Products Firms: Transaction Cost Theory and Empirical Evidence* (Boston: Harvard Business School, working paper, 1995).

p. 147   *In the oil industry . . .* : "Over-refined Europeans," *Economist*, Jul. 15, 1995, 47.

p. 147   *Vertical integration can also . . .* : Timothy J. Muris, David T. Scheffman, and Pablo T. Spiller, "Strategy and Transaction Costs," *Journal of Economics and Management Strategy*, vol. 1, no. 1 (Spring 1992), 83–128.

p. 148   *As a staff paper . . .* : John Stuckey and David White, "Vertical Integration (and Disintegration) Strategy," McKinsey staff paper no. 51 (Nov. 1990), 1.

p. 148   *Eight years later . . .* : Saul Hansell, "Citicorp Passes Off Quotron," *New York Times*, Jan. 14, 1994, D1.

p. 148   *A dubious* Wall . . . : Rajendra S. Sisodia, "A Goofy Deal," *Wall Street Journal*, Aug. 4, 1995, A8.

p. 148   *In the opinion . . .* : "Walt Disney and the Piper's Tune," *Economist*, Aug. 5, 1995, 15.

p. 148   *Notes another observer . . .* : Mark Landler and Ronald Grover, "Is Time Warner's Zigging and Zagging Leading Anywhere?" *Business Week*, Sept. 19, 1994, 38.

p. 149   *A 1996 study demonstrated . . .* : Rebecca Blumenstein, "GM's Per-Vehicle Costs Exceed Rivals' Due to In-House Parts Work, Study Says," *Wall Street Journal*, Jun. 25, 1996, A2.

p. 149   *"GM's managers . . .* : "Taking GM Apart," *Economist*, Dec. 25, 1993, 91.

p. 149   *And IBM . . .* : Andrew J. Kessler, "Is There Any Hope for IBAppleola?" *Forbes*, Dec. 19, 1994, 319.

p. 149   *Even Olympic . . .* : Thomas Boswell, "Joyner-Kersee Alone Atop Olympus," *Washington Post*, Aug. 2, 1992, A1.

p. 149 *When they stray*...: David Lei and John W. Slocum, Jr., "Global Strategy, Competence-Building and Strategic Alliances," *California Management Review,* vol. 35, no. 1 (Fall 1992), 81.

p. 149 *Quotron, for example*...: Hansell, "Citicorp Passes Off Quotron," D1, D2.

p. 150 *The reason according to* ...: Jay Greene, "Merger Monopolies," *Modern Healthcare,* Dec. 5, 1994, 38–46.

p. 150 *Small wonder that*...: Bruce Japsen, "Antitrust Battle Continues over Iowa Hospital Link," *Modern Healthcare,* Oct. 17, 1994, 18–19.

p. 150 *A 1994* Modern Healthcare ...: Greene, "Merger Monopolies," 40.

p. 150 *To the contrary*...: Jay Greene, "The Costs of Hospital Mergers," *Modern Healthcare,* Feb. 3, 1992, 36–43.

p. 151 *There is inconclusive*...: Lisa Scott, "Duplication Hard to Limit Despite Hospital Mergers," *Modern Healthcare,* Mar. 13, 1995, 42; Richard J. Bogue et al., "Hospital Reorganization After Merger," *Medical Care,* vol. 33, no. 7 (1995), 676–86.

p. 151 *In a 1992 survey*...: Greene, "Costs of Hospital Mergers," 37.

p. 151 *As one hospital*...: Karen Pallarito, "Acquisitions Tip Scales: The Hospital Industry Claims to be Slimming Down, but Critics Point to Cases of Gluttony," *Modern Healthcare,* Aug. 15, 1994, 38.

p. 151 *Explains one researcher*...: "Hospital Mergers," *HCFO News and Progress,* Mar. 1996, 3. Quoted with permission from Lisa Simonson, author.

p. 151 *Numerous researchers*...: Erwin A. Blackstone, "Hospital Mergers and Antitrust," *Journal of Health Politics, Policy, and Law,* vol. 14, no. 2 (Summer 1989), 383–403; Glenn A. Melnick et al., "The Effects of Market Structure and Bargaining Position on Hospital Prices," *Journal of Health Economics,* vol. 11 (1992), 231; David Dranove, Mark Shanley, and William D. White, "Price and Concentration in Hospital Markets," *Journal of Law and Economics,* vol. 36 (Apr. 1993), 203.

p. 151 *"highly dependent*...: Jack Zwanziger and Glenn Melnick, "Effects of Competition on the Hospital Industry," *Competitive Approaches to Health Care Reform,* edited by R. Arnould, R. Rich, and W. D. White (Washington, D.C.: Urban Institute Press, 1993), 132.

p. 151 *Indeed, an extensive*...: Gloria Bazzoli, *Effects of Horizontal Consolidation on Hospital Markets: Executive Summary* (Chicago: American Hospital Association, n.d.), 8, 9.

p. 152   *Notes David Weldon . . .* : U.S. House Judiciary Committee, *Health Care Revision Issues,* hearing, Feb. 27, 1996.

p. 152   *A* Business Week . . . : Wendy Zellner, Mike McNamee, and David Greising, "And Now, Monolith Hospital," *Business Week,* Jun. 28, 1993, 33–34.

p. 152   *For example, twenty-three physicians . . .* : Mary Chris Jaklevic, "Intermountain Settles 1 Antitrust Suit," *Modern Healthcare,* Aug. 28, 1995, 2.

p. 152   *Another group of doctors . . .* : Karen Pallarito, "N.Y. Docs File Antitrust Suit Against Aetna," *Modern Healthcare,* Aug. 28, 1995, 22.

p. 152   *For example, when . . .* : Edward Felsenthal, "Technology and Health: Columbia-HCA Merger Backed by FTC Staff," *Wall Street Journal,* Jan. 20, 1994, B7.

p. 152   *And in 1994, when . . .* : George Anders, "Technology and Health: FTC Acts to Block Hospital Merger; Wide Impact Seen," *Wall Street Journal,* Feb. 1, 1994, B7.

p. 153   *One health care . . .* : "New Competition in Dynamic Marketplace Challenges Traditional Roles," *HCFO News and Progress,* Mar. 1996, 1.

p. 153   *A 1995 study found . . .* : Gloria J. Bazzoli et al., "Federal Antitrust Merger Enforcement Standards," *Journal of Health Politics, Policy, and Law,* vol. 20, no. 1 (Spring 1995), 137–69.

p. 153   *Although these conclusions . . .* : Gregory Vistnes, "Commentary: Hospital Mergers and Antitrust Enforcement," *Journal of Health Politics, Policy, and Law,* vol. 20, no. 1 (Spring 1995), 176–90.

p. 153   *The two agencies . . .* : Gail Kursh, "Recent activities of the Antitrust Department in the Health Care Field," U.S. Department of Justice, April 5, 1995; Robert Pitofsky, "Prepared Statement Before the House Judiciary Committee," U.S. House of Representatives, Feb. 22, 1996; letter to author from Gloria Bazzoli, Oct. 1, 1996.

p. 153   *John Hickey, a consultant . . .* : Nancy P. Johnson, "Mergers Concern Benefit Managers," *Business Insurance,* Oct. 25, 1993, 7.

p. 154   *Seasoned business observers . . .* : "Large Wave: Big Is Back in Style," *Wall Street Journal,* Aug. 4, 1994, A1, A6.

Chapter 8: Resizing—the "Trade Fat for Muscle" Diet

p. 157   *No, these celebrants* . . . : James L. Heskett, *Shouldice Hospital Limited,* case no. 9-683-068, and teaching material (Boston: Harvard Business School Publishing Division, 1983).

p. 158   *twenty thousand restaurants* . . . : McDonald's Corp., *Welcome to McDonald's* (Oak Brook, Ill.: McDonald's Corp., 1996), 4.

p. 159   *With elegant simplicity* . . . : Alan O'Dell, speech at the Harvard Business School, Mar. 1996. Mr. O'Dell and Darryl Urquhart reviewed this section, July 1996.

p. 160   *Notes Dr. Byrnes Shouldice* . . . : Heskett, *Shouldice Hospital Limited,* as reprinted in Regina E. Herzlinger, *Creating New Health Care Ventures* (Gaithersburg, Md.: Aspen, 1992), 392.

p. 161   *As Professor James Heskett* . . . : Letter to author, Jul. 1996.

p. 161   *The Shouldice, a privately owned* . . . : Didier Bennert and Sue Menzel, "Shouldice Hospital," paper prepared for a Harvard Business School course, Dec. 6, 1995, 2, 11.

p. 161   *The average general surgeon* . . . : Ibid., 2.

p. 163   *Written by Wickham* . . . : Wickham Skinner, "The Focused Factory," *Harvard Business Review,* May–Jun. 1974, 113–22.

p. 163   *On the basis of* . . . : Ibid., 114.

p. 164   *To remedy these* . . . : Ibid.

p. 164   *The outsiders frequently* . . . : Keith Bradsher, "Auto Suppliers Find a Niche in Safety," *New York Times,* Feb. 29, 1996, C3.

p. 164   *George Fisher, the CEO* . . . : "Back in Focus," *Forbes,* Jan. 1, 1996, 114.

p. 165   *Take the firm* . . . : "Up from the Pits," *Forbes,* Jan. 1, 1996, 95.

p. 165   *Warren Betts* . . . : Roger Lowenstein, "Confessions of a Corporate Spin-off Junkie," *Wall Street Journal,* Mar. 28, 1996, C1.

p. 165   *When asked why* . . . : Sana Siwolop, "Outsourcing: Savings Are Just the Start," *Business Week/Enterprise,* May 13, 1996, ENT24.

p. 165   *Notes Business Week* . . . : John W. Verity, "Let's Order Out for Technology," *Business Week,* May 13, 1996, 47.

p. 166   *In retailing, for example* . . . : Peter F. Drucker, "The Retail Revolution," *Wall Street Journal,* Jul. 15, 1993, A12.

p. 166   *Jiffy Lube was chosen* . . . : Gregory Patterson, "Sears Picks Jiffy Lube to Oil Auto-Service Operations," *Wall Street Journal,* Mar. 23, 1995, B4.

p. 166   *When it closed its* ... : Susan Chandler, "Strategies for the New Mail Order," *Business Week,* Dec. 19, 1994, 83. A Sears representative reviewed this discussion.

p. 166   *Nearly $3 billion* ... : "Taking Stock of Recent IPOS," *Fortune,* May 27, 1996, 80.

p. 166   *In her vision* ... : "From Pink Lipstick to Pink Ribbons," *New York Times,* Feb. 2, 1995, C11.

p. 167   *The few existing* ... : See, for example, "Total Renal Care Adds 12 Dialysis Centers with 1,200 Patients," *Business Wire,* Aug. 1, 1996.

p. 167   *The list of "breakthrough"* ... : James L. Heskett, W. Earl Sasser, and Christopher W. L. Hart, *Service Breakthroughs* (New York: Free Press, 1990), 16.

p. 167   *The food retailer* ... : Ibid., 16–17.

p. 167   *Even the* New York ... : Stephen Drucker, "Who Is the Best Restaurateur in America?" *New York Times Magazine,* Mar. 10, 1995, 45.

p. 168   *This feat is* ... : McDonald's Corp., *Performance at a Glance* (Oak Brook, Ill.: McDonald's Corp., 1996), 3.

p. 168   *After all, not* ... : David Upton, *McDonald's Corporation 1992,* case no. 693-028 (Boston: Harvard Business School Publishing Division, 1992), 17.

p. 168   *In 1992, for example* ... : Laurie Lively Smith, *McDonald's Corporation* (Los Angeles: Seidler Amdec Securities, 1992), 16.

p. 168   *its close rival* ... : PepsiCo, *Annual Report 1994* (Purchase, N.Y.: PepsiCo, 1995), 28.

p. 169   *Now imagine that* ... : Upton, *McDonald's,* 4, 11.

p. 169   *... in each of 11,400* ... : McDonald's, *Performance at a Glance,* 2.

p. 169   *These superfryers* ... : Upton, *McDonald's,* 5.

p. 169   *(McDonald's research* ... : Ibid.

p. 169   *To obtain an adequate* ... : "The Forbes Four Hundred," *Forbes,* Oct. 16, 1995, 345.

p. 170   *McDonald's does not* ... : Upton, *McDonald's,* 5.

p. 170   *Notes one supplier* ... : Ibid., 4.

p. 170   *As a reward* ... : Ibid.

p. 170   *By 1991, the operations* ... : Ibid., 3.

p. 170 *Potatoes are to be* . . . : W. Earl Sasser, *McDonald's Corporation,* case no. 681-044 (Boston, Mass.: Harvard Business School, 1980), 6.

p. 171 *The techniques of process* . . . : Smith, *McDonald's,* 8.

p. 171 *They participate in* . . . : Sarah Anderson King and Michael J. King, "Hamburger University," in *Ronald Revisited,* edited by Scratch Fishwick (Bowling Green, Oh.: Bowling Green University Popular Press, 1983), 96.

p. 171 *While many of its* . . . : Upton, *McDonald's,* 6.

p. 171 *It obtains and analyzes* . . . : Ibid., 3.

p. 171 *Employee training focuses* . . . : Smith, *McDonald's,* 8.

p. 171 *McDonald's first franchisee* . . . : Phillip Fitzell, "The Man Who Sold the First McDonald's Hamburger," in *Ronald Revisited,* 77–78.

p. 173 *Consider diabetes* . . . : Elizabeth C. Meszaros, "Diabetes Management by Patients," *Managed Healthcare,* Jun. 1995, DSM12.

p. 173 *Yet, a careful review* . . . : Jonathan P. Weiner et al., "A Claims-Based Profile of Care Provided to Medicare Patients with Diabetes," *Journal of the American Medical Association,* vol. 273, no. 19 (May 17, 1995), 1503–08.

p. 173 *Thirteen million Americans* . . . : National Center for Health Statistics, *Vital and Health Statistics: Current Estimates from the National Health Interview Survey* (Washington, D.C.: Government Printing Office, 1994), 95.

p. 173 *It accounted for* . . . : John Borzilleri, *Pharmaceutical Industry—No Turning Back* (New York: Dean Witter, 1994), 41.

p. 174 Managed Healthcare *estimates* . . . : Karen Southwick, "Strategies for Managing Asthma," *Managed Healthcare,* Jun. 1995, DSM7.

p. 174 *When one consultant* . . . : Boston Consulting Group, *JDHC Disease Management Strategies* (New York: Boston Consulting Group, 1993), 56, 59.

p. 174 *Their use of hospitals* . . . : Ibid., 56.

p. 174 *Practicing physicians concur* . . . : Southwick, "Strategies," DSM8.

p. 174 *Compliance with guidelines* . . . : Ibid., DSM7.

p. 174 *"Up to 75 percent* . . . : Ibid., DSM8.

p. 174 *Notes another pharmacy professor* . . . : Paula Moyer, "Low Hanging Fruit," *Managed Healthcare,* Sept. 1995, S11.

p. 175   *For example, a study* . . . : David W. Bates et al., "Incidence of Adverse
Drug Events and Potential Adverse Drug Events," *Journal of the American
Medical Association,* vol. 274, no. 1 (Jul. 5, 1995), 29–30.

p. 175   *A study of elderly* . . . : Edward F. Ellerbeck et al., "Quality of Care
for Medicare Patients with Acute Myocardial Infarction," *Journal of
the American Medical Association,* vol. 273, no. 19 (May 17, 1995),
1509–14.

p. 175   *For example, physicians* . . . : Weiner, "Claims-Based Profile," 1504.

p. 175   *Because the average physician* . . . : Dr. Joseph A. Haas, letter to author,
Oct. 1, 1996.

p. 176   *For example, one study* . . . : Kevin Grumbach et al., "Regionalization of
Cardiac Care in the United States and Canada," *Journal of the American
Medical Association,* vol. 274, no. 16 (Oct. 25, 1995), 1282–88.

p. 176   *Similarly, there were* . . . : Stephen E. Kimmel, Jesse A. Berlin, and
Warren K. Laskey, "The Relationship Between Coronary Angioplasty
Procedure Volume and Major Complications," *Journal of the American
Medical Association,* vol. 274, no. 14 (Oct. 11, 1995), 113–42.

p. 176   *One study estimated* . . . : Harold S. Luft and Patrick S. Romano,
"Chance, Continuity, and Change in Hospital Mortality Rates," *Journal
of the American Medical Association,* vol. 270, no. 3 (Jul. 21, 1993), 331.

p. 176   *The per-patient differences* . . . : Margaret Arndt, Robert C. Bradbury,
and Joseph H. Golec, "Surgeon Volume and Hospital Resource Utilization," *Inquiry,* vol. 32, no. 4 (Winter 1995–96), 407–17.

p. 176   *Out of the hundreds* . . . : HCIA, Inc. and William M. Mercer, Inc., "Top
100 Hospitals: Benchmarks for Success," *Medical Benefits,* Jan. 15,
1996, 2–3.

p. 176   *One study found* . . . : Arndt et al., "Surgeon Volume," p. 415.

p. 176   *One exception is* . . . : Lucian L. Leape et al., "Systems Analysis of
Adverse Drug Events," *Journal of the American Medical Association,*
vol. 274, no. 1 (Jul. 5, 1995), 35.

p. 177   *As Dr. Lucian Leape* . . . : Ibid.

p. 177   *The American Pain* . . . : American Pain Society, Quality of Care Committee, "Quality Improvement Guidelines for the Treatment of Acute
Pain and Cancer Pain," *Journal of the American Medical Association,*
vol. 274, no. 23 (Dec. 20, 1995), 1875.

p. 177   *They called for recognizing* . . . : Ibid., 1874–79.

p. 178   *Some of the current*...: Allen R. Myerson, "It's a Business. No, It's a Religion," *New York Times,* Feb. 13, 1994, D1, D6.

p. 178   *Few details are too small*...: Dr. Denton Cooley, letter to author, Jul. 31, 1996.

p. 178   *Other early-stage*...: George Anders, "On Sale Now at Your HMO: Organ Transplants," *Wall Street Journal,* Jan. 17, 1995, B1, B5.

p. 179   *J.P. Morgan calculated*...: Joseph Chiarelli, *National Surgery Centers, Inc.* (New York: J.P. Morgan, 1995), 16.

p. 179   *For this reason*...: Lori M. Price and Kathleen Baxley, *Health Care Services: Medical Care America* (New York: Oppenheimer & Co., Inc., Feb. 16, 1994), 3.

p. 180   *Although its services*...: Dr. Gerald Rosen, letter to author, May 16, 1995.

p. 180   *For these reasons*...: Mary C. O'Connell, *Salick Health, Inc.* (New York: Louis Nicoud & Associates, Jun. 24, 1994), 10.

p. 180   *Its size also*...: Ibid., 8–9.

p. 181   *Strict achievement of*...: Mari Edlin, "Cardiologists Join Forces to Create National Network," *Managed Healthcare,* Nov. 1993, 57–58.

p. 181   *A regional program*...: Gerald T. O'Connor et al., "A Regional Intervention to Improve the Hospital Mortality Associated with Coronary Artery Bypass Graft Surgery," *Journal of the American Medical Association,* vol. 275, no. 11 (Mar. 20, 1996), 841–46.

p. 182   *Clinical paths are*...: "Clinical Path Survey," *Medical Benefits,* Feb. 2, 1996, 11.

p. 183   *Small wonder that*...: Jay Greene, "Retooling Without Layoffs," *Modern Healthcare,* Feb. 26, 1996, 76.

p. 183   *Eighty percent*...: "More Budget Cuts Ahead at Hospitals—Survey," *Modern Healthcare,* Apr. 29, 1996, 6.

p. 184   *A health and information*...: "Hospitals Expand Via Mall Centers," *Modern Healthcare,* Jun. 3, 1996, 50.

p. 184   *As one textbook*...: Robert W. Hall, *Attaining Manufacturing Excellence* (Homewood, Ill.: Dow Jones-Irwin, 1987), 63.

p. 184   *The approximate validity of*...: Heskett, Sasser, and Hart, *Service Breakthroughs,* 119.

p. 185   *Observation: Ten diagnostic*...: "Medical Care Spending—United States," *Medical Benefits,* Oct. 15, 1994, 2.

p. 185 *Observation: Thirty-three percent...*: Boston Consulting Group, *JDHC Disease Management Strategies,* 59, 61.

p. 185 *Similarly, 10 percent...*: "The Concentration of Health Expenditures: An Update," *Intramural Research Highlights—Agency for Health Care Policy and Research,* Jun. 1994, 2.

p. 185 *Infants account for...*: "Expenditures for Pregnancy and Infant Medical Care, 1987," *Intramural Research Highlights—Agency for Health Care Policy and Research,* Jun. 1994, 1–3.

p. 186 *Six types of surgical...*: Health Insurance Association of America (HIAA), *Sourcebook of Health Insurance Data—1993* (Washington, D.C.: HIAA, 1994), 114.

p. 186 *Four conditions account...*: "Prevalence of Disabilities and Associated Health Conditions," *Medical Benefits,* Nov. 15, 1994, 5.

p. 186 *Twenty-five diagnostic-episode...*: Douglas G. Cave, "Pattern-of-Treatment Differences Among Primary Care Physicians in Alternative Systems of Care," *Benefits Quarterly* (Third Quarter 1994), 10–13.

p. 186 *The world-famous Mayo...*: Mayo Clinic, letter to author, May 31, 1996.

p. 186 *As one Mayo physician...*: Victor Johnson, *Mayo Clinic: Its Growth and Progress* (Bloomington, Minn.: Voyageur Press, 1984), 148.

p. 187 *All the specialists...*: Mayo Clinic, letter to author, May 31, 1996.

p. 189 *For example, Nike...*: James Brian Quinn and Frederick G. Hilmer, "Strategic Outsourcing," *Sloan Management Review,* Summer 1994, 43.

p. 189 *In 1993, venture...*: Sandy Lutz, "Venture Capitalists Up Interests in Niche Healthcare Services Firms," *Modern Healthcare,* Jun. 6, 1994, 42.

p. 189 *but in 1995...*: Ad by Welsh, Carson, Anderson, and Stowe, *Modern Healthcare,* Feb. 5, 1996, 27.

p. 189 *Their interest lies...*: Sandy Lutz, "Venture Capitalists Up Interests in Niche Healthcare Services Firms," 42.

p. 190 *Procedure-based focused...*: Karen Pallorito, "Survey Finds No Uniformity in Packaged-Price Services," *Modern Healthcare,* Jan. 23, 1995, 19.

p. 190 *For example, Dallas...*: Geoffrey Leavenworth, "Making a Dent in Specialty Care Costs," *Business and Health,* Mar. 1994, 43–44.

p. 190 *Many physician groups...*: Cathy Tokarski, "Entrée into World of Managed Care," *American Medical News,* vol. 39, no. 17 (May 6, 1996), 1, 25.

p. 191   *MedPartners, for example* . . . : Milt Freudenheim, "$2.3 Billion Deal Creates Giant in Managing of Doctors' Offices," *New York Times,* May 15, 1996, A1, D7.

p. 191   *MedPartners, which had estimated* . . . : Thomas M. Burton and Douglas A. Blackmon, "MedPartners—Caremark Pact Is Likely to Fuel a Debate," *Wall Street Journal,* May 15, 1996, B4.

p. 191   *Some physician groups* . . . : Mari Edlin, "Doing It the Doc's Way," *Managed Healthcare,* Sept. 1995, 33.

p. 191   *Notes one member* . . . : Ibid., 34.

p. 191   *A survey found that* . . . : Rachel Kreier, "HMOs Without Gatekeepers," *American Medical News,* Aug. 5, 1996, 1, 50.

p. 192   *The process of forming* . . . : Ibid., 34.

p. 192   *MedPartners' formation of* . . . : Kathy Seal, "Dual-service Capitation a Go in California," *Managed Healthcare,* Apr. 1996, 10.

p. 192   *As a recent issue* . . . : Tokarski, "Entrée into World," 25.

p. 192   *Early stage capitated* . . . : James C. Robinson and Lawrence P. Casalino, "The Growth of Medical Groups Paid Through Capitation in California," *New England Journal of Medicine,* vol. 333, no. 25 (Dec. 21, 1995), 1684–87.

p. 193   *She has chosen* . . . : "Focus on Managing High-Cost Disease," *Medical Benefits,* Apr. 30, 1996, 10. The DMC described does not exist, as yet. The description is based on the sources that follow.

p. 194   *She has chosen the* . . . : U.S. Department of Health and Human Services, *Health United States, 1994* (Washington, D.C.: Government Printing Office, 1994), 184, 186.

p. 194   *They can treat all* . . . : Dr. Gordon Weir, letter to author, Aug. 1, 1996.

p. 195   *As new DMC* . . . : Karen Southwick, "A Roadmap for Diabetes Control," *Managed Healthcare,* Apr. 1996, S2.

p. 195   *Its proposal notes* . . . : Ibid.

p. 195   *The* Monitor *and* . . . : Ibid., S25.

p. 195   *The DMC proposal* . . . : Ibid., S18.

p. 197   *For example, while Control* . . . : Ibid., S25.

p. 197   *Many managed care* . . . : Wilkerson Group, *Integrated Health Care: Pharmaceutical Company Roles in a Seamless System of Patient Care* (New York: Wilkerson Group, 1995).

p. 197   *Further, if managed* . . . : The evidence that HMOs draw a younger, healthier population is discussed in Chapter 6.

p. 197   *Notes an executive* . . . : David R. Almos, "Digital Medicine," *Los Angeles Times,* Jul. 22, 1996, D1.

p. 198   *A representative of* . . . : Walter Alexander, "Parents of Asthmatic Children Breathe a Sigh of Relief," *Managed Healthcare,* Apr. 1996, 38–39.

p. 198   *Control Diabetes Centers* . . . : Southwick, "Roadmap," S25; and Wilkerson Group, *Integrated Health Care,* 43.

p. 198   *Notes David Lothson* . . . : Letter to author, Jul. 1996.

Chapter 9: Resizing and the Role of Technology

p. 200   *Poultry was ranked* . . . : Conference Board, *Special Consumer Report* (New York: Conference Board, 1994).

p. 200   *Now what do* . . . : Ibid.

p. 201   *It was technology* . . . : Glenn E. Bugos, "Intellectual Property Protection," *Business History Review,* vol. 66, no. 1 (Spring 1992), 127–68.

p. 201   *As Frank Perdue* . . . : Dan Lauck, "The Prince of Poultry," *Washington Post,* May 3, 1981, H1.

p. 201   *Chicken breeders ultimately perfected* . . . : Bugos, "Intellectual Property Protection," 127–68.

p. 201   *As a result* . . . : U.S. Bureau of the Census, *Statistical Abstract, 1993* (Washington, D.C.: Government Printing Office, 1993), 676, table 1144.

p. 201   *Americans liked these chickens* . . . : U.S. Bureau of the Census, *Statistical Abstract, 1995* (Washington, D.C.: Government Printing Office, 1995), 147, table 225.

p. 202   *To judge the "better"* . . . : "Thanks for the Memories?" *Consumer Reports,* vol. 61, no. 5 (May 1996), p. 6.

p. 202   *Styling improvements that reduced* . . . : John DeCicco and Marc Ross, "Improving Automotive Efficiency," *Scientific American,* vol. 271, no. 6 (Dec. 1994), 52–57.

p. 202   *Thus, while in* . . . : U.S. Bureau of the Census, *Historical Statistics of the United States, Colonial Times to 1970, Part I* (Washington, D.C.: Government Printing Office, 1975), 327, table G 798–848; Census Bureau, *Statistical Abstract, 1995,* 468, table 721.

p. 202   *As cars became cheaper* . . . : American Automobile Manufacturers Association, *AAMA Motor Vehicle Facts & Figures* (Detroit, Mich.: AAMA, 1995), 22; Census Bureau, *Statistical Abstract, 1995*, 8, table 2.

p. 203   *The PDP-1, introduced* . . . : Richard N. Langlois, "External Economies and Economic Progress: The Case of the Microcomputer Industry," *Business History Review*, vol. 66, no. 1 (Spring 1992), 1–50.

p. 203   *In 1982 Intel's 286* . . . : Otis Port et al., "Will We Keep Getting More Bits for the Buck?" *Business Week*, Jul. 4, 1994, 90–91.

p. 203   *Most 1996 personal computers* . . . : Neal Templin, "Megabyte Markdown: Memory Gets Cheaper," *Wall Street Journal*, May 6, 1996, B1.

p. 203   *In 1995 Intel's Pentium Pro* . . . : Lawrence M. Fisher, "Intel Offers Its Pentium Pro for Work Station Market," *New York Times*, Nov. 2, 1995, D2.

p. 203   *With their soaring* . . . : *The World Almanac and Book of Facts, 1996* (Mahwah, N.J.: World Almanac Books, 1996), 171.

p. 203   *Some cite the greater* . . . : See, for example, William B. Schwartz, "The Inevitable Failure of Current Cost-Containment Strategies," *Journal of the American Medical Association*, vol. 257, no. 2 (Jan. 9, 1987), 220–24; Eli Ginzberg, "High-Tech Medicine and Rising Health Care Costs," *Journal of the American Medical Association*, vol. 263, no. 13 (Apr. 4, 1990), 1820–22; Stuart H. Altman and Robert Blendon, eds., *Medical Technology: The Culprit Behind Health Care Costs?* (Washington, D.C.: Government Printing Office, 1979). But, for a later different view, see William B. Schwartz, "In the Pipeline: A Wave of Valuable Medical Technology," *Health Affairs* (Summer 1994), 70–80.

p. 204   *The cost data* . . . : Michael D. Samols, "Transition Systems, Inc." (San Francisco, Calif.: Robertson, Stephens & Co., 1996), 2.

p. 204   *But because the* . . . : Larry M. Manheim, Gloria J. Bazzoli, and Min-Woong Sohn, "Local Hospital Competition in Large Metropolitan Areas," *Journal of Economics and Management Strategy*, vol. 3, no. 1 (Spring 1994), 143–67.

p. 205   *Do you remember* . . . : Helen Thomas, "Backstairs at the White House," UPI, Sept. 3, 1983.

p. 206   *In 1984 a surgeon* . . . : Health Insurance Association of America, *Source Book of Health Insurance Data 1984–85* (Washington, D.C.: HIAA, 1985), 43–44, 59–60; Dr. Walter Wildstein, letter to author, Sept. 1996.

p. 206   *The resulting expenditure . . .* : Census Bureau, *Statistical Abstract, 1995,* 469, table 724.

p. 207   *These computer-based devices . . .* : Dr. James Rhea, letter to author, Jul. 16, 1996 and Aug. 5, 1996.

p. 207   *Dr. Jonathan Kleefield . . .* : Dr. Jonathan Kleefield, letter to author, Jul. 16, 1996.

p. 208   *When these important systems . . .* : Henrik Kehlet, ed., *Practice in Post-operative Pain: Effect of Regional Anaesthesia and Pain Management on Surgical Outcome* (Westborough, Mass.: Astra USA, 1992), 5–20; Dr. George Battit, letter to author.

p. 208   *Various regional anesthesia . . .* : Ibid., 17–20.

p. 208   *may reduce the severity . . .* : Ibid., 13–16.

p. 208   *diminish death from . . .* : Ibid., 9–12.

p. 208   *and may well deter . . .* : Ibid., 5–8.

p. 209   *Regional anesthesia can . . .* : Dr. Peter Madras, letter to author, Jul. 1996.

p. 209   *For example, 80 to 90 percent . . .* : Pieter Halter, "Minimally Invasive Surgery," *Medical Device and Diagnostic Industry,* Jan. 1994, 68–72; Dr. Walter Wildstein, letter to author, Sept. 1996.

p. 209   *Of the estimated . . .* : "Outpatient Surgery: Empires Strike Back," *MedPro Month IV,* Mar. 1994, 37.

p. 209   *In 1994 more than . . .* : Ibid., 59–60.

p. 209   *People with blocked-up . . .* : Letters to author: Dr. Walter Wildstein, Sept. 1996; Dr. George Battit, Jul., Aug. 1996; Dr. Peter Madras, various, 1995 and 1996; and Dr. Joseph Haas, Jul. 1996.

p. 210   *Small wonder the 1992 . . .* : "Market and Technology Updates," *BBI Newsletter,* vol. 17, no. 11 (Nov. 1994), 199.

p. 211   *Their rapid growth . . .* : Brand S. Mittler, "The Myth of Unnecessary Care," *Wall Street Journal,* Mar. 1, 1993, A14.

p. 211   *but a 1993 series . . .* : Steven J. Bernstein et al., "The Appropriateness of Use of Coronary Angiography in New York State," *Journal of the American Medical Association,* vol. 269, no. 6 (Feb. 10, 1993), 766–69; Lee Hilborne et al., "The Appropriateness of Use of Percutaneous Transluminal Coronary Angioplasty in New York State," *Journal of the American Medical Association,* vol. 269, no. 6 (Feb. 10, 1993), 761–65.

p. 211   *The reclogging requires . . . :* "Joint World Congress Spotlights the New-est, Brightest Developments in Cardiology Field," *BBI Newsletter,* vol. 17, no. 11 (Nov. 1994), 184.

p. 211   *In a sample of 72 . . . :* Daniel B. Mark, "The Effects of Coronary Angioplasty, Coronary Bypass Surgery and Medical Therapy on Em-ployment in Patients with Coronary Artery Disease," *Medical Benefits,* Feb. 15, 1994, 9.

p. 211   *More recently, Dr. Peter . . . :* Dr. Peter Madras, conversation with author, Aug. 28, 1995.

p. 211   *When MIS and . . . :* Cathy Read, "Trial and Error in the Operating Theatre," *New Scientist,* vol. 136, no. 1846 (Nov. 7, 1992), 12.

p. 211   *Surgeons have to learn . . . :* Nathaniel J. Soper et al., "Medical Progress: Laparoscopic General Surgery," *New England Journal of Medicine,* vol. 330, no. 6 (Feb. 10, 1994), 409–19.

p. 212   *Indeed, after reviewing . . . :* Mark A. Warner et al., "Major Morbidity and Mortality Within 1 Month of Ambulatory Surgery and Anesthe-sia," *Journal of the American Medical Association,* vol. 270, no. 12 (September 22–29, 1993), 1437–41.

p. 212   *Although the MIS . . . :* Antonio P. Legorreta et al., "Increased Cholecystectomy Rate After the Introduction of Laparoscopic Cholecystectomy," *Journal of the American Medical Association,* vol. 270, no. 12 (Sept. 22–29, 1993), 1429–32.

p. 212   *To envision what . . . :* David E. Johnson and Marshall M. Kaplan, "Pathogenesis and Treatment of Gallstones," *New England Journal of Medicine,* vol. 328, no. 6 (Feb. 11, 1993), 412–21; Dr. Walter Wildstein, letter to author, Sept. 1996.

p. 213   *Many people endured . . . :* Health Responsibility Systems, "Gallstones," America Online, In Better Health and Medical Forum, 1993.

p. 213   *And the likelihood . . . :* "Laparoscopy Technique Linked to Rise in Cholecystectomy," *Journal Watch,* vol. 15, no. 12 (Jun. 15, 1995), 96.

p. 214   *Vaccines have almost . . . :* R. A. Dershewitz, "Immunization: Good News and Bad News," *Journal Watch,* vol. 15, no. 1 (Jan. 1, 1995), 8.

p. 214   *In the 1920s . . . :* The Boston Consulting Group, *The Contribution of Pharmaceutical Companies: What's at Stake for America* (New York: Boston Consulting Group, 1993), 4.

p. 215   *A new class . . . :* Ibid., 7.

p. 215   *Lipid-lowering drugs* . . . : "Aggressive Heart Disease Therapy Pays Off," *Heart Style,* vol. 5, no. 1 (Winter 1994–95), 4.

p. 215   *Finally, a drug that helps* . . . : Michael W. Miller, "Technology & Medicine: Schizophrenia Drug Clozaril Produces Big Savings by Cutting Hospital Stays," *Wall Street Journal,* Nov. 8, 1993, B6.

p. 215   *One extensive analysis* . . . : William J. Moore and Robert J. Newman, "U.S. Medicaid Drug Formularies: Do They Work?" *Pharmaco-Economics,* supp. 1 (1992), 28–31.

p. 215   *Another study of* . . . : Stephen B. Soumerai et al., "Effects of Limiting Medicaid Drug-Reimbursement Benefits on the Use of Psychotropic Agents and Acute Mental Health Services by Patients with Schizophrenia," *New England Journal of Medicine,* vol. 331, no. 10 (Sept. 8, 1994), 650–55.

p. 216   *But au contraire* . . . : U.S. Office of Technology Assessment, *Health Care Technology and Its Assessment in Eight Countries,* OTA-BP-H-140 (Washington, D.C.: Government Printing Office, 1995), 337.

p. 216   *and Americans were admitted* . . . : Organization for Economic Cooperation and Development (OECD), *Health Care Systems in Transition: The Search for Efficiency* (Paris: OECD, 1990), 149.

p. 216   *In 1987, for example* . . . : Ibid., 150.

p. 216   *while the American* . . . : National Center for Health Statistics, *Health United States, 1994* (Hyattsville, Md.: Public Health Service, 1995), 178.

p. 216   *In the 1990s* . . . : Office of Technology Assessment, *Health Care Technology,* 338.

p. 216   *To the contrary in 1990* . . . : Organization for Economic Cooperation and Development, *Health Care Systems in Transition: The Search for Efficiency* (Paris: Organization for Economic Cooperation and Development, 1990), 44.

p. 216   *The ratio of physicians* . . . : Center for Health Policy Research, *International Health Systems: A Chartbook Perspective,* 2nd ed. (Chicago: American Medical Association), 30.

p. 216   *To the contrary* . . . : *Harvard Community Health Plan Annual Report 1990* (Brookline, Mass.: Harvard Community Health Plan, 1991), 9.

p. 216   *They find that* . . . : Ibid.

p. 217   *The 1987 annual . . .* : Organization for Economic Cooperation and Development, *Health Care Systems in Transition: The Search for Efficiency* (Paris: OECD, 1990), 131, 153, 201.

p. 217   *For example, we had . . .* : U.S. Office of Technology Assessment, *Health Care Technology and Its Assessment in Eight Countries* (Washington, D.C.: Government Printing Office, 1995), 351.

p. 217   *Similarly, in 1990 . . .* : Ibid., 350.

p. 217   *While our cardiac surgeons . . .* : Ibid., 348.

p. 217   *And while American . . .* : Ibid., 349.

p. 217   *In 1980 proportionately . . .* : Kim McPherson, "International Differences in Medical Care Practices," *Health Care Systems in Transition: The Search for Efficiency* (Paris: Organization for Economic Cooperation and Development, 1990), 22.

p. 217   *The answer is important . . .* : William B. Schwartz, "The Inevitable Failure of Current Cost-Containment Strategies: Why They Can Provide Only Temporary Relief," *Journal of the American Medical Association,* vol. 257, no. 2 (Jan. 9, 1987), 220–24.

p. 218   *In the U.K. . . . .* : "British Patient Given Artificial Heart," *New York Times,* Oct. 31, 1995, C3.

p. 218   *Many studies to be . . .* : See, for example, Jan Blustein, "High-Technology Cardiac Procedures: The Impact of Service Availability on Service Use in New York State," *Journal of the American Medical Association,* vol. 270, no. 3 (Jul. 21, 1993), 344.

p. 218   *One researcher who studied . . .* : Ibid.

p. 218   *The rate of cardiac . . .* : HIAA, *Source Book of Health Insurance Data 1994* (Washington, D.C.: Health Insurance Association of America, 1994), 141.

p. 219   *A 1994 Journal of . . .* : Elizabeth A. McGlynn et al., "Comparison of the Appropriateness of Coronary Angiography and Coronary Artery Bypass Graft Surgery Between Canada and New York State," *Journal of the American Medical Association,* vol. 272, no. 12 (Sept. 28, 1994), 934–40.

p. 219   *Presumably because of . . .* : Ibid., 937.

p. 219   *These delays not only . . .* : Ibid., 939.

p. 219   *A comparison between . . .* : Daniel B. Mark et al., "Use of Medical Resources and Quality of Life After Acute Myocardial Infarction in

Canada and the United States," *New England Journal of Medicine,* vol. 331, no. 17 (Oct. 27, 1994), 1130–35.

p. 219   *After one year . . . :* Ibid.

p. 219   *After all, in 1992 . . . :* HIAA, *Source Book of Health Insurance Data 1994,* 124.

p. 219   *The Canadian health . . . :* Eli A. Friedman, letter in *New England Journal of Medicine,* vol. 324, no. 15 (Apr. 11, 1991), 1067–68.

p. 220   *Despite lower rates . . . :* World Bank, *World Development Report 1993: Investing in Health* (Washington, D.C.: World Bank, 1993), 205.

p. 220   *the death rate for lung cancer . . . :* William E. Schmidt, "British Health System Fails Cancer Victims, Critics Say," *New York Times,* Jun. 26, 1994, A1.

p. 220   *But if technology . . . :* Dale A. Rublee, *International Health Systems: A Chartbook Perspective,* 2nd ed. (Chicago: Center for Health Policy Research, American Medical Association, 1993), 7.

p. 220   *Although we spend . . . :* David V. Axene, Richard L. Doyle, and Alan P. Feren, *Analysis of Medically Unnecessary Health Care Consumption* (Milliman & Robertson, 1991), 8–9.

p. 220   *and a 1993 average stay . . . :* John Morrissey, "Risk Management Efforts Pay Off—Study," *Modern Healthcare,* May 27, 1996, 36.

p. 220   *we also have much . . . :* Alison M. Spitz et al., "Pregnancy, Abortion, and Birth Rates Among U.S. Adolescents—1980, 1985, and 1990," *Journal of the American Medical Association,* vol. 275, no. 13 (Apr. 3, 1996), 989; "Infant Mortality—United States, 1992," *Journal of the American Medical Association,* vol. 273, no. 2 (Jan. 11, 1995), 101.

p. 220   *Our rates of teenage . . . :* Leonard A. Sagan, *The Health of Nations* (New York: Basic Books, Inc., 1987), 107.

p. 220   *and our percentage . . . :* Center for Health Policy Research, *International Health Systems: A Chartbook Perspective,* 2nd ed. (Chicago: American Medical Association), 9.

p. 220   *At that age American men . . . :* Ibid., 8.

p. 221   *A white 90-year-old . . . :* Gina Kolata, "After 80, Americans Live Longer Than Others," *New York Times,* Nov. 2, 1995, B14; Kenneth G. Manton and James W. Vaupel, "Survival After the Age of 80 in the United States, Sweden, France, England, and Japan," *The New England Journal of Medicine,* vol. 333, no. 18 (Nov. 2, 1995), 1232–35.

p. 221   *Simply put, Americans . . .* : "Health System Reform: Employers', Unions', and Citizens' Views, and a Comparative Analysis," *Medical Benefits*, Sept. 15, 1993, 8.

p. 221   *The American hospital system . . .* : Prospective Payment Assessment Commission, *Medicare and the American Health Care System: Report to Congress* (Washington, D.C.: ProPAC), Jun. 1996, 75.

p. 221   *One careful analysis . . .* : Frank Cerne and Jim Montague, "Are We Facing the Capacity Crisis?" *Medical Benefits*, Dec. 15, 1994, 9.

p. 222   *another study claimed . . .* : Elizabeth Gardner, "Eliminating Inefficiencies Could Save Hospitals $60 Billion," *Medical Benefits*, Aug. 30, 1992, 10.

p. 222   *A sophisticated analysis . . .* : Stephen Zuckerman, Jack Hadley, and Lisa Iezzoni, "Measuring Hospital Efficiency with Frontier Cost Functions," *Journal of Health Economics*, vol. 13 (1994), 263, 274.

p. 222   *Careful analyses by Jack Ashby . . .* : Prospective Payment Assessment Commission, *Report and Recommendations to the Congress* (Washington, D.C.: ProPAC, 1995), 77; Jack Ashby, letter to author, Sept. 19, 1996.

p. 222   *A 16 percent growth . . .* : Ibid., 78.

p. 222   *Both the service . . .* : Ibid., 79–80.

p. 222   *During that time . . .* : Ibid., 78.

p. 222   *Although, like other . . .* : Robert F. Graboyes, "Medical Care Price Indexes," *Federal Reserve Bank of Richmond Economic Quarterly*, vol. 80, no. 4 (Fall 1994), 69–89; reviewed by Jack Ashby, Sept. 19, 1996.

p. 222   *While the length . . .* : American Hospital Association, "Hospital Stat 1995/96: Emerging Trends in Hospitals," *Medical Benefits*, Apr. 15, 1996, 10.

p. 222   *The number of . . .* : National Center for Health Statistics, *Health United States, 1994* (Hyattsville, Md.: Public Health Service, 1995), 204, table 103.

p. 223   *Hospital administrators account . . .* : Ibid.

p. 223   *Their compensation rose . . .* : Joan G. Fitzgerald, "Execs' Compensation Rises 5.5% in 1993," *Modern Healthcare*, Jun. 20, 1994, 41.

p. 223   *Top hospital administrators . . .* : Ibid., 42.

p. 223   *In view of these statistics*...: David Shulkin et al., "Reasons for Increasing Administrative Costs in Hospitals," *Medical Benefits,* Aug. 30, 1993, 9.

p. 223   *For one thing*...: David Burda, "Hospital Profits Stable Despite Market Changes," *Modern Healthcare,* Jul. 3, 1995, 4.

p. 223   *In 1992 the U.S. hospital*...: David Burda, "A Profit By Any Other Name Would Still Give Hospitals the Fits," *Modern Healthcare,* Aug. 8, 1994, 115.

p. 223   *Meanwhile, the amount*...: Ibid., 116.

p. 223   *The simultaneous decline*...: Jay Greene, "Florida Bill Sets Charity Care Minimum," *Modern Healthcare,* Feb. 28, 1994, 18.

p. 223   *As one Missouri*...: David Burda, "States Attack Not-For-Profit Tax Breaks," *Modern Healthcare,* Feb. 20, 1995, 26.

p. 223   *In for-profit organizations*...: In a 1987 study, William Krasker and I demonstrated that for-profit hospitals are more efficient than non-profit ones. See Regina E. Herzlinger and William S. Krasker, "Who Profits from Nonprofits?" *Harvard Business Review,* Jan.–Feb. 1987. See also Rosemary Stevens, *In Sickness and In Wealth* (New York: Basic Books, 1989).

p. 224   *For example, about*...: Jeffrey D. Hosenpud et al., "The Effect of Transplant Center Volume on Cardiac Transplant Outcome," *Journal of the American Medical Association,* vol. 271, no. 23 (Jun. 15, 1994), 1845.

p. 224   *And 1992 hospital occupancy*...: National Center for Health Statistics, *Health United States, 1994* (Hyattsville, Md.: Public Health Service, 1995), 211.

p. 224   *In one tome*...: Health Care Advisory Board, *Hospital Cardiology, Volume I: Major Business Strategies* (Washington, D.C.: Advisory Board Company, 1990).

p. 224   *In another article*...: Eileen Berg, "Treating Chest Pains Brings Big Financial Gains," *Modern Healthcare,* Nov. 25, 1991, 32.

p. 225   *As recounted in*...: Kenneth H. Bacon, "Medical Waste: Hospital Construction Booms, Driving Costs of Health Care Up," *Wall Street Journal,* Jan. 10, 1990, A1. See also Walt Bogdanovich, *The Great White Lie* (New York: Simon and Schuster, 1991).

p. 226   *In 1994 only*...: Sally T. Burner and Daniel R. Waldo, "National

Health Expenditure Projections, 1994–2005," *Health Care Financing Review,* vol. 16 (Summer 1995), 238.

p. 226   *The single largest . . .* : Ibid.

p. 226   *Medicare paid $485 . . .* : Subcommittee on Health of the House Committee on Ways and Means, *Medicare: Excessive Payments Support the Proliferation of Costly Technology,* report prepared by the General Accounting Office, 102nd Cong., 2nd sess., May 27, 1992, 6.

p. 226   *Medicare's MRI payments . . .* : Ibid., 3.

p. 227   *A study of 38,000 . . .* : Mark B. Wenneker, Joel S. Weissman, and Arnold M. Epstein, "The Association of Payer with Utilization of Cardiac Procedures in Massachusetts," *Journal of the American Medical Association,* vol. 264, no. 10 (Sept. 12, 1990), 1255–60.

p. 227   *Despite the increased . . .* : Larry M. Manheim, Gloria J. Bazzoli, and Min-Woong Sohn, "Local Hospital Competition in Large Metropolitan Areas," *Journal of Economics and Management Strategy,* vol. 3, no. 1 (Spring 1994), 143.

p. 227   *In 1994 estimates . . .* : Burner and Waldo, "National Health Expenditure Projections," 238.

p. 227   *The proliferation of . . .* : For another view of this issue, see Burton A. Weisbrod, "The Health Care Quadrilemma," *Journal of Economic Literature,* vol. 39 (Jun. 1991), 523–52.

p. 227   *A study of 150 . . .* : Jeffrey D. Hosenpud et al., "Effect of Transplant Center Volume on Cardiac Transplant Outcome," *Journal of the American Medical Association,* vol. 271, no. 23 (Jun. 15, 1994), 1844–49.

p. 227   *By contrast, patients . . .* : John L. Kordash, letter to author, Oct. 2, 1996.

p. 228   *A study of nine hospitals . . .* : Elizabeth Gardner, "Study Amends Lore About CABG Volume, Cost," *Modern Healthcare,* Nov. 30, 1992, 48.

p. 228   *That cost reductions emerge . . .* : Charles J. Teplitz, *The Learning Curve Deskbook* (Westport, Conn.: Quorum Books, 1991), 9.

p. 228   *A 1992 study . . .* : Gardner, "Study Amends Lore," 48.

p. 229   *For example, in 1994 . . .* : David J. Lothson, *SciMed Life Systems* (New York: PaineWebber, 1994), 3.

p. 229   *In 1994, shortly after . . .* : Marshall S. Stanton et al., "Consistent Subcutaneous Prepectoral Implantation of a New Implantable Cardioverter Defibrillator," *Mayo Clinic Proceedings,* vol. 69 (Apr. 1994), 309–14; letter from Medtronic to author, Jul. 1996.

p. 229   *These trials alone . . .* : James M. Brophy and Lawrence Joseph, "Placing Trials in Context Using Bayesian Analysis," *Journal of the American Medical Association,* vol. 273, no. 11 (Mar. 15, 1995), 871–75; Genentech, letter from G. Kirk Raab, Jul. 25, 1996.

p. 230   *Finally, the company . . .* : FDA spokesman, personal conversation with Susan Weber, Sept. 19, 1996.

p. 230   *After all this work . . .* : U.S. Patent and Trademark Office, "What Can Be Patented," *General Information Concerning Patents* (www @uspto.gov).

p. 230   *A few years after . . .* : Hugh D'Andrade, letter to author, Jul. 22, 1996.

p. 230   *Industry analysts believe . . .* : Glenn Reicin, *Abbott Labs* (New York, N.Y.: Oppenheimer & Co., 1993), 2.

p. 230   *(Although the exact . . .* : Susan Haber, conference rapporteur, *Proceedings of a Conference on Pharmaceutical Industry Research, Innovation, and Public Policy* (Boston: Harvard University, John F. Kennedy School of Government, 1993), 1.

p. 230   *The ex-CEO . . .* : Michael Unger, "Bolar's Ex-Boss Gets 5 Years," *Newsday,* Jan. 23, 1993, 8.

p. 231   *Although pharmaceutical companies . . .* : Susan Haber, conference rapporteur, *Proceedings of a Conference on Pharmaceutical Industry Research, Innovation, and Public Policy* (Boston: Harvard University, John F. Kennedy School of Government, 1993), 7.

p. 231   *For example, Dean Witter's . . .* : John Borzilleri, *Pharmaceutical Industry—No Turning Back* (New York: Dean Witter, 1994), 4.

p. 231   *U.S. Surgical, for example, . . .* : Milt Freudenheim, "U.S. Surgical Learns Hazards of Fast Growth," *New York Times,* Feb. 22, 1994, D1.

p. 231   *The company's market . . .* : *Market value: 12/90–12/95.* In *U.S. Surgical Corporation* (Online). Available: Bloomberg's Financial Markets.

p. 231   *The daring people . . .* : Vivian Wohl, "Health Reform Act II: Moving to Zero-Day Hospital Stays" (San Francisco: Robertson Stephens & Co., 1995), 3.

p. 232   *Brilliant doctors at Boston's . . .* : Sandra Sardella, "Virtual Surgery," *Boston Sunday Herald,* May 21, 1995, Health & Fitness section, 46.

p. 232   *And a new miracle glue* . . . : Marla Matzer, "Glue 'Em," *Forbes,* Apr. 10, 1995, 106.

p. 232   *If current attempts* . . . : Robert Tjian, "Molecular Machines that Control Genes," *Scientific American,* Feb. 1995, 54–61.

p. 232   *Their magnitude can be* . . . : Robin J. Strangin, "Three Less-Invasive Surgical Procedures Save $1.9 Billion Annually," *Biomedical Market Newsletter,* vol. 5, no. 3 (Mar. 1995).

Chapter 10: How to Accomplish Resizing—The Case of Deere and Company

p. 234   *Deere began its* . . . : 1981 data: Wayne G. Broehl, Jr., *John Deere's Company* (New York: Doubleday & Co., 1984), 813. 1986 data: *Deere & Company Fact Book* (East Moline, Ill.: Deere & Co., 1994), 4.

p. 235   *In the period between* . . . : Internal data, Deere & Co.

p. 235   *and from 1983 to 1994* . . . : Ibid.

p. 235   *During the 1980 to 1994* . . . : Ibid.

p. 235   *Deere ranked seventh* . . . : "The Productivity Pacesetters," *Business Week,* Jun. 14, 1993, 79.

p. 235   *These dramatic gains* . . . : Internal data, Deere & Co.

p. 235   *Throughout the period* . . . : Ibid.

p. 235   *and from 1983 to 1994* . . . : Ibid.

p. 235   *Indeed, Deere is* . . . : Deere & Co. press release, Jan. 22, 1993.

p. 236   *Merging Deere's many* . . . : Deere & Co., letter to author from Michael S. Plunkett, Senior Vice President, Engineering, Technology and Human Resources, May 1996.

p. 236   *In Deere's judgment* . . . : Ibid.

p. 237   *The cell is loaded* . . . : "John Deere's Newest (and Oldest) Factory," *JD Journal,* vol. 23, no. 1 (1994), 10.

p. 237   *The cell unit* . . . : Frank A. Dubinskas and Ramchandran Jaikumar, *Deere & Company: CIM Planning at the Harvester Works* (Boston: Harvard Business Case Services, 1987), 7.

p. 237   *The conversion to* . . . : Ibid.

p. 237   *Notes the manager* . . . : "John Deere's Newest (and Oldest) Factory," 9–10.

p. 238   *Successful teams not...*: Michael S. Plunkett, speech before the quarterly meeting of the Manufacturers' Alliance for Productivity and Innovation, Deere & Co., Mar. 7, 1994.

p. 238   *Deere's management has also rejected...*: Deere & Co., letter to author from Michael S. Plunkett, May 1996.

p. 238   *Begun in 1989...*: Ibid.

p. 238   *Deere adopted several...*: *Deere & Company Fact Book*, 4, 10.

p. 239   *Deere was also an early...*: Gordon Shirley and Ramchandran Jaikumar, *Deere & Company (A): The Computer-Aided Manufacturing Service Division* (Boston: Harvard Business School Case Services, 1987), 10.

p. 239   *Deere also invested...*: Ibid., 5.

p. 239   *The information highway...*: Deere & Co., letter to author from Michael S. Plunkett, May 1996.

p. 239   *The parts reserved...*: Shirley and Jaikumar, *Deere & Company*, 11.

p. 239   *Deere's integrated systems...*: Plunkett, speech.

p. 240   *The employees who...*: Ibid., 5.

p. 240   *The results have been...*: Ibid., 3.

p. 241   *William Evans of...*: "The New Soul of John Deere," *Business Week*, Jan. 21, 1994, 65.

p. 241   *Deere & Company's experiences...*: Howard Gleckman, "The Giant Killers," *Enterprise 1993* (*Business Week* supplement), 69.

p. 241   *These outside manufacturers...*: "Labouring in Obscurity," *Economist*, Sept. 17, 1994, 74.

p. 241   *Thus, the steel...*: Jeffrey B. Arthur, "Effects of Human Resource Systems on Management Performance and Turnover," *Academy of Management Journal*, vol. 37, no. 3 (1994), 670–87.

Chapter 11: How to Make It Happen

p. 245   *After all, the focus...*: Ciba-Geigy Corporation, "1996 Trends and Forecasts: CibaGeneva Pharmacy Benefit Report," *Medical Benefits*, Jul. 30, 1996, 3.

p. 246   *For example, sick...*: Karen Donelan et al., "All Payer, Single Payer, Managed Care, No Payer: Patients' Perspectives in Three Nations," *Health Affairs*, vol. 15, no. 2 (Summer 1996), 254–65.

p. 246   *Indeed, the private...*: Peter Fermoy, letter to author, Mar. 12, 1993.

p. 246   *Notes the* Economist...: "Rationing Health Care," *Economist*, Apr. 23, 1994, 17–18.

p. 247   *For various forms...*: William J. Mackillop et al., "Waiting for Radiotherapy in Ontario," *International Journal of Radiation, Oncology, Biology, Physics*, vol. 30, no. 1 (Aug. 30, 1994), 221–28.

p. 247   *The physician author...*: Barry Brown, "Doctors, Patients Lament Ontario's Shortage of Cancer Treatment Facilities," *Buffalo News*, Oct. 25, 1993, 4.

p. 247   *Another physician notes...*: A. Bruce Reid, Letters to the Editor, *Journal of the American Medical Association*, vol. 272, no. 14 (Oct. 12, 1994), 1102.

p. 247   *In general, according to...*: "Waiting in Canada in 1994," *National Center for Policy Analysis Executive Alert*, Sept./Oct. 1995, 3.

p. 247   *Canadians who have...*: Tinker Ready, "Did More Cardiac Care in U.S. Produce Better Outcomes than in Canada?" *Medical Benefits*, Jan. 15, 1994, 7–8.

p. 247   *Most Canadians live...*: Storer H. Rowley, "Canadians Making a Run for Border to Shop in Niagara," *Chicago Tribune*, May 22, 1990, C1.

p. 247   *In 1991 to 1993, for example...*: Marcia Berss, "Our System Is Just Overwhelmed," *Forbes*, May 24, 1993, 40.

p. 247   *Although a positive appraisal...*: Victor R. Fuchs and James S. Hahn, "How Does Canada Do It?" *New England Journal of Medicine*, vol. 323, no. 13 (Sept. 27, 1990), 884–90.

p. 248   *a careful direct observation...*: W. Pete Welch et al., "A Detailed Comparison of Physician Services for the Elderly in the United States and Canada," *Journal of the American Medical Association*, vol. 275, no. 18 (May 8, 1996), 1410–16.

p. 248   *Significantly larger percentages...*: Karen Donelan et al., "All Payer, Single Payer, Managed Care, No Payer: Patients' Perspectives in Three Nations," *Health Affairs*, vol. 15, no. 2 (Summer 1996), 254–65.

p. 248   *For example, the smoking...*: "How to Quit," *American Medical News*, May 20, 1996, 15.

p. 249   *Although advocates of...*: Arnold S. Relman, "The United States and Canada: Different Approaches to Health Care," *New England Journal of Medicine*, vol. 315, no. 25 (Dec. 18, 1986), 1608–10.

p. 249   *At the moment when* . . . : Brian O'Reilly, "J&J is on a Roll," *Fortune,* Dec. 26, 1994, 178.

p. 249   *As a reward, J and J* . . . : Joseph Weber, "How J&J's Foresight Made Contact Lenses Pay," *Business Week,* May 4, 1992, 132.

p. 250   *After the Japanese increased* . . . : Alan K. Binder, ed., *Ward's Automotive Yearbook, 1996* (Southfield, Mich.: Ward's Communications, 1996), 198; *Ward's Automotive Yearbook, 1971* (Southfield, Mich.: Ward's Communications, 1971), 21.

p. 250   *Two obscure, seemingly* . . . : John C. Goodman and Gerald L. Musgrave, *Patient Power* (New York: CATO Institute, 1992), 275–77.

p. 251   *In 1992 the average* . . . : U.S. Bureau of the Census, *Statistical Abstract of the United States, 1994* (Washington, D.C.: Government Printing Office, 1994), 460, table 703.

p. 251   *and in 1994, Americans* . . . : Sally T. Burner and Daniel R. Waldo, "National Health Expenditure Projections, 1994–2005," *Health Care Financing Review,* vol. 16 (Summer 1995), 238.

p. 251   *Between 1982–84 and 1994* . . . : Ibid.; National Center for Health Statistics, *Health United States, 1994* (Hyattsville, Md.: Public Health Service, 1995), 222, table 118; Inflation data—CPI data are for eye care, while insured data are for eyeglasses and other medical durables. CPI for eye care is indexed at 1986 = 100, while other CPI indices are at 1982–84 = 100.

p. 252   *A 1995 report found* . . . : American Management Association and Fortis, Inc., "Employer Provided Health Care," *Medical Benefits,* Oct. 30, 1995, 4.

p. 252   *Small wonder that* . . . : Employee Benefit Research Institute, "Public Attitudes on Flexible Benefits, 1994," *Medical Benefits,* Jul. 30, 1994, 1.

p. 252   *More than 90 percent* . . . : Towers Perrin, "Navigating the Changing Health Care System," *Medical Benefits,* Oct. 30, 1995, 6.

p. 252   *Indeed, 73 percent* . . . : Colonial Life & Accident Insurance Co. and Employers Council on Flexible Compensation, "National Survey on Health Care," *Medical Benefits,* Jul. 30, 1995, 1.

p. 252   *Many surveys show* . . . : See, for example, Aragon Consulting Group, "What Americans Think About Health Insurance Reform," *Medical Benefits,* Apr. 30, 1996, 7.

p. 252   *A detailed analysis* . . . : John Hershey et al., "Health Insurance Under Competition: Would People Choose What is Expected?" *Inquiry*, vol. 21 (Winter 1984), 349–60.

p. 253   *By 1992, nearly three million* . . . : Health Insurance Association of America, *Long-Term Care Insurance in 1994* (Washington, D.C.: HIAA, 1994), 9.

p. 253   *The average 1995 premium* . . . : Health Insurance Association of America, "Who Buys Long-Term Care Insurance?" *Medical Benefits*, Feb. 15, 1996, 9.

p. 253   *The pent-up demand* . . . : Rachel Kreier, "California Long-term-care Insurance Sales Double Predictions," *American Medical News*, Jun. 17, 1996, 9.

p. 253   *Even way back in 1974* . . . : William G. Manning et al., "Health Insurance and the Demand for Medical Care: Evidence from a Randomized Experiment," *American Economic Review*, vol. 77, no. 3 (Jun. 1987), 251–77.

p. 254   *A 1996 analysis* . . . : Alan C. Monheit, Len M. Nichols, and Thomas M. Selden, "How Are Net Health Insurance Benefits Distributed in the Employment-Related Insurance Market?" *Inquiry*, vol. 32 (Winter 1995–96), 379–91.

p. 255   *For example, a group* . . . : James C. Robinson et al., "A Method for Risk-Adjusting Employer Contributions to Competing Health Insurance Plans," *Inquiry*, vol. 28 (Summer 1991), 107–16.

p. 255   *A number of purchasers* . . . : "Risk Adjustment: What Is Its Real Potential for Reducing Risk Selection?" *Health Care Financing and Organization News and Progress*, Jul. 1996, 1–3.

p. 256   *Employees receive the money* . . . : American Academy of Actuaries, *Medical Savings Accounts* (Washington, D.C.: AAA, 1995), 10–11; Judith Havemann, "House Votes to Protect Health Insurance Access," *Washington Post*, Aug. 2, 1996, A1.

p. 256   *Economists like Mark* . . . : Mark Pauly, *An Analysis of Medical Savings Accounts: Do Two Wrongs Make a Right?* (Washington, D.C.: AEI Press, 1994); "What to do About Medicare," *Heritage Foundation Reports*, Washington, D.C.: The Heritage Foundation, no. 226 (Jun. 5, 1996), 1.

p. 256   *On the other hand* . . . : John Goodman and Gerald Musgrave, *Patient Power* (Washington, D.C.: CATO Institute, 1992); Chris Warden,

"Other Paths to Health Reform," *Investor's Business Daily,* May 4, 1993, 1.

p. 258   *In a 1996 survey . . .* : Aragon Consulting Group, "What Americans Think," 7.

p. 258   *Tying health insurance . . .* : Kenneth M. Coughlin, "Pay-Related Health Care Plans Bring Equity to Cost Sharing," *Business and Health,* Feb. 1993, 39.

p. 259   *Many victims of deadly . . .* : See, for example, Don Lee, "Battle Over Unproved Treatments Escalates," *Los Angeles Times,* Nov. 24, 1992, Business section, 8.

p. 259   *and alternative medicine . . .* : Vivien Kellerman, "Growing Numbers Seek Out Alternative Medicine," *New York Times,* Apr. 4, 1993, sec. 13LI, 1.

p. 259   *Already bank credit cards . . .* : Sandy Lutz, "Credit Card Firms Charge into Health Care," *Modern Healthcare,* Oct. 30, 1995, 98.

p. 261   *For example, proponents . . .* : Meg Fletcher, "Mental Health Fight Escalates," *Business Insurance,* Apr. 29, 1996, 1.

p. 261   *business representatives argued . . .* : Jerry Geisel, "Mental Health Fight Is On," *Business Insurance,* May 13, 1996, 1.

p. 261   *The intrinsically political . . .* : Lynn Wagner, "Benefits Package Looms as Flash Point in Debate," *Modern Healthcare,* Mar. 15, 1993, 22.

p. 262   *Indeed, a 1994 survey . . .* : Steve Cook, "New Survey Shows Health Care Benefits Choice Is a Voting Issue," *U.S. Newswire,* Aug. 22, 1994.

p. 263   *One expert estimated . . .* : Steven R. Eastaugh, "Nationwide EDI System Can Trim Administrative Costs," *Medical Benefits,* Jul. 30, 1995, 11.

p. 263   *In the early 1970s . . .* : Subcommittee for Consumers of the Senate Committee on Commerce, *Symposium on the Universal Product Coding System,* hearing, 94th Cong., 1st sess., 1975.

p. 264   *In 1994 all department . . .* : John A. Ronzetti, ed., *FOR 1995 Edition, Financial and Operating Results of Retail Stores in 1994* (New York: John Wiley & Sons, 1995), 28.

p. 264   *For example, Lawrence . . .* : New York Business Group on Health Care, Conference Proceedings; *The Nation's Health Insurance System: Issues Involved in Workable Reforms* (New York: NYBGHC, 1992), 61.

p. 264   *In a 1995 editorial . . .* : Eli Ginzberg, "A Cautionary Note on Market

Reforms in Health Care," *Journal of the American Medical Association,* vol. 274, no. 20 (Nov. 22–29, 1995), 1633.

p. 264   *he cites a thirty-two* . . . : Eli Ginzberg, "Health Care Reform," *New England Journal of Medicine,* vol. 327, no. 18 (Oct. 29, 1992), 1310–12.

p. 264   *A vast body* . . . : See, for example, Amos Tversky and Daniel Kahneman, "The Framing of Decisions and the Psychology of Choice," *Science,* vol. 211 (Jan. 30, 1981), 453–58; Baruch Fischhoff, "Predicting Frames," *Journal of Experimental Psychology: Learning, Memory, and Cognition,* vol. 9, no. 1 (1983), 103–16; Daniel Kahneman and Amos Tversky, "Choices, Values, and Frames: 1983 American Psychological Association Award Address," *American Psychologist,* vol. 39, no. 4 (Apr. 1984), 341–50; Ilina Ritov and Jonathan Baron, "Status-Quo and Omission Biases," *Journal of Risk and Uncertainty,* vol. 5 (1992), 49–61; David A. Asch et al., "Omission Bias and Pertussis Vaccination," *Medical Decision Making,* vol. 14, no. 2 (Apr.–Jun. 1994), 118–23; Donald A. Redeimeier and Eldar Shafir, "Medical Decision Making in Situations that Offer Multiple Alternatives," *Journal of the American Medical Association,* vol. 273, no. 4 (Jan. 25, 1995), 302.

p. 265   *Three pieces of research* . . . : In one paper, the authors studied the existence of bias toward the status quo by examining the health insurance choices of old and new enrollees in a university's health plan. They found that old enrollees were much more likely to stick with their prior choice of an indemnity health insurance policy, while newer enrollees were more likely to favor HMOs. Although the authors maintain that this behavior shows a status quo bias, it may instead demonstrate perfectly rational behavior. New enrollees, who are new employees and may well be new to the area, understandably prefer an HMO, which provides them with an organized system of care, to an indemnity policy, which provides them with a bewildering range of provider choices. On the other hand, old enrollees, who are longer-term employees and familiar with the area, may prefer the indemnity policy because it permits them to retain established relationships with health care providers; HMOs' limited selection of providers may eliminate access to the very providers they prefer. (William Samuelson and Richard Zeckhauser, "Status Quo Bias in Decision Making," *Journal of Risk and Uncertainty,* vol. 1 (1988), 7–59.)

In another paper, the authors assert that the reason proportionately fewer New Jersey residents chose to buy an automobile insurance policy identical to one offered in Pennsylvania was primarily because of differences in what they call the "default option" of the insurance offered in the two states. Maybe so; but surely other differences in the two states can help to explain these choices, such as differences in automobile accident rates, characteristics of the citizens, and the behavior of insurance companies and the judicial system. Further, if the Pennsylvanians did indeed spend millions unnecessarily, as the authors assert, there is no evidence that they would not eventually learn about lower-priced policies and change their behavior in the future. (Eric J. Johnson, John Hershey, Jacqueline Meszaros, and Howard Kunreuther, "Framing, Probability Distortions, and Insurance Decisions," *Journal of Risk and Uncertainty,* vol. 7 (1993), 35–51.)

Finally, a paper examines the selections of enrollees in flexible spending accounts (FSAs) and concludes that the enrollees' behavior may be unduly influenced by non-normative factors. (FSAs are accounts that permit people to make tax-free contributions from their income to pay for their health care spending in the upcoming year.) The authors contend that the low explanatory power of the models they created to explain the contribution patterns of enrollees provides such evidence. But the low explanatory power of the models can also be explained by the omission of the key characteristic that determines contribution levels from the model. The authors did not have access to information about the enrollees' past medical expenditures. Yet decisions to deposit money in these accounts are clearly determined by the past and expected levels of medical expenditures. (See Randall P. Ellis, "The Effect of Prior-Year Health Expenditures on Health Coverage Plan Choice," *Advances in Health Economics and Health Services Research,* vol. 6 [1985], 166.) For example, if an enrollee spent $1,000 last year and expects to spend $1,000 on medical needs next year, he or she will deposit that amount in an FSA. Small wonder that the models had so little explanatory power—they lacked the key explanatory variable.

The authors further contend that the failure of some enrollees to deposit additional sums in their FSAs when the deductibles on their health insurance policies rose by $100 presents additional evidence of irrationality. But the value of a decision to put, say, $100 of one's income in an FSA is equal, at most, to the taxes saved by doing so. For people in a 30 percent tax bracket, the value of that decision is thus $30 a year. And for the people who use far less than $100 worth of health care per year, an FSA deposit is worth only 30 percent of this lesser amount. Thus, the authors' observation that not every enrollee deposited more money may well represent a perfectly rational response by the enrollees. They likely concluded that the time and effort required to learn about and make the deposit was simply not worth the small values to be gained. (Maurice Schweitzer, John C. Hershey, and David A. Asch, "Individual Choice in Spending Accounts," *Medical Care,* vol. 34, no. 6 (1996) 583–93.)

p. 265   *For example, one review* . . . : Johnson et al., "Framing, Probability Distortions," 35–51.

p. 265   *The FEHBP enables* . . . : Larry Stevens and Steven Findlay, "Expanding FEHBP," *Business and Health,* Sept. 1994, 26–32; "Picking a Health Plan: A Privilege or a Pain?" *Business Week,* Jun. 14, 1994, 111; "What to do About Medicare," *Backgrounder,* no. 1038 (Washington, D.C.: Heritage Foundation, 1995), 16; letter to author from James Holmes, Federal Employees Health Benefits Program, Sept. 29, 1996.

p. 266   *(Although the power* . . . : Vera Tweed, "Medical Savings Accounts: Are They a Viable Option?" *Business and Health,* Oct. 1994, 40–46.

p. 266   *In one survey* . . . : Employee Benefit Research Institute, "Public Attitudes on Benefit Trade-Offs, 1993," *Medical Benefits,* Jun. 30, 1993, 1–2.

p. 266   *Even back in the 1970s* . . . : William G. Manning et al., "Health Insurance and the Demand for Medical Care: Evidence from a Randomized Experiment," *American Economic Review,* vol. 77, no. 3 (Jun. 1987), 251–77.

p. 266   *Over two-thirds* . . . : Towers Perrin, "Navigating the Changing Health Care System," 6.

p. 268   *Indeed the SEC* . . . : David F. Hawkins, *Corporate Financial Reporting and Analysis,* 3rd ed. (Burr Ridge, Ill.: Irwin, 1986), 23–26.

p. 268   *Certified public accountants* . . . : Ibid., 3–22.

p. 269   *Most observers of J and J* . . . : Brian O'Reilly, "J&J Is On a Roll," *Fortune,* Dec. 26, 1994, 178; Robert Andrews, Johnson and Johnson, letter to author.

p. 269   *The decentralization was* . . . : "Robert Wood Johnson," *Modern Healthcare,* Sept. 10, 1990, 60.

p. 269   *The philosophy is* . . . : O'Reilly, "J&J Is On a Roll," 178.

p. 270   *A J and J company . . .* : Robert Simons, *Codman & Shurtleff, Inc.: Planning and Control System,* case no. 9-187-081 (Boston: Harvard Business School Publishing, 1993).

p. 270   *Alfred Sloan, the architect . . .* : Richard F. Vancil, *Decentralization: Managerial Ambiguity by Design* (Homewood, Ill.: Dow Jones-Irwin, 1978), 2–3.

p. 271   *Some administrators . . .* : Dr. William Butler, letter to author, Sept. 23, 1996.

p. 272   *Americans so greatly admire . . .* : Public Pulse, "Health Care Crisis: Satisfaction and Sacrifice," *Medical Benefits,* Aug. 30, 1993, 7.

p. 272   *Between 1978 and 1988 . . .* : National Science Board, *Science and Engineering Indicators—1991* (Washington, D.C.: Government Printing Office, 1991), 332.

p. 272   *In 1994 public sector . . .* : Sally F. Burner and Daniel R. Waldo, "National Health Expenditure Projections, 1994–2005," *Health Care Financing Review,* vol. 16 (Summer 1995), 238.

p. 272   *The U.S. government . . .* : National Science Board, *Science and Engineering Indicators—1991* (Washington, D.C.: Government Printing Office, 1991), 341.

p. 272   *In either case . . .* : David J. Gibson, "Technology: The Key to Controlling Health Care Costs in the Future," *American Journal of Roentgenology,* vol. 163 (1994), 1289–93.

p. 272   *In a consumer-controlled . . .* : KPMG Peat Marwick, *Health Benefits in 1994,* 15.

p. 272   *A $1000 deductible . . .* : American Academy of Actuaries, *Public Policy Monograph,* No. 4, May 1995, 10–11.

p. 273   *In cancer screening . . .* : Steven J. Katz and Timothy P. Hofer, "Socioeconomic Disparities in Preventive Care Persist Despite Universal Coverage," *Journal of the American Medical Association,* vol. 272, no. 7 (Aug. 17, 1994), 530–34.

p. 275   *In a government controlled . . .* : See also Regina E. Herzlinger, "The Quiet Health Care Revolution," *Public Interest,* no. 115 (Spring 1994), 72–90.

p. 275   *As a result, entrepreneurs . . .* : W. Pete Welch et al., "A Detailed Comparison of Physician Services for the Elderly in the United States and Canada," *Journal of the American Medical Association,* vol. 275, no. 18 (May 8, 1996), 1410–16.

p. 275   *Indeed, an innovation*...: Craig R. Waters, "Silicon Steppe," *Inc.,* Jan. 1984, 32; Mark Fineman, "For Mothering Invention, the Royal Society is Tops," *Los Angeles Times,* Jul. 3, 1990, H7.

p. 277   *For example, American cigarette*...: Gwen Kinkead, "The Still-Amazing Cigarette Game," *Fortune,* Sept. 3, 1984, 70.

p. 277   *For instance, Kaiser*...: "Transplanting Its Programs Often Proves Tricky for Kaiser," *Modern Healthcare,* Apr. 27, 1992, 32.

p. 277   *Time, for example*...: Curtis Prendergast, *The World of Time, Inc.* (New York: Atheneum, 1986), 274–75.

p. 278   *First, the Food and Drug*...: Marilyn Chase, "Hedged Bet," *Wall Street Journal,* Apr. 30, 1993, A1; G. Kirk Raab, letter to author.

p. 278   *Years after bringing*...: Ibid.

p. 279   *Kolff was advised*...: Dr. Willem Kolff, letter to author, Jul. 17, 1996.

p. 279   *A 1993 survey*...: Karen Davis et al., "Health Insurance: The Size and Shape of the Problem," *Inquiry,* vol. 32 (Summer 1995), 197.

p. 279   *Lack of health*...: Ibid.

p. 279   *A 1996 report*...: Donelan et al., "All Payer, Single Payer," 254–66.

p. 279   *The majority of*...: Davis et al., "Health Insurance," 196–203.

p. 279   *A substantial portion*...: Ibid.

p. 279   *A 1996 study showed*...: Emmett B. Keeler, "Can Medical Savings Accounts for the Nonelderly Reduce Health Care Costs?" *Journal of the American Medical Association,* vol. 275, no. 21 (Jun. 5, 1996), 1666–71.

p. 279   *A 1994 study estimated*...: Jonathan Gruber and James Poterba, "Tax Incentives and the Decision to Purchase Health Insurance: Evidence from the Self-Employed," *Quarterly Journal of Economics,* Aug. 1994, 701–33.

p. 280   *At the present time*...: Sally T. Burner and Daniel R. Waldo, "National Health Expenditure Projections, 1994–2005," *Health Care Financing Review,* vol. 16, no. 4 (Summer 1995), 238.

p. 280   *Many studies document*...: See, for example, Pamela Farley Short and Tamra J. Lair, "Health Insurance and Health Status," *Medical Benefits,* Feb. 28, 1996, 8; Beth Hahn and Ann Barry Flood, "No Insurance, Public Insurance, and Private Insurance," *Journal of Health Care for the Poor and Uninsured,* vol. 6, no. 1 (1995), 41–59.

p. 280   *Although 1996 legislative reforms* . . . : K. Beauregard, "Private Health Insurance: Persons Denied Coverage Due to Poor Health," *National Medical Expenditure Survey* (Washington, D.C.: U.S. Department of Health and Human Services, 1993); Jerry Geisel, "New Employer Duties Under Health Reforms," *Business Insurance,* Aug. 19, 1996, 1.

p. 281   *Most health care costs* . . . : Sally T. Burner and Daniel R. Waldo, "National Health Expenditure Projections, 1994–2005," *Health Care Financing Review,* vol. 16, no. 4 (Summer 1995), 221.

p. 281   *when the funds* . . . : KPMG, *Health Benefits in 1994,* 15.

Chapter 12: How to Make it Happen: The New Rules of the Game

p. 289   *Remember the university-affiliated* . . . : Lawrence K. Altman, "Big Doses of Chemotherapy Drug Killed Patient, Hurt 2nd," *New York Times,* Mar. 24, 1995, A18.

p. 289   *Remember the hospital* . . . : Doug Stanley, "Amputee Recovering After Wrong Leg Taken," *Tampa Tribune,* Feb. 28, 1995, 1.

p. 289   *Remember the religious facility* . . . : Ralph Blumenthal, "Image of Convent House is Eroded by Sex Charges," *New York Times,* Feb. 6, 1990, A1.